PLAYFAIR CRICKET COMPETITION 1987

LIMITED-OVERS CRICKET QUIZ

ENTRY FORM

Please PRINT your answers in the spaces provided and answer every question.

AF469850

1 Name the only county which has not appeared in a Lord's Cup Final. ....
2 Who is the only bowler to take a hat-trick in a Lord's Cup Final? ....
3 Which wicket-keeper has made a record eight dismissals in a limited-overs match? ....
4 The highest individual score in a Lord's Cup Final is 146. Who scored it? ....
5 Who was the first bowler to take seven wickets in a limited-overs international? ....
6 Who won the man of the match award at the first NatWest Trophy Final? ....
7 The first one-day international man of the match was John Edrich. Who was the adjudicator? ....
8 Which country did England dismiss for 45 in a World Cup match? ....
9 On which ground did Hampshire clinch their 1986 John Player League title? ....
10 In which city will the final of the 1987 World Cup be held? ....

Your name and address:

....

....

....

Your daytime telephone number: ....

Post to: PLAYFAIR CRICKET COMPETITION, Advertising Department, National Westminster Bank PLC, King's Cross House, 200 Pentonville Road, London N1 9HL.

Entries must be received before noon on 29 July 1987. All-correct entries will go into the prize-winning draw on 12 August and all winners will be notified individually.

Rules All entries must be on this official form. Proof of posting is not proof of entry. The decision of the editor regarding the answers to this quiz shall be final and binding; no correspondence may be entered into.

THE 1986 PICK-A-TEAM COMPETITION
THE WINNING TEAM

On 3 February 1986, the following England team was chosen by our selection panel of Trevor Bailey (Chairman), Fred Titmus and Pat Pocock to play a 60-overs match against a Rest of the World XI. Two of their more difficult selections were decided by superior fielding ability.

1 GRAHAM GOOCH
2 TIM ROBINSON
3 DAVID GOWER (Captain)
4 MIKE GATTING
5 ALLAN LAMB
6 IAN BOTHAM
7 RICHARD ELLISON
8 PAUL DOWNTON
9 JOHN EMBUREY
10 PHIL EDMONDS
11 NEIL FOSTER

WINNERS OF THE 1986 PICK-A-TEAM COMPETITION

There was no completely correct entry. Our congratulations go to all the prize-winners, particularly to Christopher Geddes (11) from Dalry, Ayrshire, whose only 'error' was to promote Downton above Ellison. Of limited-overs cricket he wrote: 'I like the batting in these matches – daring running, lightning singles, giant sixes, splendid catches – all make for exciting matches.' A keen Essex fan, he received his prize of £450 at a special lunch hosted by National Westminster Bank at the NatWest Tower in London on 13 January 1987.

First Prize (£450): C. GEDDES, Dalry, Ayrshire.
Second Prize (£300): M.H. WHITE, Sittingbourne, Kent.
Third Prize (£225): H. MARCELLINE, St Neots, Huntingdonshire.
Fourth Prize (£175): H. GEORGE, Acomb, York

Runners-up (£10 each):
Q. AHMED, High Wycombe, Bucks.
T. ARMSTRONG (14), Torington, Devon.
J.M. BOAKES, Truro, Cornwall.
N. COWAN, Penzance, Cornwall.
J.B. COX, Shirley, Solihull.
S. ELLIS, London SW20.
J. FISHER, Mickleover, Derby.
S.E.A. FOX, Farnborough, Hants.
R.E. GARLAND, Evesham, Worcs.
T.E. GOWER, Chislehurst, Kent.
A.F. GRAVER, Huddersfield.
C. HARCOURT, Stratford-upon-Avon.
J. HART, Southampton.
J.T. HESLOP, Leeds.
R.J. HILTON, Beeston, Nottingham.
L. JOHNSON, Buxted, Sussex.
G.W. MARCHANT, Gloucester.
S. MITTAL, Osterley, Middlesex.
S. MONK, Sketty, Swansea.
A. MUNDAY, Chingford, Essex.
D. PINDER, Salisbury.
J. PULLIN, Kingswood, Bristol.
G. ROWLANDS, Wotton-under-Edge, Glos.
T.J.W. SAUNDERS, Manchester.
D. TAYLOR, London SW1.

PLAYFAIR CRICKET ANNUAL 1987

40th edition

EDITED BY BILL FRINDALL

All statistics by the Editor unless otherwise credited

PLAYFAIR CRICKET COMPETITION 1987

LIMITED-OVERS CRICKET QUIZ

£1500 TO BE WON

PLUS NATWEST FINAL TICKETS AND HOSPITALITY

PLUS 25 CONSOLATION PRIZES

First Prize £500 + overnight accommodation (B & B) at the Westmoreland Hotel (opposite Lord's) on 4 and 5 September + TWO tickets to the 1987 NatWest Trophy Final + NatWest hospitality

Second Prize £400 + TWO tickets to the 1987 NatWest Trophy Final

Third Prize £300 + TWO tickets to the 1987 NatWest Trophy Final

Fourth Prize £200

Fifth Prize £100

Consolation prizes

Senders of the next 25 correct entries will each receive a copy of THE WISDEN BOOK OF ONE-DAY INTERNATIONAL CRICKET 1971-1985, published by John Wisden at £16.95

Closing date for entries is 12.00 noon 29 July 1987

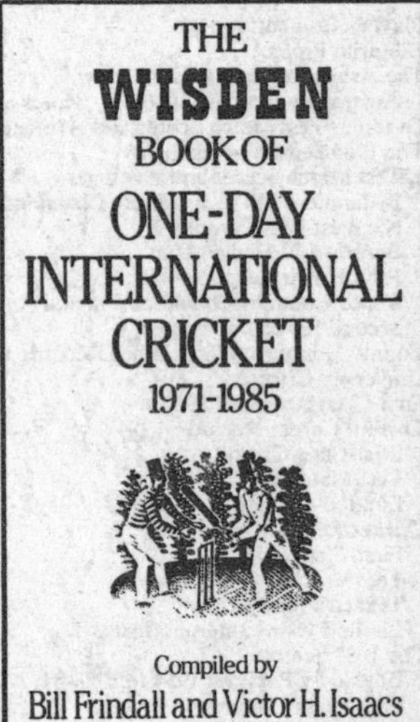

Winning entries will be drawn by the Man of the Match Adjudicator at one of the NatWest semi-finals played on Wednesday 12 August

EDITORIAL PREFACE

This fortieth edition chronicles the extremes of performance and fortune of our national team, includes a full record of the 1986 season and the scores of all 31 Tests played in the last twelve months, and previews this summer's cricket.

Congratulations to England. A highly professional campaign, shrewdly orchestrated by Messrs Lush, Stewart and Gatting, has brought much joy to those condemned to a long and dire winter at home.

Congratulations to Australia. May other Boards emulate your decision to oppose West Indian over-rates and intimidatory bowling habits by cancelling tours to the Caribbean. The ICC must not allow cricket's subtlety and charm to be further eroded by these twin menaces.

Congratulations to MCC on the 200th anniversary (on 1 June) of the first match played on Dorset Square at the first of Thomas Lord's MCC grounds. Hopefully, fine weather and attractive cricket will grace the occasion when his third ground stages the Bicentenary Match in August.

I have again tried to improve the presentation of this annual's substance without meddling with its established format. In response to your requests I have restored the lists of last season's county caps, winners of the Cricket Writers' 'Young Cricketer of the Season' award, and this year's beneficiaries. The county Who's Who section has been extended to include colts and recruits likely to appear for the first time this summer. Such has been the volume of traffic between the shires that a transfer list may soon be needed.

Glen Emanuel, Campaign Manager of NatWest, has generously increased the prizes for our annual competition – now in the form of a cricket quiz – to include NatWest Final tickets, accommodation and hospitality.

My thanks are also due to Richard Beswick of Queen Anne Press for seeing this edition safely through its many stages of production, to Geoffrey Saulez and Vic Isaacs for their contributions, and to Debbie Brown and Jeremy Gale for their help with proof-checking.

And thank you Mr Angus Henderson of Cranleigh for pointing out that the correct heading for a list of departures containing only one player is vale and not valete. My Latin master, an awesome Yorkshireman called Chadwick, would have been more proud of you than he was of me.

BILL FRINDALL

THE ASHES RETAINED STATISTICAL HIGHLIGHTS

Mike Gatting, leading his first overseas mission and one of ten players making their maiden tour of Australia, is only the fourth England captain this century (after Chapman, Hutton and Brearley) to defend the Ashes successfully abroad. At Brisbane he became the first England captain to enforce the follow-on while playing his first Test match in Australia. It was also the first time Australia had suffered this indignity in a home Ashes Test since 1965-66. At Perth, after England had registered their second-highest total in Australia – exceeded only by their 636 at Sydney in December 1928, he became the first England captain to enjoy the luxury of declaring in Australia since Illingworth (Adelaide 1970-71). At Melbourne he became the third Middlesex batsman after Hendren (3,525) and Compton (5,807) to score 3,000 runs in Test cricket, before leading England to their first three-day victory in Australia for 85 years and 105 Tests.

Broad, 'Player of the Series', joined the elite of Hobbs (who achieved the feat twice), Sutcliffe and Hammond as the only England batsmen to score three hundreds in a rubber in Australia.

Botham, whose rib injury ended an unbroken sequence of 29 Tests against Australia since 1978, held his hundredth catch to emulate Sobers by completing the Test treble. He also equalled Hadlee's world record by taking five wickets in a Test innings for the 27th time. Only Barnes (12) and Richardson (11) have exceeded Botham's nine instances against Australia.

Richards, the second Cornishman to represent England, became the third England wicket-keeper after Ames and Knott to score a century against Australia, Knott's 106 not out at Adelaide in 1975 being the only other such hundred in Australia. His five catches at Melbourne equalled the England record (shared by Parks and Taylor) for the most dismissals in an Australian innings.

Emburey became the third Middlesex bowler after Titmus and Edmonds to take 100 Test wickets, and Small is the third from Warwickshire, after Foster (Sydney 1911-12) and Hollies (Oval 1948), to take five wickets in his first Test against Australia.

Australia's only consolations were their 200th century against England (Border at Perth) and a pulsating victory at Sydney to end their record barren run of 14 matches.

AUSTRALIA v ENGLAND (1st Test)

Played at Woolloongabba, Brisbane, on 14, 15, 16, 18, 19 November 1986
Toss: Australia. Result: England won by 7 wickets
Debuts: Australia – C.D. Matthews; England – P.A.J. DeFreitas, C.J. Richards

ENGLAND

B.C. Broad c Zoehrer b Reid	8	not out	35
C.W.J. Athey c Zoehrer b C.D. Matthews	76	c Waugh b Hughes	1
*M.W. Gatting b Hughes	61	c G.R. Matthews b Hughes	12
A.J. Lamb lbw b Hughes	40	lbw b Reid	9
D.I. Gower c Ritchie b C.D. Matthews	51	not out	15
I.T. Botham c Hughes b Waugh	138		
†C.J. Richards b C.D. Matthews	0		
J.E. Emburey c Waugh b Hughes	8		
P.A.J. DeFreitas c C.D. Matthews b Waugh	40		
P.H. Edmonds not out	9		
G.R. Dilley c Boon b Waugh	0		
Extras (B3, LB19, NB3)	25	(B2, NB3)	5
Total	456	(3 wickets)	77

AUSTRALIA

G.R. Marsh c Richards b Dilley	56	(2) b DeFreitas	110
D.C. Boon c Broad b De Freitas	10	(1) lbw b Botham	14
†T.J. Zoehrer lbw b Dilley	38	(8) not out	16
D.M. Jones lbw b DeFreitas	8	(3) st Richards b Emburey	18
*A.R. Border c DeFreitas b Edmonds	7	(4) c Lamb b Emburey	23
G.M. Ritchie c Edmonds b Dilley	41	(5) lbw b DeFreitas	45
G.R.J. Matthews not out	56	(6) c and b Dilley	13
S.R. Waugh c Richards b Dilley	0	(7) b Emburey	28
C.D. Matthews c Gatting b Botham	11	lbw b Emburey	0
M.G. Hughes b Botham	0	b DeFreitas	0
B.A. Reid c Richards b Dilley	3	c Broad b Emburey	2
Extras (B2, LB8, W2, NB6)	18	(B5, LB6, NB2)	13
Total	248		282

AUSTRALIA	*O*	*M*	*R*	*W*	*O*	*M*	*R*	*W*
Reid	31	4	86	1	6	1	20	1
Hughes	36	7	134	3	5.3	0	28	2
C.D. Matthews	35	10	95	3	4	0	11	0
Waugh	21	3	76	3				
G.R. Matthews	11	2	43	0	7	1	16	0
ENGLAND								
DeFreitas	16	5	32	2	17	2	62	3
Dilley	25.4	7	68	5	19	6	47	1
Emburey	34	11	66	0	42.5	14	80	5
Edmonds	12	6	12	1	24	8	46	0
Botham	16	1	58	2	12	0	34	1
Gatting	1	0	2	0	2	0	2	0

FALL OF WICKETS

Wkt	*E 1st*	*A 1st*	*A 2nd*	*E 2nd*
1st	15	27	24	6
2nd	116	97	44	25
3rd	198	114	92	40
4th	198	126	205	—
5th	316	159	224	—
6th	324	198	262	—
7th	351	204	266	—
8th	443	239	266	—
9th	451	239	275	—
10th	456	248	282	—

Umpires: A.R. Crafter and M.W. Johnson

Test No. 1058/258

AUSTRALIA v ENGLAND (2nd Test)

Played at WACA Ground, Perth, on 28, 29, 30 November, 2, 3 December 1986
Toss: England. Result: match drawn
Debuts: nil

ENGLAND

B.C. Broad c Zoehrer b Reid	162		lbw b Waugh	16
C.W.J. Athey b Reid	96		c Border b Reid	6
A.J. Lamb c Zoehrer b Reid	0	(4)	lbw b Reid	2
*M.W. Gatting c Waugh b C.D. Matthews	14	(3)	b Waugh	70
D.I. Gower c Waugh b G.R.J. Matthews	136		c Zoehrer b Waugh	48
I.T. Botham c Border b Reid	0		c G.R.J. Matthews b Reid	6
†C.J. Richards c Waugh b C.D. Matthews	133		c Lawson b Waugh	15
P.A.J. DeFreitas lbw b C.D. Matthews	11		b Waugh	15
J.E. Emburey not out	5		not out	4
P.H. Edmonds } did not bat				
G.R. Dilley }				
Extras (B4, LB15, W3, NB13)	35		(B4, LB9, NB4)	17
Total (8 wickets declared)	592		(8 wickets declared)	199

AUSTRALIA

G.R. Marsh c Broad b Botham	15		lbw b Emburey	49
D.C. Boon b Dilley	2		c Botham b Dilley	0
S.R. Waugh c Botham b Emburey	71			
D.M. Jones c Athey b Edmonds	27	(3)	run out	69
*A.R. Border c Richards b Dilley	125	(4)	c Lamb b Edmonds	16
G.M. Ritchie c Botham b Edmonds	33	(5)	not out	24
G.R.J. Matthews c Botham b Dilley	45	(6)	not out	14
†T.M. Zoehrer lbw b Dilley	29			
G.F. Lawson b DeFreitas	13			
C.D. Matthews c Broad b Emburey	10			
B.A. Reid not out	2			
Extras (B9, LB9, NB11)	29		(B9, LB6, NB10)	25
Total	401		(4 wickets)	197

AUSTRALIA	*O*	*M*	*R*	*W*	*O*	*M*	*R*	*W*
Lawson	41	8	126	0	9	1	44	0
C.D. Matthews	29.1	4	112	3	2	0	15	0
Reid	40	8	115	4	21	3	58	3
Waugh	24	4	90	0	21.3	4	69	5
G.R. Matthews	34	3	124	1				
Border	2	0	6	0				
ENGLAND								
Botham	22	4	72	1	7.2	4	13	0
Dilley	24.4	4	79	4	15	1	53	1
Emburey	43	9	110	2	28	11	41	1
DeFreitas	24	4	67	1	13.4	2	47	0
Edmonds	21	4	55	2	27	13	25	1
Gatting					5	3	3	0
Lamb					1	1	0	0

FALL OF WICKETS

Wkt	E *1st*	A *1st*	E *2nd*	A *2nd*
1st	223	4	8	0
2nd	227	64	47	126
3rd	275	114	50	142
4th	333	128	123	152
5th	339	198	140	—
6th	546	279	172	—
7th	585	334	190	—
8th	592	360	199	—
9th	—	385	—	—
10th	—	401	—	—

Umpires: R.A. French and P.J. McConnell

Test No. 1059/259

AUSTRALIA v ENGLAND (3rd Test)

Played at Adelaide Oval on 12, 13, 14, 15, 16 December 1986
Toss: Australia. Result: match drawn
Debuts: Australia – G.C. Dyer; England – J.J. Whitaker

AUSTRALIA			
G.R. Marsh b Edmonds	43	(2) c and b Edmonds	41
D.C. Boon c Whitaker b Emburey	103	(1) lbw b DeFreitas	0
D.M. Jones c Richards b Dilley	93	c Lamb b Dilley	2
*A.R. Border c Richards b Edmonds	70	not out	100
G.M. Ritchie c Broad b DeFreitas	36	not out	46
G.R.J. Matthews not out	73		
S.R. Waugh not out	79		
P.R. Sleep, †G.C. Dyer, M.G. Hughes, B.A. Reid did not bat			
Extras (LB2, NB15)	17	(B4, LB6, NB2)	12
Total (5 wickets declared)	514	(3 wickets declared)	201

ENGLAND			
B.C. Broad c Marsh b Waugh	116	not out	15
C.W.J. Athey b Sleep	55	c Dyer b Hughes	12
*M.W. Gatting c Waugh b Sleep	100	b Matthews	0
A.J. Lamb c Matthews b Hughes	14	not out	9
D.I. Gower lbw b Reid	38		
J.E. Emburey c Dyer b Reid	49		
J.J. Whitaker c Matthews b Reid	11		
†C.J. Richards c Jones b Sleep	29		
P.A.J. DeFreitas not out	4		
P.H. Edmonds c Border b Sleep	13		
G.R. Dilley b Reid	0		
Extras (B4, LB14, W4, NB4)	26	(B2, LB1)	3
Total	455	(2 wickets)	39

ENGLAND	*O*	*M*	*R*	*W*	*O*	*M*	*R*	*W*
Dilley	32	3	111	1	21	8	38	1
DeFreitas	32	4	128	1	16	5	36	1
Emburey	46	11	117	1	22	6	50	0
Edmonds	52	14	134	2	29	7	63	1
Gatting	9	1	22	0	2	1	4	0
AUSTRALIA								
Hughes	30	8	82	1	7	2	16	1
Reid	28.4	8	64	4				
Sleep	47	14	132	4	5	5	0	0
Matthews	23	1	102	0	8	4	10	1
Border	1	0	1	0				
Waugh	19	4	56	1	3	1	10	0

FALL OF WICKETS	*A*	*E*	*A*	*E*
Wkt	*1st*	*1st*	*2nd*	*2nd*
1st	113	112	1	21
2nd	185	273	8	22
3rd	311	283	77	—
4th	333	341	—	—
5th	368	341	—	—
6th	—	361	—	—
7th	—	422	—	—
8th	—	439	—	—
9th	—	454	—	—
10th	—	455	—	—

Umpires: A.R. Crafter and S.G. Randell

Test No. 1060/260

AUSTRALIA v ENGLAND (4th Test)

Played at Melbourne Cricket Ground on 26, 27, 28 December 1986
Toss: England. Result: England won by an innings and 14 runs
Debuts: nil

AUSTRALIA

G.R. Marsh c Richards b Botham	17	(2)	run out	60
D.C. Boon c Botham b Small	7	(1)	c Gatting b Small	8
D.M. Jones c Gower b Small	59		c Gatting b DeFreitas	21
*A.R. Border c Richards b Botham	15		c Emburey b Small	34
S.R. Waugh c Botham b Small	10		b Edmonds	49
G.R.J. Matthews c Botham b Small	14		b Emburey	0
P.R. Sleep c Richards b Small	0		run out	6
†T.J. Zoehrer b Botham	5		c Athey b Edmonds	1
C.J. McDermott c Richards b Botham	0		b Emburey	1
M.G. Hughes c Richards b Botham	2		c Small b Edmonds	8
B.A. Reid not out	2		not out	0
Extras (B1, LB1, W1, NB7)	10		(LB3, W1, NB2)	6
Total	141			194

ENGLAND

B.C. Broad c Zoehrer b Hughes	112
C.W.J. Athey lbw b Reid	21
*M.W. Gatting c Hughes b Reid	40
A.J. Lamb c Zoehrer b Reid	43
D.I. Gower c Matthews b Sleep	7
I.T. Botham c Zoehrer b McDermott	29
†C.J. Richards c Marsh b Reid	3
P.A.J. DeFreitas c Matthews b McDermott	7
J.E. Emburey c and b McDermott	22
P.H. Edmonds lbw b McDermott	19
G.C. Small not out	21
Extras (B6, LB7, W1, NB11)	25
Total	349

ENGLAND	*O*	*M*	*R*	*W*	*O*	*M*	*R*	*W*
Small	22.4	7	48	5	15	3	40	2
DeFreitas	11	1	30	0	12	1	44	1
Emburey	4	1	16	0	20	5	43	2
Botham	16	4	41	5	7	1	19	0
Gatting	1	0	4	0				
Edmonds					19.4	5	45	3
AUSTRALIA								
McDermott	26.5	4	83	4				
Hughes	30	3	94	1				
Reid	28	5	78	4				
Waugh	8	4	16	0				
Sleep	28	4	65	1				

FALL OF WICKETS

Wkt	A *1st*	E *1st*	A *2nd*
1st	16	58	13
2nd	44	163	48
3rd	80	198	113
4th	108	219	153
5th	118	251	153
6th	118	273	175
7th	129	277	180
8th	133	289	185
9th	137	319	189
10th	141	349	194

Umpires: A.R. Crafter and R.A. French

Test No. 1061/261

AUSTRALIA v ENGLAND (5th Test)

Played at Sydney Cricket Ground on 10, 11, 12, 14, 15 January 1987
Toss: Australia. Result: Australia won by 55 runs
Debuts: Australia – P.L. Taylor

AUSTRALIA

G.R. Marsh c Gatting b Small	24	(2) c Emburey b Dilley	14
G.M. Ritchie lbw b Dilley	6	(1) c Botham b Edmonds	13
D.M. Jones not out	184	c Richards b Emburey	30
*A.R. Border c Botham b Edmonds	34	b Edmonds	49
D.M. Wellham c Richards b Small	17	c Lamb b Emburey	1
S.R. Waugh c Richards b Small	0	c Athey b Emburey	73
P.R. Sleep c Richards b Small	9	c Lamb b Emburey	10
†T.J. Zoehrer c Gatting b Small	12	lbw b Emburey	1
P.L. Taylor c Emburey b Edmonds	11	c Lamb b Emburey	42
M.G. Hughes c Botham b Edmonds	16	b Emburey	5
B.A. Reid b Dilley	4	not out	1
Extras (B12, LB4, W2, NB8)	26	(B5, LB7)	12
Total	343		251

ENGLAND

B.C. Broad lbw b Hughes	6	c and b Sleep	17
C.W.J. Athey c Zoehrer b Hughes	5	b Sleep	31
*M.W. Gatting lbw b Reid	0	(5) c and b Waugh	96
A.J. Lamb c Zoehrer b Taylor	24	c Waugh b Taylor	3
D.I. Gower c Wellham b Taylor	72	(3) c Marsh b Border	37
I.T. Botham c Marsh b Taylor	16	c Wellham b Taylor	0
†C.J. Richards c Wellham b Reid	46	b Sleep	38
J.E. Emburey b Taylor	69	b Sleep	22
P.H. Edmonds c Marsh b Taylor	3	lbw b Sleep	0
G.C. Small b Taylor	14	c Border b Reid	0
G.R. Dilley not out	4	not out	2
Extras (B9, LB3, W2, NB2)	16	(B8, LB6, W1, NB3)	18
Total	275		264

ENGLAND	*O*	*M*	*R*	*W*	*O*	*M*	*R*	*W*
Dilley	23.5	5	67	2	15	4	48	1
Small	33	11	75	5	8	2	17	0
Botham	23	10	42	0	3	0	17	0
Emburey	30	4	62	0	46	15	78	7
Edmonds	34	5	79	3	43	16	79	2
Gatting	1	0	2	0	2	2	0	0
AUSTRALIA								
Hughes	16	3	58	2	12	3	32	0
Reid	25	7	74	2	19	8	32	1
Waugh	6	4	6	0	6	2	13	1
Taylor	26	7	78	6	29	10	76	2
Sleep	21	6	47	0	35	14	72	5
Border					13	6	25	1

FALL OF WICKETS

	A	*E*	*A*	*E*
Wkt	*1st*	*1st*	*2nd*	*2nd*
1st	8	16	29	24
2nd	58	17	31	91
3rd	149	17	106	91
4th	184	89	110	102
5th	184	119	115	102
6th	200	142	141	233
7th	232	213	145	257
8th	271	219	243	257
9th	338	270	248	262
10th	343	275	251	264

Umpires: P.J. McConnell and S.G. Randell

Test No. 1062/262

AUSTRALIA v ENGLAND AVERAGES

AUSTRALIA – BATTING AND FIELDING

	M	I	NO	HS	Runs	Avge	100	50	Ct/St
D.M. Jones	5	10	1	184*	511	56.77	1	3	1
G.R.J. Matthews	4	7	3	73*	215	53.75	—	2	6
A.R. Border	5	10	1	125	473	52.55	2	1	4
S.R. Waugh	5	8	1	79*	310	44.28	—	3	8
G.R. Marsh	5	10	0	110	429	42.90	1	2	5
G.M. Ritchie	4	8	2	46*	244	40.66	—	—	1
D.C. Boon	4	8	0	103	144	18.00	1	—	1
T.J. Zoehrer	4	7	1	38	102	17.00	—	—	10
C.D. Matthews	2	3	0	11	21	7.00	—	—	1
P.R. Sleep	3	4	0	10	25	6.25	—	—	1
M.G. Hughes	4	6	0	16	31	5.16	—	—	2
B.A. Reid	5	7	4	4	14	4.66	—	—	—

Also batted (1 match): G.F. Lawson 13 (1 ct); C.J. McDermott 0,1 (1 ct); P.L. Taylor 11,42; D.M. Wellham 17,1 (3 ct); G.C. Dyer (2 ct) did not bat.

AUSTRALIA – BOWLING

	Overs	Mdns	Runs	Wkts	Avge	Best	5 wI	10 wM
P.L. Taylor	55	17	154	8	19.25	6-78	1	—
B.A. Reid	198.4	44	527	20	26.35	4-64	—	—
P.R. Sleep	136	43	316	10	31.60	5-72	1	—
S.R. Waugh	108.3	26	336	10	33.60	5-69	1	—
C.D. Matthews	70.1	14	233	6	38.83	3-95	—	—
M.G. Hughes	136.3	26	444	10	44.40	3-134	—	—

Also bowled: A.R. Border 16-6-32-1; G.F. Lawson 50-9-170-0; C.J. McDermott 26.5-4-83-4; G.R.J. Matthews 83-11-295-2.

ENGLAND – BATTING AND FIELDING

	M	I	NO	HS	Runs	Avge	100	50	Ct/St
B.C. Broad	5	9	2	162	487	69.57	3	—	5
D.I. Gower	5	8	1	136	404	57.71	1	2	1
M.W. Gatting	5	9	0	100	393	43.66	1	3	5
C.J. Richards	5	7	0	133	264	37.71	1	—	15/1
J.E. Emburey	5	7	2	69	179	35.80	—	1	3
C.W.J. Athey	5	9	0	96	303	33.66	—	3	3
I.T. Botham	4	6	0	138	189	31.50	1	—	10
P.A.J. DeFreitas	4	5	1	40	77	19.25	—	—	1
A.J. Lamb	5	9	1	43	144	18.00	—	—	6
G.C. Small	2	3	1	21*	35	17.50	—	—	1
P.H. Edmonds	5	5	1	19	44	11.00	—	—	2
G.R. Dilley	4	4	2	4*	6	3.00	—	—	1

Also batted (1 match): J.J. Whitaker 11 (1 ct).

ENGLAND – BOWLING

	Overs	Mdns	Runs	Wkts	Avge	Best	5 wI	10 wM
G.C. Small	78.4	23	180	12	15.00	5-48	2	—
G.R. Dilley	176.1	38	511	16	31.93	5-68	1	—
I.T. Botham	106.2	24	296	9	32.88	5-41	1	—
P.H. Edmonds	261.4	78	538	15	35.86	3-45	—	—
J.E. Emburey	315.5	86	663	18	36.83	7-78	2	—
P.A.J. DeFreitas	141.4	24	446	9	49.55	3-62	—	—

Also bowled: M.W. Gatting 23-7-39-0; A.J. Lamb 1-1-0-0.

NEW ZEALAND v AUSTRALIA (1st Test)

Played at Basin Reserve, Wellington, on 21, 22, 23, 24, 25 (no play) February 1986
Toss: New Zealand. Result: match drawn
Debuts: New Zealand – S.R. Gillespie; Australia – S.P. Davis, T.J. Zoehrer

AUSTRALIA	
D.C. Boon c Smith b Troup	70
G.R. Marsh c Coney b Chatfield	43
W.B. Phillips b Gillespie	32
*A.R. Border lbw b Hadlee	13
G.M. Ritchie b Troup	92
G.R.J. Matthews c Rutherford b Coney	130
S.R. Waugh c Smith b Coney	11
†T.J. Zoehrer c sub (J.G. Bracewell) b Coney	18
C.J. McDermott b Hadlee	2
B.A. Reid not out	0
S.P. Davis c and b Hadlee	0
Extras (B2, LB9, W4, NB9)	24
Total	435

NEW ZEALAND	
T.J. Franklin c Border b McDermott	0
B.A. Edgar c Waugh b Matthews	38
J.F. Reid c Phillips b Reid	32
S.R. Gillespie c Border b Reid	28
M.D. Crowe b Matthews	19
K.R. Rutherford c sub (R.J. Bright) b Reid	65
*J.V. Coney not out	101
R.J. Hadlee not out	72
†I.D.S. Smith, G.B. Troup, E.J. Chatfield did not bat	
Extras (B2, LB6, W1, NB15)	24
Total (6 wickets)	379

N. ZEALAND	*O*	*M*	*R*	*W*
Hadlee	37.1	5	116	3
Chatfield	36	10	96	1
Troup	28	6	86	2
Gillespie	27	2	79	1
Coney	18	7	47	3
AUSTRALIA				
McDermott	25.3	5	80	1
Davis	25	4	70	0
Reid	31	6	104	3
Matthews	37	10	107	2
Border	4	3	1	0
Waugh	4	1	9	0

FALL OF WICKETS

	A	NZ
Wkt	*1st*	*1st*
1st	104	0
2nd	143	57
3rd	166	94
4th	166	115
5th	379	138
6th	414	247
7th	418	—
8th	435	—
9th	435	—
10th	435	—

Umpires: F.R. Goodall and S.J. Woodward

Test No. 1035/19

NEW ZEALAND v AUSTRALIA (2nd Test)

Played at Lancaster Park, Christchurch, on 28 February, 1, 2, 3, 4 March 1986
Toss: New Zealand. Result: match drawn
Debuts: nil
M.D. Crowe (51) retired hurt at 117 and resumed at 190

AUSTRALIA

G.R. Marsh b Hadlee	28	(2)	lbw b Bracewell	15
D.C. Boon c Coney b Hadlee	26	(1)	c Coney b Troup	6
W.B. Phillips c Smith b Chatfield	1		b Hadlee	25
*A.R. Border b Chatfield	140		not out	114
G.M. Ritchie lbw b Hadlee	4		c Smith b Bracewell	11
G.R.J. Matthews c Smith b Hadlee	6		c sub (J.J. Crowe) b Hadlee	3
S.R. Waugh lbw b Hadlee	74		c Smith b Bracewell	1
†T.J. Zoehrer c Coney b Hadlee	30		c Rutherford b Bracewell	13
R.J. Bright c Smith b Bracewell	21		not out	21
D.R. Gilbert b Hadlee	15			
B.A. Reid not out	1			
Extras (B1, LB9, NB8)	18		(LB6, W1, NB3)	10
Total	364		(7 wickets declared)	219

NEW ZEALAND

B.A. Edgar lbw b Reid	8	c and b Matthews	9
J.G. Wright c Zoehrer b Gilbert	10	not out	4
J.F. Reid c Zoehrer b Waugh	2	not out	0
M.D. Crowe c Waugh b Reid	137		
K.R. Rutherford lbw b Gilbert	0		
*J.V. Coney c Reid b Waugh	98		
R.J. Hadlee c Zoehrer b Reid	0		
†I.D.S. Smith b Waugh	22		
J.G. Bracewell c Marsh b Reid	20		
G.B. Troup lbw b Waugh	10		
E.J. Chatfield not out	2		
Extras (B6, LB8, NB16)	30	(NB3)	3
Total	339	(1 wicket)	16

N. ZEALAND	*O*	*M*	*R*	*W*	*O*	*M*	*R*	*W*
Hadlee	44.4	8	116	7	25	4	47	2
Troup	34	4	104	0	15	0	50	1
Chatfield	36	13	56	2	17	6	29	0
Coney	9	0	28	0	3	1	10	0
Bracewell	27	9	46	1	33	12	77	4
Crowe	2	1	4	0				
Reid					1	1	0	0
AUSTRALIA								
Reid	34.3	8	90	4	4	0	7	0
Gilbert	26	4	106	2	7	4	9	0
Waugh	23	6	56	4				
Bright	18	6	51	0				
Matthews	6	1	22	0	3	3	0	1

FALL OF WICKETS

Wkt	*A 1st*	*NZ 1st*	*A 2nd*	*NZ 2nd*
1st	57	17	15	13
2nd	58	29	32	—
3rd	58	29	76	—
4th	64	48	120	—
5th	74	124	129	—
6th	251	190	130	—
7th	319	263	166	—
8th	334	311	—	—
9th	358	331	—	—
10th	364	339	—	—

Umpires: B.L. Aldridge and F.R. Goodall

Test No. 1036/20

NEW ZEALAND v AUSTRALIA (3rd Test)

Played at Eden Park, Auckland, on 13, 14, 15, 16, 17 March 1986
Toss: Australia. Result: New Zealand won by 8 wickets
Debuts: New Zealand – G.K. Robertson

AUSTRALIA

Batsman				2nd innings	
D.C. Boon c Coney b Hadlee	16	(2)	not out		58
G.R. Marsh c Coney b Hadlee	118	(1)	lbw b Hadlee		0
W.B. Phillips c Smith b Bracewell	62		c Bracewell b Chatfield		15
*A.R. Border c Smith b Chatfield	17	(5)	b Bracewell		6
†T.J. Zoehrer c Coney b Robertson	9	(4)	lbw b Chatfield		1
G.M. Ritchie c Smith b Chatfield	56		lbw b Chatfield		1
G.R.J. Matthews b Bracewell	5		st Smith b Bracewell		4
S.R. Waugh c Reid b Bracewell	1		b Bracewell		0
R.J. Bright c Smith b Hadlee	5		b Bracewell		0
C.J. McDermott lbw b Bracewell	9		b Bracewell		6
B.A. Reid not out	0		c Hadlee b Bracewell		8
Extras (B2, LB11, NB3)	16		(LB4)		4
Total	314				103

NEW ZEALAND

Batsman		2nd innings	
J.G. Wright c Zoehrer b McDermott	56	c Boon b Matthews	59
B.A. Edgar lbw b Matthews	24	b Reid	1
K.R. Rutherford b Matthews	0	not out	50
M.D. Crowe lbw b Matthews	0	not out	23
J.F. Reid c Phillips b Bright	16		
*J.V. Coney c Border b McDermott	93		
R.J. Hadlee b Reid	33		
†I.D.S. Smith b Waugh	3		
J.G. Bracewell c Boon b Bright	4		
G.K. Robertson st Zoehrer b Matthews	12		
E.J. Chatfield not out	1		
Extras (B7, LB8, NB1)	16	(B18, LB4, NB5)	27
Total	258	(2 wickets)	160

N. ZEALAND	*O*	*M*	*R*	*W*	*O*	*M*	*R*	*W*
Hadlee	31	12	60	3	20	7	48	1
Robertson	24	6	91	1				
Chatfield	29	10	54	2	18	9	19	3
Crowe	3	2	4	0				
Bracewell	43.3	19	74	4	22	8	32	6
Coney	5	0	18	0				
AUSTRALIA								
McDermott	17	2	47	2	14	3	29	0
Reid	19	2	63	1	12.4	2	30	1
Matthews	34	15	61	4	31	18	46	1
Bright	22	4	58	2	23	12	29	0
Waugh	5	1	14	1	4	1	4	0

FALL OF WICKETS

Wkt	*A 1st*	*NZ 1st*	*A 2nd*	*NZ 2nd*
1st	25	73	0	6
2nd	193	73	28	106
3rd	225	73	35	—
4th	225	103	59	—
5th	278	107	62	—
6th	293	170	71	—
7th	294	184	71	—
8th	301	203	71	—
9th	309	250	85	—
10th	314	258	103	—

Umpires: R.L. McHarg and S.J. Woodward   Test No. 1037/21

NEW ZEALAND v AUSTRALIA AVERAGES

NEW ZEALAND – BATTING AND FIELDING

	M	I	NO	HS	Runs	Avge	100	50	Ct/St
J.V. Coney	3	3	1	101*	292	146.00	1	2	7
M.D. Crowe	3	4	1	137	179	59.66	1	—	—
R.J. Hadlee	3	3	1	72*	105	52.50	—	1	2
J.G. Wright	2	4	1	59	129	43.00	—	2	—
K.R. Rutherford	3	4	1	65	115	38.33	—	2	2
J.F. Reid	3	4	1	32	50	16.66	—	—	1
B.A. Edgar	3	5	0	38	80	16.00	—	—	—
I.D.S. Smith	3	2	0	22	25	12.50	—	—	11/1
J.G. Bracewell	2	2	0	20	24	12.00	—	—	1
E.J. Chatfield	3	2	2	2*	3	—	—	—	—

Also batted: T.J. Franklin (1 match) 0; S.R. Gillespie (1 match) 28; G.K. Robertson (1 match) 12; G.B. Troup (2 matches) 10.

NEW ZEALAND – BOWLING

	Overs	Mdns	Runs	Wkts	Avge	Best	5 wI	10 wM
J.G. Bracewell	125.3	48	229	15	15.26	6-32	1	1
R.J. Hadlee	157.5	36	387	16	24.18	7-116	1	—
E.J. Chatfield	136	48	254	8	31.75	3-19	—	—
J.V. Coney	35	8	103	3	34.33	3-47	—	—
G.B. Troup	77	10	240	3	80.00	2-86	—	—

Also bowled: M.D. Crowe 5-3-8-0; S.R. Gillespie 27-2-79-1; J.F. Reid 1-1-0-0; G.K. Robertson 24-6-91-1.

AUSTRALIA – BATTING AND FIELDING

	M	I	NO	HS	Runs	Avge	100	50	Ct/St
A.R. Border	3	5	1	140	290	72.50	2	—	3
D.C. Boon	3	5	1	70	176	44.00	—	2	2
G.R. Marsh	3	5	0	118	204	40.80	1	—	1
G.M. Ritchie	3	5	0	92	164	32.80	—	2	—
G.R.J. Matthews	3	5	0	130	148	29.60	1	—	1
W.B. Phillips	3	5	0	62	135	27.00	—	1	2
S.R. Waugh	3	5	0	74	87	17.40	—	1	2
R.J. Bright	2	4	1	21*	47	15.66	—	—	—
T.J. Zoehrer	3	5	0	30	71	14.20	—	—	4/1
B.A. Reid	3	4	3	8	9	9.00	—	—	1
C.J. McDermott	2	3	0	9	17	5.66	—	—	—

Also batted: S.P. Davis (1 match) 0; D.R. Gilbert (1 match) 15.

AUSTRALIA – BOWLING

	Overs	Mdns	Runs	Wkts	Avge	Best	5 wI	10 wM
S.R. Waugh	36	9	83	5	16.60	4-56	—	—
G.R.J. Matthews	111	47	236	8	29.50	4-61	—	—
B.A. Reid	101.1	18	294	9	32.66	4-90	—	—
C.J. McDermott	56.3	10	156	3	52.00	2-47	—	—

Also bowled: A.R. Border 4-3-1-0; R.J. Bright 63-22-138-2; S.P. Davis 25-4-70-0; D.R. Gilbert 33-8-115-2.

WEST INDIES v ENGLAND (1st Test)

Played at Sabina Park, Kingston, Jamaica, on 21, 22, 23 February 1986
Toss: England. Result: West Indies won by 10 wickets
Debuts: WI – C.A. Best, B.P. Patterson; England – D.M. Smith, J.G. Thomas

ENGLAND

G.A. Gooch c Garner b Marshall	51		b Marshall	0
R.T. Robinson c Greenidge b Patterson	6		b Garner	0
*D.I. Gower lbw b Holding	16		c Best b Patterson	9
D.M. Smith c Dujon b Patterson	1	(7)	c Gomes b Marshall	0
A.J. Lamb b Garner	49		c sub (R.A. Harper) b Patterson	13
I.T. Botham c Patterson b Marshall	15		b Marshall	29
P. Willey c Dujon b Holding	0	(4)	b Garner	71
†P.R. Downton c Dujon b Patterson	2		c Haynes b Holding	3
R.M. Ellison c Haynes b Patterson	9		b Garner	11
P.H. Edmonds not out	5		lbw b Patterson	7
J.G. Thomas b Garner	0		not out	1
Extras (NB5)	5		(B5, NB3)	8
Total	159			152

WEST INDIES

C.G. Greenidge lbw b Ellison	58			
D.L. Haynes c Downton b Thomas	32	(1)	not out	4
J. Garner c Edmonds b Botham	24			
R.B. Richardson lbw b Botham	7	(2)	not out	0
H.A. Gomes lbw b Ellison	56			
C.A. Best lbw b Willey	35			
*I.V.A. Richards lbw b Ellison	23			
†P.J.L. Dujon c Gooch b Thomas	54			
M.D. Marshall c sub (J.E. Emburey) b Ellison	6			
M.A. Holding lbw b Ellison	3			
B.P. Patterson not out	0			
Extras (B2, LB4, NB3)	9		(NB1)	1
Total	307		(0 wickets)	5

WEST INDIES	*O*	*M*	*R*	*W*	*O*	*M*	*R*	*W*
Marshall	11	1	30	2	11	4	29	3
Garner	14.3	0	58	2	9	2	22	3
Patterson	11	4	30	4	10.5	0	44	3
Holding	7	0	36	2	12	1	52	1
Richards	1	1	0	0				
Richardson	1	0	5	0				
ENGLAND								
Botham	19	4	67	2				
Thomas	28.5	6	82	2	1	0	4	0
Ellison	33	12	78	5				
Edmonds	21	6	53	0				
Willey	4	0	15	1				
Gooch	2	1	6	0				
Lamb					0.0	0	1	0 (one no-ball)

FALL OF WICKETS

Wkt	*E 1st*	*WI 1st*	*E 2nd*	*WI 2nd*
1st	32	95	1	—
2nd	53	112	3	—
3rd	54	115	19	—
4th	83	183	40	—
5th	120	222	95	—
6th	127	241	103	—
7th	138	247	106	—
8th	142	299	140	—
9th	158	303	146	—
10th	159	307	152	—

Umpires: D.M. Archer and J.R. Gayle

Test No. 1038/86

WEST INDIES v ENGLAND (2nd Test)

Played at Queen's Park Oval, Port-of-Spain, Trinidad, on 7, 8, 9, 11, 12 March 1986
Toss: West Indies. Result: West Indies won by 7 wickets
Debuts: West Indies – T.R.O. Payne; England – W.N. Slack

ENGLAND			
G.A. Gooch c Best b Marshall	2	lbw b Walsh	43
W.N. Slack c Payne b Marshall	2	run out	0
*D.I. Gower lbw b Garner	66	b Walsh	47
P. Willey c Payne b Patterson	5	b Marshall	26
A.J. Lamb c Marshall b Garner	62	lbw b Walsh	40
I.T. Botham c Richardson b Marshall	2	c Payne b Marshall	1
J.E. Emburey c Payne b Garner	0	c Best b Walsh	14
†P.R. Downton c Marshall b Walsh	8	lbw b Marshall	5
R.M. Ellison lbw b Marshall	4	lbw b Marshall	36
P.H. Edmonds not out	3	c Payne b Garner	13
J.G. Thomas b Patterson	4	not out	31
Extras (LB4, NB14)	18	(B20, LB11, W1, NB27)	59
Total	176		315

WEST INDIES			
C.G. Greenidge c Lamb b Thomas	37	c Lamb b Edmonds	45
D.L. Haynes st Downton b Emburey	67	not out	39
R.B. Richardson c Downton b Emburey	102	c Gooch b Emburey	9
H.A. Gomes st Downton b Emburey	30	b Emburey	0
C.A. Best b Edmonds	22	not out	0
*I.V.A. Richards c Botham b Edmonds	34		
†T.R.O. Payne c Gower b Emburey	5		
M.D. Marshall not out	62		
J. Garner c Gooch b Emburey	12		
C.A. Walsh c Edmonds b Thomas	3		
B.P. Patterson c Gooch b Botham	9		
Extras (LB11, W1, NB4)	16	(LB2)	2
Total	399	(3 wickets)	95

WEST INDIES	O	M	R	W	O	M	R	W	FALL OF WICKETS				
Marshall	15	3	38	4	32.2	9	94	4		*E*	*WI*	*E*	*WI*
Garner	15	4	45	3	21	5	44	1	*Wkt*	*1st*	*1st*	*2nd*	*2nd*
Patterson	8.4	0	60	2	16	0	65	0	1st	2	59	2	72
Walsh	6	2	29	1	27	4	74	4	2nd	11	209	82	89
Richards					7	4	7	0	3rd	30	242	109	91
Gomes					1	1	0	0	4th	136	257	190	—
ENGLAND									5th	147	298	192	—
Botham	9.4	0	68	1					6th	148	303	197	—
Thomas	20	4	86	2	5	1	21	0	7th	153	327	214	—
Ellison	18	3	58	0	3	1	12	0	8th	163	342	214	—
Edmonds	30	5	98	2	12.3	3	24	1	9th	165	364	243	—
Emburey	27	5	78	5	10	1	36	2	10th	176	399	315	—

Umpires: D.M. Archer and C.E. Cumberbatch — Test No. 1039/87

WEST INDIES v ENGLAND (3rd Test)

Played at Kensington Oval, Bridgetown, Barbados, on 21, 22, 23, 25 March 1986
Toss: England. Result: West Indies won by an innings and 30 runs
Debuts: nil

WEST INDIES	
C.G. Greenidge c Botham b Foster	21
D.L. Haynes c Botham b Foster	84
R.B. Richardson lbw b Emburey	160
H.A. Gomes c Gower b Thomas	33
*I.V.A. Richards c Downton b Thomas	51
C.A. Best lbw b Foster	21
†P.J.L. Dujon c sub (W.N. Slack) b Botham	5
M.A. Holding b Thomas	23
M.D. Marshall run out	4
J. Garner c Gooch b Thomas	0
B.P. Patterson not out	0
Extras (B2, LB9, W3, NB2)	16
Total	418

ENGLAND				
G.A. Gooch c Dujon b Garner	53		b Patterson	11
R.T. Robinson c Dujon b Marshall	3		b Patterson	43
*D.I. Gower c Dujon b Marshall	66		c Marshall b Garner	23
P. Willey c Dujon b Marshall	5		lbw b Garner	17
A.J. Lamb c Richardson b Marshall	5		c and b Holding	6
I.T. Botham c Dujon b Patterson	14	(7)	c Dujon b Garner	21
†P.R. Downton lbw b Holding	11	(8)	c Dujon b Holding	26
J.E. Emburey c Best b Patterson	0	(9)	not out	35
P.H. Edmonds c Richardson b Patterson	4	(6)	lbw b Garner	4
N.A. Foster lbw b Holding	0		c Richardson b Holding	0
J.G. Thomas not out	4		b Patterson	0
Extras (B4, LB8, W2, NB10)	24		(LB1, NB12)	13
Total	189			199

ENGLAND	*O*	*M*	*R*	*W*	*O*	*M*	*R*	*W*
Botham	24	3	80	1				
Thomas	16.1	2	70	4				
Foster	19	0	76	3				
Edmonds	29	2	85	0				
Emburey	38	7	96	1				
WEST INDIES								
Marshall	14	1	42	4	13	1	47	0
Garner	14	4	35	1	17	2	69	4
Patterson	15	5	54	3	8.4	2	28	3
Holding	13	4	37	2	10	1	47	3
Richards	3	0	9	0	4	1	7	0

FALL OF WICKETS	*WI*	*E*	*E*
Wkt	*1st*	*1st*	*2nd*
1st	34	6	48
2nd	228	126	71
3rd	286	134	94
4th	361	141	108
5th	362	151	108
6th	367	168	132
7th	406	172	138
8th	413	181	185
9th	418	185	188
10th	418	189	199

Umpires: D.M. Archer and L.H. Barker — Test No. 1040/88

WEST INDIES v ENGLAND (4th Test)

Played at Queen's Park Oval, Port-of-Spain, Trinidad, on 3, 4, 5 April 1986
Toss: West Indies. Result: West Indies won by 10 wickets
Debuts: nil

ENGLAND

G.A. Gooch c Richards b Garner	14	c Dujon b Marshall	0
R.T. Robinson c Marshall b Garner	0	b Garner	5
*D.I. Gower c Dujon b Garner	10	lbw b Patterson	22
D.M. Smith c Greenidge b Patterson	47	lbw b Holding	32
A.J. Lamb b Holding	36	b Patterson	11
I.T. Botham b Holding	38	c Gomes b Marshall	25
P. Willey c Richardson b Garner	10	lbw b Marshall	2
†P.R. Downton c Garner b Marshall	7	not out	11
J.E. Emburey c Haynes b Marshall	8	b Holding	0
N.A. Foster c Richards b Holding	0	b Garner	14
J.G. Thomas not out	5	b Garner	0
Extras (LB3, W1, NB21)	25	(B5, LB7, NB16)	28
Total	200		150

WEST INDIES

C.G. Greenidge lbw b Emburey	42		
D.L. Haynes c Botham b Foster	25	(1) not out	17
R.B. Richardson b Emburey	32	(2) not out	22
H.A. Gomes c Downton b Foster	48		
*I.V.A. Richards lbw b Botham	87		
†P.J.L. Dujon c Downton b Botham	5		
M.D. Marshall b Emburey	5		
R.A. Harper lbw b Botham	21		
M.A. Holding b Botham	25		
J. Garner not out	5		
B.P. Patterson c Downton b Botham	3		
Extras (LB10, W3, NB1)	14		
Total	312	(0 wickets)	39

WEST INDIES	*O*	*M*	*R*	*W*	*O*	*M*	*R*	*W*
Marshall	23	4	71	2	10	2	42	3
Garner	18	3	43	4	9	3	15	3
Patterson	10	2	31	1	9	1	36	2
Holding	14.4	3	52	3	10	1	45	2
ENGLAND								
Botham	24.1	3	71	5	3	0	24	0
Thomas	15	0	101	0				
Foster	24	3	68	2	2.5	0	15	0
Emburey	27	10	62	3				

FALL OF WICKETS

Wkt	*E 1st*	*WI 1st*	*E 2nd*	*WI 2nd*
1st	8	58	0	—
2nd	29	74	30	—
3rd	31	111	30	—
4th	123	213	75	—
5th	124	244	105	—
6th	151	249	109	—
7th	168	249	115	—
8th	181	300	126	—
9th	190	306	150	—
10th	200	312	150	—

Umpires: C.E. Cumberbatch and S. Mohammed

Test No. 1041/89

WEST INDIES v ENGLAND (5th Test)

Played at Recreation Ground, St John's, Antigua, on 11, 12, 13, 15, 16 April 1986
Toss: England. Result: West Indies won by 240 runs
Debuts: nil

WEST INDIES			
C.G. Greenidge b Botham	14		
D.L. Haynes c Gatting b Ellison	131	(1) run out	70
R.B. Richardson c Slack b Emburey	24	(2) c Robinson b Emburey	31
H.A. Gomes b Emburey	24		
*I.V.A. Richards c Gooch b Botham	26	(3) not out	110
†P.J.L. Dujon b Foster	21		
M.D. Marshall c Gatting b Gooch	76		
R.A. Harper c Lamb b Foster	60	(4) not out	19
M.A. Holding c Gower b Ellison	73		
J. Garner run out	11		
B.P. Patterson not out	0		
Extras (B2, LB11, W1)	14	(B4, LB9, W1, NB2)	16
Total	474	(2 wickets declared)	246

ENGLAND			
G.A. Gooch lbw b Holding	51	lbw b Holding	51
W.N. Slack c Greenidge b Patterson	52	b Garner	8
R.T. Robinson b Marshall	12	run out	3
*D.I. Gower c Dujon b Marshall	90	(5) c Dujon b Harper	21
A.J. Lamb c and b Harper	1	(6) b Marshall	1
M.W. Gatting c Dujon b Garner	15	(7) b Holding	1
I.T. Botham c Harper b Garner	10	(8) b Harper	13
†P.R. Downton c Holding b Garner	5	(9) lbw b Marshall	13
R.M. Ellison c Dujon b Marshall	6	(4) lbw b Garner	16
J.E. Emburey not out	7	c Richardson b Harper	0
N.A. Foster c Holding b Garner	10	not out	0
Extras (B5, LB6, NB40)	51	(B10, LB10, W2, NB21)	43
Total	310		170

ENGLAND	*O*	*M*	*R*	*W*	*O*	*M*	*R*	*W*
Botham	40	6	147	2	15	0	78	0
Foster	28	5	86	2	10	0	40	0
Ellison	24.3	3	114	2	4	0	32	0
Emburey	37	11	93	2	14	0	83	1
Gooch	5	2	21	1				
WEST INDIES								
Marshall	24	5	64	3	16.1	6	25	2
Garner	21.4	2	67	4	17	5	38	2
Patterson	14	2	49	1	15	3	29	0
Holding	20	3	71	1	16	3	45	2
Harper	26	7	45	1	12	8	10	3
Richards	2	0	3	0	3	1	3	0

FALL OF WICKETS				
	WI	*E*	*WI*	*E*
Wkt	*1st*	*1st*	*2nd*	*2nd*
1st	23	127	100	14
2nd	63	132	161	29
3rd	137	157	—	84
4th	178	159	—	101
5th	232	205	—	112
6th	281	213	—	124
7th	351	237	—	147
8th	401	289	—	166
9th	450	290	—	168
10th	474	310	—	170

Umpires: L.H. Barker and C.E. Cumberbatch

Test No. 1042/90

WEST INDIES v ENGLAND AVERAGES

WEST INDIES – BATTING AND FIELDING

	M	I	NO	HS	Runs	Avge	100	50	Ct/St
D.L. Haynes	5	9	3	131	469	78.16	1	3	3
I.V.A. Richards	5	6	1	110*	331	66.20	1	2	2
R.B. Richardson	5	9	2	160	387	55.28	2	—	6
R.A. Harper	2	3	1	60	100	50.00	—	1	2
M.D. Marshall	5	5	1	76	153	38.25	—	2	4
C.G. Greenidge	5	6	0	58	217	36.16	—	1	3
H.A. Gomes	5	6	0	56	191	31.83	—	1	2
M.A. Holding	4	4	0	73	124	31.00	—	1	3
C.A. Best	3	4	1	35	78	26.00	—	—	4
P.J.L. Dujon	4	4	0	54	85	21.25	—	1	16
J. Garner	5	5	1	24	52	13.00	—	—	2
B.P. Patterson	5	5	3	9	12	6.00	—	—	1

Also batted: T.R.O. Payne (1 match) 5 (5ct); C.A. Walsh (1 match) 3.

WEST INDIES – BOWLING

	Overs	Mdns	Runs	Wkts	Avge	Best	5 wI	10 wM
J. Garner	156.1	30	436	27	16.14	4-43	—	—
M.D. Marshall	169.3	36	482	27	17.85	4-38	—	—
C.A. Walsh	33	6	103	5	20.60	4-74	—	—
B.P. Patterson	118.1	18	426	19	22.42	4-30	—	—
M.A. Holding	102.4	16	385	16	24.06	3-47	—	—

Also bowled: H.A. Gomes 1-1-0-0; R.A. Harper 38-15-55-4; I.V.A. Richards 20-7-29-0; R.B. Richardson 1-0-5-0.

ENGLAND – BATTING AND FIELDING

	M	I	NO	HS	Runs	Avge	100	50	Ct/St
D.I. Gower	5	10	0	90	370	37.00	—	3	3
G.A. Gooch	5	10	0	53	276	27.60	—	4	6
A.J. Lamb	5	10	0	62	224	22.40	—	1	3
D.M. Smith	2	4	0	47	80	20.00	—	—	—
P. Willey	4	8	0	71	136	17.00	—	1	—
I.T. Botham	5	10	0	38	168	16.80	—	—	4
W.N. Slack	2	4	0	52	62	15.50	—	1	—
R.M. Ellison	3	6	0	36	82	13.66	—	—	—
J.G. Thomas	4	8	4	31*	45	11.25	—	—	—
J.E. Emburey	4	8	2	35*	64	10.66	—	—	—
P.R. Downton	5	10	1	26	91	10.11	—	—	6/2
R.T. Robinson	4	8	0	43	72	9.00	—	—	1
P.H. Edmonds	3	6	2	13	36	9.00	—	—	2
N.A. Foster	3	6	1	14	24	4.80	—	—	—

Also batted: M.W. Gatting (1 match) 15,1 (2 ct).

ENGLAND – BOWLING

	Overs	Mdns	Runs	Wkts	Avge	Best	5 wI	10 wM
J.E. Emburey	153	34	448	14	32.00	5-78	1	—
N.A. Foster	83.5	8	285	7	40.71	3-76	—	—
R.M. Ellison	82.3	19	294	7	42.00	5-78	1	—
J.G. Thomas	86	13	364	8	45.50	4-70	—	—
I.T. Botham	134.5	16	535	11	48.63	5-71	1	—

Also bowled: P.H. Edmonds 92.3-16-260-3; G.A. Gooch 7-3-27-1; A.J. Lamb 0.0-0-1-0 (1 nb); P. Willey 4-0-15-1.

SRI LANKA v PAKISTAN (1st Test)

Played at Asgiriya Stadium, Kandy, on 23, 24, 25, 27 February 1986
Toss: Sri Lanka. Result: Pakistan won by an innings and 20 runs
Debuts: Sri Lanka – K.P.J. Warnaweera; Pakistan – Zulqarnain

SRI LANKA

S. Wettimuny lbw b Imran	0	c Ramiz b Wasim	8
†S.A.R. Silva c Zulqarnain b Wasim	3	absent hurt	–
P.A. De Silva c Zulqarnain b Imran	11	b Tausif	5
R.L. Dias b Tausif	11	b Tausif	26
*L.R.D. Mendis c Mudassar b Imran	6	c Mudassar b Tausif	4
A. Ranatunga b Tausif	18	st Zulqarnain b Tausif	33
J.R. Ratnayeke b Qadir	4	(2) b Imran	7
A.L.F. De Mel b Tausif	23	(7) b Tausif	0
R.J. Ratnayake c Salim b Qadir	4	(8) st Zulqarnain b Tausif	4
E.A.R. De Silva not out	10	(9) not out	4
K.P.J. Warnaweera c Imran b Qadir	3	(10) b Imran	0
Extras (LB7, W2, NB7)	16	(LB3, W6, NB1)	10
Total	109		101

PAKISTAN

Mudassar Nazar c Mendis b Ratnayake	81
Mohsin Khan lbw b De Mel	1
Qasim Omar lbw b Ratnayake	11
Javed Miandad lbw b E.A.R. De Silva	4
Ramiz Raja lbw b Warnaweera	3
Salim Malik c P.A. De Silva b De Mel	54
*Imran Khan c sub (R.S. Mahanama) b Ranatunga	7
Abdul Qadir b Ratnayake	11
†Zulqarnain b De Mel	5
Tausif Ahmed not out	23
Wasim Akram run out	19
Extras (B4, W7)	11
Total	230

PAKISTAN	*O*	*M*	*R*	*W*	*O*	*M*	*R*	*W*
Imran	9	0	20	3	16	5	29	2
Wasim	8	3	21	1	5	3	5	1
Tausif	13	4	32	3	15	7	45	6
Qadir	12.4	3	29	3	7	1	19	0
SRI LANKA								
De Mel	16.2	5	50	3				
Ratnayeke	10	1	26	0				
Ratnayake	23	2	57	3				
Warnaweera	8.3	2	26	1				
E.A.R. De Silva	18	7	37	1				
Ranatunga	14.3	6	30	1				

FALL OF WICKETS

Wkt	*SL 1st*	*P 1st*	*SL 2nd*
1st	0	1	14
2nd	14	28	19
3rd	25	49	31
4th	37	52	43
5th	44	154	74
6th	59	167	74
7th	69	173	80
8th	78	181	100
9th	100	191	101
10th	109	230	—

Umpires: A.C. Felsinger and S. Ponnadurai

Test No. 1043/7

SRI LANKA v PAKISTAN (2nd Test)

Played at Colombo Cricket Club Ground, Colombo, on 14, 15, 16, 18 March 1986
Toss: Sri Lanka. Result: Sri Lanka won by 8 wickets
Debuts: Sri Lanka – S.D. Anurasiri, A.K. Kuruppuarachchi, R.S. Mahanama

PAKISTAN

Mudassar Nazar c de Alwis b Kuruppuarachchi	3		lbw b Kuruppuarachchi	1
Mohsin Khan lbw b Kuruppuarachchi	35		c De Silva b De Mel	2
Qasim Omar lbw b De Mel	3		c de Alwis b Ratnayeke	52
Javed Miandad c de Alwis b De Mel	0	(5)	lbw b Ratnayeke	36
Ramiz Raja lbw b De Mel	32	(4)	c de Alwis b Ratnayeke	21
Salim Malik c Mahanama b Kuruppuarachchi	42		c Wettimuny b Ratnayeke	30
*Imran Khan c Mendis b Ratnayeke	8		c De Silva b De Mel	0
Tausif Ahmed b Ratnayeke	0	(9)	lbw b Ratnayeke	1
Wasim Akram c De Mel b Kuruppuarachchi	0	(8)	c Ranatunga b De Mel	0
†Zulqarnain c De Silva b Kuruppuarachchi	1		lbw b Kuruppuarachchi	5
Mohsin Kamal not out	1		not out	13
Extras (LB4, W2, NB1)	7		(B1, LB6, NB4)	11
Total	132			172

SRI LANKA

S. Wettimuny c Zulqarnain b Mudassar	37	c Salim b Imran	7
R.S. Mahanama run out	10	c Zulqarnain b Imran	8
A.P. Gurusinha c Imran b Wasim	23	not out	9
P.A. De Silva c sub (Shoaib Mohammad) b Mohsin Kamal	37	not out	1
A. Ranatunga c Qasim b Wasim	77		
*L.R.D. Mendis c Mohsin Khan b Imran	5		
J.R. Ratnayeke c Imran b Wasim	38		
†R.G. de Alwis c Miandad b Mohsin Kamal	10		
A.L.F. De Mel c Zulqarnain b Imran	11		
S.D. Anurasiri c Ramiz b Wasim	4		
A.K. Kuruppuarachchi not out	0		
Extras (B7, LB3, W4, NB7)	21	(B2, LB2, W1, NB2)	7
Total	273	(2 wickets)	32

SRI LANKA	*O*	*M*	*R*	*W*	*O*	*M*	*R*	*W*
De Mel	16	6	39	3	16	1	79	3
Kurup	14.5	2	44	5	10.3	1	41	2
Ratnayeke	17.4	8	29	2	17	3	37	5
Ranatunga	1	0	12	0				
Anurasiri	2	1	4	0	2	0	8	0
PAKISTAN								
Imran	27	5	78	2	7	2	18	2
Wasim	27.3	9	55	4	6	1	10	0
M. Kamal	15	0	52	2				
Mudassar	14	2	36	1				
Tausif	11	2	40	0				
Salim	1	0	2	0				

FALL OF WICKETS

Wkt	*P 1st*	*SL 1st*	*P 2nd*	*SL 2nd*
1st	3	40	6	19
2nd	12	69	6	31
3rd	12	82	72	—
4th	74	130	93	—
5th	78	137	131	—
6th	124	227	136	—
7th	124	248	136	—
8th	130	265	145	—
9th	131	272	154	—
10th	132	273	172	—

Umpires: K.T. Francis and D.C.C. Perera   Test No. 1044/8

SRI LANKA v PAKISTAN (3rd Test)

Played at P. Saravanamuttu Stadium, Colombo, on 22, 23, 24, 26, 27 March 1986
Toss: Sri Lanka. Result: match drawn
Debuts: Sri Lanka – K.N. Amalean; Pakistan – Zakir Khan

SRI LANKA			
S. Wettimuny c Ramiz b Wasim	0	c Ramiz b Wasim	14
R.S. Mahanama c Zulqarnain b Qadir	41	b Imran	4
A.P. Gurusinha c Zulqarnain b Imran	39	not out	116
A. Ranatunga c Imran b Zakir	53	(5) not out	135
P.A. De Silva c Mohsin b Zakir	16	(4) c Miandad b Imran	25
*L.R.D. Mendis c Zulqarnain b Imran	58		
J.R. Ratnayeke c Miandad b Zakir	7		
†R.G. de Alwis b Imran	18		
A.L.F. De Mel not out	14		
S.D. Anurasiri b Imran	8		
K.N. Amalean lbw b Qadir	2		
Extras (B7, LB9, W6, NB3)	25	(B19, LB7, W1, NB2)	29
Total	281	(3 wickets)	323

PAKISTAN	
Mudassar Nazar c de Alwis b De Mel	8
Mohsin Khan lbw b Amalean	12
Qasim Omar c de Alwis b Ratnayeke	19
Javed Miandad lbw b Amalean	23
Ramiz Raja lbw b Ratnayeke	122
Salim Malik c sub (S.M.S. Kaluperuma) b Ratnayeke	29
*Imran Khan c de Alwis b Ranatunga	33
Abdul Qadir b Amalean	20
†Zulqarnain b de Alwis b Ratnayeke	13
Wasim Akram run out	11
Zakir Khan not out	0
Extras (B10, LB7, W1, NB10)	28
Total	318

PAKISTAN	*O*	*M*	*R*	*W*	*O*	*M*	*R*	*W*
Imran	32	11	69	4	25	4	56	2
Wasim	22	8	41	1	29	11	72	1
Zakir	24	6	80	3	21	4	70	0
Mudassar	7	2	19	0	10	2	29	0
Qadir	23.5	3	56	2	22	5	70	0
Salim					1	1	0	0
SRI LANKA								
De Mel	27	3	91	1				
Amalean	18.2	1	59	3				
Ratnayeke	30	4	116	4				
Anurasiri	15	11	9	0				
Ranatunga	11	5	26	1				

FALL OF WICKETS	*SL*	*P*	*SL*
Wkt	*1st*	*1st*	*2nd*
1st	12	24	18
2nd	79	32	18
3rd	109	49	83
4th	149	87	—
5th	202	158	—
6th	218	234	—
7th	251	278	—
8th	260	305	—
9th	272	318	—
10th	281	318	—

Umpires: D.P. Buultjens and H.C. Felsinger. Test No. 1045/9

SRI LANKA v PAKISTAN AVERAGES

SRI LANKA – BATTING AND FIELDING

	M	I	NO	HS	Runs	Avge	100	50	Ct/St
A.P. Gurusinha	2	4	2	116*	187	93.50	1	—	—
A. Ranatunga	3	5	1	135*	316	79.00	1	2	1
P.A. De Silva	3	6	1	37	95	19.00	—	—	4
L.R.D. Mendis	3	4	0	58	73	18.25	—	1	2
A.L.F. De Mel	3	4	1	23	48	16.00	—	—	1
R.S. Mahanama	2	4	0	41	63	15.75	—	—	1
J.R. Ratnayeke	3	4	0	38	56	14.00	—	—	—
S. Wettimuny	3	6	0	37	66	11.00	—	—	1

Also batted: K.N. Amalean (1 match) 2; S.D. Anurasiri (2 matches) 4,8; R.G. de Alwis (2 matches) 10,18 (8 ct); E.A.R. De Silva (1 match) 10*,4*; R.L. Dias (1 match) 11,26; A.K. Kuruppuarachchi (1 match) 0*; R.J. Ratnayake (1 match) 4,4; S.A.R. Silva (1 match) 3; K.P.J. Warnaweera (1 match) 3,0.

SRI LANKA – BOWLING

	Overs	Mdns	Runs	Wkts	Avge	Best	5 wI	10 wM
A.K. Kuruppuarachchi	25.2	3	85	7	12.14	5-44	1	—
J.R. Ratnayeke	74.4	14	208	11	18.90	5-37	1	—
A.L.F. De Mel	75.2	15	259	10	25.90	3-39	—	—

Also bowled: K.N. Amalean 18.2-1-59-3; S.D. Anurasiri 19-12-21-0; E.A.R. De Silva 18-7-37-1; A. Ranatunga 26.3-11-68-2; R.J. Ratnayake 23-2-57-3; K.P.J. Warnaweera 8.3-2-26-1.

PAKISTAN – BATTING AND FIELDING

	M	I	NO	HS	Runs	Avge	100	50	Ct/St
Ramiz Raja	3	4	0	122	178	44.50	1	—	4
Salim Malik	3	4	0	54	155	38.75	—	1	2
Mudassar Nazar	3	4	0	81	93	23.25	—	1	2
Qasim Omar	3	4	0	52	85	21.25	—	1	1
Javed Miandad	3	4	0	36	63	15.75	—	—	3
Mohsin Khan	3	4	0	35	50	12.50	—	—	2
Imran Khan	3	4	0	33	48	12.00	—	—	4
Tausif Ahmed	2	3	1	23*	24	12.00	—	—	—
Wasim Akram	3	4	0	19	30	7.50	—	—	—
Zulqarnain	3	4	0	13	24	6.00	—	—	8/2

Also batted: Abdul Qadir (2 matches) 11,20; Mohsin Kamal (1 match) 1*,13*; Zakir Khan (1 match) 0*

PAKISTAN – BOWLING

	Overs	Mdns	Runs	Wkts	Avge	Best	5 wI	10 wM
Tausif Ahmed	39	13	117	9	13.00	6-45	1	—
Imran Khan	116	27	270	15	18.00	4-69	—	—
Wasim Akram	97.3	35	204	8	25.50	4-55	—	—
Abdul Qadir	65.3	12	174	5	34.80	3-29	—	—

Also bowled: Mohsin Kamal 15-0-52-2; Mudassar Nazar 31-6-84-1; Salim Malik 2-1-2-0; Zakir Khan 45-10-150-3.

INDIA v AUSTRALIA (1st Test)

Played at Chidambaram Stadium, Chepauk, Madras, on 18, 19, 20, 21, 22 September 1986
Toss: Australia. Result: match tied
Debuts: nil

AUSTRALIA

D.C. Boon c Kapil b Sharma	122	(2)	lbw b Maninder	49
G.R. Marsh c Kapil Dev b Yadav	22	(1)	b Shastri	11
D.M. Jones b Yadav	210		c Azharuddin b Maninder	24
R.J. Bright c Shastri b Yadav	30			
*A.R. Border c Gavaskar b Shastri	106	(4)	b Maninder	27
G.M. Ritchie run out	13	(5)	c Pandit b Shastri	28
G.R.J. Matthews c Pandit b Yadav	44	(6)	not out	27
S.R. Waugh not out	12	(7)	not out	2
†T.J. Zoehrer } did not bat				
C.J. McDermott } did not bat				
B.A. Reid } did not bat				
Extras (B1, LB7, W1, NB6)	15		(LB1, NB1)	2
Total (7 wickets declared)	574		(5 wickets declared)	170

INDIA

S.M. Gavaskar c and b Matthews	8		c Jones b Bright	90
K. Srikkanth c Ritchie b Matthews	53		c Waugh b Matthews	39
M. Amarnath run out	1		c Boon b Matthews	51
M. Azharuddin c and b Bright	50		c Ritchie b Bright	42
R.J. Shastri c Zoehrer b Matthews	62	(7)	not out	48
C.S. Pandit c Waugh b Matthews	35	(5)	b Matthews	39
*Kapil Dev c Border b Matthews	119	(6)	c Bright b Matthews	1
†K.S. More c Zoehrer b Waugh	4	(9)	lbw b Bright	0
C. Sharma c Zoehrer b Reid	30	(8)	c McDermott b Bright	23
N.S. Yadav c Border b Bright	19		b Bright	8
Maninder Singh not out	0		lbw b Matthews	0
Extras (B1, LB9, NB6)	16		(B1, LB3, NB2)	6
Total	397			347

INDIA	*O*	*M*	*R*	*W*	*O*	*M*	*R*	*W*
Kapil Dev	18	5	52	0	1	0	5	0
Sharma	16	1	70	1	6	0	19	0
Maninder	39	8	135	0	19	2	60	3
Yadav	49.5	9	142	4	9	0	35	0
Shastri	47	8	161	1	14	2	50	2
Srikkanth	1	0	6	0				
AUSTRALIA								
McDermott	14	2	59	0	5	0	27	0
Reid	18	4	93	1	10	2	48	0
Matthews	28.2	3	103	5	39.5	7	146	5
Bright	23	3	88	2	25	3	94	5
Waugh	11	2	44	1	4	1	16	0
Border					3	0	12	0

FALL OF WICKETS

	A	*I*	*A*	*I*
Wkt	*1st*	*1st*	*2nd*	*2nd*
1st	48	62	31	55
2nd	206	65	81	158
3rd	282	65	94	204
4th	460	142	125	251
5th	481	206	165	253
6th	544	220	—	291
7th	574	245	—	331
8th	—	330	—	334
9th	—	387	—	344
10th	—	397	—	347

Umpires: D.N. Dotiwalla and V. Raju

Test No. 1052/43

INDIA v AUSTRALIA (2nd Test)

Played at Feroz Shah Kotla, Delhi, on 26‡, 27‡, 28‡, 29, 30 September 1986
Toss: Australia. Result: match drawn
Debuts: nil

AUSTRALIA

G.R. Marsh c Pandit b Sharma	11
D.C. Boon c Maninder b Shastri	67
D.M. Jones st Pandit b Shastri	29
S.R. Waugh not out	39
†T.J. Zoehrer not out	52
*A.R. Border, G.M. Ritchie, G.R.J. Matthews, R.J. Bright, C.J. McDermott, D.R. Gilbert did not bat	
Extras (LB2, W4, NB3)	9
Total (3 wickets declared)	207

INDIA

S.M. Gavaskar b Gilbert	4
K. Srikkanth run out	26
M. Azharuddin c Zoehrer b Waugh	24
D.B. Vengsarkar not out	22
†C.S. Pandit not out	26
M. Amarnath, R. J. Shastri, *Kapil Dev, C. Sharma, N.S. Yadav, Maninder Singh did not bat	
Extras (LB5)	5
Total (3 wickets)	107

INDIA	*O*	*M*	*R*	*W*
Kapil Dev	14	5	27	0
Sharma	8	1	34	1
Shastri	21.4	4	44	2
Maninder	19	4	54	0
Yadav	13	1	46	0
AUSTRALIA				
McDermott	6	1	24	0
Gilbert	11	1	44	1
Waugh	6	0	29	1
Boon	2	0	5	0
Jones	1	1	0	0

FALL OF WICKETS

	A	*I*
Wkt	*1st*	*1st*
1st	34	9
2nd	110	57
3rd	118	59
4th	—	—
5th	—	—
6th	—	—
7th	—	—
8th	—	—
9th	—	—
10th	—	—

‡ (no play)

Umpires: V.K. Ramaswamy and P.D. Reporter

Test No. 1053/44

INDIA v AUSTRALIA (3rd Test)

Played at Wankhede Stadium, Bombay, on 15, 16, 17, 18, 19 October 1986
Toss: Australia. Result: match drawn
Debuts: India – R.R. Kulkarni

AUSTRALIA			
G.R. Marsh c Gavaskar b Kulkarni	101	b Shastri	20
D.C. Boon c Gavaskar b Kulkarni	47	c More b Shastri	40
D.M. Jones c sub (L. Sivaramakrishnan) b Yadav	35	not out	73
*A.R. Border st More b Maninder	46	not out	66
G.M. Ritchie run out	31		
G.R.J. Matthews b Yadav	20		
S.R. Waugh b Yadav	6		
†T.J. Zoehrer c and b Maninder	21		
R.J. Bright lbw b Kulkarni	8		
D.R. Gilbert c sub (L. Sivaramakrishnan) b Yadav	1		
B.A. Reid not out	2		
Extras (B5, LB12, NB10)	27	(B5, LB5, NB7)	17
Total	345	(2 wickets)	216

INDIA	
S.M. Gavaskar c Ritchie b Matthews	103
K. Srikkanth c Marsh b Bright	24
†K.S. More c Jones b Matthews	15
M. Amarnath c sub‡ b Matthews	35
D.B. Vengsarkar not out	164
M. Azharuddin c sub‡ b Matthews	10
R.J. Shastri not out	121
*Kapil Dev, N.S. Yadav, R.R. Kulkarni, Maninder Singh — did not bat	
Extras (B9, LB15, NB21)	45
Total (5 wickets declared)	517

INDIA	*O*	*M*	*R*	*W*	*O*	*M*	*R*	*W*
Kulkarni	23	2	85	3	6	0	29	0
Kapil Dev	6	1	16	0	6	1	24	0
Shastri	42	16	68	0	30	8	60	2
Yadav	41.4	8	84	4	23	7	52	0
Maninder	33	10	72	2	20	7	31	0
Srikkanth	2	0	3	0	3	0	10	0
AUSTRALIA								
Reid	32	5	81	0				
Gilbert	24	3	75	0				
Matthews	52	8	158	4				
Bright	38	6	109	1				
Border	10	3	29	0				
Waugh	14	2	41	0				

FALL OF WICKETS

	A	*I*	*A*
Wkt	*1st*	*1st*	*2nd*
1st	76	53	64
2nd	151	119	70
3rd	241	194	—
4th	252	205	—
5th	295	219	—
6th	304	—	—
7th	308	—	—
8th	340	—	—
9th	340	—	—
10th	345	—	—

‡ (M.R.J. Veletta)

Umpires: J.D. Ghosh and R.B. Gupta

Test No. 1054/45

INDIA v AUSTRALIA AVERAGES

INDIA - BATTING AND FIELDING

	M	I	NO	HS	Runs	Avge	100	50	Ct/St
R.J. Shastri	3	3	2	121*	231	231.00	1	1	1
S.M. Gavaskar	3	4	0	103	205	51.25	1	1	3
C.S. Pandit	2	3	1	39	100	50.00	—	—	3/1
K. Srikkanth	3	4	0	53	142	35.50	—	1	—
M. Azharuddin	3	4	0	50	126	31.50	—	1	1
M. Amarnath	3	3	0	51	87	29.00	—	1	—
K.S. More	2	3	0	15	19	6.33	—	—	1/1

Also batted (3 matches): Kapil Dev 119,1 (2 ct); Maninder Singh 0*,0 (2 ct); N.S. Yadav 19,8. (2 matches): C. Sharma 30,23; D.B. Vengsarkar 22*,164*. R.R. Kulkarni (1 match) did not bat.

INDIA – BOWLING

	Overs	Mdns	Runs	Wkts	Avge	Best	5 wI	10 wM
N.S. Yadav	136.3	25	359	8	44.87	4-84	—	—
R.J. Shastri	154.4	38	383	7	54.71	2-44	—	—
Maninder Singh	130	31	352	5	70.40	3-60	—	—

Also bowled: Kapil Dev 45-12-124-0; R.R. Kulkarni 29-2-114-3; C. Sharma 30-2-123-2; K. Srikkanth 6-0-19-0.

AUSTRALIA - BATTING AND FIELDING

	M	I	NO	HS	Runs	Avge	100	50	Ct/St
D.M. Jones	3	5	1	210	371	92.75	1	1	2
A.R. Border	3	4	1	106	245	81.66	1	1	2
D.C. Boon	3	5	0	122	325	65.00	1	1	1
S.R. Waugh	3	4	3	39*	59	59.00	—	—	2
G.R.J. Matthews	3	3	1	44	91	45.50	—	—	1
G.R. Marsh	3	5	0	101	165	33.00	1	—	1
G.M. Ritchie	3	3	0	31	72	24.00	—	—	3

Also batted (3 matches): R.J. Bright 30,8 (2 ct); T.J. Zoehrer 52*,21 (4 ct). (2 matches): D.R. Gilbert 1; C.J. McDermott did not bat (1 ct); B.A. Reid 2*.

AUSTRALIA – BOWLING

	Overs	Mdns	Runs	Wkts	Avge	Best	5 wI	10 wM
G.R.J. Matthews	120.1	18	407	14	29.07	5-103	2	1
R.J. Bright	86	12	291	8	36.37	5-94	1	—

Also bowled: D.C. Boon 2-0-5-0; A.R. Border 13-3-41-0; D.R. Gilbert 35-4-119-1; D.M. Jones 1-1-0-0; C.J. McDermott 25-3-110-0; B.A. Reid 60-11-222-1; S.R. Waugh 35-5-130-2.

PAKISTAN v WEST INDIES (1st Test)

Played at Iqbal Stadium, Faisalabad, on 24, 26, 27, 28, 29 October 1986
Toss: Pakistan. Result: Pakistan won by 186 runs
Debuts: West Indies – A.H. Gray
In Pakistan's first innings, Salim Malik retired hurt at 90

PAKISTAN

Mohsin Khan lbw b Marshall	2		c Haynes b Walsh	40
Mudassar Nazar c Richardson b Marshall	26		c Haynes b Marshall	2
Ramiz Raja lbw b Marshall	0		c Gray b Patterson	13
Javed Miandad c Dujon b Patterson	1	(6)	c sub (A.L. Logie) b Gray	30
Qasim Omar hit wkt b Gray	3		lbw b Walsh	48
Salim Malik retired hurt	21	(11)	not out	3
*Imran Khan c and b Gray	61		c Harper b Marshall	23
Abdul Qadir c and b Patterson	14		lbw b Gray	2
†Salim Yousuf lbw b Gray	0	(4)	c Greenidge b Harper	61
Wasim Akram c Richardson b Gray	0	(9)	st Dujon b Harper	66
Tausif Ahmed not out	9	(10)	b Walsh	8
Extras (B1, LB11, NB10)	22		(B7, LB8, W2, NB15)	32
Total	159			328

WEST INDIES

G.C. Greenidge lbw b Wasim	10		lbw b Imran	12
D.L. Haynes lbw b Imran	40		lbw b Imran	0
R.B. Richardson b Tausif	54		c Ramiz b Qadir	14
H.A. Gomes c sub (Manzoor Elahi) b Qadir	33		b Qadir	2
†P.J.L. Dujon c Ramiz b Tausif	0	(6)	lbw b Imran	0
R.A. Harper c Salim Yousuf b Wasim	28	(7)	c sub (Shoaib Mohd) b Qadir	2
M.D. Marshall c Salim Yousuf b Wasim	5	(8)	c and b Qadir	10
*I.V.A. Richards c Salim Yousuf b Wasim	33	(5)	c Ramiz b Qadir	0
A.H. Gray not out	12		b Qadir	5
C.A. Walsh lbw b Wasim	4		b Imran	0
B.P. Patterson lbw b Wasim	0		not out	6
Extras (B9, LB8, NB12)	29		(LB2)	2
Total	248			53

WEST INDIES	*O*	*M*	*R*	*W*	*O*	*M*	*R*	*W*
Marshall	10	2	48	3	26	3	83	2
Patterson	12	1	38	2	19	3	63	1
Gray	11.5	3	39	4	22	4	82	2
Walsh	5	0	22	0	23	6	49	3
Harper					27.5	9	36	2
PAKISTAN								
Wasim	25	3	91	6	3	0	5	0
Imran	21	8	32	1	13	5	30	4
Qadir	15	1	58	1	9.3	1	16	6
Tausif	22	5	50	2				

FALL OF WICKETS

Wkt	*P 1st*	*WI 1st*	*P 2nd*	*WI 2nd*
1st	12	12	2	5
2nd	12	103	19	16
3rd	19	124	113	19
4th	37	124	124	19
5th	37	178	208	20
6th	119	192	218	23
7th	120	223	224	36
8th	120	243	258	42
9th	159	247	296	43
10th	—	248	328	53

Umpires: Khizar Hayat and Mian Mohammad Aslam

Test No. 1055/20

PAKISTAN v WEST INDIES (2nd Test)

Played at Gaddafi Stadium, Lahore, on 7, 8, 9 November 1986
Toss: Pakistan. Result: West Indies won by an innings and 10 runs
Debuts: Pakistan – Asif Mujtaba
In Pakistan's second innings, Qasim Omar retired hurt at 26

PAKISTAN

Mohsin Khan b Marshall	0	(2)	lbw b Gray	1
Rizwan-uz-Zaman c Richardson b Marshall	2	(1)	b Marshall	1
Qasim Omar lbw b Marshall	4		retired hurt	10
Javed Miandad c Greenidge b Walsh	46		b Walsh	19
Ramiz Raja b Gray	15		lbw b Gray	1
Asif Mujtaba b Marshall	8		lbw b Richards	6
†Salim Yousuf lbw b Walsh	8	(8)	lbw b Gray	13
Abdul Qadir run out	12	(9)	b Walsh	2
Wasim Akram lbw b Marshall	1	(11)	c Harper b Walsh	0
*Imran Khan not out	13	(7)	c Dujon b Walsh	2
Tausif Ahmed c Dujon b Walsh	0	(10)	not out	6
Extras (B9, LB4, NB9)	22		(B4, LB9, W1, NB2)	16
Total	131			77

WEST INDIES

G.C. Greenidge lbw b Qadir	75
D.L. Haynes b Tausif	18
R.B. Richardson lbw b Qadir	4
H.A. Gomes lbw b Imran	9
*I.V.A. Richards c Salim b Qadir	44
†P.J.L. Dujon b Imran	2
R.A. Harper lbw b Qadir	6
M.D. Marshall not out	13
C.G. Butts c Salim b Imran	6
A.H. Gray b Imran	10
C.A. Walsh b Imran	8
Extras (B15, LB5, NB3)	23
Total	218

WEST INDIES	*O*	*M*	*R*	*W*	*O*	*M*	*R*	*W*
Marshall	18	5	33	5	8	3	14	1
Gray	13	0	28	1	17	7	20	3
Walsh	21.4	3	56	3	14.5	5	21	4
Harper	1	0	1	0				
Richards					5	2	9	1
PAKISTAN								
Imran	30.5	4	59	5				
Wasim	9	2	16	0				
Qadir	32	5	96	4				
Tausif	19	6	27	1				

FALL OF WICKETS

	P	*WI*	*P*
Wkt	*1st*	*1st*	*2nd*
1st	0	49	3
2nd	6	71	3
3rd	9	107	33
4th	46	153	44
5th	75	160	54
6th	95	172	63
7th	98	179	69
8th	99	189	71
9th	129	204	77
10th	131	218	—

Umpires: V.K. Ramaswamy and P.D. Reporter

Test No. 1056/21

PAKISTAN v WEST INDIES (3rd Test)

Played at National Stadium, Karachi, on 20, 21, 22, 24, 25 November 1986
Toss: West Indies. Result: match drawn
Debut: Pakistan – Salim Jaffer

WEST INDIES

C.G. Greenidge c Salim Yousuf b Mudassar	27	b Qadir	8
D.L. Haynes lbw b Imran	3	not out	88
R.B. Richardson c Asif b Salim Jaffer	44	c Ramiz b Qadir	32
H.A. Gomes lbw b Qadir	18	lbw b Qadir	5
*I.V.A. Richards c Ramiz b Tausif	70	c Salim Yousuf b Imran	28
†P.J.L. Dujon c Salim Yousuf b Qadir	19	c Salim Yousuf b Salim Jaffer	6
R.A. Harper lbw b Imran	9	b Imran	4
M.D. Marshall b Tausif	4	lbw b Imran	0
C.G. Butts lbw b Qadir	17	c Mohsin b Imran	12
A.H. Gray c Imran b Qadir	0	b Imran	0
C.A. Walsh not out	0	b Imran	0
Extras (B14, LB11, W1, NB3)	29	(B7, LB13, W1, NB7)	28
Total	240		211

PAKISTAN

Mudassar Nazar b Gray	16	(6) lbw b Butts	25
Mohsin Khan c Richards b Marshall	1	c Greenidge b Marshall	4
Ramiz Raja c Harper b Butts	62	(4) b Butts	29
Javed Miandad run out	76	(5) b Marshall	4
*Imran Khan lbw b Butts	1	(8) not out	15
Asif Mujtaba c Dujon b Marshall	12	(7) c Dujon b Walsh	6
Qasim Omar c Richardson b Butts	5	(1) c Dujon b Gray	1
†Salim Yousuf c Walsh b Butts	22	(3) c Haynes b Marshall	10
Tausif Ahmed c Richardson b Gray	3	not out	7
Salim Jaffer b Gray	9		
Abdul Qadir not out	8		
Extras (B9, LB12, W1, NB2)	24	(B17, LB6, W1)	24
Total	239	(7 wickets)	125

PAKISTAN	*O*	*M*	*R*	*W*	*O*	*M*	*R*	*W*
Imran	19	4	32	2	22.3	2	46	6
Salim Jaffer	15	5	34	1	14	4	23	1
Mudassar	4	0	15	1				
Qadir	31.5	3	107	4	44	9	84	3
Tausif	17	7	27	2	12	2	36	0
Asif					3	2	2	0
WEST INDIES								
Marshall	33	9	57	2	19	5	31	3
Gray	21.1	6	40	3	14	7	18	1
Harper	7	0	31	0	1	0	1	0
Walsh	11	2	17	0	22	11	30	1
Butts	38	15	73	4	22	9	22	2

FALL OF WICKETS

Wkt	*WI 1st*	*P 1st*	*WI 2nd*	*P 2nd*
1st	14	19	36	3
2nd	55	29	107	16
3rd	94	140	128	19
4th	110	145	159	25
5th	172	172	171	73
6th	204	179	185	95
7th	210	215	185	95
8th	227	218	209	—
9th	234	222	211	—
10th	240	239	211	—

Umpires: V.K. Ramaswamy and P.D. Reporter   Test No. 1057/22

PAKISTAN v WEST INDIES AVERAGES

PAKISTAN – BATTING AND FIELDING

	M	I	NO	HS	Runs	Avge	100	50	Ct/St
Javed Miandad	3	6	0	76	176	29.33	—	1	—
Imran Khan	3	6	2	61	115	28.75	—	1	1
Ramiz Raja	3	6	0	62	120	20.00	—	1	5
Salim Yousuf	3	6	0	61	114	19.00	—	1	9
Mudassar Nazar	2	4	0	26	69	17.25	—	—	—
Wasim Akram	2	4	0	66	67	16.75	—	1	—
Qasim Omar	3	6	1	48	71	14.20	—	—	—
Tausif Ahmed	3	6	3	9*	33	11.00	—	—	—
Abdul Qadir	3	5	1	14	38	9.50	—	—	1
Mohsin Khan	3	6	0	40	48	8.00	—	—	1
Asif Mujtaba	2	4	0	12	32	8.00	—	—	1

Also batted (1 match): Rizwan-uz-Zaman 2,1; Salim Jaffer 9; Salim Malik 21*,3*.

PAKISTAN – BOWLING

	Overs	Mdns	Runs	Wkts	Avge	Best	5 wI	10 wM
Imran Khan	106.2	23	199	18	11.05	6-46	2	—
Wasim Akram	37	5	112	6	18.66	6-91	1	—
Abdul Qadir	132.2	19	361	18	20.05	6-16	1	—
Tausif Ahmed	70	22	140	5	28.00	2-27	—	—

Also bowled: Asif Mujtaba 3-2-2-0; Mudassar Nazar 4-0-15-1; Salim Jaffer 29-5-57-2.

WEST INDIES – BATTING AND FIELDING

	M	I	NO	HS	Runs	Avge	100	50	Ct/St
D.L. Haynes	3	5	1	88*	149	37.25	—	1	3
I.V.A. Richards	3	5	0	70	175	35.00	—	1	1
R.B. Richardson	3	5	0	54	148	29.60	—	1	5
C.G. Greenidge	3	5	0	75	132	26.40	—	1	3
H.A. Gomes	3	5	0	33	67	13.40	—	—	—
C.G. Butts	2	3	0	17	35	11.66	—	—	—
R.A. Harper	3	5	0	28	49	9.80	—	—	3
M.D. Marshall	3	5	1	13*	32	8.00	—	—	—
A.H. Gray	3	5	1	12*	27	6.75	—	—	2
P.J.L. Dujon	3	5	0	19	27	5.40	—	—	6/1
C.A. Walsh	3	5	1	8	12	3.00	—	—	1

Also batted (1 match): B.P. Patterson 0,6* (1 ct).

WEST INDIES – BOWLING

	Overs	Mdns	Runs	Wkts	Avge	Best	5 wI	10 wM
C.G. Butts	60	24	95	6	15.83	4-73	—	—
A.H. Gray	99	27	227	14	16.21	4-39	—	—
M.D. Marshall	114	27	266	16	16.62	5-33	1	—
C.A. Walsh	97.3	27	195	11	17.72	4-21	—	—

Also bowled: R.A. Harper 36.5-9-69-2; B.P. Patterson 31-4-101-3; I.V.A. Richards 5-2-9-1.

INDIA v SRI LANKA (1st Test)

Played at Green Park, Kanpur, on 17, 18 (no play), 20, 21, 22 December 1986
Toss: Sri Lanka. Result: match drawn
Debuts: India – B. Arun, R. Lamba; Sri Lanka – G.F. Labrooy

SRI LANKA	
S. Wettimuny lbw b Sharma	79
J.R. Ratnayeke lbw b Kapil Dev	93
P.A. De Silva b Arun	26
A.P. Gurusinha b Kapil Dev	19
R.L. Dias c Azharuddin b Arun	50
*L.R.D. Mendis lbw b Sharma	1
A. Ranatunga lbw b Maninder	52
†R.G. de Alwis b Maninder	13
A.L.F. De Mel c Arun b Shastri	25
E.A.R. De Silva lbw b Arun	21
G.F. Labrooy not out	5
Extras (B1, LB10, W6, NB19)	36
Total	420

INDIA	
S.M. Gavaskar c Wettimuny b Labrooy	176
K. Srikkanth c de Alwis b Ratnayeke	18
R. Lamba run out	24
D.B. Vengsarkar c Gurusinha b De Mel	57
M. Azharuddin lbw b Ratnayeke	199
R.J. Shastri lbw b Ratnayeke	6
*Kapil Dev lbw b Ratnayeke	163
B. Arun not out	2
†K.S. More, C. Sharma, Maninder Singh } did not bat	
Extras (B1, LB11, W1, NB18)	31
Total (7 wickets)	676

INDIA	*O*	*M*	*R*	*W*
Kapil Dev	30	11	81	2
Arun	27	7	76	3
Sharma	31	4	122	2
Maninder	32	12	89	2
Shastri	17	6	37	1
Srikkanth	1	0	4	0
SRI LANKA				
De Mel	31	4	119	1
Labrooy	35	4	164	1
Ratnayeke	37.1	2	132	4
E.A.R. De Silva	40	7	133	0
Ranatunga	15	4	58	0
Gurusinha	7	0	42	0
Wettimuny	2	0	16	0

FALL OF WICKETS

	SL	*I*
Wkt	*1st*	*1st*
1st	159	50
2nd	217	100
3rd	217	217
4th	286	380
5th	292	399
6th	355	671
7th	355	676
8th	389	—
9th	394	—
10th	420	—

Umpires: R.B. Gupta and V.K. Ramaswamy

Test No. 1063/5

INDIA v SRI LANKA (2nd Test)

Played at Vidarbha C.A. Ground, Nagpur, on 27, 28, 30, 31 December 1986
Toss: Sri Lanka. Result: India won by an innings and 106 runs
Debuts: nil

SRI LANKA

S. Wettimuny c Amarnath b Sharma	6		c Srikkanth b Kapil Dev	6
J.R. Ratnayeke c Shastri b Kapil Dev	17		c Gavaskar b Maninder	54
A.P. Gurusinha c Amarnath b Yadav	29		c and b Yadav	15
R.L. Dias b Maninder	6		b Maninder	2
P.A. De Silva lbw b Yadav	33		c sub (Madan Lal) b Maninder	6
A. Ranatunga c Amarnath b Yadav	59	(7)	c Gavaskar b Maninder	5
*L.R.D. Mendis c Srikkanth b Maninder	1	(6)	b Maninder	38
B.R. Jurangpathy b Maninder	0		c Vengsarkar b Yadav	0
†R.G. de Alwis c Vengsarkar b Yadav	1	(11)	c More b Maninder	0
R.J. Ratnayake not out	32		not out	4
E.A.R. De Silva c Shastri b Yadav	16	(9)	c Srikkanth b Maninder	0
Extras (B2, LB1, NB1)	4		(B4, LB5, NB2)	11
Total	204			141

INDIA

K. Srikkanth c de Alwis b Ratnayeke	4
R. Lamba c Jurangpathy b E.A.R. De Silva	53
M. Amarnath c sub‡ b Jurangpathy	131
D.B. Vengsarkar c Jurangpathy b Ratnayake	153
S.M. Gavaskar c E.A.R. De Silva b Gurusinha	74
*Kapil Dev not out	11
R.J. Shastri c sub‡ b Gurusinha	12
†K.S. More, C. Sharma, N.S. Yadav, Maninder Singh — did not bat	
Extras (LB4, W1, NB8)	13
Total (6 wickets declared)	451

INDIA	*O*	*M*	*R*	*W*	*O*	*M*	*R*	*W*
Kapil Dev	10	3	29	1	6	1	16	1
Sharma	5	0	26	1	5	0	14	0
Maninder	20	6	56	3	17.4	4	51	7
Yadav	19.1	4	76	5	14	6	21	2
Shastri	5	2	14	0	6	0	30	0
SRI LANKA								
Ratnayake	35	4	139	2				
Ratnayeke	28	4	89	0				
Ranatunga	6	1	34	0				
E.A.R. De Silva	38	5	91	1				
Jurangpathy	21	3	69	1				
Gurusinha	5	0	25	2				

FALL OF WICKETS

Wkt	*SL 1st*	*I 1st*	*SL 2nd*
1st	7	5	15
2nd	38	131	42
3rd	52	304	47
4th	66	420	57
5th	105	428	122
6th	110	451	132
7th	110	—	137
8th	129	—	137
9th	160	—	141
10th	204	—	141

‡(R.S. Mahanama)

Umpires: R. Mehra and P.D. Reporter

Test No. 1064/6

INDIA v SRI LANKA (3rd Test)

Played at Barabati Stadium, Cuttack, on 4, 5, 6, 7 January 1987
Toss: India. Result: India won by an innings and 67 runs
Debuts: nil

INDIA	
S.M. Gavaskar lbw b Ratnayeke	5
K. Srikkanth b Ratnayake	40
M. Amarnath b Anurasiri	39
D.B. Vengsarkar lbw b Ratnayeke	166
R. Lamba lbw b Ratnayeke	24
R.J. Shastri c E.A.R. De Silva b Ratnayeke	19
*Kapil Dev b Anurasiri	60
B. Arun c Ranatunga b Anurasiri	2
†K.S. More not out	6
N.S. Yadav st de Alwis b Anurasiri	3
Maninder Singh lbw b Ratnayeke	2
Extras (B8, LB19, NB7)	34
Total	400

SRI LANKA				
S. Wettimuny c Kapil Dev b Maninder	6		b Shastri	12
J.R. Ratnayeke c Srikkanth b Yadav	20		c Srikkanth b Yadav	22
A.P. Gurusinha c Lamba b Arun	40		c Arun b Yadav	10
E.A.R. De Silva b Kapil Dev	1	(9)	st More b Yadav	19
*L.R.D. Mendis b Kapil Dev	9		lbw b Shastri	27
A. Ranatunga lbw b Kapil Dev	30		lbw b Maninder	2
R.L. Dias c Kapil Dev b Maninder	49		b Shastri	9
P.A. De Silva lbw b Maninder	21		c Shastri b Maninder	8
R.J. Ratnayake lbw b Maninder	0	(4)	b Kapil Dev	24
†R.G. de Alwis c Srikkanth b Kapil Dev	0		lbw b Shastri	0
S.D. Anurasiri not out	0		not out	0
Extras (B1, LB11, NB3)	15		(B2, LB5, NB2)	9
Total	191			142

SRI LANKA	O	M	R	W	O	M	R	W
Ratnayake	30	5	98	1				
Ratnayeke	27.3	3	85	5				
E.A.R. De Silva	40	6	114	0				
Anurasiri	26	3	71	4				
Ranatunga	4	2	5	0				
INDIA								
Kapil Dev	26	3	69	4	16	4	36	1
Arun	13	5	26	1	2	0	14	0
Maninder	17.1	6	41	4	17	5	42	2
Yadav	15	6	21	1	13	3	32	3
Shastri	5	0	22	0	11	4	11	4

FALL OF WICKETS	I	SL	SL
Wkt	*1st*	*1st*	*2nd*
1st	18	27	35
2nd	70	33	45
3rd	164	38	51
4th	225	56	91
5th	272	96	94
6th	383	125	112
7th	385	188	121
8th	387	190	121
9th	397	191	124
10th	400	191	142

Umpires: R.B. Gupta and V.K. Ramaswamy

Test No. 1065/7

INDIA v SRI LANKA AVERAGES

INDIA – BATTING AND FIELDING

	M	*I*	*NO*	*HS*	*Runs*	*Avge*	*100*	*50*	*Ct/St*
D.B. Vengsarkar	3	3	0	166	376	125.33	2	1	2
Kapil Dev	3	3	1	163	234	117.00	1	1	2
S.M. Gavaskar	3	3	0	176	255	85.00	1	1	2
M. Amarnath	2	2	0	131	170	85.00	1	—	3
R. Lamba	3	3	0	53	101	33.66	—	1	1
K. Srikkanth	3	3	0	40	62	20.66	—	—	6
R.J. Shastri	3	3	0	19	37	12.33	—	—	3
B. Arun	2	2	1	2*	4	4.00	—	—	2

Also batted: (3 matches): K.S. More 6* (1 ct, 1 st); Maninder Singh 2. (2 matches): N.S. Yadav 3 (1 ct). (1 match) M. Azharuddin 199 (1 ct). C. Sharma (2 matches) did not bat.

INDIA – BOWLING

	Overs	*Mdns*	*Runs*	*Wkts*	*Avge*	*Best*	*5 wI*	*10 wM*
N.S. Yadav	61.1	19	150	11	13.63	5-76	1	—
Maninder Singh	103.5	33	279	18	15.50	7-51	1	1
R.J. Shastri	44	12	114	5	22.80	4-11	—	—
Kapil Dev	88	22	231	9	25.66	4-69	—	—
B. Arun	42	12	116	4	29.00	3-76	—	—
C. Sharma	41	4	162	3	54.00	2-122	—	—

Also bowled: K. Srikkanth 1-0-4-0.

SRI LANKA – BATTING AND FIELDING

	M	*I*	*NO*	*HS*	*Runs*	*Avge*	*100*	*50*	*Ct/St*
J.R. Ratnayeke	3	5	0	93	206	41.20	—	2	—
R.J. Ratnayake	2	4	2	32*	60	30.00	—	—	—
A. Ranatunga	3	5	0	59	148	29.60	—	2	1
R.L. Dias	3	5	0	50	116	23.20	—	1	—
A.P. Gurusinha	3	5	0	40	113	22.60	—	—	1
S. Wettimuny	3	5	0	79	109	21.80	—	1	1
P.A. De Silva	3	5	0	33	94	18.80	—	—	—
L.R.D. Mendis	3	5	0	38	76	15.20	—	—	—
E.A.R. De Silva	3	5	0	21	57	11.40	—	—	2
R.G. de Alwis	3	5	0	13	14	2.80	—	—	2/1
B.R. Jurangpathy	1	2	0	0	0	0.00	—	—	2
S.D. Anurasiri	1	2	2	0*	0	—	—	—	—

Also batted: (1 match): A.L.F. De Mel 25; G.F. Labrooy 5*.

SRI LANKA – BOWLING

	Overs	*Mdns*	*Runs*	*Wkts*	*Avge*	*Best*	*5 wI*	*10 wM*
S.D. Anurasiri	26	3	71	4	17.75	4-71	—	—
A.P. Gurusinha	8.5	0	67	2	33.50	2-25	—	—
J.R. Ratnayeke	92.4	9	306	9	34.00	5-85	1	—
R.J. Ratnayake	65	9	237	3	79.00	2-139	—	—

Also bowled: A.L.F. De Mel 31-4-119-1; E.A.R. De Silva 118-18-338-1; B.R. Jurangpathy 21-3-69-1; G.F. Labrooy 35-4-164-1; A. Ranatunga 25-7-97-0; S. Wettimuny 2-0-16-0.

THE 1986 FIRST-CLASS SEASON STATISTICAL HIGHLIGHTS

HIGHEST INNINGS TOTALS

590-7 dec	Kent v Oxford University	Oxford
519-7 dec	New Zealanders v D.B. Close's XI	Scarborough
503	Northamptonshire v Gloucestershire	Northampton
500-9 dec	Surrey v Worcestershire	The Oval

LOWEST INNINGS TOTALS

44	Essex v Northamptonshire	Colchester
58	Nottinghamshire v Leicestershire	Leicester
64	Surrey v Hampshire	Basingstoke
65	Warwickshire v Kent	Folkestone
70	Middlesex v Sussex	Lord's

MOST EXTRAS IN AN INNINGS

53	Gloucestershire v Derbyshire	Chesterfield

FIRST TO INDIVIDUAL TARGETS

1000 RUNS	G.A. Hick	Worcestershire	July 17
2000 RUNS	C.G. Greenidge	Hampshire	September 10

At 20 years 112 days G.A. Hick became the youngest to score 2000 runs in a season

100 WICKETS	C.A. Walsh	Gloucestershire	August 11

TRIPLE HUNDRED AND 300 RUNS IN A DAY

K.R. Rutherford	317	New Zealanders v D.B. Close's XI	Scarborough

DOUBLE HUNDREDS

R.J. Bailey (2)	200*	Northamptonshire v Yorkshire	Luton
	224*	Northamptonshire v Glamorgan	Swansea
C.G. Greenidge	222	Hampshire v Northamptonshire	Northampton
R.A. Harper	234	Northamptonshire v Gloucestershire	Northampton
G.A. Hick (2)	227*	Worcestershire v Nottinghamshire	Worcester
	219*	Worcestershire v Glamorgan (*In successive innings*)	Neath
T.E. Jesty	221	Surrey v Essex	The Oval
P.M. Roebuck	221*	Somerset v Nottinghamshire	Nottingham
J.J. Whitaker	200*	Leicestershire v Nottinghamshire	Leicester

FOUR HUNDREDS IN SUCCESSIVE INNINGS

C.G. Greenidge (Hampshire) 222 v Nh, 103 and 180* v D, 126 v Sx

HUNDRED IN EACH INNINGS

C.G. Greenidge	103	180*	Hampshire v Derbyshire	Derby
M.D. Moxon	123	112*	Yorkshire v Indians	Scarborough

FASTEST HUNDRED (WALTER LAWRENCE TROPHY)

I.V.A. Richards	48 balls	Somerset v Glamorgan	Taunton

In 57 minutes and including 6 sixes and 12 fours

HUNDRED BEFORE LUNCH

		Day		
M. Amarnath	101*	2	Indians v Northamptonshire	Northampton
C.G. Greenidge	125*	1	Hampshire v Sussex	Hove
I.V.A. Richards	102	2	Somerset v Glamorgan	Taunton
K.R. Rutherford	101*	2	New Zealanders v D.B. Close's XI	Scarborough

Rutherford added a further 199 between lunch and tea*

HUNDRED ON FIRST-CLASS DEBUT

R.J. Bartlett	117*	Somerset v Oxford University	Oxford
P.D. Bowler	100*	Leicestershire v Hampshire	Leicester
I.L. Philip	145	Scotland v Ireland	Glasgow

CARRYING BAT THROUGH COMPLETED INNINGS

G.S. Clinton	84*	Surrey (171) v Yorkshire	Leeds
W.N. Slack	105*	Middlesex (252) v Yorkshire	Leeds

FIFTY BOUNDARIES IN AN INNINGS

K.R. Rutherford (45×4, 8×6) New Zealanders v D.B. Close's XI Scarborough

TWELVE SIXES IN AN INNINGS

R.A. Harper Northamptonshire v Gloucestershire Northampton

NOTABLE PARTNERSHIPS † *County record*

First Wicket

282	M.D. Moxon/A.A. Metcalfe, Yorkshire v Lancashire	Manchester
273*	N.A. Felton/P.M. Roebuck, Somerset v Hampshire	Taunton
250†	C.G. Greenidge/V.P. Terry, Hampshire v Northants	Northampton

A.J. Moles and P.A. Smith shared opening partnerships of 161 and 155 for Warwickshire v Somerset at Weston-super-Mare.

Second Wicket

344†	G. Cook/R.J. Boyd-Moss, Northamptonshire v Lancashire	Northampton
287*†	T.S. Curtis/G.A. Hick, Worcestershire v Glamorgan	Neath

Fourth Wicket

273*	P. Willey/P.D. Bowler, Leicestershire v Hampshire	Leicester
264	P. Willey/J.J. Whitaker, Leicestershire v Nottinghamshire	Leicester

Fifth Wicket

319	K.R. Rutherford/E.J. Gray, N. Zealanders v D.B. Close's XI	Scarborough

Seventh Wicket

193	R.A. Harper/D. Ripley, Northamptonshire v Glos	Northampton

Tenth Wicket

132†	A. Hill/M. Jean-Jacques, Derbyshire v Yorkshire	Sheffield

TEN OR MORE WICKETS IN A MATCH

J.A. Afford	10-103	Nottinghamshire v Kent	Nottingham
T.M. Alderman (3)	10-135	Kent v Gloucestershire	Gloucester
	11-130	Kent v Derbyshire	Derby
	14-144	Kent v Leicestershire	Canterbury
J.G. Bracewell	10-77	N. Zealanders v Combined U	Cambridge
J.H. Childs (3)	10-98	Essex v Glamorgan	Swansea
	11-95	Essex v Gloucestershire	Colchester
	10-123	Essex v Kent	Folkestone
P.A.J. DeFreitas	13-86	Leicestershire v Essex	Southend
G.R. Dilley	10-110	Kent v Lancashire	Canterbury
N.A. Foster (2)	10-154	Essex v Nottinghamshire	Chelmsford
	11-157	Essex v Worcestershire	Southend
A.H. Gray	12-113	Surrey v Warwickshire	The Oval
R.J. Hadlee (2)	10-72	Nottinghamshire v Surrey	Nottingham
	10-140	N. Zealand v Eng (2nd Test)	Nottingham
E.E. Hemmings (2)	10-164	Nottinghamshire v Essex	Chelmsford
	10-175	Nottinghamshire v Lancashire	Southport
P.W. Jarvis (2)	11-92	Yorkshire v Middlesex	Lord's
	10-108	Yorkshire v Surrey	Leeds
M. Jean-Jacques	10-125	Derbyshire v Kent	Derby
V.J. Marks	14-212	Somerset v Glamorgan	Cardiff
K.T. Medlycott	10-155	Surrey v Middlesex	Uxbridge
P.J. Newport	11-100	Worcestershire v Hampshire	Worcester
R.C. Ontong	13-127	Glamorgan v Nottinghamshire	Cardiff
B.P. Patterson	10-89	Lancashire v Essex	Manchester
N.V. Radford (3)	10-129	Worcestershire v Northants	Northampton
	10-169	Worcestershire v Sussex	Worcester
	11-129	Worcestershire v Somerset	Worcester
C. Sharma	10-188	India v Eng (3rd Test)	Birmingham
J. Simmons	10-145	Lancashire v Glamorgan	Lytham St Annes
C.A. Walsh (4)	11-94	Gloucestershire v Hampshire	Bournemouth
	11-113	Gloucestershire v Surrey	Bristol
	10-114	Gloucestershire v Somerset	Bristol
	12-124	Gloucestershire v Hampshire	Cheltenham

EIGHT OR MORE WICKETS IN AN INNINGS

T.M. Alderman (2)	8-46	Kent v Derbyshire	Derby
	8-70	Kent v Leicestershire	Canterbury
P. Bainbridge	8-53	Gloucestershire v Somerset	Bristol
J.H. Childs (2)	8-61	Essex v Northamptonshire	Colchester
	8-58	Essex v Gloucestershire (*In successive innings*)	Colchester
Imran Khan	8-34	Sussex v Middlesex	Lord's
M. Jean-Jacques	8-77	Derbyshire v Kent	Derby
V.J. Marks	8-100	Somerset v Glamorgan	Cardiff
R.C. Ontong	8-101	Glamorgan v Nottinghamshire	Cardiff
N.V. Radford	9-70	Worcestershire v Somerset	Worcester
A. Sidebottom	8-72	Yorkshire v Leicestershire	Middlesbrough
C.A. Walsh	9-72	Gloucestershire v Somerset	Bristol

HAT-TRICKS

A.M. Babington	Sussex v Gloucestershire	Bristol
G.R. Dilley	Kent v Essex	Chelmsford

OUTSTANDING ANALYSES

D.L. Underwood	35.5	29	11	7	Kent v Warwicks	Folkestone
D.J. Wild	6.3	4	4	4	Northants v Camb U	Cambridge
J.K. Lever	9	9	0	2	Essex v Camb U	Cambridge

1000 RUNS AND 50 WICKETS

V.J. Marks (Somerset) – 1057 runs and 59 wickets

SIX WICKET-KEEPING DISMISSALS IN AN INNINGS

6	S.A. Marsh	(5 ct, 1 st)	Kent v Warwickshire	Folkestone
6	R.J. Parks	(5 ct, 1 st)	Hampshire v Notts	Southampton

FIVE CATCHES IN THE FIELD

5	R.J. Bailey	Northamptonshire v Worcestershire	Northampton
5	M. Azharuddin	Indians v Somerset	Taunton
5	C.S. Cowdrey	Kent v Warwickshire	Folkestone

HAT-TRICK OF CATCHES

R.C. Russell	Gloucestershire v Surrey	The Oval

COUNTY CAPS AWARDED IN 1986

Derbyshire	J.E. Morris, O.H. Mortensen, P.G. Newman, B. Roberts
Essex	A.R. Border, J.H. Childs, A.W. Lilley, P.J. Prichard
Glamorgan	H. Morris, J.G. Thomas
Hampshire	R.J. Maru
Kent	S.A. Marsh
Lancashire	C. Maynard, G.D. Mendis
Leicestershire	T.J. Boon, R.A. Cobb, P.A.J. DeFreitas, J.J. Whitaker
Northamptonshire	D.J. Capel, R.A. Harper, D.J. Wild
Nottinghamshire	P. Johnson
Somerset	N.A. Felton
Sussex	A.N. Jones, D.A. Reeve, A.P. Wells
Warwickshire	P.A. Smith
Worcestershire	G.A. Hick, R.K. Illingworth, P.J. Newport, S.J. Rhodes, M.J. Weston
Yorkshire	P.W. Jarvis, A.A. Metcalfe

No caps were awarded by Gloucestershire, Middlesex or Surrey.

ENGLAND v INDIA (1st Test)

Played at Lord's, London, on 5, 6, 7, 9, 10 June 1986
Toss: India. Result: India won by 5 wickets
Debuts: India – K.S. More

ENGLAND				
G.A. Gooch b Sharma	114		lbw b Kapil Dev	8
R.T. Robinson c Azharuddin b Maninder	35		c Amarnath b Kapil Dev	11
*D.I. Gower c More b Sharma	18		lbw b Kapil Dev	8
M.W. Gatting b Sharma	0		b Sharma	40
A.J. Lamb c Srikkanth b Sharma	6		c More b Shastri	39
D.R. Pringle b Binny	63		c More b Kapil Dev	6
J.E. Emburey c Amarnath b Kapil Dev	7	(9)	c and b Maninder	1
†P.R. Downton lbw b Sharma	5	(7)	c Shastri b Maninder	29
R.M. Ellison c Kapil Dev b Binny	12	(8)	c More b Binny	19
G.R. Dilley c More b Binny	4		not out	2
P.H. Edmonds not out	7		c Binny b Maninder	7
Extras (LB15, W1, NB7)	23		(LB6, W1, NB3)	10
Total	294			180

INDIA				
S.M. Gavaskar c Emburey b Dilley	34		c Downton b Dilley	22
K. Srikkanth c Gatting b Dilley	20		c Gooch b Dilley	0
M. Amarnath c Pringle b Edmonds	69		lbw b Pringle	8
D.B. Vengsarkar not out	126		b Edmonds	33
M. Azharuddin c and b Dilley	33		run out	14
R.J. Shastri c Edmonds b Dilley	1		not out	20
R.M.H. Binny lbw b Pringle	9			
*Kapil Dev c Lamb b Ellison	1	(7)	not out	23
C. Sharma b Pringle	2			
†K.S. More lbw b Pringle	25			
Maninder Singh c Lamb b Emburey	6			
Extras (LB5, W1, NB9)	15		(B1, LB9, W1, NB5)	16
Total	341		(5 wickets)	136

INDIA	*O*	*M*	*R*	*W*	*O*	*M*	*R*	*W*
Kapil Dev	31	8	67	1	22	7	52	4
Binny	18.2	4	55	3	15	3	44	1
Sharma	32	10	64	5	17	4	48	1
Maninder	30	15	45	1	20.4	12	9	3
Amarnath	7	1	18	0	2	2	0	0
Shastri	10	3	30	0	20	8	21	1
ENGLAND								
Dilley	34	7	146	4	10	3	28	2
Ellison	29	11	63	1	6	0	17	0
Emburey	27	13	28	1				
Edmonds	22	7	41	1	11	2	51	1
Pringle	25	7	58	3	15	5	30	1

FALL OF WICKETS				
	E	*I*	*E*	*I*
Wkt	*1st*	*1st*	*2nd*	*2nd*
1st	66	31	18	10
2nd	92	90	23	31
3rd	92	161	35	76
4th	98	232	108	78
5th	245	238	113	110
6th	264	252	121	—
7th	269	253	164	—
8th	271	264	170	—
9th	287	303	170	—
10th	294	341	180	—

Umpires: K.E. Palmer and D.R. Shepherd — Test No. 1046/73

NURSERY END

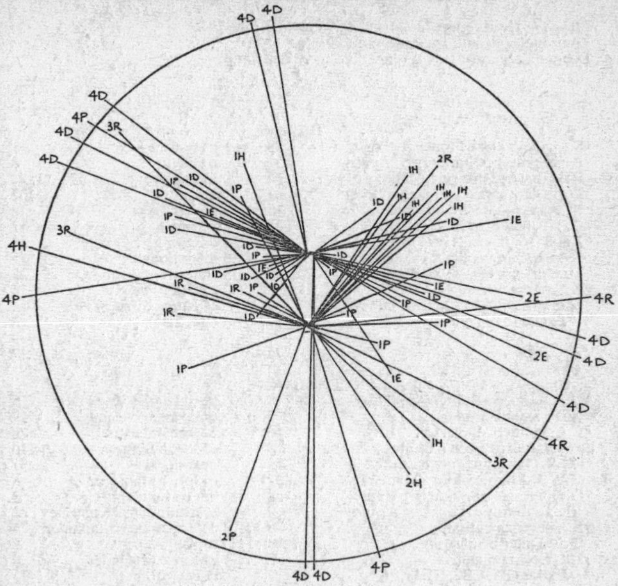

PAVILION END

BOWLER	Symbol	RUNS 1	2	3	4	Total
DILLEY	D	14	—	—	10	54
EDMONDS	H	9	1	—	1	15
ELLISON	R	3	1	3	2	22
EMBUREY	E	5	2	—	—	9
PRINGLE	P	12	1	—	3	26
TOTAL		43	5	3	16	126

D.B. VENGSARKAR at Lord's

126 RUNS (not out)
213 BALLS
327 MINUTES

DILIP VENGSARKAR became the first batsman to score three hundreds against England at Lord's.

ENGLAND v INDIA (2nd Test)

Played at Headingley, Leeds, on 19, 20, 21, 23 June 1986
Toss: India. Result: India won by 279 runs
Debuts: England – B.N. French; India – C.S. Pandit

INDIA				
S.M. Gavaskar c French b Pringle	35		c French b Lever	1
K. Srikkanth c Emburey b Pringle	31		b Dilley	8
R.J. Shastri c Pringle b Dilley	32		lbw b Lever	3
D.B. Vengsarkar c French b Lever	61		not out	102
M. Azharuddin lbw b Gooch	15		lbw b Lever	2
C.S. Pandit c Emburey b Pringle	23		b Pringle	17
*Kapil Dev lbw b Lever	0	(8)	c Gatting b Lever	31
R.M.H. Binny c Slack b Emburey	6	(10)	lbw b Pringle	26
Madan Lal c Gooch b Dilley	20	(9)	run out	22
†K.S. More not out	36	(7)	c Slack b Pringle	16
Maninder Singh c Gooch b Dilley	3		c Gatting b Pringle	1
Extras (LB5, NB5)	10		(B4, LB4)	8
Total	272			237

ENGLAND				
G.A. Gooch c Binny b Kapil Dev	8		c Srikkanth b Kapil Dev	5
W.N. Slack b Madan Lal	0		c Gavaskar b Binny	19
C.L. Smith b Madan Lal	6		c More b Shastri	28
A.J. Lamb c Pandit b Binny	10		c More b Binny	10
*M.W. Gatting c More b Binny	13		not out	31
C.W.J. Athey c More b Madan Lal	32		c More b Maninder	8
D.R. Pringle c Srikkanth b Binny	8	(8)	lbw b Maninder	8
J.E. Emburey c Kapil Dev b Binny	0	(9)	c Azharuddin b Kapil Dev	1
†B.N. French b Binny	8	(10)	c Vengsarkar b Maninder	5
G.R. Dilley b Shastri	10	(11)	run out	2
J.K. Lever not out	0	(7)	c More b Maninder	0
Extras (B1, LB2, NB4)	7		(LB9, NB2)	11
Total	102			128

ENGLAND	*O*	*M*	*R*	*W*	*O*	*M*	*R*	*W*
Dilley	24.2	7	54	3	17	2	71	1
Lever	30	4	102	2	23	5	64	4
Pringle	27	6	47	3	22.3	6	73	4
Emburey	17	4	45	1	7	3	9	0
Gooch	6	0	19	1	7	2	12	0
INDIA								
Kapil Dev	18	7	36	1	19.2	7	24	2
Madan Lal	11.1	3	18	3	9.4	2	30	0
Binny	13	1	40	5	8	1	18	2
Shastri	3	1	5	1	10	3	21	1
Maninder					16.3	6	26	4

FALL OF WICKETS	*I*	*E*	*I*	*E*
Wkt	*1st*	*1st*	*2nd*	*2nd*
1st	64	4	9	12
2nd	75	14	9	46
3rd	128	14	29	63
4th	163	38	35	77
5th	203	41	70	90
6th	203	63	102	90
7th	211	63	137	101
8th	213	71	173	104
9th	267	100	233	109
10th	272	102	237	128

Umpires: J. Birkenshaw and D.J. Constant

Test No. 1047/74

ENGLAND v INDIA (3rd Test)

Played at Edgbaston, Birmingham, on 3, 4, 5, 7, 8 July 1986
Toss: England. Result: match drawn
Debuts: England – M.R. Benson, N.V. Radford

ENGLAND			
G.A. Gooch c More b Kapil Dev	0	lbw b Sharma	40
M.R. Benson b Maninder	21	b Shastri	30
C.W.J. Athey c More b Kapil Dev	0	c More b Sharma	38
D.I. Gower lbw b Sharma	49	c Gavaskar b Sharma	26
*M.W. Gatting not out	183	lbw b Sharma	26
D.R. Pringle c Amarnath b Shastri	44	c More b Maninder	7
J.E. Emburey c Shastri b Maninder	38	not out	27
N.A. Foster b Binny	17	run out	0
P.H. Edmonds b Sharma	18	c Binny b Maninder	10
†B.N. French b Sharma	8	c More b Sharma	1
N.V. Radford c Gavaskar b Sharma	0	c Azharuddin b Sharma	1
Extras (LB7, NB5)	12	(B10, LB6, W2, NB11)	29
Total	390		235

INDIA			
S.M. Gavaskar b Pringle	29	c French b Foster	54
K. Srikkanth c Pringle b Radford	23	c Pringle b Edmonds	23
M. Amarnath b Edmonds	79	c French b Edmonds	16
D.B. Vengsarkar c Gooch b Radford	38	c French b Edmonds	0
M. Azharuddin c French b Foster	64	not out	29
R.J. Shastri c Gooch b Foster	18	c Emburey b Edmonds	0
*Kapil Dev c French b Foster	26		
†K.S. More c French b Emburey	48	(7) not out	31
R.M.H. Binny c Gower b Emburey	40		
C. Sharma c Gower b Pringle	9		
Maninder Singh not out	0		
Extras (B1, LB9, W1, NB5)	16	(B1, LB15, W1, NB4)	21
Total	390	(5 wickets)	174

INDIA	*O*	*M*	*R*	*W*	*O*	*M*	*R*	*W*
Kapil Dev	31	6	89	2	7	1	38	0
Binny	17	1	53	1	16	1	41	0
Sharma	29.3	2	130	4	24	4	58	6
Maninder	25	3	66	2	22	5	41	2
Shastri	14	1	45	1	23	8	39	1
Amarnath					2	1	2	0
ENGLAND								
Radford	35	3	131	2	3	0	17	0
Foster	41	9	93	3	22	9	48	1
Pringle	21	2	61	2	16	5	33	0
Edmonds	24	7	55	1	28	11	31	4
Emburey	18.5	7	40	2	7	1	19	0
Gatting					2	0	10	0

FALL OF WICKETS

	E	*I*	*E*	*I*
Wkt	*1st*	*1st*	*2nd*	*2nd*
1st	0	53	49	58
2nd	0	58	102	101
3rd	61	139	152	101
4th	88	228	163	104
5th	184	266	190	105
6th	278	275	190	—
7th	327	302	190	—
8th	367	370	217	—
9th	384	385	229	—
10th	390	390	235	—

Umpires: H.D. Bird and B.J. Meyer

Test No. 1048/75

ENGLAND v INDIA AVERAGES

ENGLAND – BATTING AND FIELDING

	M	I	NO	HS	Runs	Avge	100	50	Ct/St
M.W. Gatting	3	6	2	183*	293	73.25	1	—	3
G.A. Gooch	3	6	0	114	175	29.16	1	—	5
D.I. Gower	2	4	0	49	101	25.25	—	—	2
D.R. Pringle	3	6	0	63	136	22.66	—	1	4
C.W.J. Athey	2	4	0	38	78	19.50	—	—	—
A.J. Lamb	2	4	0	39	65	16.25	—	—	2
J.E. Emburey	3	6	1	38	74	14.80	—	—	4
P.H. Edmonds	2	4	1	18	42	14.00	—	—	1
G.R. Dilley	2	4	1	10	18	6.00	—	—	1
B.N. French	2	4	0	8	22	5.50	—	—	9

Played in one Test: M.R. Benson 21,30; P.R. Downton 5,29 (1 ct); R.M. Ellison 12,19; N.A. Foster 17,0; J.K. Lever 0*,0; N.V. Radford 0,1; R.T. Robinson 35,11; W.N. Slack 0,19 (2 ct); C.L. Smith 6,28.

ENGLAND – BOWLING

	Overs	Mdns	Runs	Wkts	Avge	Best	5 wI	10 wM
D.R. Pringle	126.3	31	302	13	23.23	4-73	—	—
P.H. Edmonds	85	27	178	7	25.42	4-31	—	—
J.K. Lever	53	9	166	6	27.66	4-64	—	—
G.R. Dilley	85.2	19	299	10	29.90	4-146	—	—
J.E. Emburey	76.5	28	141	4	35.25	2-40	—	—
N.A. Foster	63	18	141	4	35.25	3-93	—	—

Also bowled: R.M. Ellison 35-11-80-1; M.W. Gatting 2-0-10-0; G.A. Gooch 13-2-31-1; N.V. Radford 38-3-148-2.

INDIA – BATTING AND FIELDING

	M	I	NO	HS	Runs	Avge	100	50	Ct/St
D.B. Vengsarkar	3	6	2	126*	360	90.00	2	1	1
K.S. More	3	5	2	48	156	52.00	—	—	16
M. Amarnath	2	4	0	79	172	43.00	—	2	3
M. Azharuddin	3	6	1	64	157	31.40	—	1	3
S.M. Gavaskar	3	6	0	54	175	29.16	—	1	3
R.M.H. Binny	3	4	0	40	81	20.25	—	—	3
Kapil Dev	3	5	1	31	81	20.25	—	—	2
K. Srikkanth	3	6	0	31	105	17.50	—	—	3
R.J. Shastri	3	6	1	32	74	14.80	—	—	2
C. Sharma	2	2	0	9	11	5.50	—	—	—
Maninder Singh	3	4	1	6	10	3.33	—	—	1

Played in one Test: Madan Lal 20,22; C.S. Pandit 23,17 (1 ct).

INDIA – BOWLING

	Overs	Mdns	Runs	Wkts	Avge	Best	5 wI	10 wM
Maninder Singh	114.1	41	187	12	15.58	4-26	—	—
C. Sharma	102.3	20	300	16	18.75	6-58	2	1
R.M.H. Binny	87.2	11	251	12	20.91	5-40	1	—
Kapil Dev	128.2	36	306	10	30.60	4-52	—	—
R.J. Shastri	80	24	161	5	32.20	1-5	—	—

Also bowled: M. Amarnath 11-4-20-0; Madan Lal 20.5-5-48-3.

ENGLAND v NEW ZEALAND (1st Test)

Played at Lord's, London, on 24, 25, 26, 28, 29 July 1986
Toss: England. Result: match drawn
Debuts: England – M.D. Moxon; New Zealand – W. Watson

ENGLAND

G.A. Gooch c Smith b Hadlee	18	c Watson b Bracewell	183
M.D. Moxon lbw b Hadlee	74	lbw b Hadlee	5
C.W.J. Athey c J.J. Crowe b Hadlee	44	b Gray	16
D.I. Gower c M.D. Crowe b Bracewell	62	b Gray	3
*M.W. Gatting b Hadlee	2	c M.D. Crowe b Gray	26
P. Willey lbw b Watson	44	b Bracewell	42
P.H. Edmonds c M.D. Crowe b Hadlee	6	not out	9
†B.N. French retired hurt	0		
G.R. Dilley c Smith b Hadlee	17		
N.A. Foster b Watson	8		
N.V. Radford not out	12		
Extras (B6, LB7, NB7)	20	(LB6, W1, NB4)	11
Total	307	(6 wickets declared)	295

NEW ZEALAND

J.G. Wright b Dilley	0	(2) c Gower b Dilley	0
B.A. Edgar c Gatting b Gooch	83	(1) c Gower b Foster	0
K.R. Rutherford c Gooch b Dilley	0	not out	24
M.D. Crowe c and b Edmonds	106	not out	11
J.J. Crowe c Gatting b Edmonds	18		
*J.V. Coney c Gooch b Radford	51		
E.J. Gray c Gower b Edmonds	11		
R.J. Hadlee b Edmonds	19		
†I.D.S. Smith c Edmonds b Dilley	18		
J.G. Bracewell not out	1		
W. Watson lbw b Dilley	1		
Extras (B4, LB9, W6, NB15)	34	(LB4, NB2)	6
Total	342	(2 wickets)	41

N. ZEALAND	*O*	*M*	*R*	*W*	*O*	*M*	*R*	*W*
Hadlee	37.5	11	80	6	27	3	78	1
Watson	30	7	70	2	17	2	50	0
M.D. Crowe	8	1	38	0	4	0	13	0
Coney	4	0	12	0				
Bracewell	26	8	65	1	23.4	7	57	2
Gray	13	9	29	0	46	14	83	3
Rutherford					3	0	8	0
ENGLAND								
Dilley	35.1	9	82	4	6	3	5	1
Foster	25	6	56	0	3	1	13	1
Radford	25	4	71	1				
Edmonds	42	10	97	4	5	0	18	0
Gooch	13	6	23	1				
Gower					1	0	1	0

FALL OF WICKETS

	E	NZ	E	NZ
Wkt	*1st*	*1st*	*2nd*	*2nd*
1st	27	2	9	0
2nd	102	5	68	8
3rd	196	215	72	—
4th	198	218	136	—
5th	237	274	262	—
6th	258	292	295	—
7th	271	310	—	—
8th	285	340	—	—
9th	307	340	—	—
10th	—	342	—	—

Umpires: H.D. Bird and A.G.T. Whitehead

Test No. 1049/61

ENGLAND v NEW ZEALAND (2nd Test)

Played at Trent Bridge, Nottingham, on 7, 8, 9, 11, 12 August 1986
Toss: New Zealand. Result: New Zealand won by 8 wickets
Debuts: England – G.C. Small

ENGLAND

G.A. Gooch lbw b Hadlee	18		c Coney b Bracewell	17
M.D. Moxon b Hadlee	9		c Smith b Hadlee	23
C.W.J. Athey lbw b Watson	55	(4)	c Smith b Bracewell	6
D.I. Gower lbw b Gray	71	(5)	c J.J. Crowe b Bracewell	26
*M.W. Gatting b Hadlee	17	(6)	c Smith b Gray	4
D.R. Pringle c Watson b Stirling	21	(7)	c Gray b Stirling	9
J.E. Emburey c Smith b Hadlee	8	(8)	c M.D. Crowe b Hadlee	75
P.H. Edmonds c Smith b Hadlee	0	(3)	lbw b Hadlee	20
J.G. Thomas b Hadlee	28		c Gray b Stirling	10
†B.N. French c Coney b Watson	21		not out	12
G.C. Small not out	2		lbw b Hadlee	12
Extras (B1, LB3, NB2)	6		(B4, LB9, W1, NB2)	16
Total	256			230

NEW ZEALAND

J.G. Wright c Athey b Small	58		b Emburey	7
B.A. Edgar lbw b Thomas	8			
J.J. Crowe c French b Small	23	(2)	lbw b Small	2
M.D. Crowe c Edmonds b Emburey	28	(3)	not out	48
*J.V. Coney run out	24	(4)	not out	20
E.J. Gray c Athey b Edmonds	50			
R.J. Hadlee c Gooch b Thomas	68			
J.G. Bracewell c Moxon b Emburey	110			
†I.D.S. Smith lbw b Edmonds	2			
D.A. Stirling b Small	26			
W. Watson not out	8			
Extras (LB4, W2, NB2)	8			
Total	413		(2 wickets)	77

N. ZEALAND	*O*	*M*	*R*	*W*	*O*	*M*	*R*	*W*
Hadlee	32	7	80	6	33.1	15	60	4
Stirling	17	3	62	1	18	5	48	2
Gray	13	4	30	1	24	9	55	1
Watson	16.5	6	51	2	9	3	25	0
Coney	7	1	18	0				
Bracewell	4	1	11	0	11	5	29	3
ENGLAND								
Small	38	12	88	3	8	3	10	1
Thomas	39	5	124	2	4	0	16	0
Pringle	20	1	58	0	2	0	16	0
Edmonds	28	11	52	2	4	1	16	0
Emburey	42.5	17	87	2	6	1	15	1
Gooch	2	2	0	0				
Gower					0.0	0	4	0

FALL OF WICKETS

Wkt	*E 1st*	*NZ 1st*	*E 2nd*	*NZ 2nd*
1st	18	39	23	5
2nd	43	85	47	19
3rd	126	92	63	—
4th	170	142	87	—
5th	176	144	98	—
6th	191	239	104	—
7th	191	318	178	—
8th	205	326	203	—
9th	240	391	203	—
10th	256	413	230	—

Umpires: D.J. Constant and K.E. Palmer

Test No. 1050/62

RADCLIFFE ROAD END

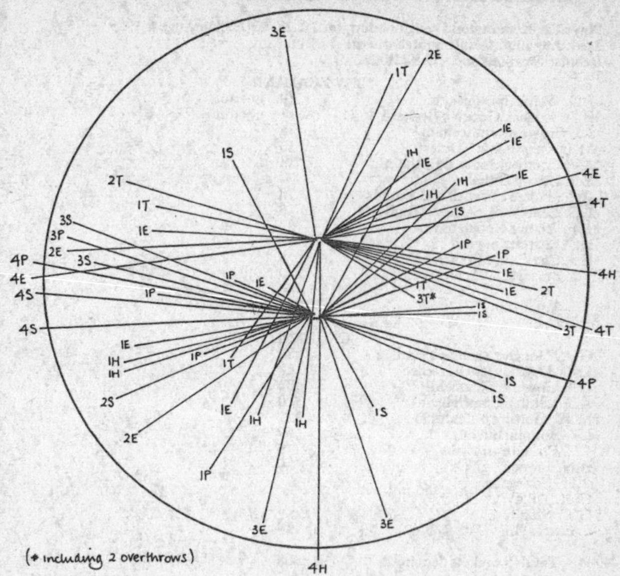

PAVILION END

BOWLER	Symbol	RUNS 1	2	3	4	Total
EDMONDS	H	7	—	—	2	15
EMBUREY	E	10	3	3	2	33
PRINGLE	P	6	—	1	2	17
SMALL	S	7	1	2	2	23
THOMAS	T	4	2	2	2	22
TOTAL		34	6	8	10	110

J.G. BRACEWELL at Trent Bridge

110 RUNS
200 BALLS
270 MINUTES

JOHN BRACEWELL's maiden Test hundred defied a batting average of 16 and was a vital contribution to New Zealand's first series win in England.

ENGLAND v NEW ZEALAND (3rd Test)

Played at Kennington Oval, London, on 21, 22, 23, 25, 26 August 1986
Toss: England. Result: match drawn
Debuts: New Zealand – T.E. Blain

NEW ZEALAND

J.G. Wright b Edmonds	119	not out	7
B.A. Edgar c Gooch b Botham	1	not out	0
J.J. Crowe lbw b Botham	8		
M.D. Crowe lbw b Dilley	13		
*J.V. Coney c Gooch b Botham	38		
E.J. Gray b Dilley	30		
R.J. Hadlee c French b Edmonds	6		
J.G. Bracewell c Athey b Emburey	3		
†T.E. Blain c Gooch b Dilley	37		
D.A. Stirling not out	18		
E.J. Chatfield c French b Dilley	5		
Extras (B1, W1, NB7)	9		
Total	287	(0 wickets)	7

ENGLAND

G.A. Gooch c Stirling b Hadlee		32
C.W.J. Athey lbw b Hadlee		17
D.I. Gower b Chatfield		131
A.J. Lamb b Chatfield		0
*M.W. Gatting b Chatfield		121
I.T. Botham not out		59
J.E. Emburey not out		9
†B.N. French	did not bat	
P.H. Edmonds	did not bat	
G.R. Dilley	did not bat	
G.C. Small	did not bat	
Extras (LB9, W5, NB5)		19
Total (5 wickets declared)		388

ENGLAND	*O*	*M*	*R*	*W*	*O*	*M*	*R*	*W*
Dilley	28.2	4	92	4				
Small	18	5	36	0				
Botham	25	4	75	3	1	0	7	0
Emburey	31	15	39	1				
Edmonds	22	10	29	2				
Gooch	4	1	15	0				
N. ZEALAND								
Hadlee	23.5	6	92	2				
Stirling	9	0	71	0				
Chatfield	21	7	73	3				
Gray	21	4	74	0				
Bracewell	11	1	51	0				
Coney	5	0	18	0				

FALL OF WICKETS

Wkt	*NZ 1st*	*E 1st*	*NZ 2nd*
1st	17	38	—
2nd	31	62	—
3rd	59	62	—
4th	106	285	—
5th	175	326	—
6th	192	—	—
7th	197	—	—
8th	251	—	—
9th	280	—	—
10th	287	—	—

Umpires: H.D. Bird and D.R. Shepherd

Test No. 1051/63

ENGLAND v NEW ZEALAND AVERAGES

ENGLAND – BATTING AND FIELDING

	M	*I*	*NO*	*HS*	*Runs*	*Avge*	*100*	*50*	*Ct/St*
D.I. Gower	3	5	0	131	293	58.60	1	2	3
G.A. Gooch	3	5	0	183	268	53.60	1	—	6
J.E. Emburey	2	3	1	75	92	46.00	—	1	—
M.W. Gatting	3	5	0	121	170	34.00	1	—	2
B.N. French	3	3	2	21	33	33.00	—	—	3
M.D. Moxon	2	4	0	74	111	27.75	—	1	1
C.W.J. Athey	3	5	0	55	138	27.60	—	1	3
G.C. Small	2	2	1	12	14	14.00	—	—	—
P.H. Edmonds	3	4	1	20	35	11.66	—	—	3

Played in two Tests: G.R. Dilley 17. *Played in one Test*: I.T. Botham 59*; N.A. Foster 8; A.J. Lamb 0; D.R. Pringle 21,9; N.V. Radford 12*; J.G. Thomas 28,10; P. Willey 44,42.

ENGLAND – BOWLING

	Overs	*Mdns*	*Runs*	*Wkts*	*Avge*	*Best*	*5 wI*	*10 wM*
G.R. Dilley	69.3	16	179	9	19.88	4-82	—	—
P.H. Edmonds	101	32	212	8	26.50	4-97	—	—
G.C. Small	64	20	134	4	33.50	3-88	—	—
J.E. Emburey	79.5	33	141	4	35.25	2-87	—	—

Also bowled: I.T. Botham 26-4-82-3; N.A. Foster 28-7-69-1; G.A. Gooch 19-9-38-1; D.I. Gower 1-0-5-0; D.R. Pringle 22-1-74-0; N.V. Radford 25-4-71-1; J.G. Thomas 43-5-140-2.

NEW ZEALAND – BATTING AND FIELDING

	M	*I*	*NO*	*HS*	*Runs*	*Avge*	*100*	*50*	*Ct/St*
M.D. Crowe	3	5	2	106	206	68.66	1	—	4
J.G. Bracewell	3	3	1	110	114	57.00	1	—	—
J.V. Coney	3	4	1	51	133	44.33	—	1	2
D.A. Stirling	2	2	1	26	44	44.00	—	—	1
J.G. Wright	3	6	1	119	191	38.20	1	1	—
R.J. Hadlee	3	3	0	68	93	31.00	—	1	—
E.J. Gray	3	3	0	50	91	30.33	—	1	2
B.A. Edgar	3	5	1	83	92	23.00	—	1	—
J.J. Crowe	3	4	0	23	51	12.75	—	—	2
I.D.S. Smith	2	2	0	18	20	10.00	—	—	7
W. Watson	2	2	1	8*	9	9.00	—	—	2

Played in one Test: T.E. Blain 37; E.J. Chatfield 5; K.R. Rutherford 0,24*.

NEW ZEALAND – BOWLING

	Overs	*Mdns*	*Runs*	*Wkts*	*Avge*	*Best*	*5 wI*	*10 wM*
R.J. Hadlee	153.5	42	390	19	20.52	6-80	2	1
J.G. Bracewell	75.4	22	213	6	35.50	3-29	—	—
W. Watson	72.5	18	196	4	49.00	2-51	—	—
E.J. Gray	117	40	271	5	54.20	3-83	—	—

Also bowled: E.J. Chatfield 21-7-73-3; J.V. Coney 16-1-48-0; M.D. Crowe 12-1-51-0; K.R. Rutherford 3-0-8-0; D.A. Stirling 44-8-181-3.

THE YEAR OF CHILDS

Essex won their third Championship in four seasons with something to spare. On their now customary visit to Buckingham Palace, they were duly received by the Lord's Taverners' Twelfth Man, Prince Philip. He could be excused for thinking that no other county competes in cricket's oldest competition. Essex are to the Eighties what Surrey were to the Fifties.

It was a marvellous performance by Essex who gained their ninth trophy and fourth championship in eight seasons after winning absolutely nothing in their first 103. They clinched the title at 3.49 pm on 10 September – when the season still had six days to run. Shrugging off injuries, Test calls and the premature abdication of their Australian eminence, they battled through a mockery of a summer to finish 28 points ahead of Gloucestershire who had made most of the early and middle running.

The only player associated with both counties was John Childs; 1986 was indisputably his year – as *Wisden* has affirmed. The previous season, after ten moderate summers with Gloucestershire, he moved to Essex, whereupon he played in four matches and claimed three Championship wickets for 377 runs. Now he proved that 35 was the optimum age for a left-arm spinner by taking 89 wickets at 16.28 apiece. In seven matches between 6 August and 2 September he took 48 wickets for 12.37 runs each, including 16 in two successive innings at Colchester. Ironically this mayhem prevented his first adopted county – he was born in Plymouth – from claiming their first official title. Gloucestershire have been credited with some on media assessment before 1890 when the competition was officially constituted.

One did not need to watch Essex in the field for many overs before realising that operations were still being monitored and frequently directed by the Wise Old Gnome. It is highly fortunate for Essex that Keith Fletcher has shrugged off his brutal treatment by England's selectors and has retained all his youthful zest for the county game. Graham Gooch is usually the first to give his former captain full credit and the pair have moulded into a most harmonious partnership.

Once again one wondered why anyone bothered to invent anything so pernickety as the present bonus points system. Inevitably the side winning most matches wins the Championship.

The Championship produced some outstanding performances. Gordon Greenidge, after being rebuked for a public go-slow, thundered his way to four hundreds in successive innings, the last of them at a pre-lunch gallop. Viv Richards, in probably his final season of county cricket, won the Walter Lawrence Trophy for the fastest hundred by using only 48 balls from Glamorgan's bowlers to complete the task. A young batsman called Bowler became the first to score a hundred for Leicestershire on his first-class debut. For the 23rd consecutive season no bowler took all ten wickets in an innings; Neil Radford and Courtney Walsh came closest. And Derek Underwood, celebrated his testimonial year by recording the slightly grudging analysis of 35.5 overs, 29 maidens, 11 runs and 7 wickets against Warwickshire at Folkestone.

BRITANNIC ASSURANCE COUNTY CHAMPIONSHIP 1986 FINAL TABLE

Win = 16 points*					*1st Inns Points*		*Total*
	P	*W*	*L*	*D*	*Bat*	*Bowl*	*Points*
1 **ESSEX** (4)	24	10	6	8	51	76	287
2 Gloucestershire (3)	24	9	3	12	50	65	259
3 Surrey (6)	24	8	6	10	54	66	248
4 Nottinghamshire (8)	24	7	2	15	55	80	247
5 Worcestershire (5)	24	7	5	12	58	72	242
6 Hampshire (2)	23	7	4	12	54	69	235
7 Leicestershire (16)	24	5	7	12	55	67	202
8 Kent (9)	24	5	7	12	42	75	197
9 Northamptonshire (10)	24	5	3	16	53	60	193
10 Yorkshire (11)	24	4	5	15	62	59	193
11 Derbyshire (13)	24	5	5	14	42	70	188
12 {Middlesex (1)	24	4	9	11	47	65	176
12 {Warwickshire (15)	24	4	5	15	61	51	176
14 Sussex (7)	23	4	7	12	46	56	166
15 Lancashire (14)	23	4	5	14	41	51	156
16 Somerset (17)	23	3	7	13	52	52	152
17 Glamorgan (12)	24	2	7	15	39	47	118

1985 final positions are shown in brackets.

* Yorkshire's total includes eight points for levelling the scores in a drawn match. Derbyshire gained 12 points for winning a match reduced to one innings. Where sides are equal on points, the one with the most wins has priority.

The following two matches were abandoned and are not included in the above table: May 31, June 2, 3 – Sussex v Somerset at Horsham; September 13, 15, 16 – Hampshire v Lancashire at Southampton.

COUNTY CHAMPIONS

The English County Championship was not officially constituted until December 1889. Prior to that date there was no generally accepted method of awarding the title; although the 'least matches lost' method existed, it was not consistently applied. Rules governing playing qualifications were not agreed until 1873, and the first unofficial points system was not introduced until 1888. Recent research has produced a list of champions dating back to 1826, but at least seven different versions exist for the period from 1864 to 1889 (see *The Wisden Book of Cricket Records*). Only from 1890 can any authorised list of county champions commence. From 1977 to 1983 the Championship was sponsored by Schweppes. BRITANNIC ASSURANCE have been its benefactors since 1984.

1890	Surrey
1891	Surrey
1892	Surrey
1893	Yorkshire
1894	Surrey
1895	Surrey
1896	Yorkshire
1897	Lancashire
1898	Yorkshire
1899	Surrey
1900	Yorkshire
1901	Yorkshire
1902	Yorkshire
1903	Middlesex
1904	Lancashire
1905	Yorkshire
1906	Kent
1907	Nottinghamshire
1908	Yorkshire
1909	Kent
1910	Kent
1911	Warwickshire
1912	Yorkshire
1913	Kent
1914	Surrey
1919	Yorkshire
1920	Middlesex
1921	Middlesex
1922	Yorkshire
1923	Yorkshire
1924	Yorkshire
1925	Yorkshire
1926	Lancashire
1927	Lancashire
1928	Lancashire
1929	Nottinghamshire
1930	Lancashire
1931	Yorkshire
1932	Yorkshire
1933	Yorkshire
1934	Lancashire
1935	Yorkshire
1936	Derbyshire
1937	Yorkshire
1938	Yorkshire
1939	Yorkshire
1946	Yorkshire
1947	Middlesex
1948	Glamorgan
1949	Middlesex Yorkshire
1950	Lancashire Surrey
1951	Warwickshire
1952	Surrey
1953	Surrey
1954	Surrey
1955	Surrey
1956	Surrey
1957	Surrey
1958	Surrey
1959	Yorkshire
1960	Yorkshire
1961	Hampshire
1962	Yorkshire
1963	Yorkshire
1964	Worcestershire
1965	Worcestershire
1966	Yorkshire
1967	Yorkshire
1968	Yorkshire
1969	Glamorgan
1970	Kent
1971	Surrey
1972	Warwickshire
1973	Hampshire
1974	Worcestershire
1975	Leicestershire
1976	Middlesex
1977	Kent Middlesex
1978	Kent
1979	Essex
1980	Middlesex
1981	Nottinghamshire
1982	Middlesex
1983	Essex
1984	Essex
1985	Middlesex
1986	Essex

SUSSEX RECLAIM THEIR HERITAGE

Sussex, thrice winners of the old Gillette Cup, won the NatWest Trophy for the first time and with something to spare. After three last-ball results within five finals, ten balls and seven wickets seemed rather a lot to spare. They owed much to Dermot Reeve, the Man of the Match, whose bustling swing bowling undid a sound start by Lancashire and set up a victory which his batsmen had little trouble in completing. Crucially he removed Clive Lloyd. Applauded to the wicket by a standing capacity Lord's, poor Hubert was all too soon trudging back after playing across his fourth ball. The heart went out of the crowd with that dismissal and the game seemed unable to inspire the usual fervour of these finals.

Ken Suttle, who appeared in a record 423 consecutive championship matches for Sussex, as well as in both of the very first two Lord's finals, remembered being awarded a £5 bonus for winning in 1963. 'We did much better the next year. They gave us £7 and ten shillings!'

A major miracle in a very minor summer came to pass on 25 June when the monsoons receded for a day and allowed all 16 first round matches to be completed according to schedule. The next three stages fared less happily. The Worcestershire–Sussex semi-final went well into a third day and involved a helicopter being used to dry the square for the first time in these matches.

GILLETTE CUP WINNERS

1963	Sussex	1969	Yorkshire	1975	Lancashire
1964	Sussex	1970	Lancashire	1976	Northamptonshire
1965	Yorkshire	1971	Lancashire	1977	Middlesex
1966	Warwickshire	1972	Lancashire	1978	Sussex
1967	Kent	1973	Gloucestershire	1979	Somerset
1968	Warwickshire	1974	Kent	1980	Middlesex

NATWEST BANK TROPHY WINNERS

1981	Derbyshire	1983	Somerset	1985	Essex
1982	Surrey	1984	Middlesex	1986	Sussex

THE NATWEST BANK TROPHY 1986

FIRST ROUND 25 June	SECOND ROUND 9, 10 July	QUARTER-FINALS 30, 31 July, 1 August	SEMI-FINALS 13, 14, 15 August	FINAL 6 September	
LANCASHIRE† Cumberland	LANCASHIRE	LANCASHIRE	LANCASHIRE	Lancashire (£9,500)	SUSSEX (£19,000)
SOMERSET† Dorset	Somerset†				
LEICESTERSHIRE† Ireland	LEICESTERSHIRE	Leicestershire† (£2,250)			
GLOUCESTERSHIRE Berkshire†	Gloucestershire†				
SURREY Cheshire†	SURREY	SURREY†	Surrey† (£4,500)		
DERBYSHIRE† Cornwall	Derbyshire†				
NOTTINGHAMSHIRE Devon†	NOTTINGHAMSHIRE†	Nottinghamshire (£2,250)			
KENT Scotland†	Kent				
HAMPSHIRE† Hertfordshire	Hampshire†	WORCESTERSHIRE†	Worcestershire† (£4,500)	SUSSEX	
WORCESTERSHIRE† Oxfordshire	WORCESTERSHIRE				
ESSEX Northumberland†	Essex	Warwickshire (£2,250)			
WARWICKSHIRE† Durham	WARWICKSHIRE†				
GLAMORGAN Staffordshire†	Glamorgan	SUSSEX	SUSSEX		
SUSSEX† Suffolk	SUSSEX†				
MIDDLESEX Northamptonshire†	Middlesex	Yorkshire† (£2,250)			
YORKSHIRE† Cambridgeshire	YORKSHIRE†				

† Home team. Winning teams are in capitals. Amounts in brackets show prize-money won by that county.

1986 NATWEST TROPHY FINAL

LANCASHIRE v SUSSEX

Played at Lord's, London, on 6 September
Toss: Sussex. Result: Sussex won by 7 wickets
Match Award: D.A. Reeve (adjudicator: Sir Leonard Hutton)

LANCASHIRE	RUNS	MINS	BALLS	6s	4s
G.D. Mendis lbw b Reeve	17	71	47	—	1
G. Fowler c Gould b C.M. Wells	24	55	44	—	3
J. Abrahams c Pigott b Reeve	20	53	45	—	3
*C.H. Lloyd lbw b Reeve	0	2	4	—	—
N.H. Fairbrother b Pigott	63	153	108	—	5
S.J. O'Shaughnessy b Reeve	4	23	23	—	—
A.N. Hayhurst c Gould b Imran	49	87	75	—	5
†C. Maynard c Gould b Imran	14	9	7	—	3
M. Watkinson not out	15	18	11	1	—
J. Simmons not out	6	13	9	—	—
P.J.W. Allott did not bat					
Extras (B1, LB17, W6, NB6)	30				
Total (60 overs; 251 minutes)	242-8 Closed				

SUSSEX	RUNS	MINS	BALLS	6s	4s
R.I. Alikhan b Allott	6	33	27	—	—
A.M. Green st Maynard b Simmons	62	152	131	—	8
P.W.G. Parker c Abrahams b Hayhurst	85	146	112	1	9
Imran Khan not out	50	62	61	—	3
C.M. Wells not out	17	34	22	1	1
A.P. Wells, *†I.J. Gould, G.S. Le Roux, D.A. Reeve, A.C.S. Pigott, A.N. Jones — did not bat					
Extras (LB17, W6)	23				
Total (58.2 overs; 216 minutes)	243-3				

SUSSEX	*O*	*M*	*R*	*W*
Imran	12	2	43	2
Le Roux	9	0	43	0
Jones	3	0	25	0
C.M. Wells	12	3	34	1
Reeve	12	4	20	4
Pigott	12	1	59	1
LANCASHIRE				
Watkinson	11.2	0	40	0
Allott	11	3	34	1
O'Shaughnessy	6	0	52	0
Hayhurst	12	2	38	1
Simmons	12	2	31	1
Abrahams	3	0	15	0
Fairbrother	3	0	16	0

FALL OF WICKETS

Wkt	*La*	*Sx*
1st	50	19
2nd	56	156
3rd	56	190
4th	85	—
5th	100	—
6th	203	—
7th	205	—
8th	217	—
9th	—	—
10th	—	—

Umpires: H.D. Bird and K.E. Palmer

*Captain †Wicket-keeper

NATWEST BANK TROPHY PRINCIPAL RECORDS 1963-86

(*Including The Gillette Cup*)

Highest Total	392-5	Warwicks v Oxon	Birmingham	1984
Highest Total in a Final	317-4	Yorks v Surrey	Lord's	1965
Highest Total by a Minor County	256	Oxon v Warwicks	Birmingham	1983
Highest Total Batting Second	306-6	Glos v Leics	Leicester	1983
Highest Losing Total	302-5	Leics v Glos	Leicester	1983
Lowest Total	39	Ire v Sussex	Hove	1985
Lowest Total in a Final	118	Lancs v Kent	Lord's	1974
Lowest Total to Win Batting First	98	Worcs v Durham	Chester-le-S	1968
Highest Score	206 A.I. Kallicharran	Warwicks v Oxon	Birmingham	1984
HS (Minor County)	132 G. Robinson	Lincs v Northumb	Jesmond	1971

Hundreds 145 have been scored in GC (93) and NWT (52) matches

Fastest Hundred	77 min – R.E. Marshall	Hants v Beds	Bedford	1968

Highest Partnerships for Each Wicket

1st	227	R.E. Marshall/B.L. Reed	Hants v Beds	Bedford	1968
2nd	286	I.S. Anderson/A. Hill	Derbys v Cornwall	Derby	1986
3rd	209	P. Willey/D.I. Gower	Leics v Ireland	Leicester	1986
4th	234*	D. Lloyd/C.H. Lloyd	Lancs v Glos	Manchester	1978
5th	166	M.A. Lynch/G.R.J. Roope	Surrey v Durham	The Oval	1982
6th	105	G. St A. Sobers/R.A. White	Notts v Worcs	Worcester	1974
7th	160*	C.J. Richards/I.R. Payne	Surrey v Lincs	Sleaford	1983
8th	69	S.J. Rouse/D.J. Brown	Warwicks v Middx	Lord's	1977
9th	87	M.A. Nash/A.E. Cordle	Glam v Lincs	Swansea	1974
10th	81	S. Turner/R.E. East	Essex v Yorks	Leeds	1982

Most Wickets	7-15	A.L. Dixon	Kent v Surrey	The Oval	1967
	7-30	P.J. Sainsbury	Hants v Norfolk	Southampton	1965
	7-32	S.P. Davis	Durham v Lancs	Chester-le-S	1983
	7-33	R.D. Jackman	Surrey v Yorks	Harrogate	1970
	7-37	N.A. Mallender	Northants v Worcs	Northampton	1984

Hat Tricks	J.D.F. Larter	Northants v Sussex	Northampton	1963
	D.A.D. Sydenham	Surrey v Cheshire	Hoylake	1964
	R.N.S. Hobbs	Essex v Middlesex	Lord's	1968
	N.M. McVicker	Warwicks v Lincs	Birmingham	1971
	G.S. Le Roux	Sussex v Ireland	Hove	1985

Most Wicket-Keeping Dismissals

6 (5 ct, 1 st)	R.W. Taylor	Derbys v Essex	Derby	1981
6 (4 ct, 2 st)	T. Davies	Glam v Staffs	Stone	1986

Most Catches in the Field

4	A.S. Brown	Glos v Middx	Bristol	1963
4	G. Cook	Northants v Glam	Northampton	1972
4	C.G. Greenidge	Hants v Cheshire	Southampton	1981
4	D.C. Jackson	Durham v Northants	Darlington	1984
4	T.S. Smith	Herts v Somerset	St Albans	1984

Most Match Awards: 8 C.H. Lloyd (Lancs); 7 Imran Khan (Worcs & Sussex); 6 B.L. D'Oliveira (Worcs), T.E. Jesty (Hants & Surrey), B. Wood (Lancs); 5 G. Cook (Northants), M.C. Cowdrey (Kent), G.A. Gooch (Essex), A.W. Greig (Sussex), R.D.V. Knight (Glos & Surrey), P. Willey (Northants & Leics), Zaheer Abbas (Glos).

MIDDLESEX WIN A CLASSIC FINAL

At 7.32 pm in near darkness and steady drizzle Middlesex won an extraordinary Benson and Hedges Cup Final when Dilley failed to hit the final ball from Hughes for six. It was a classic one-day match with several outstanding performances culminating in a last-ball climax.

The result gave a much-needed fillip to Middlesex. Reigning county champions, they had been severely hampered by injuries and Test calls and were currently languishing in 16th position in the county table. Clive Radley, at the ripe age of 42, and John Emburey ensured that the metropolitans would have some reward from the season's toils. Emburey's immaculate all-round performance, which included supremely accurate bowling and a snorting right-handed slip catch at full stretch, gained him the Gold Award. A rousing innings by Graham Cowdrey ensured the regulation dramatic finish and made David Gower's task as adjudicator a more than usually testing one.

Kent won a vital toss on a morning of such mist and murk that most pundits were predicting either the pre-lunch loss of eight wickets or the total abandonment of play. Middlesex managed an interval score of 89 for 4 from 34 overs thanks to Miller surviving some testing bowling by Kent and much manic calling by his opening partner. This was just the platform for Radley, and Middlesex were always slight favourites to win their second Benson and Hedges title after his 46-run partnership with Downton.

BENSON AND HEDGES CUP WINNERS

1972	Leicestershire	1977	Gloucestershire	1982	Somerset
1973	Kent	1978	Kent	1983	Middlesex
1974	Surrey	1979	Essex	1984	Lancashire
1975	Leicestershire	1980	Northamptonshire	1985	Leicestershire
1976	Kent	1981	Somerset	1986	Middlesex

1986 BENSON AND HEDGES CUP

GROUP A	*P*	*W*	*L*	*Pts*	*Rate*†
DERBYSHIRE	4	4	0	8	31.82
NORTHAMPTONSHIRE	4	3	1	6	52.64
Warwickshire	4	2	2	4	44.58
Leicestershire	4	1	3	2	40.43
Minor Counties	4	0	4	0	49.30
GROUP B					
WORCESTERSHIRE	4	3	1	6	37.76
NOTTINGHAMSHIRE	4	3	1	6	54.29
Yorkshire	4	2	2	4	36.29
Lancashire	4	1	3	2	49.84
Scotland	4	1	3	2	51.12
GROUP C					
ESSEX	4	4	0	8	38.64
SUSSEX	4	3	1	6	29.48
Gloucestershire	4	2	2	4	38.06
Somerset	4	1	3	2	41.25
Glamorgan	4	0	4	0	51.60
GROUP D					
MIDDLESEX	4	4	0	8	32.53
KENT	4	2	2	4	36.69
Hampshire	4	2	2	4	41.24
Surrey	4	2	2	4	56.82
Combined Universities	4	0	4	0	105.87

† Total balls bowled divided by wickets taken.

FINAL ROUNDS

QUARTER-FINALS 28, 29 May	SEMI-FINALS 11 June	FINAL 12 July	
KENT Derbyshire† (£2,250)	KENT	Kent (£9,500)	MIDDLESEX (£19,000)
WORCESTERSHIRE† Northamptonshire (£2,250)	Worcestershire† (£4,500)		
NOTTINGHAMSHIRE† Essex (£2,250)	Nottinghamshire (£4,500)	MIDDLESEX	
MIDDLESEX† Sussex (£2,250)	MIDDLESEX†		

† Home team. Winning teams are in capitals. Prize-money in brackets.

1986 BENSON AND HEDGES CUP FINAL

KENT v MIDDLESEX

Played at Lord's, London, on 12 July
Toss: Kent. Result: Middlesex won by 2 runs
Match Award: J.E. Emburey (adjudicator: D.I. Gower)

MIDDLESEX	**RUNS**	**MINS**	**BALLS**	**6s**	**4s**
W.N. Slack b Dilley	0	10	8	—	—
A.J.T. Miller c Marsh b C.S. Cowdrey	37	124	73	—	3
*M.W. Gatting c Marsh b Ellison	25	68	66	—	3
R.O. Butcher c Marsh b Ellison	0	1	1	—	—
C.T. Radley run out (Marsh)	54	117	93	—	6
†P.R. Downton lbw b Ellison	13	39	30	—	—
J.E. Emburey b Baptiste	28	50	45	—	1
P.H. Edmonds not out	15	21	13	—	1
S.P. Hughes not out	4	7	5	—	—
N.G. Cowans, W.W. Daniel } did not bat					
Extras (LB8, W11, NB4)	23				
Total (55 overs; 226 minutes)	199-7 Closed				

KENT	**RUNS**	**MINS**	**BALLS**	**6s**	**4s**
M.R. Benson c Downton b Cowans	1	34	23	—	—
S.G. Hinks lbw b Cowans	13	56	35	—	1
C.J. Tavaré c Downton b Daniel	3	12	15	—	—
N.R. Taylor c Miller b Edmonds	19	88	78	—	1
*C.S. Cowdrey c Emburey b Hughes	19	57	45	—	—
G.R. Cowdrey c Radley b Hughes	58	86	70	2	3
E.A.E. Baptiste b Edmonds	20	42	35	—	—
R.M. Ellison b Edmonds	29	22	18	1	1
†S.A. Marsh not out	14	13	9	1	—
G.R. Dilley not out	4	9	3	—	—
D.L. Underwood did not bat					
Extras (LB9, W8)	17				
Total (55 overs; 218 minutes)	197-8 Closed				

KENT	*O*	*M*	*R*	*W*	FALL OF WICKETS *Wkt*	*M*	*K*
Dilley	11	2	19	1	1st	6	17
Baptiste	11	0	61	1	2nd	66	20
C.S. Cowdrey	11	0	48	1	3rd	66	20
Ellison	11	2	27	3	4th	85	62
Underwood	11	4	36	0	5th	131	72
MIDDLESEX					6th	163	141
Cowans	9	2	18	2	7th	183	178
Daniel	11	1	43	1	8th	—	182
Gatting	4	0	18	0	9th	—	—
Hughes	9	3	34	2	10th	—	—
Emburey	11	4	17	0			
Edmonds	11	1	58	3			

Umpires: D.J. Constant and D.R. Shepherd

*Captain †Wicket-keeper

BENSON AND HEDGES CUP

PRINCIPAL RECORDS 1972-86

Highest Total	350-3	Essex v Comb U	Chelmsford	1979
Highest Total Batting Second / **Highest Losing Total**	294-7	Glos v Somerset	Taunton	1982
Lowest Total	56	Leics v Minor C	Wellington	1982
Highest Score	198*G.A. Gooch	Essex v Sussex	Hove	1982

Hundreds 129 have been scored in Benson and Hedges Cup matches

Fastest Hundred	62 min – M.A. Nash	Glam v Hants	Swansea	1976

Highest Partnerships for Each Wicket

1st	241	S.M. Gavaskar/B.C. Rose	Somerset v Kent	Canterbury	1980
2nd	285*	C.G. Greenidge/D.R. Turner	Hants v Minor C (S)	Amersham	1973
3rd	268*	G.A. Gooch/K.W.R. Fletcher	Essex v Sussex	Hove	1982
4th	184*	D. Lloyd/B.W. Reidy	Lancs v Derbys	Chesterfield	1980
5th	160	A.J. Lamb/D.J. Capel	Northants v Leics	Northampton	1986
6th	114	Majid Khan/G.P. Ellis	Glam v Glos	Bristol	1975
7th	149*	J.D. Love/C.M. Old	Yorks v Scotland	Bradford	1981
8th	109	R.E. East/N. Smith	Essex v Northants	Chelmsford	1977
9th	85	P.G. Newman/M.A. Holding	Derbys v Notts	Nottingham	1985
10th	80*	D.L. Bairstow/M. Johnson	Yorks v Derbys	Derby	1981

Most Wickets	7-12	W.W. Daniel	Middx v Minor C (E)	Ipswich	1978
	7-22	J.R. Thomson	Middx v Hants	Lord's	1981
	7-32	R.G.D. Willis	Warwicks v Yorks	Birmingham	1981
Hat Tricks		G.D. McKenzie	Leics v Worcs	Worcester	1972
		K. Higgs	Leics v Surrey	Lord's	1974
		A.A. Jones	Middx v Essex	Lord's	1977
		M.J. Procter	Glos v Hants	Southampton	1977
		W. Larkins	Northants v Comb U	Northampton	1980
		E.A. Moseley	Glam v Kent	Cardiff	1981
		G.C. Small	Warwicks v Leics	Leicester	1984

Most Wicket-Keeping Dismissals

8 (8 ct)	D.J.S. Taylor	Somerset v Comb U	Taunton	1982

Most Catches in the Field

5	V.J. Marks	Comb U v Kent	Oxford	1976

Most Match Awards: 12 G.A. Gooch (Essex); 11 B. Wood (Lancs & Derbys); 10 J.C. Balderstone (Leics); 9 G. Boycott (Yorks), J.H. Edrich (Surrey), T.E. Jesty (Hants & Surrey); 8 K.W.R. Fletcher (Essex), M.W. Gatting (Middx), C.G. Greenidge (Hants), Imran Khan (Worcs, Sussex & Comb U) C.E.B. Rice (Notts).

JOHN PLAYER LEAGUE 1986

HAMPSHIRE WIN SUNDAY LEAGUE

Hampshire became the 18th and final holders of the John Player League Trophy when they narrowly defeated Surrey at The Oval on the penultimate Sunday of the competition. They thus emulated the record of Essex and Kent by winning this title three times.

It was a fitting reward for a team which has recently specialised in near-misses. Incredibly for a side containing Greenidge and Marshall, the most prolific opening batsman and bowler currently playing international cricket, this was Hampshire's first major trophy since 1978 – when they last won this competition. Although they have been semi-finalists six times they remain the only county never to have reached a Lord's final.

Essex, winners in the previous two seasons, were hampered by Test calls and the early departure of Border. Sussex finished in the first-four prize-money bracket for the sixth successive year.

Hampshire will keep the trophy for a year, after which period it will be presented by the sponsors to the TCCB for permanent display at Lord's.

This season the competition will remain unchanged but with a new trophy and new sponsors. Welcome Refuge Assurance.

JOHN PLAYER LEAGUE FINAL TABLE

		P	*W*	*L*	*T*	*NR*	*Pts*	*6s*	*4w*
1	**HAMPSHIRE** (3)	16	12	3	0	1	50	37	5
2	Essex (1)	16	11	4	0	1	46	37	3
3	Nottinghamshire (12)	16	10	5	0	1	42	23	5
4	Sussex (2)	16	10	6	0	0	40	28	6
5	Northamptonshire (5)	16	9	5	0	2	40	33	2
6	Somerset (10)	16	8	6	0	2	36	61	1
	Kent (10)	16	7	5	1	3	36	18	5
8	Yorkshire (6)	16	7	6	1	2	34	26	3
9	Derbyshire (4)	16	7	9	0	0	28	35	—
	Warwickshire (6)	16	5	7	2	2	28	13	1
	Middlesex (12)	16	5	7	1	3	28	10	1
12	Lancashire (14)	16	6	9	0	1	26	29	—
	Glamorgan (14)	16	6	9	0	1	26	19	4
	Surrey (17)	16	5	8	1	2	26	20	2
15	Leicestershire (6)	16	5	10	0	1	22	18	4
16	Worcestershire (6)	16	5	11	0	0	20	21	2
17	Gloucestershire (6)	16	3	11	0	2	16	8	—

For the first four places only, the final positions for teams finishing with equal points are decided by the most wins. 1985 final positions are shown in brackets.

P.C.A. 1987.—3

JOHN PLAYER LEAGUE

(REFUGE ASSURANCE LEAGUE from 1987)

PRINCIPAL RECORDS 1969-86

Highest Total	310-5	Essex v Glam	Southend	1983
Highest Total Batting Second	301-6	Warwicks v Essex	Colchester	1982
Lowest Total	23	Middx v Yorks	Leeds	1974
Highest Score 176 G.A. Gooch		Essex v Glam	Southend	1983

Hundreds 283 have been scored in Sunday League matches

Highest Partnerships for Each Wicket

1st	239	G.A. Gooch/B.R. Hardie	Essex v Notts	Nottingham	1985
2nd	273	G.A. Gooch/K.S. McEwan	Essex v Notts	Nottingham	1983
3rd	215	W. Larkins/R.G. Williams	Northants v Worcs	Luton	1982
4th	178	J.J. Whitaker/P. Willey	Leics v Glam	Swansea	1984
5th	185*	Asif Din/B.M. McMillan	Warwicks v Essex	Chelmsford	1986
6th	121	C.P. Wilkins/A.J. Borrington	Derbys v Warwicks	Chesterfield	1972
7th	101	S.J. Windaybank/D.A. Graveney	Glos v Notts	Nottingham	1981
8th	95*	D. Breakwell/K.F. Jennings	Somerset v Notts	Nottingham	1976
9th	105	D.G. Moir/R.W. Taylor	Derbys v Kent	Derby	1984
10th	57	D.A. Graveney/J.B. Mortimore	Glos v Lancs	Tewkesbury	1973

Most Wickets	8-26	K.D. Boyce	Essex v Lancs	Manchester	1971
	7-15	R.A. Hutton	Yorks v Worcs	Leeds	1969
	7-39	A. Hodgson	Northants v Somerset	Northampton	1976

Four Wickets in Four Balls	A. Ward	Derbys v Sussex	Derby	1970

Hat Tricks: 16 bowlers have achieved this feat in League matches: Derbyshire – A. Ward (1970), C.J. Tunnicliffe (1979); Essex – K.D. Boyce (1971); Glamorgan – M.A. Nash (1975), A.E. Cordle (1979); Hampshire – J.M. Rice (1975), M.D. Marshall (1981); Kent – R.M. Ellison (1983); Leicestershire – G.D. McKenzie (1972); Northamptonshire – A. Hodgson (1976); Somerset – R. Palmer (1970), I.V.A. Richards (1982); Sussex – A. Buss (1974); Warwickshire – R.G.D. Willis (1973), W. Blenkiron (1974); Yorkshire – P.W. Jarvis (1982).

Most Economical Analysis

O	*M*	*R*	*W*				
8	8	0	0	B.A. Langford	Somerset v Essex	Yeovil	1969

Most Expensive Analyses

O	*M*	*R*	*W*				
7.5	0	89	3	G. Miller	Derbys v Glos	Gloucester	1984
8	0	88	1	E.E. Hemmings	Notts v Somerset	Nottingham	1983

Most Wicket-Keeping Dismissals

7 (6 ct, 1 st)	R.W. Taylor	Derbys v Lancs	Manchester	1975

Most Catches in the Field

5	J.M. Rice	Hants v Warwicks	Southampton	1978

JOHN PLAYER LEAGUE CHAMPIONS

1969	Lancashire	1975	Hampshire	1981	Essex
1970	Lancashire	1976	Kent	1982	Sussex
1971	Worcestershire	1977	Leicestershire	1983	Yorkshire
1972	Kent	1978	Hampshire	1984	Essex
1973	Kent	1979	Somerset	1985	Essex
1974	Leicestershire	1980	Warwickshire	1986	Hampshire

MINOR COUNTIES CHAMPIONSHIP

FINAL TABLE 1986

EASTERN DIVISION (Points:)		*Played*	*Won* (10)	*Tied* (5)	*Lost*	*Won 1st Inns* (3)	*Tied 1st Inns* (2)	*Lost 1st Inns* (1)	*No Result* (2)	*Points*
Cumberland	NW	9	5	—	1	3	—	—	—	59
Staffordshire	NW	9	3	—	—	2	—	4	—	40
Cambridgeshire	NW	9	2	—	1(a)	3	—	3	—	35
Hertfordshire	NW	9	2	—	3(b)	2	—	2	—	34
Northumberland	NW	9	2	—	1	3	—	2	1	33
Durham	NW	9	1	—	1(a)	5	—	—	2	32
Suffolk	NW	9	2	—	3(c)	2	—	2	—	30
Bedfordshire		9	1	—	1(a)	2	1	4	—	25
Lincolnshire		9	—	—	2(a)	1	—	4	2	14
Norfolk		9	—	—	5(a)	—	1	2	1	9

WESTERN DIVISION		*Played*	*Won*	*Tied*	*Lost*	*Won 1st Inns*	*Tied 1st Inns*	*Lost 1st Inns*	*No Result*	*Points*
Oxfordshire	NW	9	4	—	1(a)	1	—	2	1	50
Dorset	NW	9	3	—	1(a)	3	—	1	1	45
Wiltshire	NW	9	3	—	1	3	—	2	—	41
Somerset II		9	3	—	—	1	—	4	1	39
Cheshire	NW	9	2	—	2(a)	3	—	2	—	34
Buckinghamshire	NW	9	2	—	1	3	—	3	—	32
Devon	NW	9	1	—	2(c)	3	1	2	—	25
Berkshire		9	1	—	1	2	1	3	1	23
Shropshire		9	—	—	4(d)	3	—	2	—	19
Cornwall		9	—	—	6(a)	1	—	2	—	8

(a) 1st Innings points in 1 match lost.
(b) 1st Innings points in 2 matches lost.
(c) Tie on 1st innings in 1 match lost.
(d) 1st Innings points in 2 matches lost *and* Tie on 1st Innings in 1 match lost.
NW Qualified for 1987 NatWest Trophy

MINOR COUNTIES CHAMPIONSHIP 1986 FINAL

Played at Worcester on 13, 14 September 1986
Toss: Cumberland. Result: Cumberland won by two wickets and became Champions for the first time

OXFORDSHIRE		
G.C. Ford	b Scothern	4
M.D. Nurton	c and b Woods	36
P.A. Fowler	b Scothern	3
*P.J. Garner	c Clarke b Woods	36
C.J. Clements	b Halliwell	28
†A. Crossley	b Halliwell	1
G.R. Hobbins	run out	27
S.R. Porter	b Reidy	0
R.N. Busby	c Hodgson b Halliwell	17
K.A. Arnold	b Reidy	2
I.J. Curtis	not out	0
Extras		12
Total (54.3 overs)		166

CUMBERLAND		
M.D. Woods	c Fowler b Porter	14
C.J. Stockdale	lbw b Busby	11
G.D. Hodgson	lbw b Hobbins	57
B.W. Reidy	c Hobbins b Porter	23
G.J. Clarke	c Ford b Garner	12
*J.R. Moyes	b Garner	17
S. Sharp	b Garner	9
R.I. Cooper	run out	5
†S.M. Dutton	not out	6
D. Halliwell	not out	0
M.G. Scothern	did not bat	
Extras		15
Total (54.5 overs – 8 wickets)		169

CUMBERLAND	*O*	*M*	*R*	*W*
Halliwell	10.3	3	27	3
Scothern	11	4	32	2
Sharp	11	3	34	0
Reidy	11	1	34	2
Woods	11	1	29	2
OXFORDSHIRE				
Busby	11	6	10	1
Arnold	8	1	31	0
Hobbins	8	2	19	1
Porter	11	0	41	2
Curtis	11	2	34	0
Garner	5.5	1	23	3

FALL OF WICKETS

Wkt	*Ox*	*Cm*
1st	15	18
2nd	19	38
3rd	75	94
4th	87	118
5th	89	143
6th	139	157
7th	142	163
8th	154	163
9th	162	—
10th	166	—

Umpires: D.B. Harrison and C. Smith

MINOR COUNTIES CHAMPIONSHIP

LEADING AVERAGES 1986

BATTING

(Qualifications: 8 innings, average 25.00)

		I	*NO*	*HS*	*Runs*	*Avge*
P.D. Atkins	Bucks	11	3	160*	488	61.00
N.A. Riddell	Durham	14	5	101	537	59.67
M.D. Nurton	Oxon	15	3	104*	694	57.83
N. Priestley	Lincs	14	2	144*	679	56.58
S. Burrow	Bucks	13	4	84*	480	53.33
N.R. Williams	Somerset II	11	2	109*	472	52.44
A. Kennedy	Dorset	14	2	100	624	52.00
M.G. Stephenson	Cambs	10	7	34*	156	52.00
G.R.J. Roope	Berks	16	4	78	620	51.67
S.G. Plumb	Norfolk	17	1	116*	796	49.75
C. Stone	Dorset	13	9	30	189	47.25
S.R. Atkinson	Durham	8	1	61	329	47.00
R.J. Lanchbury	Wilts	16	4	105*	553	46.08
A.R. Harwood	Bucks	9	2	127*	310	44.29
D.G. Ottley	Herts	12	1	108	486	44.18
J.G. Wyatt	Somerset II	12	1	86	483	43.91
C.M. Old	N'land	12	3	86*	390	43.33
M.S.T. Dunstan	Cornwall	13	2	118*	474	43.09
I. Cockbain	Cheshire	16	2	83*	598	42.71
J.P. Addison	Staffs	10	3	78*	290	41.43
D.A. Banks	Staffs	12	2	116	413	41.30
B.W. Reidy	Cumb'land	14	1	107	533	41.00
J. Foster	Shrops	18	1	137	683	40.18
J.W. Lister	Durham	15	1	132	558	39.86
N.R. Gaywood	Devon	15	3	79	473	39.42
D.J. Mercer	Wilts	18	2	121	630	39.38
P.A. Fowler	Oxon	10	2	76	312	39.00
M.R. Davies	Shrops	14	2	96*	464	38.67
S.C. Yates	Cheshire	10	2	103*	307	38.38
R.J. Bartlett	Somerset II	13	1	86	458	38.17
M.A. Garnham	Cambs	17	2	93	566	37.73
S.T. Crawley	Cheshire	12	1	134	414	37.64
N.A. Folland	Devon	10	1	78	327	36.33
D. Lloyd	Cumberland	9	0	109	326	36.22
G.E. Loveday	Berks	13	1	85	430	35.83
P.A. Todd	Lincs	16	0	180	572	35.75
M. Olive	Devon	15	1	118*	497	35.50
M. Morgan	Beds	17	2	83	503	33.53
M.A. Fell	Lincs	16	1	99	503	33.53
A.S. Pearson	Beds	13	1	93	402	33.50
P.R. Butler	Lincs	14	6	51*	268	33.50
M.G. Lickley	Berks	17	1	102	535	33.44
N.T. Gadsby	Cambs	17	1	147*	534	33.38
E.G. Willcock	Cornwall	18	1	112	567	33.35
J.J. Hitchmough	Cheshire	11	3	96*	266	33.25
J.A. Waterhouse	Staffs	11	4	73*	231	33.00
J.S. Johnson	Shrops	17	0	118	557	32.76

MINOR COUNTIES AVERAGES – *cont.*

Batting (*cont.*)		*I*	*NO*	*HS*	*Runs*	*Avge*
M.S.A. McEvoy	Suffolk	15	0	127	490	32.67
P.J. Hayes	Suffolk	15	7	65*	255	31.88
M.C.G. Wright	Herts	10	4	45	190	31.67
K.V. Jones	Beds	12	2	68*	315	31.50
S.A. Dean	Herts	16	2	129*	439	31.36
G.V. Palmer	Somerset II	14	3	39*	345	31.36
S.C. Gale	Shrops	12	2	84	313	31.30
P.G. Cormack	N'land	9	2	79*	219	31.29
M.C. Seaman	Wilts	16	0	76	500	31.25
B. Wood	Cheshire	16	0	114	496	31.00
C.J. Stockdale	Cumb'land	14	0	102	430	30.71
M.L. Simmons	Berks	9	3	62*	183	30.50
P.J. Caley	Suffolk	15	1	79	426	30.43
R.V. Lewis	Dorset	11	1	72	303	30.30
G. Morgan	Suffolk	13	1	100	362	30.17
S.M. Clements	Suffolk	17	1	124	479	29.94
S.J. Edwards	Bucks	11	3	60	238	29.75
P.J. Garner	Oxon	15	3	81*	353	29.42
G.D. Halliday	N'land	10	0	75	293	29.30
S. Sharp	Cumb'land	12	4	45	230	28.75
R.P. Merriman	Dorset	17	2	84	431	28.73
J. Whitehead	Norfolk	11	2	37	253	28.11
G.R. Morris	N'land	15	3	58	334	27.83
N.J. Archer	Staffs	13	3	272	75	27.20
R.C. Cooper	Wilts	15	2	70	351	27.00
P.J. Ringwood	Norfolk	8	2	50	162	27.00
K. Pearson	N'land	12	2	74*	268	26.80
K.G. Rice	Devon	15	1	119*	375	26.79
T.M. Thomas	Cornwall	13	2	85	293	26.64
R. Dreyer	N'land	12	1	102	291	26.45
S. Greensword	Durham	14	2	72	316	26.33
J.D.R. Benson	Cambs	17	3	59*	368	26.29
B.H. White	Wilts	16	1	64	394	26.27
A.S. Patel	Durham	14	6	50*	208	26.00

BOWLING

(Qualification: 20 wickets, average 25.00)

		O	*M*	*R*	*W*	*Avge*
G.R.J. Roope	Berks	123	32	316	22	14.36
R.C. Green	Suffolk	160.4	38	397	27	14.70
R.A. Bunting	Norfolk	154	31	453	29	15.62
M.G. Stephenson	Cambs	206.3	74	459	29	15.83
R.N. Busby	Oxon	220.4	54	588	36	16.33
J.E. Benjamin	Staffs	140.3	20	439	26	16.88
I.E.W. Sanders	Dorset	145.3	29	411	24	17.13
B. Wood	Cheshire	175	60	381	22	17.32
P.J. Lewington	Berks	319.5	111	721	40	18.03
W.G. Merry	Herts	190	50	515	28	18.39
S.J. Edwards	Bucks	225	47	669	36	18.58
D. Halliwell	Cumb'land	284.3	75	826	44	18.77
D.C. Wing	Cambs	180.4	49	484	25	19.36
J. Johnston	Durham	174.2	40	446	23	19.39
T.S. Smith	Herts	218.1	69	545	28	19.46
C. Stone	Dorset	259.4	70	722	37	19.51

MINOR COUNTIES AVERAGES – *cont.*

Bowling (*cont.*)		*O*	*M*	*R*	*W*	*Avge*
S.R. Porter	Oxon	131.2	28	431	22	19.59
G.V. Palmer	Somerset II	157	29	446	22	20.27
R.W. Flower	Staffs	160	55	426	21	20.29
C. Lethbridge	Cambs	282.2	49	813	40	20.33
J.A. Sutton	Cheshire	227	69	543	26	20.88
B.W. Reidy	Cumb'land	211.1	59	578	27	21.41
J.A. Smith	Shrops	216.2	47	665	31	21.45
C.M. Old	N'land	223	67	521	24	21.71
I.J. Curtis	Oxon	198.1	61	589	26	22.65
N.T. O'Brien	Cheshire	158	41	487	21	23.19
B.J. Perry	Shrops	158.4	25	655	27	24.26

SECOND XI CHAMPIONSHIP FINAL TABLE 1986

					Bonus Points		*Total*	*Avge*
Position	*P*	*W*	*L*	*D*	*Bt*	*Bw*	*Points*	*Points*
1 Lancashire (5)	18	9	0	9	40	47	227*	12.61
2 Warwickshire (7)	16	6	5	5	31	47	174	10.87
3 Essex (6)	13	4	3	6	35	37	136	10.46
4 Middlesex (3)	15	5	3	7	36	39	155*	10.33
5 Yorkshire (12)	16	5	1	10	43	38	157*	9.81
6 Leicestershire (11)	14	4	3	7	26	40	130	9.28
7 Somerset (14)	10	3	5	2	16	23	87	8.70
8 Worcestershire (10)	12	3	5	4	19	36	103	8.58
9 Derbyshire (15)	14	3	3	8	26	38	112	8.00
10 Surrey (2)	16	2	2	12	43	48	123	7.68
11 Nottinghamshire (1)	15	3	4	8	27	37	112	7.46
12 Northamptonshire (16)	14	2	4	8	33	37	102	7.28
13 Kent (8)	15	2	3	10	27	49	108	7.20
14 Hampshire (13)	13	1	3	9	31	39	86	6.61
15 Sussex (4)	12	1	5	6	23	37	76	6.33
16 Gloucestershire (17)	13	1	3	9	25	36	77	5.92
17 Glamorgan (9)	16	1	3	12	28	32	72*	4.50

*Includes 12 points for win in one-innings match.
1985 final positions are shown in brackets.

SECOND XI CHAMPIONS

1959	Gloucestershire	1969	Kent	1979	Warwickshire
1960	Northamptonshire	1970	Kent	1980	Glamorgan
1961	Kent	1971	Hampshire	1981	Hampshire
1962	Worcestershire	1972	Nottinghamshire	1982	Worcestershire
1963	Worcestershire	1973	Essex	1983	Leicestershire
1964	Lancashire	1974	Middlesex	1984	Yorkshire
1965	Glamorgan	1975	Surrey	1985	Nottinghamshire
1966	Surrey	1976	Kent	1986	Lancashire
1967	Hampshire	1977	Yorkshire		
1968	Surrey	1978	Sussex		

THE FIRST-CLASS COUNTIES HONOURS, WHO'S WHO, RECORDS AND 1986 AVERAGES

Records are complete to the end of the 1986 English season (16 September).

ABBREVIATIONS

General

*	not out/unbroken partnership	f-c	first-class
b	born	HS	Highest Score
BB	Best innings bowling analysis	LOI	Limited-Overs Internationals
Cap	Awarded 1st XI County Cap	Tests	Official Test Matches
Tours	Overseas tours involving first-class appearances		

Awards

BHC	Benson and Hedges Cup 'Gold' Award
NWT	NatWest Trophy or Gillette Cup 'Man of the Match' Award
Wisden 1986	One of *Wisden Cricketers' Almanack*'s Five Cricketers of 1986
YC 1986	Cricket Writers' Club Young Cricketer of 1986

Competitions

BHC	Benson and Hedges Cup
GC	Gillette Cup
JPL	John Player League
NWT	NatWest Trophy

Playing Categories

LB	Bowls right-arm leg-breaks
LF	Bowls left-arm fast
LFM	Bowls left-arm fast-medium
LHB	Bats left-handed
LM	Bowls left-arm medium pace
LMF	Bowls left-arm medium fast
OB	Bowls right-arm off-breaks
RHB	Bats right-handed
RM	Bowls right-arm medium pace
RMF	Bowls right-arm medium-fast
RF	Bowls right-arm fast
RFM	Bowls right-arm fast-medium
SLA	Bowls left-arm leg-breaks
WK	Wicket-keeper

Education

BHS	Boys' High School
BS	Boys' School
C	College
CE	College of Education
CFE	College of Further Education
CHE	College of Higher Education
CPE	College of Physical Education
CS	Comprehensive School
GS	Grammar School
HS	High School
LSE	London School of Economics
RGS	Royal Grammar School
S	School
SFC	Sixth Form College
SS	Secondary School
TC	Technical College
TGS	Technical Grammar School
THS	Technical High School
U	University

Teams/Countries Toured *(Also see p. 167)*

Cav	Cavaliers	ND	Northern Districts
DHR	D.H. Robins' XI	NSW	New South Wales
DN	Duke of Norfolk's XI	OFS	Orange Free State
Eng Co	English Counties XI	PIA	Pakistan International Airlines
GW	Griqualand West	RW	Rest of the World XI
Int XI	International XI	SAB	South African Breweries XI
IW	International Wanderers	Zim	Zimbabwe (Rhodesia)

DERBYSHIRE

Formation of Present Club: 4 November 1870
Colours: Chocolate, Amber and Pale Blue
Badge: Rose and Crown
Championships: (1) 1936
NatWest Trophy/Gillette Cup Winners: (1) 1981
Benson and Hedges Cup Winners: (0) Finalists 1978
John Player League Champions: (0) Third 1970
Match Awards: NWT 23; BHC 37

Chief Executive: R. Pearman, County Ground, Nottingham Road, Derby DE2 6DA
Captain: K.J. Barnett
Scorer: S.W. Tacey
Scores/Prospects: ☎ Derby (0332) 383211; Chesterfield (0246) 73090

ANDERSON, Iain Stuart (Dovecliff GS; Wulfric S), b Derby 24 Apr 1960. 6'0". RHB, OB. Debut 1978. Cap 1985. Boland 1983-84. 1000 runs (1): 1233 (1983). HS 112 v Kent (Chesterfield) 1983. BB 4-35 v Australians (Derby) 1981. **NWT:** HS 134 v Cornwall (Derby) 1986 (sharing with A. Hill in record county limited-overs second-wicket partnership of 286). **BHC:** HS 42 v Warwicks (Birmingham) 1986. **JPL:** HS 64 v Somerset (Derby) 1985. BB 2-15 v Northants (Derby) 1983.

BARNETT, Kim John (Leek HS), b Stoke-on-Trent 17 Jul 1960. 6'1". RHB, LB. Debut 1979. Cap 1982. Captain 1983-. Staffordshire 1976. Boland 1982-85. Tours: NZ 1979-80 (DHR); SL 1985-86 (Eng B). 1000 runs (4); most – 1734 (1984). HS 144 v Middx (Derby) 1984. BB 6-115 v Yorks (Bradford) 1985. Awards: NWT 2; BHC 2. **NWT:** HS 88 v Middx (Derby) 1983. BB 6-24 v Cumberland (Kensal) 1984. **BHC:** HS 86 v Glos (Chesterfield) 1985. BB 1-10 v Worcs (Worcester) 1984. **JPL:** HS 131* v Essex (Derby) 1984. BB 3-39 v Yorks (Chesterfield) 1979.

BROWN, Andrew Mark (Aldercar CS; SE Derbyshire C), b Heanor 6 Nov 1964. 5'9". LHB, OB. Debut 1985. HS 74 v Warwicks (Chesterfield). **JPL:** HS 2*.

FINNEY, Roger John (Lady Manners S, Bakewell), b Darley Dale 2 Aug 1960. 6'1". RHB, LM. Debut 1982. Cap 1985. HS 82 v Glos (Derby) 1985. BB 7-54 v Leics (Chesterfield) 1986. Awards: BHC 1. **NWT:** HS 14* v Suffolk (Bury St Edmunds) 1983. BB 2-8 v Cumberland (Kensal) 1984. **BHC:** HS 46 v Lancs (Derby) 1984. BB 5-40 v Scotland (Aberdeen) 1985. **JPL:** HS 50* v Worcs (Worcester) 1984. BB 4-38 v Northants (Northampton) 1984.

HOLDING, Michael Anthony (Kingston College HS), b Kingston, Jamaica 16 Feb 1954. 6'3". RHB, RF. Jamaica 1972-86. *Wisden* 1976. Lancashire 1981. Tasmania 1982-83. Derbyshire debut/cap 1983. **Tests** (WI): 59 (1975-76 to 1985-86); HS 73 v Eng (St John's) 1985-86; BB 8-92 v Eng (Oval) 1976. LOI (WI): 99. Tours (WI): Eng 1976, 1980, 1984; Aus 1975-76, 1979-80, 1981-82, 1984-85, 1986-87; NZ 1979-80, 1986-87; Ind 1983-84; Pak 1980-81, 1981-82 (Int XI). HS 80 v Yorks (Chesterfield) 1985. BB 8-92 (Tests). Derbyshire BB 7-97 v Worcs (Derby) 1986. **NWT:** HS 27 v Durham (Derby) 1985. BB 3-35 Lancs v Hants (Southampton) 1981. **BHC:** HS 69 and BB 2-13 v Leics (Chesterfield) 1986. **JPL:** HS 58 v Sussex (Hove) 1985. BB 3-16 v Yorks (Chesterfield) 1986.

JEAN-JACQUES, Martin (Aylestone SS, London), b Soufriere, Dominica 2 Jul 1960. 6'0". RHB, RMF. Debut 1986 (scoring 73 and sharing County 10th wicket record stand of 132 with A. Hill). Buckinghamshire 1983-85. HS 73 v Yorks (Sheffield) 1986. BB 8-77 v Kent (Derby) 1986. **NWT:** HS 16 and BB 3-43 v Surrey (Derby) 1986. **JPL:** HS 1. BB 3-36 v Worcs (Worcester) 1986.

MAHER, Bernard Joseph Michael (Abbotsfield CS; Bishopshalt GS; Loughborough U), b Hillingdon, Middlesex 11 Feb 1958. 5'10". RHB, WK. Debut 1981. HS 126 v NZ (Derby) 1986. BB 2-69 v Glam (Abergavenny) 1986. **BHC:** HS 2*. **JPL:** HS 45 v Glam (Ebbw Vale) 1986.

MALCOLM, Devon Eugene (Richmond C, Sheffield), b Kingston, Jamaica 22 Feb 1963. 6'2". RHB, RF. Debut 1984. HS 29* and BB 5-42 v Glos (Gloucester) 1986. **JPL:** HS 16 and BB 2-40 v Northants (Finedon) 1986.

MORRIS, John Edward (Shavington CS; Dane Bank CFE), b Crewe, Cheshire 1 Apr 1964. 5'10". RHB, RM. Debut 1982. Cap 1986. 1000 runs (1): 1739 (1986). HS 191 v Kent (Derby) 1986. BB 1-35. **NWT:** HS 12* v Cornwall (Derby) 1986. **BHC:** HS 65 v Kent (Derby) 1986. **JPL:** HS 104 v Glos (Gloucester) 1984.

MORTENSEN, Ole Henrek (Brondbyoster S; Abedore C, Copenhagen), b Vejle, Denmark 29 Jan 1958. 6'3". RHB, RFM. Debut 1983. Cap 1986. Denmark 1975-82. HS 40* v Glam (Derby) 1984. BB 6-27 v Yorks (Sheffield) 1983. **NWT:** HS 11 v Surrey (Derby) 1986. BB 3-16 v Suffolk (Bury St Edmunds) 1983. **BHC:** HS 2. BB 3-17 v Leics (Chesterfield) 1986. **JPL:** HS 5. BB 4-10 v Leics (Chesterfield) 1985.

NEWMAN, Paul Geoffrey (Alderman Newton's GS, Leicester), b Evington, Leicester 10 Jan 1959. 6'2½". RHB, RFM. Debut 1980. Tour: Zim 1984-85 (Eng Co). HS 115 v Leics (Chesterfield) 1985. BB 7-104 v Surrey (Oval) 1984. **NWT:** HS 35 v Leics (Leicester) 1984. BB 3-23 v Notts (Derby) 1981. **BHC:** HS 56* v Notts (Nottingham) 1985. BB 4-48 v Worcs (Worcester) 1982. **JPL:** HS 46 v Worcs (Knypersley) 1985. BB 4-21 v Hants (Derby) 1983.

ROBERTS, Bruce (Peterhouse; Prince Edward S, Salisbury), b Lusaka, N Rhodesia 30 May 1962. 6'2". RHB, RM, WK. Transvaal B 1982-87. Derbyshire debut 1984. Cap 1986. 1000 runs (1): 1128 (1985). HS 124* v Somerset (Chesterfield) 1986. BB 4-32 Transvaal B v OFS (Jo'burg) 1982-83. Derbys BB 4-77 v Essex (Ilford) 1984. Awards: BHC 1. **NWT:** HS 13 v Durham (Derby) 1985. BB 2-73 v Leics (Leicester) 1984. **BHC:** HS 86* v Northants (Northampton) 1986. BB 2-47 v Minor C (Shrewsbury) 1984. **JPL:** HS 77* v Notts (Heanor) 1985. BB 4-29 v Lancs (Derby) 1984.

RUDD, Christopher Francis Baines Paul (Douai S), b Sutton Coldfield, Warwicks 9 Dec 1963. 5'11". RHB, OB. Debut 1986. HS 1.

SHARMA, Rajeshwar (**'Reg'**) (Parklands S, Sidcup; Bexley and Erith TS), b Nairobi, Kenya 27 Jun 1962. 6'3". RHB, RM/OB. Debut 1985. HS 71 and BB 3-72 v Warwicks (Birmingham) 1986. **NWT:** HS 11 v Durham (Derby) 1985. BB 4-29 v Cornwall (Derby) 1986. **BHC:** HS 2. **JPL:** HS 37 v Hants (Heanor) 1986. BB 1-39.

TAYLOR, Jonathan **Paul** (Pingle S, Swadlincote), b Ashby-de-la-Zouch 8 Aug 1964. 6'2". LHB, LFM. Debut 1984. HS 11 v Middx (Derby) 1984. BB 4-81 v Glos (Chesterfield) 1986. **JPL:** HS 4. BB 3-14 v Glos (Gloucester) 1986.

WARNER, Alan Esmond (Tabernacle S, St Kitts), b Birmingham 12 May 1957. 5'7". RHB, RFM. Worcestershire 1982-84. Derbyshire debut 1985. HS 91 v Leics (Chesterfield) 1986. BB 5-27 Worcs v Glam (Worcester) 1984. Derbys BB 5-51 v Essex (Colchester). **NWT:** HS 17 v Durham (Derby) 1985. BB 1-38 Worcs v Notts (Worcester) 1983. **BHC:** HS 24* Worcs v Derbys (Worcester) 1982. BB 3-67 v Warwicks (Birmingham) 1986. **JPL:** HS 68 v Hants (Heanor) 1986. BB 5-39 v Worcs (Knypersley) 1985.

WOOD, Lindsay Jonathan (Simon Langton GS; King Alfred's C, Winchester), b Ruislip, Middlesex 12 May 1961. LHB, SLA. Kent 1981-82. Derbyshire debut 1986. HS 5. BB 4-124 Kent v Essex (Chelmsford) 1981. Derbys BB 2-82 v Essex (Derby) 1986.

WRIGHT, John Geoffrey (Christ's C, Christchurch; Otago U), b Darfield, NZ 5 July 1954. 6'1". LHB, RM. N Districts 1975-86. Derbys debut/cap 1977. Benefit 1987. **Tests** (NZ): 49 (1977-78 to 1986). HS 141 v Aus (Christchurch) 1981-82. LOI (NZ): 86. Tours (NZ): Eng 1978, 1983, 1986; Aus 1980-81, 1985-86; WI 1982-83 (Int XI), 1984-85; Pak 1984-85; SL 1977-78 (DHR), 1983-84. 1000 runs (6+1); most – 1830 (1982). HS 190 v Yorks (Derby) 1982. BB 1-4. Awards: NWT 1; BHC 3. **NWT:** HS 87* v Sussex (Hove) 1977. **BHC:** 102 v Worcs (Chesterfield) 1977. **JPL:** 108 v Warwicks (Coventry) 1983.

SALVE

KRIKKEN, Karl Matthew, b Bolton, Lancs, 9 Apr 1969. RHB, WK.

VALETE

HILL, Alan (New Mills GS; Chester CE), b Buxworth 29 Jun 1950. 6'0". RHB, OB. Debut 1972. Cap 1976. OFS 1976-77. Benefit 1986. 1000 runs (5); most – 1438 (1986). HS 172* v Yorks (Sheffield) 1986. BB 3-5 OFS v N Transvaal (Pretoria) 1976-77. Awards: NWT 3; BHC 2. Now 2nd XI captain and coach.

MARPLES, Christopher (Tupton Hall CS), b Chesterfield 3 Aug 1964. 5'11". RHB, WK. Debut 1985. HS 57 v Lancs (Liverpool) 1986.

MILLER, G. – see ESSEX.

DERBYSHIRE RECORDS

FIRST-CLASS CRICKET

Highest Total	For	645		v	Hampshire	Derby	1898
	V	662		by	Yorkshire	Chesterfield	1898
Lowest Total	For	16		v	Notts	Nottingham	1879
	V	23		by	Hampshire	Burton upon T	1958
Highest Innings	For	274	G. Davidson	v	Lancashire	Manchester	1896
	V	343*	P.A. Perrin	for	Essex	Chesterfield	1904

Highest Partnerships

Wkt						
1st	322	H. Storer/J. Bowden	v	Essex	Derby	1929
2nd	349	C.S. Elliott/J.D. Eggar	v	Notts	Nottingham	1947
3rd	291	P.N. Kirsten/D.S. Steele	v	Somerset	Taunton	1981
4th	328	P. Vaulkhard/D. Smith	v	Notts	Nottingham	1946
5th	203	C.P. Wilkins/I.R. Buxton	v	Lancashire	Manchester	1971
6th	212	G.M. Lee/T.S. Worthington	v	Essex	Chesterfield	1932
7th	241*	G.H. Pope/A.E.G. Rhodes	v	Hampshire	Portsmouth	1948
8th	182	A.H.M. Jackson/W. Carter	v	Leics	Leicester	1922
9th	283	A. Warren/J. Chapman	v	Warwicks	Blackwell	1910
10th	132	A.Hill/M. Jean-Jacques	v	Yorkshire	Sheffield	1986

Best Bowling	For	10-40	W. Bestwick	v	Glamorgan	Cardiff	1921
(Innings)	V	10-47	T.F. Smailes	for	Yorkshire	Sheffield	1939
Best Bowling	For	17-103	W. Mycroft	v	Hampshire	Southampton	1876
(Match)	V	16-101	G. Giffen	for	Australians	Derby	1886

Most Runs – Season	2,165	D.B. Carr	(av 48.11)	1959
Most Runs – Career	20,516	D. Smith	(av 31.41)	1927-1952
Most 100s – Season	8	P.N. Kirsten		1982
Most 100s – Career	30	D. Smith		1927-1952
Most Wkts – Season	168	T.B. Mitchell	(av 19.55)	1935
Most Wkts – Career	1,670	H.L. Jackson	(av 17.11)	1947-1963

LIMITED-OVERS CRICKET

Highest Total	NWT	365-3		v	Cornwall	Derby	1986
	BHC	284-6		v	Worcs	Worcester	1982
	JPL	292-9		v	Worcs	Knypersley	1985
Lowest Total	NWT	79		v	Surrey	The Oval	1967
	BHC	102		v	Yorkshire	Bradford	1975
	JPL	70		v	Surrey	Derby	1972
Highest Innings	NWT	153	A. Hill	v	Cornwall	Derby	1986
	BHC	111*	P.J. Sharpe	v	Glamorgan	Chesterfield	1976
	JPL	131*	K.J. Barnett	v	Essex	Derby	1984
Best Bowling	NWT	6-18	T.J.P. Eyre	v	Sussex	Chesterfield	1969
	BHC	6-33	E.J. Barlow	v	Glos	Bristol	1978
	JPL	6-7	M. Hendrick	v	Notts	Nottingham	1972

DERBYSHIRE 1986

RESULTS SUMMARY

	Place	*Won*	*Lost*	*Drew*	*Abandoned*
Britannic Assurance Championship	**11th**	5	5	14	
All First-class Matches		5	5	15	
John Player League	**9th**	7	9		
NatWest Bank Trophy	Lost to Surrey (2nd Round)				
Benson and Hedges Cup	Lost to Kent (Quarter-Final)				

BRITANNIC ASSURANCE CHAMPIONSHIP AVERAGES

BATTING AND FIELDING

Cap		*M*	*I*	*NO*	*HS*	*Runs*	*Avge*	*100*	*50*	*Ct/St*
1986	J.E. Morris	24	38	3	191	1654	47.25	4	10	8
1976	A. Hill	24	40	6	172*	1438	42.29	3	7	9
1982	K.J. Barnett	24	42	3	143	1484	38.05	2	10	23
—	B.J.M. Maher	13	23	5	77*	626	34.77	—	5	23
1986	P.G. Newman	3	4	2	34	62	31.00	—	—	1
—	R. Sharma	15	17	6	71	321	29.18	—	2	14
—	A.E. Warner	19	27	6	91	543	25.85	—	5	6
1985	R.J. Finney	16	16	5	54	275	25.00	—	1	2
1986	B. Roberts	24	36	3	124*	771	23.36	1	2	12/1
—	M. Jean-Jacques	9	12	3	73	208	23.11	—	1	1
—	C. Marples	14	23	3	57	442	22.10	—	2	30/3
1985	I.S. Anderson	13	23	1	93	449	20.40	—	2	6
1976	G. Miller	19	26	2	65	461	19.20	—	2	13
1983	M.A. Holding	14	20	2	36*	295	16.38	—	—	6
—	D.E. Malcolm	8	6	4	29*	30	15.00	—	—	2
1986	O.H. Mortensen	16	17	9	31*	69	8.62	—	—	1
—	J.P. Taylor	3	4	1	6	9	3.00	—	—	1

Also batted: A.M. Brown (1 match) 21,9*; C.F.B.P. Rudd (1 match) 1; L.J. Wood (2 matches) 5,2; J.G. Wright (2 matches – cap 1977) 3,7,4 (1 ct).

BOWLING

	O	*M*	*R*	*W*	*Avge*	*Best*	*5 wI*	*10 wM*
M.A. Holding	388.1	110	1045	52	20.09	7-97	4	—
O.H. Mortensen	416.2	111	1082	46	23.52	5-35	1	—
D.E. Malcolm	203.2	35	735	27	27.22	5-42	1	—
M. Jean-Jacques	159	16	599	22	27.22	8-77	1	1
R.J. Finney	301.4	58	986	28	35.21	7-54	1	—
R. Sharma	140.5	33	407	11	37.00	3-72	—	—
G. Miller	604.2	180	1340	32	41.87	5-37	2	—
A.E. Warner	341.1	66	1186	28	42.35	4-38	—	—

Also bowled: K.J. Barnett 95-25-333-5; A. Hill 9-3-22-1; B.J.M. Maher 33-2-151-3; C. Marples 4-0-48-0; J.E. Morris 44.4-5-245-1; P.G. Newman 73.1-16-198-9; B. Roberts 22-5-53-2; C.F.B.P. Rudd 28.3-7-90-0; J.P. Taylor 72-10-254-6; L.J. Wood 39-10-95-2.

The First-Class Averages (pp. 167–182) give the records of Derbyshire players in all first-class county matches (their other opponents being the New Zealanders), with the exception of J.G. Wright, whose full county figures are as above, and: K.J. Barnett 25-43-3-143-1502-37.55-2-10-23 ct. 104-28-359-6-59.83-1/8. J.E. Morris 25-39-3-191-1703-47.30-4-10-8 ct. 44.4-5-245-1-245.00-1/103.

ESSEX

Formation of Present Club: 14 January 1876
Colours: Blue, Gold and Red
Badge: Three Seaxes above Scroll bearing 'Essex'
Championships: (4) 1979, 1983, 1984, 1986
NatWest Trophy/Gillette Cup Winners: (1) 1985
Benson and Hedges Cup Winners: (1) 1979
John Player League Champions: (3) 1981, 1984, 1985
Match Awards: NWT 26; BHC 45

Secretary/Manager: P.J. Edwards, County Cricket Ground, New Writtle Street, Chelmsford CM2 0PG
Captain: G.A. Gooch
Scorer: C.F. Driver
Scores/Prospects: Chelmsford matches only ☎ (0245) 87921

ACFIELD, David Laurence (Brentwood S; Christ's, Cambridge), b Chelmsford 24 Jul 1947. 5'9½". RHB, OB. Cambridge U and Essex debuts 1966. Blue 1967-68. Cap 1970. Benefit 1981. HS 42 CU v Leics (Leicester) 1967. Essex HS 38 v Notts (Chelmsford) 1973. BB 8-55 v Kent (Canterbury) 1981. **NWT:** HS 4*. BB 3-9 v Scotland (Chelmsford) 1984. **BHC:** HS 6*. BB 2-14 v Combined Univs (Chelmsford) 1979. **JPL:** HS 9*. BB 5-14 v Northants (Northampton) 1970.

CHILDS, John Henry (Audley Park SMS, Torquay), b Plymouth, Devon 15 Aug 1951. 6'0". LHB, SLA. Gloucestershire 1975-84 (cap 1977). Essex debut 1985. Cap 1986. *Wisden* 1986. Devon 1973-74. HS 34* Glos v Notts (Cheltenham) 1982. Essex HS 34 v NZ (Chelmsford) 1986. BB 9-56 Glos v Somerset (Bristol) 1981. Essex BB 8-58 v Glos (Colchester) 1986. Awards: BHC 1. **NWT:** HS 14* Glos v Hants (Bristol) 1983. BB 2-15 Glos v Ire (Dublin) 1981. **BHC:** HS 10 Glos v Somerset (Bristol) 1979. BB 3-36 Glos v Glam (Bristol) 1982. **JPL:** HS 16* Glos v Warwicks (Bristol) 1981. BB 4-15 Glos v Northants (Northampton) 1976.

EAST, David Edward (Hackney Downs S; E Anglia U), b Clapton 27 Jul 1959. 5'9". RHB, WK. Debut 1981. Cap 1982. HS 131 v Glos (Southend) 1985. Set world first-class record by catching the FIRST eight wickets to fall in an innings (v Somerset at Taunton 1985 on his 26th birthday). Awards: NWT 1. **NWT:** HS 28 v Northumberland (Jesmond) 1986. **BHC:** HS 33 v Glos (Chelmsford) 1984. **JPL:** HS 43 v Derbys (Derby) 1982.

FLETCHER, Keith William Robert (Comberton Village C, Cambs), b Worcester 20 May 1944. 5'9". RHB, LB. Debut 1962. Cap 1963. *Wisden* 1973. Benefit 1973. Captain 1974-85. Testimonial 1982. OBE 1985. **Tests:** 59 (1968 to 1981-82, 7 as captain); HS 216 v NZ (Auckland) 1974-75; BB 1-6. LOI: 24. Tours: Aus 1970-71, 1974-75, 1976-77; WI 1964-65 (Cav), 1973-74; NZ 1970-71, 1974-75; Ind and SL 1967-68 (Int XI), 1972-73, 1976-77, 1981-82 (captain); Pak 1966-67 (MCC U-25), 1967-68 (Int XI), 1968-69, 1972-73; SL 1968-69, 1969-70. 1000 runs (20); most – 1890 (1968). HS 228* v Sussex (Hastings) 1968. BB 5-41 v Middx (Colchester) 1979. Awards: NWT 2; BHC 8. **NWT:** HS 97 v Kent (Chelmsford) 1982. BB 1-16. **BHC:** HS 101* v Sussex (Hove) 1982. BB 1-25. **JPL:** HS 99* v Notts (Ilford) 1974. BB 1-4.

FOSTER, Neil Alan (Philip Morant CS), b Colchester 6 May 1962. 6'3". RHB, RFM. Debut 1980. Cap 1983. YC 1983. **Tests:** 14 (1983 to 1986); HS 18* v NZ (Auckland) 1983-84; BB 6-104 v Ind (Madras) 1984-85. LOI: 23. Tours: Aus 1986-87; WI 1985-86; NZ/Pak 1983-84; Ind/SL 1984-85. 100 wickets (1): 105 (1986).

HS 74* Eng XI v Queensland (Brisbane) 1986-87. Essex HS 63 v Lancs (Ilford) 1985. BB 6-30 Eng XI v ND (Hamilton) 1983-84. Essex BB 6-46 v Sussex (Ilford) 1983. Awards: BHC 2. **NWT:** HS 20 v Warwicks (Birmingham) 1986. BB 3-19 v Dorset (Bournemouth) 1983. **BHC:** HS 23* v Middx (Chelmsford) 1985. BB 5-32 v Surrey (Oval) 1985. **JPL:** HS 38 v Surrey (Chelmsford) 1986. BB 5-17 v Derbys (Derby) 1986.

GLADWIN, Christopher (Langdon CS, Newham), b East Ham 10 May 1962. 5'11". LHB, RM. Debut 1981. Cap 1984. 1000 runs (1): 1396 (1984). HS 162 v CU (Cambridge) 1984. **NWT:** HS 15 v Middx (Chelmsford) 1985. **BHC:** HS 41 v Surrey (Chelmsford) 1984. **JPL:** HS 75 v Middx (Lord's) 1984.

GOOCH, Graham Alan (Norlington Jr HS), b Leytonstone 23 Jul 1953. 6'0". RHB, RM. Debut 1973. Cap 1975. *Wisden* 1979. Benefit 1985. Captain 1986. W Province 1982-84. **Tests:** 59 (1975 to 1986); HS 196 v Aus (Oval) 1985; BB 2-12 v Ind (Delhi) 1981-82. LOI: 48. Tours: Aus 1978-79, 1979-80; SA 1981-82 (SAB); WI 1980-81, 1985-86; Ind 1979-80, 1981-82; SL 1981-82. 1000 runs (10+1); most – 2559 (1984). HS 227 v Derbys (Chesterfield) 1984. BB 7-14 v Worcs (Ilford) 1982. Awards: NWT 5; BHC 12 (record). **NWT:** HS 133 v Scot (Chelmsford) 1984. BB 3-31 v Warwicks (Birmingham) 1986. **BHC:** HS 198* v Sussex (Hove) 1982. BB 3-24 v Sussex (Hove) 1982. **JPL:** HS 176 v Glam (Southend) 1983. BB 4-33 v Worcs (Chelmsford) 1984.

HARDIE, Brian Ross (Larbert HS), b Stenhousemuir 14 Jan 1950. 5'11". RHB, RM. Brother of K.M. (Scotland 1966-76). Scotland 1970-72. Essex debut 1973. Cap 1974. Benefit 1983. 1000 runs (10); most – 1522 (1975). HS 162 v Warwicks (Birmingham) 1975, and 162 v Somerset (Southend) 1985. BB 2-39 v Glamorgan (Ilford) 1979. Awards: NWT 1; BHC 1. **NWT:** HS 110 v Notts (Lord's) 1985. BB 1-16. **BHC:** HS 119* v Sussex (Hove) 1986. **JPL:** HS 109 v Northants (Colchester) 1986. BB 1-4.

LEVER, John Kenneth (Dane SM), b Stepney 24 Feb 1949. 6'0½". RHB, LFM. Debut 1967. Cap 1970. *Wisden* 1978. Benefit 1980. Natal 1982-85. **Tests:** 21 (1976-77 to 1986); HS 53 and BB 7-46 (10-70 match) v India (Delhi) 1976-77 on debut. LOI: 22. Tours: Aus 1976-77, 1978-79, 1979-80; SA 1972-73 (DHR), 1973-74 (DHR), 1981-82 (SAB); NZ 1977-78; Ind/SL 1976-77, 1981-82; Ind 1979-80, 1980-81 (Overseas XI); Pak 1977-78; SL 1977-78 (DHR). 100 wickets (4); most – 116 (1984). HS 91 v Glamorgan (Cardiff) 1970. BB 8-37 v Glos (Bristol) 1984. Awards: NWT 4; BHC 2. **NWT:** HS 15* v Surrey (Chelmsford) 1984. BB 5-8 v Middx (Westcliff) 1972. **BHC:** HS 13 v Lancs (Chelmsford) 1984. BB 5-13 v Middx (Lord's) 1985. **JPL:** HS 23 v Worcs (Worcester) 1974. BB 5-13 v Glam (Ebbw Vale) 1975.

LILLEY, Alan William (Caterham HS, Ilford), b Ilford 8 May 1959. 5'11". RHB, RM. Debut 1978 scoring 22 and 100* v Notts (Nottingham). Cap 1986. HS 100* (on debut). BB 3-116 v Glamorgan (Swansea) 1985. Awards: NWT 1; BHC 1. **NWT:** HS 113 v Northumberland (Jesmond) 1986. BB 2-19 v Scotland (Chelmsford) 1984. **BHC:** HS 119 v Cambridge U (Chelmsford) 1979. BB 1-4. **JPL:** HS 60 v Northants (Chelmsford) 1980. BB 2-0 v Glos (Bristol) 1984.

PONT, Ian Leslie (Sir Anthony Browne's S), b Brentwood 28 Aug 1961. 6'2½". RHB, RFM. Brother of K.R. Notts 1982. Essex debut 1985. Natal 1985-86. HS 43 v NZ (Chelmsford) 1986. BB 5-103 v Somerset (Taunton) 1985. **NWT:** HS 7*. BB 1-54. **BHC:** HS 13* Minor C v Essex (Slough) 1983. BB 1-42. **JPL:** BB 2-18 v Somerset (Taunton) 1985.

PRICHARD, Paul John (Brentwood HS), b Billericay 7 Jan 1965. 5'10". RHB. Debut 1984. Cap 1986. 1000 runs (1): 1342 (1986). HS 147* v Notts (Chelmsford) 1986. **NWT:** HS 94 v Oxon (Chelmsford) 1985. **BHC:** HS 52 v Glos (Chelmsford) 1986. **JPL:** HS 103* v Lancs (Manchester) 1986.

PRINGLE, Derek Raymond (Felsted S; Fitzwilliam C, Cambridge), b Nairobi, Kenya 18 Sep 1958. 6'4½". RHB, RMF. Son of D.J. (East Africa). Debut 1978. Cap 1982. Cambridge U 1979-82; blue 1979-80-81 (capt 1982). **Tests:** 14 (1982 to 1986); HS 63 v Ind (Lord's) 1986; BB 5-108 v WI (Birmingham) 1984. LOI: 13. Tours: Aus 1982-83; SL 1985-86 (Eng B). HS 127* CU v Worcs (Cambridge) 1981. Essex HS 121* v Surrey (Oval) 1985. BB 7-32 v Middx (Chelmsford) 1983. Awards: NWT 1; BHC 3. **NWT:** HS 55 and BB 5-12 v Oxon (Chelmsford) 1985. **BHC:** HS 68 Comb Us v Som (Taunton) 1982. BB 5-35 v Lancs (Chelmsford) 1984. **JPL:** HS 81* v Warwicks (Birmingham) 1985. BB 5-41 v Glos (Southend) 1985.

STEPHENSON, John Patrick (Felsted S), b Stebbing 14 Mar 1965. 6'1". RHB, RM. Debut 1985. HS 85 v Worcs (Southend) 1986. **NWT:** HS 55 v Warwicks (Birmingham) 1986. **JPL:** HS 45 v Lancs (Manchester) 1986.

TOPLEY, Thomas **Donald** (Royal Hospital S, Holbrook, Suffolk), b Canterbury 25 Feb 1964. 6'3". RHB, RMF. Brother of P.A. (Kent 1972-75). Surrey (v CU) and Essex debuts 1985. Norfolk 1984-85. HS 45 v NZ (Chelmsford) 1986. BB 5-52 v Sussex (Ilford) 1986. **NWT:** HS 9. BB 2-3 v Norfolk v Leics (Norwich) 1985. **BHC:** BB 2-34 v Glam (Chelmsford) 1986. **JPL:** 8*. BB 2-19 v Sussex (Eastbourne) 1986.

SALVETE

FIELD-BUSS, Michael Gwyn (Wanstead HS), b Mtarfa, Malta 23 Sep 1964. 5'9". RHB, OB.

HUSSAIN, Nasser (Forest S, Snaresbrook; Durham U), b Madras, India 28 Mar 1968. Brother of M. (Worcs 1985). 5'11". RHB, LB. England YC to Sri Lanka 1987.

MILLER, Geoffrey (Chesterfield GS), b Chesterfield 8 Sep 1952. 6'1". RHB, OB. Derbyshire 1973-86 (Cap 1976; Captain 1979-81; Benefit 1985). YC 1976. Natal 1983-84. **Tests:** 34 (1976 to 1984); HS 98* v Pak (Lahore) 1977-78; BB 5-44 v Aus (Sydney) 1978-79. LOI: 25. Tours: Aus 1976-77, 1978-79, 1979-80, 1982-83; WI 1980-81; NZ 1977-78; Ind and SL 1976-77; Pak 1977-78. HS 130 v Lancs (Manchester) 1984. BB 8-70 v Leics (Coalville) 1982. Awards: BHC 4. **NWT:** HS 59* v Worcs (Worcester) 1978. BB 3-28 v Suffolk (Bury St Edmunds) 1983. **BHC:** HS 88* v Minor C (Derby) 1982. BB 3-23 v Surrey (Derby) 1979. **JPL:** HS 84 v Somerset (Chesterfield) 1980. BB 4-22 v Yorks (Huddersfield) 1978.

PAGF, Hugh Ashton (King Edward S), b Salisbury, Rhodesia 3 Jul 1962. LHB, LFM. Transvaal 1981-86. HS 57 Transvaal B v Natal B (Johannesburg) 1984-85. BB 5-31 Transvaal v Border (East London) 1985-86.

REDPATH, Ian (Woodlands S; Bastable S), b Basildon 12 Sep 1965. 5'8". RHB, RM/LB.

VALETE

BORDER, Allan Robert (N Sydney BHS), b Cremorne, Sydney, Aus 27 Jul 1955. 5'9". LHB, SLA. NSW 1976-80. Queensland 1980-86, captain since 1983-84. Glos 1977 (1 match). Essex debut/cap 1986. **Tests** (Aus): 89 (1978-79 to 1986-87, 26 as captain); HS 196 v Eng (Lord's) 1985. BB 3-20 v NZ (Christchurch) 1981-82. LOI (Aus): 136. Tours (Aus) (C = captain): Eng 1980, 1981, 1985C; WI 1983-84; NZ 1981-82, 1985-86C; Ind 1979-80, 1986-87C; Pak 1979-80, 1982-83; SL 1982-83. 1000 runs (2+4); most – 1385 (1986). HS 200 NSW v Queensland (Brisbane) 1979-80. Essex HS 150 v Glam (Swansea) 1986. BB 4-61 Queensland v NSW (Sydney) 1980-81. Essex BB 1-8.

BURNS, N.D. – see SOMERSET.

PONT, Keith Rupert (St Martin's SM, Hutton), b Wanstead 16 Jan 1953. 6'2½". RHB, RFM. Brother of I.L. Debut 1970. Cap 1976. HS 125* v Glamorgan (Southend) 1983. BB 5-17 v Glamorgan (Cardiff) 1982. Awards: BHC 2.

TURNER, Stuart (Epping SM), b Chester 18 Jul 1943. 6'0½. RHB, RMF. Debut 1965. Cap 1970. Benefit 1979. Natal 1976-78. Tour: SA 1974-75 (DHR). HS 121 v Som (Taunton) 1970. BB 6-26 v Northants (Northampton) 1977. Awards: BHC 4.

ESSEX RECORDS

FIRST-CLASS CRICKET

Highest Total	For	692		v	Somerset	Taunton	1895
	V	803-4d		by	Kent	Brentwood	1934
Lowest Total	For	30		v	Yorkshire	Leyton	1901
	V	14		by	Surrey	Chelmsford	1983
Highest Innings	For	343*	P.A. Perrin	v	Derbyshire	Chesterfield	1904
	V	332	W.H. Ashdown	for	Kent	Brentwood	1934

Highest Partnerships

Wkt						
1st	270	A.V. Avery/T.C. Dodds	v	Surrey	The Oval	1946
2nd	321	G.A. Gooch/K.S. McEwan	v	Northants	Ilford	1978
3rd	343	P.A. Gibb/R. Horsfall	v	Kent	Blackheath	1951
4th	298	A.V. Avery/R. Horsfall	v	Worcs	Clacton	1948
5th	287	C.T. Ashton/J. O'Connor	v	Surrey	Brentwood	1934
6th	206	J.W.H.T. Douglas/J. O'Connor	v	Glos	Cheltenham	1923
6th	206	B.R. Knight/R.A.G. Luckin	v	Middlesex	Brentwood	1962
7th	261	J.W.H.T. Douglas/J. Freeman	v	Lancashire	Leyton	1914
8th	263	D.R. Wilcox/R.M. Taylor	v	Warwicks	Southend	1946
9th	251	J.W.H.T. Douglas/S.N. Hare	v	Derbyshire	Leyton	1921
10th	218	F.H. Vigar/T.P.B. Smith	v	Derbyshire	Chesterfield	1947

Best Bowling (Innings)	For	10-32	H. Pickett	v	Leics	Leyton	1895
	V	10-40	E.G. Dennett	for	Glos	Bristol	1906
Best Bowling (Match)	For	17-119	W. Mead	v	Hampshire	Southampton	1895
	V	17-56	C.W.L. Parker	for	Glos	Gloucester	1925

Most Runs – Season	2,559	G.A. Gooch	(av 67.34)	1984
Most Runs – Career	29,172	P.A. Perrin	(av 36.19)	1896-1928
Most 100s – Season	9	J. O'Connor		1934
	9	D.J. Insole		1955
Most 100s – Career	71	J. O'Connor		1921-1939
Most Wkts – Season	172	T.P.B. Smith	(av 27.13)	1947
Most Wkts – Career	1,610	T.P.B. Smith	(av 26.68)	1929-1951

LIMITED-OVERS CRICKET

Highest Total	NWT	327-6		v	Scotland	Chelmsford	1984
	BHC	350-3		v	Comb Univs	Chelmsford	1979
	JPL	310-5		v	Glamorgan	Southend	1983
Lowest Total	NWT	100		v	Derbyshire	Brentwood	1965
	BHC	123		v	Kent	Canterbury	1973
	JPL	69		v	Derbyshire	Chesterfield	1974
Highest Innings	NWT	133	G.A. Gooch	v	Scotland	Chelmsford	1984
	BHC	198*	G.A. Gooch	v	Sussex	Hove	1982
	JPL	176	G.A. Gooch	v	Glamorgan	Southend	1983
Best Bowling	NWT	5-8	J.K. Lever	v	Middlesex	Westcliff	1972
	BHC	5-13	J.K. Lever	v	Middlesex	Lord's	1985
	JPL	8-26	K.D. Boyce	v	Lancashire	Manchester	1971

ESSEX 1986

RESULTS SUMMARY

	Place	*Won*	*Lost*	*Drew*	*Abandoned*
Britannic Assurance Championship	**1st**	10	6	8	
All First-class Matches		10	7	9	
John Player League	**2nd**	11	4		1
NatWest Bank Trophy	Lost to Warwickshire (2nd Round)				
Benson and Hedges Cup	Lost to Nottinghamshire (Quarter-Final)				

BRITANNIC ASSURANCE CHAMPIONSHIP AVERAGES

BATTING AND FIELDING

Cap		*M*	*I*	*NO*	*HS*	*Runs*	*Avge*	*100*	*50*	*Ct/St*
1986	A.R. Border	18	29	4	150	1287	51.48	4	8	14
1975	G.A. Gooch	13	21	0	151	778	37.04	1	5	11
1986	P.J. Prichard	24	40	3	147*	1165	31.48	1	8	18
1963	K.W.R. Fletcher	19	27	5	91	691	31.40	—	6	25
1974	B.R. Hardie	21	33	4	113*	831	28.65	2	4	19
1986	A.W. Lilley	14	24	2	87	557	25.31	—	3	5
—	J.P. Stephenson	13	23	1	85	551	25.04	—	3	6
—	I.L. Pont	2	4	3	14*	24	24.00	—	—	—
1983	N.A. Foster	21	27	7	53*	433	21.65	—	2	12
1982	D.E. East	23	37	4	100*	712	21.57	1	2	61/19
1982	D.R. Pringle	15	22	2	97	370	18.50	—	1	7
1984	C. Gladwin	7	13	0	73	178	13.69	—	1	4
1970	J.K. Lever	21	25	5	38	199	9.95	—	—	1
1986	J.H. Childs	20	21	6	30	149	9.93	—	—	4
—	T.D. Topley	7	9	2	23	58	8.28	—	—	7
1976	K.R. Pont	6	11	1	31	79	7.90	—	—	1
1970	D.L. Acfield	17	17	9	10	41	5.12	—	—	4

Also batted: N.D. Burns (2 matches) 18,7,29 (2 ct, 2 st); S. Turner (1 match – cap 1970) 32,25*.

BOWLING

	O	*M*	*R*	*W*	*Avge*	*Best*	*5 wI*	*10 wM*
J.H. Childs	566.3	186	1278	85	15.03	8-58	5	3
T.D. Topley	207.1	46	651	31	21.00	5-52	2	—
N.A. Foster	715.2	154	2139	100	21.39	6-57	10	2
D.R. Pringle	336.1	85	946	41	23.07	7-46	2	—
D.L. Acfield	327.1	78	765	25	30.60	4-50	—	—
J.K. Lever	564.1	130	1812	58	31.24	6-57	3	—

Also bowled: A.R. Border 21-2-100-1; D.E. East 0.2-0-1-0; G.A. Gooch 127.4-34-329-7; B.R. Hardie 12-0-58-0; A.W. Lilley 18.3-1-104-2; I.L. Pont 32.2-2-130-3; K.R. Pont 31.5-7-85-4; J.P. Stephenson 2-0-5-0; S. Turner 21-5-72-1.

The First-Class Averages (pp. 167–182) give the records of Essex players in all first-class county matches (their other opponents being the New Zealanders and Cambridge U.), with the exception of N.A. Foster and G.A. Gooch, whose full county figures are as above, and: J.K. Lever 22-25-5-38-199-9.95-0-0-1 ct. 585.1-145-1824-64-28.50-6/57-3-0. D.R. Pringle 16-24-4-97-445-22.25-0-2-9 ct. 358-96-972-43-22.60-7/46-2-0.

GLAMORGAN

Formation of Present Club: 6 July 1888
Colours: Blue and Gold
Badge: Gold Daffodil
Championships: (2) 1948, 1969
NatWest Trophy/Gillette Cup Winners: (0) Finalists 1977
Benson and Hedges Cup Winners: (0) Quarter-Finalists five times
John Player League Champions: (0) Eighth 1977
Match Awards: NWT 17; BHC 28

Secretary: P.G. Carling, Sophia Gardens, Cardiff, CF1 9XR
Captain: H. Morris
Scorer: B.T. Denning
Scores/Prospects: ☎ Cardiff (0222) 43478; Swansea (0792) 466321

BARWICK, Stephen Royston (Cwrt Sart CS; Dwr-y-Felin CS), b Neath 6 Sep 1960. 6'2". RHB, RMF. Debut 1981. HS 29 v Somerset (Cardiff) 1985. BB 8-42 v Worcs (Worcester) 1983. Awards: BHC 1. **NWT:** HS 6. BB 4-14 v Hants (Bournemouth) 1981. **BHC:** HS 18 v Kent (Canterbury) 1984. BB 4-11 v Minor C (Swansea) 1985. **JPL:** HS 29* v Worcs (Worcester) 1986. BB 3-35 v Lancs (Manchester) 1985.

BASE, Simon John (Fish Hoek HS, Cape Town), b Maidstone, Kent 2 Jan 1960. 6'2". RHB, RMF. Western Province B 1981-84. Glamorgan debut 1986. HS 15* v Somerset (Taunton) 1986. BB 4-74 v Yorks (Leeds) 1986. **NWT:** HS 2 and BB 2-49 v Sussex (Hove) 1986. **BHC:** HS 4*. BB 2-34 v Glos (Swansea) 1986. **JPL:** HS 1 and BB 3-31 v Surrey (Oval) 1986.

CANN, Michael James (St Illtyds C, Cardiff; Swansea U), b Cardiff 4 July 1965. 5'9". LHB, OB. Debut 1986. HS 16* v Essex (Chelmsford) 1986.

COTTEY, Phillip Anthony (Bishopston CS, Swansea), Swansea 2 Jun 1966. 5'4". RHB. Debut 1986. HS 9*. Soccer for Swansea City **JPL:** HS 2*.

DAVIES, Terry (Townsend SS, St Albans), b St Albans, Herts 25 Oct 1960. 5'6". RHB, WK. Debut 1979. Cap 1985. HS 75 v Middx (Cardiff) 1985. **NWT:** HS 30* v Staffs (Stone) 1986. **BHC:** HS 23 v Sussex (Hove) 1984. **JPL:** HS 46* v Kent (Cardiff) 1983.

DERRICK, John (Blaengwawr CS), b Cwmaman 15 Jan 1963. 6'1". RHB, RM. Debut 1983. HS 78* v Derbys (Abergavenny) 1986. BB 4-60 v Northants (Wellingborough) 1985. **NWT:** HS 4. BB 4-14 v Scot (Edinburgh) 1985. **BHC:** HS 42 v Kent (Cardiff) 1985. BB 2-34 v Glos (Swansea) 1986. **JPL:** HS 26 v Northants (Northampton) 1983 and 26 v Kent (Maidstone) 1986. BB 4-48 v Derbys (Ebbw Vale) 1986.

HOLMES, Geoffrey Clark (West Denton HS), b Newcastle-upon-Tyne 16 Sep 1958. 5'10". RHB, RM. Debut 1978. Cap 1985. 1000 runs (3); most – 1129 (1985). HS 112 v Leics (Leicester) 1985. BB 5-86 v Surrey (Oval) 1980. Awards: NWT 1. **NWT:** HS 45 v Sussex (Hove) 1986. BB 5-24 v Scotland (Edinburgh) 1985. **BHC:** HS 70 v Somerset (Taunton) 1985. BB 3-26 v Minor C (Swansea) 1985. **JPL:** HS 73 v Warwicks (Birmingham) 1984. BB 5-2 v Derbys (Ebbw Vale) 1984.

HOPKINS, John Anthony (Ynysawdre CS; Trinity CE), b Maesteg 16 Jun 1953. 5'10". RHB, WK. Brother of J.D. (Middlesex 1969-72). Debut 1970. Cap 1977. E

Province 1981-82. 1000 runs (7); most – 1500 (1984). HS 230 v Worcs (Worcester) 1977. Awards: NWT 1; BHC 4. **NWT:** HS 63 v Leics (Swansea) 1977. **BHC:** HS 103* v Minor C (Swansea) 1980. **JPL:** HS 130* v Somerset (Bath) 1983.

JAMES, Stephen Peter (Monmouth S; Swansea U), b Lydney, Glos 7 Sep 1967. 5'11". RHB. Debut 1985. Did not bat or field – rain.

JONES, Alan Lewis (Ystalyfera GS, Cwmtawe CS, Cardiff C of Ed), b Alltwen 1 Jun 1957. 5'8½". LHB. Debut 1973 aged 16 years 99 days. Cap 1983. 1000 runs (2); most – 1811 (1984). HS 132 v Hants (Cardiff) 1984. BB 1-60. **NWT:** HS 60* v Scot (Edinburgh) 1985. **BHC:** HS 36 v Worcs (Cardiff) 1979. **JPL:** HS 82 v Warwicks (Birmingham) 1982.

MAYNARD, Matthew Peter (Ysgol David Hughes, Anglesey), b Oldham, Lancs 21 March 1966. 5'10½". RHB, RM. Debut 1985 scoring 102 out of 117 in 87 minutes v Yorks (Swansea), and completing hundred with three sixes off successive balls. First Glamorgan hundred on debut since 1921 (F.B. Pinch). 1000 runs (1): 1002 (1986). HS 148 v Oxford U (Oxford) 1986. **NWT:** HS 9. **BHC:** HS 0. **JPL:** HS 31 v Glos (Cardiff) 1986.

MORRIS, Hugh (Blundell's S), b Cardiff 5 Oct 1963. 5'8". LHB, RM. Debut 1981. Cap 1986. Captain 1986-. 1000 runs (1): 1522 (1986). HS 128* v Kent (Maidstone) 1986. BB 1-45. **NWT:** HS 75 v Worcs (Swansea) 1985. **BHC:** HS 51 v Somerset (Taunton) 1986. **JPL:** HS 100 v Derbys (Ebbw Vale) 1986.

NORTH, Philip David (St Julian's CS; Nash CFE), b Newport 16 May 1965. 5'5". RHB, SLA. Debut 1985. HS 17* v Lancs (Lytham) 1986. BB 4-49 v Lancs (Lytham) 1986.

ONTONG, Rodney Craig (Selbourne C, East London, SA), b Johannesburg, SA 9 Sep 1955. 5'11". RHB, OB. Border 1972-76 (debut aged 17 years 7 months), and 1982-85 (captain 1983-85). Transvaal 1976-78. Northern Transvaal 1978-82 and 1985-87. Glamorgan debut 1975. Cap 1979. Captain 1984-86. 1000 runs (5); most – 1320 in 1984. HS 204* v Middx (Swansea) 1984. BB 8-67 (13-106 and 130 in match) v Notts (Nottingham) 1985. Awards: NWT 2; BHC 3. **NWT:** HS 64 v Somerset (Cardiff) 1978. BB 4-49 v Norfolk (Norwich) 1983. **BHC:** HS 81 v Somerset (Swansea) 1984. BB 5-30 v Somerset (Taunton) 1985. **JPL:** HS 100 v Northants (Abergavenny) 1982. BB 4-28 v Glos (Cardiff) 1986.

PAULINE, Duncan Brian (Bishop Fox S, East Molesey), b Aberdeen 15 Dec 1960. 5'10". RHB, RM. Surrey 1979-85. Glamorgan debut 1986. HS 115 Surrey v Sussex (Oval) 1983. Glam HS 97 v Worcs (Neath) 1986. BB 5-52 Surrey v Derbys (Derby) 1985. 2-48 v Northants (Swansea) 1986. **NWT:** HS 10 Surrey v Durham (Oval) 1982. **BHC:** HS 69* and BB 2-28 Surrey v Comb Us (Oval) 1985. **JPL:** HS 92 Surrey v Worcs (Oval) 1981. BB 3-34 Surrey v Lancs (Oval) 1985.

ROBERTS, Martin Leonard (Helston CS), b Mullion, Cornwall 12 Apr 1966. 6'1". RHB, WK. Debut 1985. Cornwall 1983-84. HS 8. **JPL:** HS 6*.

SMITH, Ian (Ryton CS), b Chopwell, Co Durham 11 Mar 1967. 6'2". RHB, RM. Debut 1985. HS 12 v Derbys (Derby) 1985. BB 1-18. **JPL:** HS 3*.

THOMAS, John **Gregory** (Cwmtawe HS; Cardiff CE), b Trebanos 12 Aug 1960. 6'3". RHB, RF. Debut 1979. Cap 1986. Border 1983-87. **Tests:** 5 (1985-86 and 1986); HS 31* v WI (P-of-S) 1985-86; BB 4-70 v WI (Bridgetown) 1985-86. LOI: 2. Tour: WI 1985-86. HS 84 v Surrey (Guildford) 1982. BB 5-56 v Somerset (Cardiff) 1984. Awards: NWT 1. **NWT:** HS 24 v Hants (Swansea) 1983. BB 5-17 v Sussex (Cardiff) 1985. **BHC:** HS 17 v Kent (Canterbury) 1984. BB 4-38 v Hants (Southampton) 1985. **JPL:** HS 37 v Notts (Nottingham) 1983. BB 5-38 v Yorks (Cardiff) 1983.

WATKIN, Steven Llewellyn (Cymer Afan CS; South Glamorgan CHE), b Maesteg 15 Sep 1964. 6'3". RHB, RMF. Debut 1986. Did not bat. BB 2-74 v Worcs (Worcester) 1986. **JPL:** HS 7. BB 1-37.

SALVETE

BUTCHER, Alan Raymond (Heath Clark GS); b Croydon 7 Jan 1954. 5'8½". LHB, SLA/LM. Brother of I.P. (Leics 1980-) and M.S. (Surrey 1982). Surrey 1972-86; cap 1975; benefit 1985. **Tests:** 1 (1979); HS 20 v India (Oval). LOI: 1. Tours: WI 1982-83 (Int XI); Ind 1980-81 (Overseas XI). 1000 runs (7); most – 1713 (1980). HS 216* v CU (Cambridge) 1980. BB 6-48 v Hants (Guildford) 1972. Awards: NWT 1; BHC 5. **NWT:** HS 86* Warwicks (Lord's) 1982. BB 1-27. **BHC:** HS 80 v Sussex (Oval) 1982. BB 4-36 v Middx (Lord's) 1985. **JPL:** HS 113* v Warwicks (Birmingham) 1978. BB 5-19 v Glos (Bristol) 1975.

MONKHOUSE, Steven (Derby TGS; Peel C, Bury), b Bury, Lancs 24 Nov 1962. 6'3". RHB, LFM. Warwickshire 1985-86. HS 5. BB 1-34.

SHASTRI, Ravishankar Jayadritha (Don Bosco HS, Bombay), b Bombay, India 27 May 1962. 6'3". RHB, SLA. Bombay 1979-87. Tests (Ind): 49 (1980-81 to 1986-87); HS 142 v Eng (Bombay) 1984-85; BB 5-75 v Pak (Nagpur) 1983-84. LOI (Ind): 74. Tours (Ind): Eng 1982, 1986; Aus 1985-86; WI 1982-83; NZ 1980-81; Pak 1982-83, 1984–85; SL 1985-86. 1000 runs (0+1). HS 200* Bombay v Baroda (Bombay) 1984-85 (including 6 sixes off one over and 200 in 113 minutes – world records). BB 9-101 Bombay v The Rest (Indore) 1981-82.

VAN ZYL, Cornelius Johannes Petrus Gerhardus (**'Corrie'**) (Grey C; U of OFS), b Bloemfontein, South Africa 1 Oct 1961. RHB, RFM. OFS 1981-87. HS 49 OFS v Natal B (Bloemfontein) 1984-85. BB 8-84 OFS v N Transvaal B (Bloemfontein) 1984-85.

VALETE

HICKEY, Denis Jon (Chisholm Institute of Technology), b Mooropana, Victoria, Australia 31 December 1964. 6'2". RHB, RFM. Victoria 1985-86. Glamorgan 1986 (on Esso scholarship). HS 9*. BB 7-81 Victoria v S Aus (Adelaide) 1985-86. Glam BB 5-57 v Oxford U (Oxford) 1986.

STEELE, John Frederick (Endon SS), b Stafford 23 Jul 1946. 5'10½". RHB, SLA. Brother of D.S. (Northants, Derbys and England 1963-84). Leics 1970-83 (cap 1971). Benefit 1983. Glamorgan debut/cap 1984. Natal 1973-78. Staffs 1965-69. Tour: SA 1974-75 (DHR). 1000 runs (6); most – 1347 (1972). HS 195 Leics v Derbys (Leicester) 1971. BB 7-29 Natal B v GW (Umzinto) 1973-74, and 7-29 Leics v Glos (Leicester) 1980. Awards: NWT 3; BHC 5. Now Assistant Sec.

YOUNIS AHMED, Mohammad (Moslem HS, Lahore), b Jullundur, India 20 Oct 1947. 5'10½". LHB, LM/SLA. Half-brother of Saeed Ahmed (Lahore and Pakistan 1954-72). Debut 1961-62 for Pakistan Inter Board Schools XI at age of 14 years 4 months. Appeared for Lahore, Karachi and PIA 1961-70. Surrey 1965-78; cap 1969. South Australia 1972-73. Worcestershire 1979-83; cap 1979. Glamorgan 1984-86; cap 1985. **Tests** (Pakistan): 2 (1969-70); HS 62 v NZ (Karachi). Tours: SA (Int Wanderers) 1974-75, 1975-76, (DHR) 1973-74, 1974-75; WI 1969-70 (Cavs); Pak 1970-71 (Cwlth). 1000 runs (13); most – 1760 (1969). HS 221* Worcs v Notts (Nottingham) 1979. BB 4-10 Surrey v CU (Cambridge) 1975. Awards: BHC 3.

GLAMORGAN RECORDS

FIRST-CLASS CRICKET

Highest Total	For	587-8d		v	Derbyshire	Cardiff	1951
	V	653-6d		by	Glos	Bristol	1928
Lowest Total	For	22		v	Lancashire	Liverpool	1924
	V	33		by	Leics	Ebbw Vale	1965
Highest Innings	For	287*	D.E. Davies	v	Glos	Newport	1939
	V	302*	W.R. Hammond	for	Glos	Bristol	1934
		302	W.R. Hammond	for	Glos	Newport	1939

Highest Partnerships

Wkt						
1st	330	A. Jones/R.C. Fredericks	v	Northants	Swansea	1972
2nd	238	A. Jones/A.R. Lewis	v	Sussex	Hastings	1962
3rd	313	D.E. Davies/W.E. Jones	v	Essex	Brentwood	1948
4th	306*	Javed Miandad/Younis Ahmed	v	Australians	Neath	1985
5th	264	M. Robinson/S.W. Montgomery	v	Hampshire	Bournemouth	1949
6th	230	W.E. Jones/B.L. Muncer	v	Worcs	Worcester	1953
7th	195*	W. Wooller/W.E. Jones	v	Lancashire	Liverpool	1947
8th	202	D. Davies/J.J. Hills	v	Sussex	Eastbourne	1928
9th	203*	J.J. Hills/J.C. Clay	v	Worcs	Swansea	1929
10th	143	T. Davies/S.A.B. Daniels	v	Glos	Swansea	1982

Best Bowling (Innings)	For	10-51	J. Mercer	v	Worcs	Worcester	1936
	V	10-18	G. Geary	for	Leics	Pontypridd	1929
Best Bowling (Match)	For	17-212	J.C. Clay	v	Worcs	Swansea	1937
	V	16-96	G. Geary	for	Leics	Pontypridd	1929

Most Runs – Season	2,083	Javed Miandad	(av 69.43)	1981
Most Runs – Career	34,056	A. Jones	(av 33.03)	1957-1983
Most 100s – Season	8	Javed Miandad		1981
Most 100s – Career	52	A. Jones		1957-1983
Most Wkts – Season	176	J.C. Clay	(av 17.34)	1937
Most Wkts – Career	2,174	D.J. Shepherd	(av 20.95)	1950-1972

LIMITED-OVERS CRICKET

Highest Total	**NWT**	283-3		v	Warwicks	Birmingham	1976
	BHC	245-7		v	Hampshire	Swansea	1976
	JPL	277-6		v	Derbyshire	Ebbw Vale	1984
Lowest Total	**NWT**	76		v	Northants	Northampton	1968
	BHC	68		v	Lancashire	Manchester	1973
	JPL	42		v	Derbyshire	Swansea	1979
Highest Innings	**NWT**	124*	A. Jones	v	Warwicks	Birmingham	1976
	BHC	103*	M.A. Nash	v	Hampshire	Swansea	1976
		103*	J.A. Hopkins	v	Minor C	Swansea	1980
	JPL	130*	J.A. Hopkins	v	Somerset	Bath	1983
Best Bowling	**NWT**	5-17	J.G. Thomas	v	Sussex	Cardiff	1985
	BHC	5-17	A.H. Wilkins	v	Worcs	Worcester	1978
	JPL	6-29	M.A. Nash	v	Worcs	Worcester	1975

GLAMORGAN 1986

RESULTS SUMMARY

	Place	Won	Lost	Drew	Abandoned
Britannic Assurance Championship	**17th**	2	7	15	
All First-class Matches		3	7	16	
John Player League	**12th**	6	9		1
NatWest Bank Trophy	Lost to Sussex (2nd Round)				
Benson and Hedges Cup	Failed to qualify for Quarter-Final				

BRITANNIC ASSURANCE CHAMPIONSHIP AVERAGES

BATTING AND FIELDING

Cap		*M*	*I*	*NO*	*HS*	*Runs*	*Avge*	*100*	*50*	*Ct/St*
1985	Younis Ahmed	15	23	2	105*	845	40.23	1	4	4
1986	H. Morris	24	42	2	128*	1512	37.80	2	11	8
—	J. Derrick	16	22	6	78*	496	31.00	—	4	3
—	M.P. Maynard	20	32	4	129	838	29.92	1	6	12
1983	A.L. Jones	12	20	4	50	413	25.81	—	1	6
1986	J.G. Thomas	19	25	6	70	485	25.52	—	2	6
1985	G.C. Holmes	24	42	5	107	939	25.37	1	4	17
1977	J.A. Hopkins	14	25	0	93	596	23.84	—	3	8
—	D.B. Pauline	11	19	0	97	435	22.89	—	3	3
1979	R.C. Ontong	24	37	4	80*	744	22.54	—	6	8
1985	T. Davies	22	28	13	41	316	21.06	—	—	25/7
1984	J.F. Steele	11	16	4	41*	251	20.91	—	—	7
1981	E.A. Moseley	6	8	1	19	55	7.85	—	—	—
—	S.J. Base	11	11	4	13*	53	7.57	—	—	3
—	P.D. North	4	5	2	17*	22	7.33	—	—	—
—	S.R. Barwick	10	8	2	9	33	5.50	—	—	3
—	D.J. Hickey	12	9	5	9*	19	4.75	—	—	3

Also batted: M.J. Cann (1 match) 16* (1 ct); P.A. Cottey (2 matches) 2,0,7 (1 ct); M.L. Roberts (2 matches) 8 (2 ct, 1 st); I. Smith (3 matches) 0,0 (1 ct). S.L. Watkin (1 match) did not bat.

BOWLING

	O	*M*	*R*	*W*	*Avge*	*Best*	*5 wI*	*10 wM*
R.C. Ontong	606.4	153	1774	64	27.71	8-101	2	1
S.R. Barwick	256.4	56	838	23	36.43	3-25	—	—
J.G. Thomas	397.5	60	1478	39	37.89	4-56	—	—
S.J. Base	199.5	34	727	19	38.26	4-74	—	—
E.A. Moseley	124.3	14	447	11	40.63	4-70	—	—
J. Derrick	213.2	39	705	16	44.06	3-19	—	—
D.J. Hickey	243.5	29	996	17	58.58	3-87	—	—

Also bowled: M.J. Cann 1-1-0-0; G.C. Holmes 107-14-427-9; J.A. Hopkins 1.5-0-12-0; M.P. Maynard 4-0-13-0; H. Morris 11-4-44-0; P.D. North 43.4-11-92-4; D.B. Pauline 14-0-67-2; I. Smith 24-3-111-1; J.F. Steele 134-20-534-6; S.L. Watkin 16-1-82-2; Younis Ahmed 20-4-82-0.

The First-Class Averages (pp. 167–182) give the records of Glamorgan players in all first-class county matches (their other opponents being the New Zealanders and Oxford U.), with the exception of: J.G. Thomas 21-25-6-70-485-25.52-0-2-7 ct. 435.5-65-1606-43-37.34-4/56.

GLOUCESTERSHIRE

Formation of Present Club: 1871
Colours: Blue, Gold, Brown, Silver, Green and Red
Badge: Coat of Arms of the City and County of Bristol
Championships (since 1890): (0) Runners-up 1930, 1931, 1947, 1959, 1969, 1986
NatWest Trophy/Gillette Cup Winners: (1) 1973
Benson and Hedges Cup Winners: (1) 1977
John Player League Champions: (0) Sixth 1969, 1973, 1977, 1985
Match Awards: NWT 26; BHC 31

Secretary: P.G.M. August, Phoenix County Ground, Nevil Road, Bristol BS7 9EJ
Captain: D.A. Graveney
Scorer: A.G. Avery
Scores/Prospects: ☎ Bristol (0272) 48461; Cheltenham College (0242) 522000, Gloucester (0452) 423011; Swindon (0793) 23088

ALLEYNE, Mark Wayne (Harrison C, Barbados; Cardinal Pole S, London E9; Haringey C), b Tottenham, London N 17, 23 May 1968. 5'10". RHB. Debut 1986. HS 116* v Sussex (Bristol) 1986. England YC v Sri Lanka 1986 and to Sri Lanka 1987. **JPL:** HS 46 v Worcs (Hereford) 1986.

ATHEY, Charles William Jeffrey (Stainsby SS; Acklam Hall HS), b Middlesbrough 27 Sep 1957. 5'9½". RHB, RM. Yorkshire 1976-83 (cap 1980). Glos debut 1984. Cap 1985. **Tests:** 13 (1980 to 1986-87); HS 96 v Aus (Perth) 1986–87. LOI: 7. Tours: Aus 1986-87; WI 1980-81; NZ 1979-80 (DHR); SL 1985-86 (Eng B). 1000 runs (5); most – 1812 (1984). HS 184 England B v Sri Lanka (Galle) 1985-86. Glos HS 171* v Northants (Northampton) 1986. BB 3-3 v Hants (Bristol) 1985. Awards: NWT 3; BHC 3. **NWT:** 115 Yorks v Kent (Leeds) 1980. BB 1-18. **BHC:** HS 94* Yorks v Warwicks (Leeds) 1983. BB 4-48 v Comb Us (Bristol) 1984. **JPL:** HS 121* v Worcs (Moreton) 1985. BB 5-35 Yorks v Derbys (Chesterfield) 1981.

BAINBRIDGE, Philip (Hanley HS; Stoke-on-Trent SFC, Borough Road CE), b Sneyd Green, Stoke-on-Trent 16 Apr 1958. RHB, RM. 5'10". Debut 1977. Cap 1981. *Wisden* 1985. Tour: Zim 1984-85 (Eng Co). 1000 runs (6); most – 1644 (1985). HS 151* v Derbys (Derby) 1985. BB 8-53 v Somerset (Bristol) 1986. Awards: NWT 1. **NWT:** HS 75 and BB 3-49 v Scotland (Bristol) 1983. **BHC:** HS 80 v Somerset (Taunton) 1982. BB 3-21 v Notts (Gloucester) 1981. **JPL:** HS 106 v Somerset (Bristol) 1986. BB 4-27 v Middx (Cheltenham) 1980.

BRASSINGTON, Andrew James (Endon SS), b Bagnall, Staffs 9 Aug 1954. 5'11". RHB, WK. Debut 1974. Cap 1978. HS 35 v Sussex (Hastings) 1982. **NWT:** HS 20 v Hants (Bristol) 1979. **BHC:** HS 9*. **JPL:** HS 14* v Northants (Bristol) 1982.

BURROWS, Dean Andrew (Shotton Hall Co S), b Peterlee, Co Durham 20 Jun 1966. RHB, RMF. Debut 1984. Durham 1984. No appearances 1985 or 1986. HS 0. **JPL:** HS 1*. BB 1-32.

CURRAN, Kevin Malcolm (Marandellas HS), b Rusape, S Rhodesia 7 Sep 1959. 6'1". RHB, RFM. Son of K.P. (Rhodesia 1947-54). Irish-born grandparents. Zimbabwe 1980-85. Glos debut/cap 1985. LOI (Zim): 6. Tours (Zim): Eng 1982; SL 1983-84. 1000 runs (1): 1353 (1986). HS 117* v Notts (Cheltenham) 1986. BB 5-35 v Australians (Bristol) 1985. Awards: NWT 1; BHC 1. **NWT:** HS 38 v Berks (Reading) 1986. BB 4-34 v Northants (Bristol) 1985. **BHC:** HS 53* v Scotland (Bristol) 1985. BB 3-45 v Notts (Bristol) 1985. **JPL:** HS 71* v Notts (Nottingham) 1986. BB 4-11 v Leics (Cheltenham) 1985.

GRAVENEY, David Anthony (Millfield S), b Bristol 2 Jan 1953. 6'4". RHB, SLA. Son of J.K. (Glos 1947-64). Debut 1972. Cap 1976. Captain 1981-. HS 119 v OU (Oxford) 1980. BB 8-85 v Notts (Cheltenham) 1974. **NWT:** HS 44 v Surrey (Bristol) 1973. BB 5-11 v Ireland (Dublin) 1981. **BHC:** HS 49* v Somerset (Taunton) 1982. BB 3-13 v Scot (Glasgow) 1983. **JPL:** HS 56* v Notts (Bristol) 1985. BB 4-22 v Hants (Lydney) 1974.

LAWRENCE, David Valentine (Linden S), b Gloucester 28 Jan 1964. 6'2". RHB, RF. Debut 1981. Cap 1985. YC 1985. Tour: SL 1985-86 (Eng B). HS 41 v Notts (Nottingham) 1985. BB 7-48 v Sussex (Hove) 1985. Awards: NWT 1; BHC 1. **NWT:** HS 1*. BB 4-36 v Berks (Reading) 1986. **BHC:** HS 22* v Scot (Bristol) 1985. BB 5-48 v Hants (Bristol) 1984. **JPL:** HS 21* v Leics (Leicester) 1986. BB 4-32 v Lancs (Moreton) 1984.

LLOYDS, Jeremy William (Blundell's S), b Penang, Malaya 17 Nov 1954. 6'0". LHB, OB. Somerset 1979-84 (cap 1982). OFS 1983-84. Gloucestershire debut/cap 1985. 1000 runs (1): 1295 (1986). HS 132* Somerset v Northants (Northampton) 1982. Glos HS 111 v Derbys (Gloucester) 1986. BB 7-88 Somerset v Essex (Chelmsford) 1982. Glos BB 5-37 v Notts (Cheltenham) 1985. **NWT:** HS 40 v Northants (Bristol) 1985. BB 2-35 v Berks (Reading) 1986. **BHC:** HS 51 Somerset v Sussex (Taunton) 1983. BB 3-21 v Glam (Swansea) 1986. **JPL:** HS 45* v Kent (Canterbury) 1986. BB 2-1 Somerset v Hants (Taunton) 1981.

ROMAINES, Paul William (Leeholm S), b Bishop Auckland, Co Durham 25 Dec 1955. 6'0". RHB. Northants 1975-76. Gloucestershire debut 1982. Cap 1983. Griqualand West 1984-85. Durham 1977-81. 1000 runs (2); most – 1844 (1984). HS 186 v Warwicks (Nuneaton) 1982. BB 3-42 v Surrey (Oval) 1985. Awards: BHC 2. **NWT:** HS 82 v Hants (Bristol) 1983. **BHC:** HS 125 v Notts (Bristol) 1985. **JPL:** HS 105 v Northants (Northampton) 1985.

RUSSELL, Robert Charles (**Jack**) (Archway CS), b Stroud 15 Aug 1963. 5'8½". LHB, WK. Debut 1981. Cap 1985. HS 71 v Surrey (Oval) 1986. Award: BHC 1. **NWT:** HS 39 v Leics (Bristol) 1986. **BHC:** HS 36* v Scotland (Glasgow) 1983. **JPL:** HS 108 v Worcs (Hereford) 1986.

SAINSBURY, Gary Edward (Beal GS, Bath U), b Wanstead 17 Jan 1958. 6'2". RHB, LMF. Essex 1979-80. Gloucestershire debut 1983. HS 14* v Yorks (Bristol) 1986. BB 7-38 v Northants (Northampton) 1985. **NWT:** HS 3. BB 3-58 v Lancs (Bristol) 1984. **BHC:** HS 4. BB 4-28 v Northants (Northampton) 1983. **JPL:** HS 7*. BB 3-19 v Notts (Nottingham) 1984.

STOVOLD, Andrew Willis (Filton HS; Loughborough C), b Bristol 19 Mar 1953. 5'8". RHB, WK. Brother of Martin (Glos 1979-82). Debut 1973. Cap 1976. Benefit 1987. Orange Free State 1974-76. 1000 runs (7); most – 1671 (1983). HS 212* v Northants (Northampton) 1982. BB 1-0. Awards: NWT 2; BHC 6. **NWT:** HS 82 v Scot (Bristol) 1983. **BHC:** HS 123 v Comb Us (Oxford) 1982. **JPL:** HS 98* v Kent (Cheltenham) 1977.

TOMLINS, Keith Patrick (St Benedict's, Ealing; Durham U), b Kingston upon Thames 23 Oct 1957. 5'9". RHB, RM. Middlesex 1977-85; cap 1983. Glos debut 1986. Tour: Zim 1980-81 (Middx). HS 146 Middx v OU (Oxford) 1982. Glos HS 75 v Worcs (Worcester) 1986. BB 2-28 Middx v Kent (Lord's) 1982. **NWT:** HS 80 Middx v Cambs (Wisbech) 1983. **BHC:** HS 40 Middx v Somerset (Taunton) 1984. **JPL:** HS 59 Middx v Somerset (Bath) 1984. BB 4-24 Middx v Notts (Lord's) 1978.

WALSH, Courtney Andrew (Excelsior HS), b Kingston, Jamaica 30 Oct 1962. 6'5½". RHB, RF. Jamaica 1981-86. Gloucestershire debut 1984. Cap 1985. *Wisden* 1986. **Tests** (WI): 10 (1984-85 to 1986-87); HS 18* v Aus (Melbourne) 1984-85; BB 4-21 v Pak (Lahore) 1986-87. LOI (WI): 24. Tours (WI): Eng 1984; Aus 1984-85; Pak 1986-87; Zim 1983-84 (Young WI). 100 wickets (1): 118 (1986). HS 52 v Yorks (Bristol) 1986. BB 9-72 v Somerset (Bristol) 1986. **NWT:** HS 25* v Berks (Reading) 1986. BB 2-20 v Beds (Luton) 1985. **BHC:** HS 8*. BB 2-19 v Scotland 1985. **JPL:** HS 35 v Glam (Cardiff) 1986. BB 3-28 v Northants (Northampton) 1985.

WRIGHT, Anthony John (Alleyn's GS) b Stevenage, Herts 27 Jun 1962. 6'0". RHB, RM. Gloucestershire debut 1982. HS 139 v Surrey (Cheltenham) 1984. **NWT:** HS 51 v Berks (Reading) 1986. **BHC:** HS 7. **JPL:** HS 52 v Essex (Cheltenham) 1982.

SALVETE

GREENE, Victor Sylvester (**'Vibert'**), b Barbados 24 Sep 1960. RHB, RMF. Barbados 1985-86.

SMITH, Oliver Charles Kennedy (Cotham GS; York U), b Meriden, Warwicks 29 Oct 1967. 5'11". LHB, OB. England YC to Sri Lanka 1987.

TAYLOR, Duncan John, b Keynsham 19 Feb 1969. RHB, OB.

VALETE

PAYNE, Ian Roger (Emanuel S), b Kennington, London 9 May 1958. 6'0". RHB, RM. Surrey 1977-84. Gloucestershire debut 1985. HS 43 Surrey v Essex (Oval) 1983. BB 5-13 Surrey v Glos (Oval) 1983. Awards: BHC 2.

TWIZELL, Peter Henry (Ponteland HS), b Rothbury, Northumberland 18 Jun 1959. 6'2". RHB, RFM. Debut 1985. Northumberland 1978-84. HS 0. BB 2-65 v Zimbabweans (Bristol) 1985.

GLOUCESTERSHIRE RECORDS

FIRST-CLASS CRICKET

Highest Total	For	653-6d		v	Glamorgan	Bristol	1928
	V	774-7d		by	Australians	Bristol	1948
Lowest Total	For	17		v	Australians	Cheltenham	1896
	V	12		by	Northants	Gloucester	1907
Highest Innings	For	318*	W.G. Grace	v	Yorkshire	Cheltenham	1876
	V	296	A.O. Jones	for	Notts	Nottingham	1903

Highest Partnerships

Wkt						
1st	395	D.M. Young/R.B. Nicholls	v	Oxford U	Oxford	1962
2nd	256	C.T.M. Pugh/T.W. Graveney	v	Derbyshire	Chesterfield	1960
3rd	336	W.R. Hammond/B.H. Lyon	v	Leics	Leicester	1933
4th	321	W.R. Hammond/W.L. Neale	v	Leics	Gloucester	1937
5th	261	W.G. Grace/W.O. Moberley	v	Yorkshire	Cheltenham	1876
6th	320	G.L. Jessop/J.H. Board	v	Sussex	Hove	1903
7th	248	W.G. Grace/E.L. Thomas	v	Sussex	Hove	1896
8th	239	W.R. Hammond/A.E. Wilson	v	Lancashire	Bristol	1938
9th	193	W.G. Grace/S.A.P. Kitcat	v	Sussex	Bristol	1896
10th	131	W.R. Gouldsworthy/J.G. Bessant	v	Somerset	Bristol	1923

Best Bowling	For	10-40	E.G. Dennett	v	Essex	Bristol	1906
(Innings)	V	10-66	A.A. Mailey	for	Australians	Cheltenham	1921
	V	10-66	K. Smales	for	Notts	Stroud	1956
Best Bowling	For	17-56	C.W.L. Parker	v	Essex	Gloucester	1925
(Match)	V	15-87	A.J. Conway	for	Worcs	Moreton-in-M	1914

Most Runs – Season	2,860	W.R. Hammond	(av 69.75)	1933
Most Runs – Career	33,664	W.R. Hammond	(av 57.05)	1920-1951
Most 100s – Season	13	W.R. Hammond		1938
Most 100s – Career	113	W.R. Hammond		1920-1951
Most Wkts – Season	222	T.W.J. Goddard	(av 16.80)	1937
	222	T.W.J. Goddard	(av 16.37)	1947
Most Wkts – Career	3,170	C.W.L. Parker	(av 19.43)	1903-1935

LIMITED-OVERS CRICKET

Highest Total	**NWT**	327-7		v	Berkshire	Reading	1966
	BHC	300-4		v	Comb Univs	Oxford	1982
	JPL	272-4		v	Middlesex	Lord's	1983
Lowest Total	**NWT**	85		v	Essex	Bristol	1981
	BHC	62		v	Hampshire	Bristol	1975
	JPL	49		v	Middlesex	Bristol	1978
Highest Innings	**NWT**	158	Zaheer Abbas	v	Leics	Leicester	1983
	BHC	154*	M.J. Procter	v	Somerset	Taunton	1972
	JPL	131	Sadiq Mohd	v	Somerset	Bristol (Imp)	1975
Best Bowling	**NWT**	5-11	D.A. Graveney	v	Ireland	Dublin	1981
	BHC	6-13	M.J. Procter	v	Hampshire	Southampton	1977
	JPL	6-52	D.J. Shepherd	v	Kent	Bristol	1983

GLOUCESTERSHIRE 1986

RESULTS SUMMARY

	Place	Won	Lost	Drew	Abandoned
Britannic Assurance Championship	**2nd**	9	3	12	
All First-class Matches		9	3	14	
John Player League	**17th**	3	11		2
NatWest Bank Trophy	Lost to Leicestershire (2nd Round)				
Benson and Hedges Cup	Failed to qualify for Quarter-Final				

BRITANNIC ASSURANCE CHAMPIONSHIP AVERAGES

BATTING AND FIELDING

Cap		*M*	*I*	*NO*	*HS*	*Runs*	*Avge*	*100*	*50*	*Ct/St*
1985	C.W.J. Athey	13	21	1	171*	994	49.70	1	6	17
1985	J.W. Lloyds	24	36	9	111	1232	45.62	1	8	22
1985	K.M. Curran	24	37	6	117*	1181	38.09	3	6	28
—	M.W. Alleyne	10	16	5	116*	336	30.54	1	1	4
1976	A.W. Stovold	24	40	4	118	1072	29.77	1	7	7
—	K.P. Tomlins	15	27	4	75	676	29.39	—	4	1
1985	R.C. Russell	24	31	9	71	585	26.59	—	2	51/4
1981	P. Bainbridge	24	41	4	105	941	25.43	1	5	11
—	A.J. Wright	14	24	0	87	530	22.08	—	4	14
1983	P.W. Romaines	13	24	4	67*	429	21.45	—	2	4
1985	C.A. Walsh	23	24	6	52	221	12.27	—	1	7
1976	D.A. Graveney	20	17	8	30*	93	10.33	—	—	19
1985	D.V. Lawrence	22	25	5	34*	198	9.90	—	—	5
—	I.R. Payne	9	10	2	12	53	6.62	—	—	6

Also batted: G.E. Sainsbury (4 matches) 1*,14*,13; P.H. Twizell (1 match) 0.

BOWLING

	O	*M*	*R*	*W*	*Avge*	*Best*	*5 wI*	*10 wM*
C.A. Walsh	789.5	193	2145	118	18.17	9-72	12	4
P. Bainbridge	381.1	81	1095	41	26.70	8-53	2	—
J.W. Lloyds	329.2	61	1119	34	32.91	5-111	2	—
D.A. Graveney	418	125	942	27	34.88	4-17	—	—
I.R. Payne	160.3	35	459	13	35.30	3-48	—	—
D.V. Lawrence	542.1	78	2134	59	36.16	5-84	1	—

Also bowled: C.W.J. Athey 7-1-46-0; K.M. Curran 18-3-50-0; P.W. Romaines 21.1-0-152-0; G.E. Sainsbury 109.1-25-376-8; A.W. Stovold 26-1-132-2; K.P. Tomlins 6-0-34-0; P.H. Twizell 11.1-3-38-0; A.J. Wright 1-0-10-0.

The First-Class Averages (pp. 167–182) give the records of Gloucestershire players in all first-class county matches (their other opponents being the Indians and Oxford U.), with the exception of: C.W.J. Athey 14-22-1-171*-1017-48.42-1-6-18 ct. 18-5-60-1-60.00-1/14. D.V. Lawrence 23-25-5-34*-198-9.90-0-0-5 ct. 563.1-81-2214-61-36.29-5/84-1-0. R.C. Russell 26-31-9-71-585-26.59-0-2-53 ct/4 st.

HAMPSHIRE

Formation of Present Club: 12 August 1863
Colours: Blue, Gold and White
Badge: Tudor Rose and Crown
Championships: (2) 1961, 1973
NatWest Trophy/Gillette Cup Semi-Finalists: (4) 1966, 1976, 1983, 1985
Benson and Hedges Cup Semi-Finalists: (2) 1975, 1977
John Player League Champions: (3) 1975, 1978, 1986
Match Awards: NWT 33; BHC 35

Chief Executive: A.F. Baker, County Cricket Ground, Northlands Road, Southampton SO9 2TY.
Captain: M.C.J. Nicholas
Scorer: V.H. Isaacs
Scores/Prospects: ☎ Southampton (0703) 333788/9; Basingstoke (0256) 3646; Bournemouth (0202) 25872

ANDREW, Stephen Jon Walter (Milton Abbey S; Portchester SS), b London 27 Jan 1966. 6'3". RHB, RMF. Debut 1984. HS 7. BB 6-43 v Glos (Bournemouth) 1985. Award: BHC 1. **NWT:** BB 1-28. **BHC:** HS 1*. BB 3-12 v Surrey (Oval) 1984. **JPL:** BB 3-38 v Northants (Southampton) 1984.

BAKKER, Paul-Jan (Hugo De Groot C, The Hague), b Vlaardingen, Holland 19 Aug 1957. 5'11". RHB, RMF. Debut 1986. HS 3*. BB 2-15 v Cambridge U (Cambridge) 1986. **BHC:** BB 2-19 v Comb Us (Oxford) 1986. **JPL:** BB 2-46 v Sussex (Bournemouth) 1986.

CHIVERS, Ian James (Richard Taunton SFC, Southampton), b Southampton 5 Nov 1964. 5'9". RHB, OB. Debut 1985. Did not bat. BB 1-5.

CONNOR, Cardigan Adolphus (The Valley SS, Anguilla; Langley C, Berkshire), b The Valley, Anguilla 24 Mar 1961. 5'9". RHB, RFM. Debut 1984. Buckinghamshire 1979-83. HS 36 v Northants (Northampton) 1985. BB 7-37 v Kent (Bournemouth) 1984. **NWT:** HS 5. BB 3-52 v Essex (Southampton) 1985. **BHC:** HS 4*. BB 4-27 v Kent (Canterbury) 1985. **JPL:** HS 2*. BB 4-16 v Yorks (Bournemouth) 1984.

COWLEY, Nigel Geoffrey (Dutchy Manor SS, Mere), b Shaftesbury, Dorset 1 Mar 1953. 5'7". RHB, OB. Debut 1974. Cap 1978. Dorset 1972. 1000 runs (1): 1042 (1984). HS 109* v Somerset (Taunton) 1977. BB 6-48 v Leics (Southampton) 1982. Award: NWT 1. **NWT:** HS 63* v Glos (Bristol) 1979. BB 5-24 v Norfolk (Norwich) 1984. **BHC:** HS 59 v Glos (Southampton) 1977. BB 3-39 v Sussex (Bournemouth) 1982. **JPL:** HS 74 v Warwicks (Birmingham) 1981. BB 4-42 v Surrey (Portsmouth) 1983.

GREENIDGE, Cuthbert **Gordon** (St Peter's BS, Barbados; Sutton SS, Reading), b St Peter, Barbados 1 May 1951. 5'9½". RHB, RM. Debut 1970. Cap 1972. Barbados 1972-86. *Wisden* 1976. Benefit 1983. MBE 1985. **Tests** (WI): 74 (1974-75 to 1986-87); HS 223 v Eng (Manchester) 1984. LOI (WI): 81. Tours (WI): Eng 1976, 1980, 1984; Aus 1975-76, 1979-80, 1981-82, 1984-85, 1986-87; NZ 1979-80, 1986-87; Ind 1974-75, 1983-84; Pak 1974-75; 1980-81, 1986-87; SL 1974-75. 1000 (15+1); most – 2035 (1986). HS 273* D.H. Robins' XI v Pakistanis (Eastbourne) 1974. Hants HS 259 v

Sussex (Southampton) 1975. BB 5-49 v Surrey (Southampton) 1971. Awards: NWT 4. BHC 8. **NWT:** HS 177 v Glamorgan (Southampton) 1975. **BHC:** HS 173* v Minor C (S) (Amersham) 1973. **JPL:** HS 163* v Warwicks (Birmingham) 1979. BB 1-36.

JAMES, Kevan David (Edmonton County HS), b Lambeth 18 Mar 1961. 6'0". LHB, LMF. Middlesex 1980-84. Wellington 1982-83. Hampshire debut 1985. HS 124 v Somerset (Taunton) 1985. BB 6-22 v Australians (Southampton) 1985. **NWT:** HS 19 v Worcs (Southampton) 1986. BB 2-19 v Herts (Southampton) 1986. **BHC:** HS 27 v Leics (Southampton) 1985. BB 2-31 Middx v Kent (Canterbury) 1983. **JPL:** HS 54* v Surrey (Oval) 1986. BB 4-23 v Lancs (Southampton) 1986.

MARSHALL, Malcolm Denzil (Parkinson CS, Barbados), b St Michael, Barbados 18 Apr 1958. 5'11". RHB, RF. Barbados 1977-86. Hampshire debut 1979. Cap 1981. *Wisden* 1982. Benefit 1987. **Tests** (WI): 48 (1978-79 to 1986-87); HS 92 v Ind (Kanpur) 1983-84; BB 7-53 v Eng (Leeds) 1984. LOI (WI): 79. Tours: Eng 1980, 1984; Aus 1979-80, 1981-82, 1984-85, 1986-87; NZ 1979-80, 1986-87; Ind 1978-79, 1983-84; Pak 1980-81, 1986-87; SL 1978-79; Zim 1981-82 (Young WI). 100 wickets (1): 134 (1982). HS 116* v Lancs (Southampton) 1982. BB 8-71 v Worcs (Southampton) 1982. **NWT:** HS 32 v Worcs (Southampton) 1986. BB 4-15 v Kent (Canterbury) 1983. **BHC:** HS 33 v Kent (Southampton) 1986. BB 4-26 v Kent (Canterbury) 1983. **JPL:** HS 46 v Leics (Leicester) 1982. BB 5-13 v Glam (Portsmouth) 1979.

MARU, Rajesh Jamandass (Rook's Heath HS, Harrow; Pinner SFC), b Nairobi, Kenya 28 Oct 1962. 5'6". RHB, SLA. Middlesex 1980-82. Hampshire debut 1984. Cap 1986. Tour: Zim 1980-81 (Middx). HS 62 v Sussex (Portsmouth) 1985. BB 7-79 v Middx (Bournemouth) 1984. **JPL:** HS 3*. BB 2-41 Middx v Kent (Lord's) 1980.

MIDDLETON, Tony Charles (Montgomery of Alamein S, and Peter Symonds SFC, Winchester), b Winchester 1 Feb 1964. 5'10½". RHB, SLA. Debut 1984. HS 68* v Somerset (Taunton) 1986. BB 1-13.

NICHOLAS, Mark Charles Jefford (Bradfield C), b London 29 Sep 1957. 5'11" RHB, RM. Grandson of F.W.H. (Essex 1912-29). Debut 1978. Cap 1982. Captain 1985-. Tours: SL 1985-86 (Eng B; captain); Zim 1984-85 (Eng Co; captain). 1000 runs (4); most – 1559 (1984). HS 206* v OU (Oxford) 1982. BB 5-45 v Worcs (Southampton) 1983. Award: BHC 1. **NWT:** HS 63 v Norfolk (Norwich) 1984. BB 2-39 v Berks (Southampton) 1985. **BHC:** HS 74 v Glam (Southampton) 1985. BB 4-34 v Minor C (Reading) 1985. **JPL:** HS 108 v Glos (Bristol) 1984. BB 4-41 v Northants (Southampton) 1986.

PARKS, Robert James (Eastbourne GS; Southampton Inst of Technology), b Cuckfield, Sussex 15 Jun 1959. 5'8". RHB, WK. Son of J.M. (Sussex, Somerset and England 1949-76) and grandson of J.H. (Sussex and England 1924-52). Debut 1980. Cap 1982. Tour: Zim 1984-85 (Eng Co). Held 10 catches in match v Derbys (Portsmouth) 1981. HS 89 v CU (Cambridge) 1984. Awards: BHC 1. **NWT:** HS 25 v Kent (Southampton) 1984. **BHC:** HS 16 v Kent (Southampton) 1986. **JPL:** HS 36* v Leics (Leics) 1982.

SCOTT, Richard James, b Bournemouth 2 Nov 1963. LHB, RM. No f-c matches. **JPL:** HS 8*.

SMITH, Christopher Lyall ('Kippy') (Northlands HS, Durban), b Durban, South Africa 15 Oct 1958. 5'10". RHB, OB. Brother of R.A. and grandson of Dr V.L. Shearer (Natal). Natal 1977-83. Glamorgan 1979. Hampshire debut 1980. Cap 1981. *Wisden* 1983. **Tests:** 8 (1983 to 1986); HS 91 v NZ (Auckland) 1983-84; 2-31 v NZ

(Nottingham) 1983. LOI: 4. Tours: NZ 1983-84; Pak 1983-84; SL 1985-86 (Eng B). 1000 runs (5); most – 2000 (1985). HS 193 v Derbys (Derby) 1983. BB 3-35 v Glam (Southampton) 1983. Awards: NWT 1; BHC 2. **NWT:** HS 101* v Glos (Bristol) 1983. BB 3-32 v Berks (Southampton) 1985. **BHC:** HS 82* v Comb Us (Southampton) 1984. **JPL:** HS 95 v Leics (Basingstoke) 1984. BB 2-3 v Glos (Bristol) 1984.

SMITH, Robin Arnold (Northlands HS), b Durban, South Africa 13 Sep 1963. 5'11". RHB, LB. Brother of C.L. and grandson of Dr V.L. Shearer (Natal). Natal 1980-85. Hampshire debut 1982. Cap 1985. 1000 (2); – most 1533 (1985). HS 140* v Derbys (Basingstoke) 1985. BB 2-11 v Surrey (Southampton) 1985. Award: NWT 1. **NWT:** HS 110 v Somerset (Taunton) 1985. BB 2-13 v Berks (Southampton) 1985. **BHC:** HS 81 v Leics (Southampton) 1985. **JPL:** HS 104 v Glam (Cardiff) 1984, 104 v Surrey (Southampton) 1985.

TERRY, Vivian Paul (Millfield S), b Osnabruck, West Germany 14 Jan 1959. 6'0". RHB, RM. Debut 1978. Cap 1983. **Tests:** 2 (1984); HS 8. Tour: Zim 1984-85 (Eng Co). 1000 runs (3); most – 1284 (1985). HS 175* v Glos (Bristol) 1985. Awards: NWT 2. **NWT:** HS 165* v Berks (Southampton) 1985. **BHC:** HS 72 v Kent (Canterbury) 1983, 72 v Essex (Southampton) 1984. **JPL:** HS 142 v Leics (Southampton) 1986.

TREMLETT, Timothy Maurice (Bellemoor SS; Richard Taunton SFC, Southampton), b Wellington, Somerset 26 Jul 1956. 6'2". RHB, RMF. Son of M.F. (Somerset, Central Districts and England 1947-60). Debut 1976. Cap 1983. Tours: SL 1985-86 (Eng B); Zim 1984-85 (Eng Co). HS 102* v Somerset (Taunton) 1985. BB 6-82 v Derbys (Portsmouth) 1983. Award: BHC 1. **NWT:** HS 28* v Worcs (Southampton) 1986. BB 4-38 v Kent (Canterbury) 1983. **BHC:** HS 36* v Kent (Southampton) 1986. BB 4-30 v Surrey (Oval) 1986. **JPL:** HS 35 v Worcs (Worcester) 1984. BB 5-28 v Kent (Canterbury) 1985.

TURNER, David Roy (Chippenham BHS), b Chippenham, Wiltshire 5 Feb 1949. 5'6". LHB, RM. Debut 1966. Cap 1970. Western Province 1977-78. Benefit 1981. Tour: SA 1972-73 (DHR). 1000 runs (7); most – 1365 (1984). HS 181* v Surrey (Oval) 1969. BB 2-7 v Glam (Bournemouth) 1981. Awards: NWT 1; BHC 4. **NWT:** HS 86 v Northants (Southampton) 1976. **BHC:** HS 123* v Minor C (S) (Amersham) 1973. **JPL:** HS 114 v Essex (Colchester) 1984.

SALVETE

AYLING, Jonathan Richard (Portsmouth GS), b Portsmouth 13 Jun 1967. 6'4". RHB, RM.

AYMES, Adrian Nigel (Bellemoor SS), b Southampton 4 Jun 1964. 6'0". RHB, WK.

NEWTON, Mark Roy (Peter Symonds C, Winchester), b Winchester 17 Dec 1967. 6'1". RHB, SLA. EYC to Sri Lanka 1987.

VALE

GOLDIE, Christopher Frederick Evelyn (St Paul's S; Pembroke C, Cambridge) b Johannesburg, South Africa 2 Nov 1960. 5'6". RHB, WK. Cambridge U 1981-82; blue 1981-82. Hampshire debut 1983. HS 77 v OU (Lord's) 1981.

HAMPSHIRE RECORDS

FIRST-CLASS CRICKET

Highest Total	For	672-7d		v	Somerset	Taunton	1899
	V	742		by	Surrey	The Oval	1909
Lowest Total	For	15		v	Warwicks	Birmingham	1922
	V	23		by	Yorkshire	Middlesbrough	1965
Highest Innings	For	316	R.H. Moore	v	Warwicks	Bournemouth	1937
	V	302*	P. Holmes	for	Yorkshire	Portsmouth	1920

Highest Partnerships

Wkt						
1st	250	C.G. Greenidge/V.P. Terry	v	Northants	Northampton	1986
2nd	321	G. Brown/E.I.M. Barrett	v	Glos	Southampton	1920
3rd	344	C.P. Mead/G. Brown	v	Yorks	Portsmouth	1927
4th	263	R.E. Marshall/D.A. Livingstone	v	Middlesex	Lord's	1970
5th	235	G. Hill/D.F. Walker	v	Sussex	Portsmouth	1937
6th	411	R.M. Poore/E.G. Wynyard	v	Somerset	Taunton	1899
7th	325	G. Brown/C.H. Abercrombie	v	Essex	Leyton	1913
8th	227	K.D. James/T.M. Tremlett	v	Somerset	Taunton	1985
9th	230	D.A. Livingstone/A.T. Castell	v	Surrey	Southampton	1962
10th	192	H.A.W. Bowell/W.H. Livsey	v	Worcs	Bournemouth	1921

Best Bowling (Innings)	For	9-25	R.M.H. Cottam	v	Lancashire	Manchester	1965
	V	10-46	W. Hickton	for	Lancashire	Manchester	1870
Best Bowling (Match)	For	16-88	J.A. Newman	v	Somerset	Weston-s-M	1927
	V	17-119	W. Mead	for	Essex	Southampton	1895

Most Runs – Season	2,854	C.P. Mead	(av 79.27)	1928
Most Runs – Career	48,892	C.P. Mead	(av 48.84)	1905-1936
Most 100s – Season	12	C.P. Mead		1928
Most 100s – Career	138	C.P. Mead		1905-1936
Most Wkts – Season	190	A.S. Kennedy	(av 15.61)	1922
Most Wkts – Career	2,669	D. Shackleton	(av 18.23)	1948-1969

LIMITED-OVERS CRICKET

Highest Total	NWT	371-4		v	Glamorgan	Southampton	1975
	BHC	321-1		v	Minor C (S)	Amersham	1973
	JPL	292-1		v	Surrey	Portsmouth	1983
Lowest Total	NWT	98		v	Lancashire	Manchester	1975
	BHC	94		v	Glamorgan	Swansea	1973
	JPL	43		v	Essex	Basingstoke	1972
Highest Innings	NWT	177	C.G. Greenidge	v	Glamorgan	Southampton	1975
	BHC	173*	C.G. Greenidge	v	Minor C (S)	Amersham	1973
	JPL	166*	T.E. Jesty	v	Surrey	Portsmouth	1983
Best Bowling	NWT	7-30	P.J. Sainsbury	v	Norfolk	Southampton	1965
	BHC	5-24	R.S. Herman	v	Glos	Bristol	1975
	BHC	5-24	K.StJ.D. Emery	v	Essex	Chelmsford	1982
	JPL	6-20	T.E. Jesty	v	Glamorgan	Cardiff	1975

HAMPSHIRE 1986

RESULTS SUMMARY

	Place	Won	Lost	Drew	Abandoned
Britannic Assurance Championship	6th	7	4	12	1
All First-class Matches		7	4	14	1
John Player League	1st	12	3		1
NatWest Bank Trophy	Lost to Worcestershire (2nd Round)				
Benson and Hedges Cup	Failed to qualify for Quarter-Final				

BRITANNIC ASSURANCE CHAMPIONSHIP AVERAGES

BATTING AND FIELDING

Cap		M	I	NO	HS	Runs	Avge	100	50	Ct/St
1972	C.G. Greenidge	19	32	4	222	1916	68.42	8	5	17
1981	C.L. Smith	17	25	8	114*	964	56.70	2	7	13
1985	R.A. Smith	23	34	6	128*	1100	39.28	2	7	19
1983	T.M. Tremlett	19	21	11	59*	317	31.70	—	2	2
1970	D.R. Turner	9	13	0	96	403	31.00	—	2	2
—	T.C. Middleton	8	14	3	68*	316	28.72	—	1	7
1978	N.G. Cowley	17	18	6	78*	329	27.41	—	2	4
1986	R.J. Maru	15	9	5	23	108	27.00	—	—	10
—	K.D. James	12	13	2	62	275	25.00	—	1	5
1982	R.J. Parks	23	21	4	80	419	24.64	—	3	68/6
1983	V.P. Terry	21	33	3	80	704	23.46	—	4	16
1982	M.C.J. Nicholas	21	28	2	55	489	18.80	—	2	12
1981	M.D. Marshall	23	23	2	51*	263	12.52	—	1	5
—	C.A. Connor	20	13	5	16	41	5.12	—	—	3
—	S.J.W. Andrew	5	5	2	7	15	5.00	—	—	2

Also batted: P.J. Bakker (1 match) 3*,3.

BOWLING

	O	M	R	W	Avge	Best	5 wI	10 wM
M.D. Marshall	656.3	171	1508	100	15.08	6-51	5	—
R.J. Maru	438.3	132	1177	41	28.70	4-33	—	—
N.G.Cowley	345.2	69	949	33	28.75	5-17	1	—
T.M. Tremlett	424.4	103	1175	40	29.37	5-46	1	—
K.D. James	228.4	55	692	21	32.95	5-34	1	—
C.A. Connor	541.4	123	1616	49	32.97	5-60	1	—
S.J.W. Andrew	97.2	15	331	10	33.10	3-25	—	—

Also bowled: P.J. Bakker 24-5-73-1; T.C. Middleton 8-1-39-1; M.C.J. Nicholas 57-11-171-2; R.J. Parks 23-1-110-0; C.L. Smith 37-4-177-1; R.A. Smith 42.4-7-189-2; V.P. Terry 1-1-0-0; D.R. Turner 3-1-6-0.

The First-Class Averages (pp. 167–182) give the records of Hampshire players in all first-class county matches (their other opponents being the Indians and Cambridge U.), with the exception of: M.C.J. Nicholas 23-31-2-55-544-18.75-0-2-13 ct. 64-13-198-3-66.00-1/27. C.L. Smith 19-28-8-114*-1027-51.35-2-7-16 ct. 40-7-177-1-177.00-1/54.

KENT

Formation of Present Club: 1 March 1859
Substantial Reorganisation: 6 December 1870
Colours: Maroon and White
Badge: White Horse on a Red Ground
Championships: (6) 1906, 1909, 1910, 1913, 1970, 1978.
Joint Championships: (1) 1977
NatWest Trophy/Gillette Cup Winners: (2) 1967, 1974
Benson and Hedges Cup Winners: (3) 1973, 1976, 1978
John Player League Champions: (3) 1972, 1973, 1976
Match Awards: NWT 36; BHC 50

Secretary: D.B. Dalby, St Lawrence Ground, Canterbury, CT1 3NZ
Captain: C.S. Cowdrey
Scorer: C. Lewis
Scores/Prospects: ☎ Canterbury (0227) 457323/4

ASLETT, Derek George (Dover GS; Leicester U), b Dover 12 Feb 1958. 5'11". RHB, LB. Debut 1981 scoring 146* and 20* v Hampshire at Bournemouth. Cap 1983. 1000 runs (2); most – 1491 (1984). HS 221* v Sri Lankans (Canterbury) 1984. BB 4-119 v Sussex (Hove) 1982. **NWT:** HS 67 v Hants (Southampton) 1984. BB 1-0. **BHC:** HS 49 v Hants (Canterbury) 1985. **JPL:** HS 100 v Somerset (Taunton) 1983.

BAPTISTE, Eldine Ashworth Elderfield (All Saints SS, Liberta), b Liberta, Antigua 12 Mar 1960. 6'0". RHB, RFM. Debut 1981. Cap 1983. Leeward Is 1981-86. **Tests** (WI): 9 (1983-84 to 1984); HS 87* v Eng (Birmingham) 1984; BB 3-31 v Eng (Manchester) 1984. LOI: 29. Tours (WI): Eng 1984; Aus 1984-85; Ind 1983-84. HS 136* v Yorks (Sheffield) 1983. BB 6-42 v Northants (Northampton) 1985. Awards: NWT 1; BHC 1. **NWT:** HS 22 v Warwicks (Canterbury) 1985. BB 5-20 v Hants (Canterbury) 1983. **BHC:** HS 43* v Somerset (Taunton) 1985. BB 5-30 v Glam (Cardiff) 1985. **JPL:** HS 60 v Warwicks (Canterbury) 1985. BB 4-22 v Surrey (Canterbury) 1986.

BENSON, Mark Richard (Sutton Valence S), b Shoreham, Sussex 6 Jul 1958. 5'10". LHB, OB. Debut 1980. Cap 1981. **Tests:** 1 (1986); HS 30 v Ind (Birmingham) 1986. LOI: 1. 1000 runs (5); most – 1515 (1983). HS 162 v Hants (Southampton) 1985. BB 2-55 v Surrey (Dartford) 1986. Awards: NWT 2. **NWT:** HS 113* v Warwicks (Birmingham) 1984. **BHC:** HS 65 v Surrey (Canterbury) 1982 and 65 v Hants (Southampton) 1986. **JPL:** HS 97 v Surrey (Oval) 1982.

COWDREY, Christopher Stuart (Tonbridge S), b Farnborough, Kent 20 Oct 1957. 6'1". RHB, RM. Brother of G.R., son of M.C. (Kent and England 1950-76) and grandson of E.A. (Europeans). Kent 2nd XI debut when aged 15. Debut 1977. Cap 1979. Captain 1985-. **Tests:** 5 (1984-85); HS 38 v Ind (Delhi) 1984-85; BB 2-65 v Ind (Madras) 1984-85. LOI: 3. Tours: NZ 1979-80 (DHR); Ind/SL 1984-85; SL 1977-78 (DHR). 1000 runs (3); most – 1364 (1983). HS 159 v Surrey (Canterbury) 1985. BB 5-69 v Hants (Canterbury) 1986. Awards: NWT 3; BHC 3. **NWT:** HS 122* v Essex (Chelmsford) 1983. BB 4-36 v Hants (Canterbury) 1983. **BHC:** HS 114 v Sussex (Canterbury) 1977. BB 3-38 v Hants (Canterbury) 1985. **JPL:** HS 95 v Worcs (Canterbury) 1983. BB 5-28 v Leics (Canterbury) 1984.

COWDREY, Graham Robert (Tonbridge S; Durham U), b Farnborough, Kent 27 Jun 1964. 5'11". RHB, RM. Brother of C.S., son of M.C. (Kent and England 1950-76) and grandson of E.A. (Europeans). Debut 1984. HS 75 v Northants (Canterbury) 1986. BB 1-17. Award: BHC 1. **NWT:** HS 22 v Notts (Nottingham) 1986. BB 1-30. **BHC:** HS 65 v Surrey (Canterbury) 1986. **JPL:** HS 48 v Somerset (Canterbury) 1986.

DAVIS, Richard Peter (King Ethelbert's S, Birchington; Thanet TC), b Westbrook, Margate 18 Mar 1966. 6'3". RHB, SLA. Debut 1986. HS 0*. BB 3-38 v Warwicks (Folkestone) 1986.

ELLISON, Richard Mark (Tonbridge S; Exeter U), b Ashford, Kent 21 Sep 1959. 6'2". LHB, RMF. Brother of C.C. (Cambridge U). Debut 1981. Cap 1983. *Wisden* 1985. Tasmania 1986-87. **Tests:** 11 (1984 to 1986); HS 41 v Sri Lanka (Lord's) 1984; BB 6-77 v Aus (Birmingham) 1985. LOI: 14. Tours: WI 1985-86; Ind/SL 1984-85. HS 108 v OU (Oxford) 1984. BB 7-87 v Northants (Maidstone) 1985. Awards: NWT 1; BHC 4. **NWT:** HS 49* v Warwicks (Birmingham) 1984. BB 4-19 v Cheshire (Canterbury) 1983. **BHC:** HS 72 v Middx (Lord's) 1984. BB 4-28 v Glam (Canterbury) 1984. **JPL:** HS 84 v Glos (Canterbury) 1984. BB 4-25 v Hants (Canterbury) 1983.

HINKS, Simon Graham (St George's S, Gravesend), b Northfleet, Kent 12 Oct 1960. 6'2". LHB, RM. Debut 1982. Cap 1985. 1000 (1): 1536 (1985). HS 131 v Hants (Canterbury) 1986. BB 1-10. Award: NWT 1. **NWT:** HS 95 v Surrey (Canterbury) 1985. **BHC:** HS 49 v Glam (Cardiff) 1985. BB 1-15. **JPL:** HS 99 v Glam (Maidstone) 1986. BB 1-3.

IGGLESDEN, Alan Paul (Churchill S, Westerham), b Farnborough, Kent 8 Oct 1964. 6'5". RHB, RFM. Debut 1986. HS 8*. BB 4-46 v Surrey (Oval) 1986.

JARVIS, Kevin Bertram Sidney (Springhead S, Northfleet; Thames Polytechnic) b Dartford 23 Apr 1953. 6'3". RHB, RFM. Debut 1975. Cap 1977. Benefit 1987. Tours: WI 1982-83 (Int XI); SL 1977-78 (DHR). HS 19 v Derbys (Maidstone) 1984. BB 8-97 v Worcs (Worcester) 1978. Awards: NWT 1; BHC 1. **NWT:** HS 5*. BB 4-19 v Warwicks (Canterbury) 1983. **BHC:** HS 4*. BB 4-34 v Worcs (Lord's) 1976. **JPL:** HS 8*. BB 5-24 v Notts (Nottingham) 1985.

MARSH, Steven Andrew (Walderslade SS; Mid-Kent CFE), b Westminster 27 Jan 1961. 5'10". RHB, WK. Debut 1982. Cap 1986. HS 70 v Warwicks (Folkestone) 1986. **NWT:** HS 1. **BHC:** HS 15 v Middx (Canterbury) 1986. **JPL:** HS 22* v Somerset (Bath) 1986.

PENN, Christopher (Dover GS), b Dover 19 Jun 1963. 6'1". LHB, RFM. Debut 1982. HS 115 v Lancs (Manchester) 1984. BB 5-65 v Somerset (Maidstone) 1986. **NWT:** HS 5. BB 1-34. **BHC:** HS 17 v Somerset (Canterbury) 1984. BB 4-34 v Surrey (Canterbury) 1982. **JPL:** HS 40 v Sussex (Maidstone) 1982. BB 3-35 v Yorks (Canterbury) 1982.

TAVARÉ, Christopher James (Sevenoaks S; St John's, Oxford), b Orpington, Kent 27 Oct 1954. 6'1½". RHB, RM. Debut 1974. Oxford U 1975-77; blue 1975-76-77. Cap 1978. Captain 1983-84. Benefit 1988. **Tests:** 30 (1980 to 1984); HS 149 v Ind (Delhi) 1981-82. LOI: 29. Tours: Aus 1982-83; NZ 1983-84; Ind/SL 1981-82; Pak 1983-84. 1000 runs (10); most – 1770 (1981). HS 168* v Essex (Chelmsford) 1982. BB 1-3. Awards: NWT 3; BHC 6. **NWT:** HS 118* v Yorks (Canterbury) 1981. **BHC:** HS 143 v Somerset (Taunton) 1985. **JPL:** HS 136* v Glos (Canterbury) 1978.

TAYLOR, Neil Royston (Cray Valley THS), b Orpington, Kent 21 Jul 1959. 6'1". RHB, OB. Debut 1979 scoring 110 and 11 v Sri Lankans at Canterbury. Cap 1982. 1000 runs (4); most – 1340 (1982). HS 155* v Glam (Cardiff) 1983. BB 2-20 v Somerset (Canterbury) 1985. Awards: BHC 5. **NWT:** HS 51 v Essex (Chelmsford) 1985. **BHC:** HS 121 v Sussex (Hove) 1982 and 121 v Somerset (Canterbury) 1982. **JPL:** HS 75 v Derbys (Derby) 1986.

UNDERWOOD, Derek Leslie (Beckenham and Penge GS), b Bromley 8 Jun 1945. 5'11". RHB, LM. Debut 1963 – youngest to take 100 wickets in first season. Cap 1964. YC 1966. *Wisden* 1968. Benefit 1975. Testimonial 1986. MBE 1981. **Tests:** 86 (1966 to 1981-82); HS 45* v Aus (Leeds) 1968; BB 8-51 (13-71 match) v Pak (Lord's) 1974. LOI: 26. Tours: Aus 1970-71, 1974-75, 1976-77, 1979-80; SA 1975-76 (Int Wan), 1981-82 (SAB); WI 1969-70 (Cav/DN), 1973-74; NZ 1970-71, 1974-75; Ind 1979-80; Ind/SL 1967-68, 1972-73, 1976-77, 1981-82; Pak 1966-67 (MCC U-25), 1968-69, 1972-73; SL 1968-69. 100 wickets (10); most – 157 (1966). HS 111 v Sussex (Hastings) 1984. BB 9-28 v Sussex (Hastings) 1964. Awards: BHC 2. **NWT:** HS 28 v Sussex (Tunbridge Wells) 1963. BB 4-57 v Leics (Canterbury) 1974. **BHC:** HS 27 v Surrey (Canterbury) 1983. BB 5-35 v Surrey (Oval) 1976. **JPL:** HS 22 v Worcs (Dudley) 1969. BB 6-12 v Sussex (Hastings) 1984.

WARD, Trevor Robert (Hextable CS, nr Swansea), b Farningham 18 Jan 1968. 5'11". RHB, RM. Debut 1986. HS 29 v Hants (Southampton) 1986. England YC v Sri Lanka YC 1986 and to Sri Lanka 1987.

SALVETE

FARBRACE, Paul (Geoffrey Chaucer S, Canterbury), b Ash, Kent 7 Jul 1967. 5'10". RHB, WK.

GOLDSMITH, Steven Clive (Simon Langton GS, Canterbury), b Ashford 19 Dec 1964. 5'10". RHB, RM.

KELLEHER, Daniel John Michael (St Mary's GS, Sidcup; Erith TC), b Southwark, London 5 May 1966. Nephew of H.R.A. (Surrey 1955, Northants 1956-58). 6'1". RHB, RMF.

SABINE, David John, b Papakura, Auckland, NZ 2 Jun 1966. RHB, RM.

VALETE

ALDERMAN, Terence Michael (Aquinas C and Churchlands C, Perth), b Subiaco, Perth, Australia 12 Jun 1956. 6'2½". RHB, RFM. Western Australia 1974-85. *Wisden* 1981. Kent debut/cap 1984. **Tests** (Aus): 22 (1981 to 1984-85); HS 23 and BB 6-128 v WI (Perth) 1984-85. LOI: 23. Tours (Aus): Eng 1981; SA (Aus XI) 1985-86, 1986-87; WI 1983-84; NZ 1981-82; Pak 1982-83. HS 52* v Sussex (Hastings) 1984. BB 8-46 v Derbys (Derby) 1986.

DALE, Christopher Stephen, b Canterbury 15 Dec 1961. RHB, OB. Gloucestershire 1984. Kent 1986. HS 49 Glos v Yorks (Bradford) 1984. BB 3-10 Glos v Oxford U (Oxford) 1984.

DILLEY, G.R. – see WORCESTERSHIRE.

KENT RECORDS

FIRST-CLASS CRICKET

Highest Total	For	803-4d		v	Essex	Brentwood	1934
	V	676		by	Australians	Canterbury	1921
Lowest Total	For	18		v	Sussex	Gravesend	1867
	V	16		by	Warwicks	Tonbridge	1913
Highest Innings	For	332	W.H. Ashdown	v	Essex	Brentwood	1934
	V	344	W.G. Grace	for	MCC	Canterbury	1876

Highest Partnerships

Wkt						
1st	283	A.E. Fagg/P.R. Sunnucks	v	Essex	Colchester	1938
2nd	352	W.H. Ashdown/F.E. Woolley	v	Essex	Brentwood	1934
3rd	321*	A. Hearne/J.R. Mason	v	Notts	Nottingham	1899
4th	297	H.T.W. Hardinge/ A.P.F. Chapman	v	Hampshire	Southampton	1926
5th	277	F.E. Woolley/L.E.G. Ames	v	New Zealand	Canterbury	1931
6th	284	A.P.F. Chapman/G.B. Legge	v	Lancashire	Maidstone	1927
7th	248	A.P. Day/E. Humphreys	v	Somerset	Taunton	1908
8th	157	A.L. Hilder/A.C. Wright	v	Essex	Gravesend	1924
9th	161	B.R. Edrich/F. Ridgway	v	Sussex	Tunbridge W	1949
10th	235	F.E. Woolley/A. Fielder	v	Worcs	Stourbridge	1909

Best Bowling	For	10-30	C. Blythe	v	Northants	Northampton	1907
(Innings)	V	10-48	C.H.G. Bland	for	Sussex	Tonbridge	1899
Best Bowling	For	17-48	C. Blythe	v	Northants	Northampton	1907
(Match)	V	17-106	T.W.J. Goddard	for	Glos	Bristol	1939

Most Runs – Season	2,894	F.E. Woolley	(av 59.06)	1928
Most Runs – Career	47,868	F.E. Woolley	(av 41.77)	1906-1938
Most 100s – Season	10	F.E. Woolley		1928
	10	F.E. Woolley		1934
Most 100s – Career	122	F.E. Woolley		1906-1938
Most Wkts – Season	262	A.P. Freeman	(av 14.74)	1933
Most Wkts – Career	3,340	A.P. Freeman	(av 17.64)	1914-1936

LIMITED-OVERS CRICKET

Highest Total	**NWT**	297-3		v	Worcs	Canterbury	1970
	BHC	293-6		v	Somerset	Taunton	1985
	JPL	281-5		v	Warwicks	Folkestone	1983
Lowest Total	**NWT**	60		v	Somerset	Taunton	1979
	BHC	73		v	Middlesex	Canterbury	1979
	JPL	83		v	Middlesex	Lord's	1984
Highest Innings	**NWT**	129*	B.W. Luckhurst	v	Durham	Canterbury	1974
	BHC	143	C.J. Tavaré	v	Somerset	Taunton	1985
	JPL	142	B.W. Luckhurst	v	Somerset	Weston-s-M	1970
Best Bowling	**NWT**	7-15	A.L. Dixon	v	Surrey	The Oval	1967
	BHC	5-21	B.D. Julien	v	Surrey	The Oval	1973
	JPL	6-9	R.A. Woolmer	v	Derbyshire	Chesterfield	1979

KENT 1986

RESULTS SUMMARY

	Place	*Won*	*Lost*	*Drew*	*Tied*	*Aban*
Britannic Assurance Championship	**8th**	5	7	12		
All First-class Matches		5	7	14		
John Player League	**6th**	7	5		1	3
NatWest Bank Trophy	Lost to Nottinghamshire (2nd Round)					
Benson and Hedges Cup	Lost to Middlesex (Final)					

BRITANNIC ASSURANCE CHAMPIONSHIP AVERAGES

BATTING AND FIELDING

Cap		*M*	*I*	*NO*	*HS*	*Runs*	*Avge*	*100*	*50*	*Ct/St*
1981	M.R. Benson	20	34	1	123	1229	37.24	1	7	5
1978	C.J. Tavaré	24	40	4	105	1086	30.16	1	5	21
1986	S.A. Marsh	24	34	6	70	829	29.60	—	6	48/3
1979	C.S. Cowdrey	21	32	3	100	820	28.27	1	4	31
1982	N.R. Taylor	24	40	5	88	981	28.02	—	6	10
1985	S.G. Hinks	21	35	1	131	893	26.26	2	2	15
1983	R.M. Ellison	19	27	6	62*	521	24.80	—	2	5
1983	D.G. Aslett	17	23	0	63	517	22.47	—	3	17
1983	E.A.E. Baptiste	5	6	0	80	134	22.33	—	1	1
—	G.R. Cowdrey	15	24	1	75	353	15.34	—	3	9
1980	G.R. Dilley	13	20	6	30	179	12.78	—	—	6
1964	D.L. Underwood	23	26	5	29	243	11.57	—	—	2
1984	T.M. Alderman	19	21	8	25	102	7.84	—	—	9
—	A.P. Igglesden	5	5	2	8*	22	7.33	—	—	2
1977	K.B.S. Jarvis	5	6	4	4	9	4.50	—	—	1
—	C. Penn	5	6	1	9	11	2.20	—	—	2

Also batted: C.S. Dale (2 matches) 0*,2,16; R.P. Davis (1 match) 0* (1 ct); T.R. Ward (1 match) 29,12.

BOWLING

	O	*M*	*R*	*W*	*Avge*	*Best*	*5 wI*	*10 wM*
T.M. Alderman	610	139	1882	98	19.20	8-46	9	3
E.A.E. Baptiste	137	38	327	13	25.15	4-53	—	—
G.R. Dilley	350.3	51	1156	44	26.27	6-57	3	1
C. Penn	100.5	18	369	14	26.35	5-65	1	—
D.L. Underwood	627.1	251	1368	51	26.82	7-11	1	—
A.P. Igglesden	125	25	372	11	33.81	4-46	—	—
C.S. Cowdrey	258.2	43	886	26	34.07	5-69	1	—
R.M. Ellison	350.4	79	1023	22	46.50	4-36	—	—
K.B.S. Jarvis	139.2	33	472	10	47.20	2-48	—	—

Also bowled: D.G. Aslett 35-3-187-4; M.R. Benson 7-0-55-2; G.R. Cowdrey 7-1-26-1; C.S. Dale 34-5-142-0; R.P. Davis 59.5-22-121-6; C.J. Tavaré 27-6-107-2; N.R. Taylor 76.3-8-252-3.

The First-Class Averages (pp. 167–182) give the records of Kent players in all first-class county matches (their other opponents being the Indians and Oxford U.), with the exception of R.M. Ellison, whose full county figures are as above, and: M.R. Benson 22-37-2-128-1410-40.28-2-7-5 ct. 7-0-55-2-27.50-2/55. G.R. Dilley 14-21-7-30-183-13.07-0-0-6 ct. 350.3-51-1156-44-26.27-6/57-3-1.

LANCASHIRE

Formation of Present Club: 12 January 1864
Colours: Red, Green and Blue
Badge: Red Rose
Championships (since 1890): (7) 1897, 1904, 1926, 1927, 1928, 1930, 1934
Joint Championships: (1) 1950
NatWest Trophy/Gillette Cup Winners: (4) 1970, 1971, 1972, 1975
Benson and Hedges Cup Winners: (1) 1984
John Player League Champions: (2) 1969, 1970
Match Awards: NWT 45; BHC 39

Secretary: C.D. Hassell, Old Trafford, Manchester M16 0PX
Captain: D.P. Hughes
Scorer: W. Davies
Scores/Prospects: ☎ Manchester (061) 872 0261

ABRAHAMS, John (Heywood GS), b Cape Town, South Africa 21 Jul 1952. 5′8″. LHB, OB. Debut 1973. Cap 1982. Captain 1984-85. 1000 runs (4); most – 1261 (1983). HS 201* v Warwicks (Nuneaton) 1984. BB 3-27 v Worcs (Manchester) 1981. Awards: NWT 1; BHC 2. **NWT:** HS 67* and BB 2-26 v Cumberland (Manchester) 1986. **BHC:** HS 66* v Minor C (Bowdon) 1984. BB 1-11. **JPL:** HS 103* v Somerset (Taunton) 1986. BB 2-11 v Kent (Canterbury) 1986.

ALLOTT, Paul John Walter (Altrincham GS; Durham U), b Altrincham, Cheshire 14 Sep 1956. 6′4″. RHB, RFM. Debut 1978. Cap 1981. Cheshire 1976. **Tests:** 13 (1981 to 1985); HS 52* v Aus (Manchester) 1981 – on debut. BB 6-61 v WI (Leeds) 1984. LOI: 13. Tours: WI 1982-83 (Int XI); Ind/SL 1981-82, 1984-85. HS 78 v Glos (Bristol) 1985. BB 8-48 v Northants (Northampton) 1981. Award: BHC 1. **NWT:** HS 19* v Worcs (Worcester) 1980. BB 4-28 v Leics (Leicester) 1986. **BHC:** HS 23* v Notts (Liverpool) 1986. BB 3-15 v Warwicks (Lord's) 1984. **JPL:** HS 32* v Yorks (Leeds) 1983. BB 4-28 v Kent (Manchester) 1985.

CHADWICK, Mark Robert (Roch Valley HS, Milnrow), b Rochdale 9 Feb 1963. 6′1″. RHB, RM. Debut 1983. HS 132 v Somerset (Manchester) 1985. Award: BHC 1. **NWT:** HS 43 v Worcs (Manchester) 1985. **BHC:** HS 87 v Notts (Nottingham) 1984. **JPL:** HS 10 v Glos (Bristol) 1983.

DAVIDSON, Ian Charles (Ellesmere Park HS; Eccles SFC), b Roe Green, Worsley 21 Dec 1964. 5′8″. RHB, OB. Debut 1985. HS 13 and BB 2-24 v Warwicks (Birmingham) 1985.

FAIRBROTHER, Neil Harvey (Lymm GS), b Warrington 9 Sep 1963. 5′8″. LHB, LM. Debut 1982. Cap 1985. 1000 runs (3); most – 1395 (1985). HS 164* v Hants (Liverpool) 1985. BB 1-3. Awards: NWT 2. **NWT:** HS 93* v Leics (Leicester) 1986. **BHC:** HS 47 v Worcs (Worcester) 1986. **JPL:** HS 79 v Notts (Nottingham) 1986.

FOLLEY, Ian (Mansfield HS; Colne C), b Burnley 9 Jan 1963. 5′9½″. RHB, SLA. Debut 1982. HS 69 v Yorks (Manchester) 1985. BB 6-8 v OU (Oxford) 1985. **NWT:** HS 3*. BB 2-10 v Lancs (Chester-le-St) 1983. **BHC:** HS 11* v Notts (Nottingham) 1982. BB 4-18 v Middx (Lord's) 1982. **JPL:** HS 11* v Somerset (Manchester) 1983. BB 2-26 v Notts (Manchester) 1983.

FOWLER, Graeme (Accrington GS; Durham U), b Accrington 20 Apr 1957. 5′9½″. LHB, RM. Debut 1979. Cap 1981. **Tests:** 21 (1982 to 1984-85); HS 201 v Ind (Madras) 1984-85. LOI: 26. Tours: Aus 1982-83; WI 1982-83 (Int XI); NZ 1983-84; Ind/SL 1984-85; Pak 1983-84. 1000 runs (5); most – 1560 (1981). HS 226 v Kent

(Maidstone) 1984. BB 2-34 v Warwicks (Manchester) 1986. Awards: NWT 2; BHC 2. **NWT:** HS 122 v Glos (Bristol) 1984. **BHC:** HS 97 v Northants (Manchester) 1983. **JPL:** HS 112 v Kent (Canterbury) 1986.

HAYES, Kevin Anthony (Queen Elizabeth's GS, Blackburn; Merton C, Oxford), b Thurnscoe, Yorks 26 Sep 1962. 5'7". RHB, RM. Debut 1980. Oxford U 1981-84; blue 1981-82-83-84 (capt 1984). HS 152 OU v Warwicks (Oxford) 1982. Lancs HS 117 v Somerset (Manchester) 1985. BB 6-58 OU v Warwicks (Birmingham) 1983. **BHC:** HS 67 Comb Us v Hants (Southampton) 1984. BB 3-40 Comb Us v Glos (Bristol) 1984. **JPL:** HS 53 v Glos (Moreton) 1984.

HAYHURST, Andrew Neil (Worsley Wardley HS; Eccles SFC; Leeds Polytechnic), b Davyhulme, Manchester 23 Nov 1962. 5'11". RHB, RM. Debut 1985. HS 31 v Somerset (Manchester) 1986. BB 4-69 v Yorks (Manchester) 1986. **NWT:** HS 49 v Sussex (Lord's) 1986. BB 4-40 v Leics (Leicester) 1986. **BHC:** HS 12* v Surrey (Oval) 1985. **JPL:** HS 34 v Leics (Leicester) 1986. BB 1-17.

HEGG, Warren Kevin (Unsworth HS, Bury; Stand C, Whitefield), b Whitefield 23 Feb 1968. 5'8". RHB, WK. Debut 1986. England YC to Sri Lanka 1987.

HENRIKSEN, Soren, b Rodoure, Copenhagen, Denmark 1 Dec 1964. 6'3". RHB, RFM. Debut 1985. HS 10*. BB 1-26. **NWT:** HS 1*. BB 2-51 v Worcs (Manchester) 1985. **JPL:** HS 1. BB 1-35.

HUGHES, David Paul (Newton-le-Willows GS), b Newton-le-Willows 13 May 1947. 5'11". RHB, SLA. Debut 1967. Cap 1970. Captain 1987. Tasmania 1975-77. Benefit 1981. Tour: SA 1972-73 (DHR). 1000 runs (2); most – 1303 (1982). HS 153 v Glam (Manchester) 1983. BB 7-24 v OU (Oxford) 1970. Awards: NWT 1; BHC 1. **NWT:** HS 71 v Durham (Chester-le-St) 1983. BB 4-61 v Somerset (Manchester) 1972. **BHC:** HS 52 v Derbys (Manchester) 1981. BB 5-23 v Minor C (W) (Watford) 1978. **JPL:** HS 92 v Kent (Maidstone) 1984. BB 6-29 v Somerset (Manchester) 1977.

MAKINSON, David John (St Mary's HS, Leyland) b Eccleston 12 Jan 1961. 6'3". RHB, LFM. Debut 1984. HS 58* v Northants (Lytham) 1985. BB 5-60 v Derbys (Manchester) 1985. **NWT:** HS 17 v Worcs (Manchester) 1985. BB 2-49 v Somerset (Taunton) 1986. **BHC:** HS 5. BB 3-36 v Worcs (Worcester) 1986. **JPL:** HS 13 v Hants (Manchester) 1985. BB 4-28 v Derbys (Manchester) 1985.

MAYNARD, Christopher (Bishop Vesey's GS, Sutton Coldfield), b Haslemere, Surrey 8 Apr 1958. 5'11". RHB, WK. Warwickshire 1978-1982. Registered for Lancashire in mid-season 1982. Cap 1986. Tour: NZ 1979-80 (DHR). HS 132* v Yorks (Leeds) 1986. **NWT:** HS 22 v Surrey (Oval) 1986. **BHC:** HS 60 v Notts (Nottingham) 1982. **JPL:** HS 49* v Middx (Manchester) 1986.

MENDIS, Gehan Dixon (St Thomas C, Colombo; Brighton, Hove & Sussex GS; Durham U), b Colombo, Ceylon 24 Apr 1955. 5'9". RHB, RM. Sussex 1974-85 (cap 1980). Lancashire debut/cap 1986. Tours: WI 1982-83 (Int XI); Pak 1981-82 (Int XI). 1000 runs (7); most – 1756 (1985). HS 209* Sussex v Somerset (Hove) 1984. Lancs HS 108 v Notts (Nottingham) 1986. BB 1-65. Awards: NWT 3; BHC 3. **NWT:** HS 141* Sussex v Warwicks (Hove) 1980. **BHC:** HS 109 Sussex v Glos (Hove) 1980. **JPL:** HS 125* Sussex v Glos (Hove) 1981.

MURPHY, Anthony John (Xaverian C, Swansea U), b Manchester 6 Aug 1962. 6'0". RHB, RMF. Debut 1985. Cheshire 1984-85. HS 6. BB 3-67 v Notts (Southport) 1986. **JPL:** 2*. BB 1-33.

O'SHAUGHNESSY, Steven Joseph (Harper Green SS, Farnworth), b Bury 9 Sep 1961. 5'10½". RHB, RM. Debut 1980. Cap 1985. Scored 100 in 35 minutes to equal world record v Leics (Manchester) 1983. 1000 runs (1): 1167 (1984). HS 159* v Somerset (Bath) 1984. BB 4-66 v Notts (Nottingham) 1982. Awards: BHC 2. **NWT:** HS 62 v Surrey (Oval) 1986. BB 3-28 v Suffolk (Bury St Edmunds) 1985. **BHC:** HS 90 v Worcs (Worcester) 1985. BB 4-17 v Leics (Manchester) 1985. **JPL:** HS 101* v Leics (Leicester) 1984. BB 3-18 v Middx (Manchester) 1984.

PATTERSON, Balfour **Patrick** (Happy Grove HS; Wolmer's HS), b Portland, Jamaica 15 Sep 1961. 6'2½". RHB, RFM. Jamaica 1982-86. Lancashire debut 1984. **Tests** (WI): 6 (1985-86 to 1986-87); HS 9; BB 4-30 v Eng (Kingston) 1985-86. LOI (WI): 6. Tour (WI): Pak 1986-87. HS 22 v Northants (Lytham) 1985. BB 7-24 Jamaica v Guyana (Kingston) 1985-86. Lancs BB 7-49 v OU (Oxford) 1985. **NWT:** HS 4. BB 1-69. **BHC:** HS 15* v Leics (Manchester) 1985. BB 3-31 v Scotland (Perth) 1986. **JPL:** HS 3*.

SIMMONS, Jack (Accrington TS; Blackburn TC), b Clayton-le-Moors 28 Mar 1941. 6'1½". RHB, OB. Debut 1968. Cap 1971. Tasmania 1972-79. Benefit 1980. *Wisden* 1984. Tour: Ind 1980-81 (Overseas XI). HS 112 v Sussex (Hove) 1970. BB 7-59 Tasmania v Queensland (Brisbane) 1978-79. Lancs BB 7-64 v Hants (Southport) 1973. Awards: NWT 1; BHC 2. **NWT:** HS 54* v Essex (Manchester) 1979. BB 5-37 v Glos (Bristol) 1984. **BHC:** HS 64 v Derbys (Manchester) 1978. BB 4-31 v Yorks (Manchester) 1975. **JPL:** HS 65 v Essex (Manchester) 1980. BB 5-17 v Worcs (Worcester) 1982.

STANWORTH, John (Chadderton GS; N Cheshire C), b Oldham 30 Sep 1960. 5'10". RHB, WK. Debut 1983. HS 50* v Glos (Bristol) 1985. **BHC:** HS 8*. **JPL:** HS 2.

VAREY, David William (Birkenhead S; Pembroke C, Cambridge), b Darlington, Co Durham 15 Oct 1961. 6'2". RHB. Twin of J.G. (Oxford 1982-83). Cambridge U 1981-83; blue 1982-83. Lancs debut 1984. Cheshire 1982-83. HS 156* CU v Northants (Camb) 1982. Lancs HS 112 v OU (Oxford) 1985. **BHC:** HS 27 v Worcs (Manchester) 1984. **JPL:** HS 3.

WATKINSON, Michael (Rivington and Blackrod HS, Horwich), b Westhoughton 1 Aug 1961. 6'1". RHB, RMF. Debut 1982. Cheshire 1982. 106 v Surrey (Southport) 1985. BB 6-39 v Leics (Leicester) 1984. **NWT:** HS 56 v Worcs (Manchester) 1985. BB 3-44 v Somerset (Taunton) 1986. **BHC:** HS 34 v Leics (Manchester) 1985. BB 4-39 v Notts (Manchester) 1983. **JPL:** HS 34* v Kent (Manchester) 1985 and 34* v Somerset (Taunton) 1986. BB 3-25 v Essex (Manchester) 1984.

SALVETE

ATHERTON, Michael Andrew (Manchester GS; Downing C, Cambridge), b Manchester 23 Mar 1968. 5'11". RHB, LB. Captain England YC to Sri Lanka 1987

CRAWLEY, Mark Andrew (Manchester GS; Oriel C, Oxford), b Newton-le-Willows 16 Dec 1967. 6'3". RHB. England YC to Sri Lanka 1987. Soccer blue 1986.

LLOYD, Graham David, b Accrington 1 Jul 1969. Son of D. Lloyd (Lancs and England) – see 1987 Umpires. RHB.

VALE

LLOYD, Clive Hubert (Chatham HS, Georgetown), b Georgetown, British Guiana 31 Aug 1944. 6'4½". LHB, RM. British Guiana/Guyana 1963-83. Lancashire debut 1968. Cap 1969. *Wisden* 1970. Benefit 1977. Captain 1981-83, 1986. **Tests** (WI): 110 (1966-67 to 1984-85); HS 242* v Ind (Bombay) 1974-75; BB 2-13. Most matches (74) and most wins (36) as captain. LOI (WI): 87. Tours (WI) (C = Captain): Eng 1969, 1973, 1976C, 1980C, 1984C; Aus 1968-69, 1971-72 (RW), 1975-76C, 1979-80C, 1981-82C, 1984-85C; NZ 1968-69, 1979-80C· Ind/SL 1966-67, 1974-75C, 1983-84C; Pak 1970-71 (RW), 1973-74 (RW), 1974-75C, 1980-81C. 1000 runs (10+4); most – 1603 (1970). HS 242* (Tests). Lancs HS 217* v Warwicks (Manchester) 1971. BB 4-48 v Leics (Manchester) 1970. Awards: NWT 8; BHC 1.

LANCASHIRE RECORDS

FIRST-CLASS CRICKET

Highest Total	For	801		v	Somerset	Taunton	1895
	V	634		by	Surrey	The Oval	1898
Lowest Total	For	25		v	Derbyshire	Manchester	1871
	V	22		by	Glamorgan	Liverpool	1924
Highest Innings	For	424	A.C. MacLaren	v	Somerset	Taunton	1895
	V	315*	T.W. Hayward	for	Surrey	The Oval	1898

Highest Partnerships

Wkt						
1st	368	A.C. MacLaren/R.H. Spooner	v	Glos	Liverpool	1903
2nd	371	F.B. Watson/G.E. Tyldesley	v	Surrey	Manchester	1928
3rd	306	E. Paynter/N. Oldfield	v	Hampshire	Southampton	1938
4th	324	A.C. MacLaren/J.T. Tyldesley	v	Notts	Nottingham	1904
5th	249	B. Wood/A. Kennedy	v	Warwicks	Birmingham	1975
6th	278	J. Iddon/H.R.W. Butterworth	v	Sussex	Manchester	1932
7th	245	A.H. Hornby/J. Sharp	v	Leics	Manchester	1912
8th	158	J. Lyon/R.M. Ratcliffe	v	Warwicks	Manchester	1979
9th	142	L.O.S. Poidevin/A. Kermode	v	Sussex	Eastbourne	1907
10th	173	J. Briggs/R. Pilling	v	Surrey	Liverpool	1885

Best Bowling (Innings)	For	10-46	W. Hickton	v	Hampshire	Manchester	1870
	V	10-40	G.O.B. Allen	for	Middlesex	Lord's	1929
Best Bowling (Match)	For	17-91	H. Dean	v	Yorkshire	Liverpool	1913
	V	16-65	G. Giffen	for	Australians	Manchester	1886

Most Runs – Season	2,633	J.T. Tyldesley	(av 56.02)	1901
Most Runs – Career	34,222	G.E. Tyldesley	(av 45.20)	1909-1936
Most 100s – Season	11	C. Hallows		1928
Most 100s – Career	90	G.E. Tyldesley		1909-1936
Most Wkts – Season	198	E.A. McDonald	(av 18.55)	1925
Most Wkts – Career	1,816	J.B. Statham	(av 15.12)	1950-1968

LIMITED-OVERS CRICKET

Highest Total	**NWT**	349-6		v	Glos	Bristol	1984
	BHC	290-5		v	Northants	Manchester	1983
	JPL	255-5		v	Somerset	Manchester	1970
Lowest Total	**NWT**	59		v	Worcs	Worcester	1963
	BHC	82		v	Yorkshire	Bradford	1972
	JPL	76		v	Somerset	Manchester	1972
Highest Innings	**NWT**	131	A. Kennedy	v	Middlesex	Manchester	1978
	BHC	124	C.H. Lloyd	v	Warwicks	Manchester	1981
	JPL	134*	C.H. Lloyd	v	Somerset	Manchester	1970
Best Bowling	**NWT**	5-28	J.B. Statham	v	Leics	Manchester	1963
	BHC	6-10	C.E.H. Croft	v	Scotland	Manchester	1982
	JPL	6-29	D.P. Hughes	v	Somerset	Manchester	1977

LANCASHIRE 1986

RESULTS SUMMARY

	Place	Won	Lost	Drew	Abandoned
Britannic Assurance Championship	**15th**	4	5	14	1
All First-class Matches		5	5	14	1
John Player League	**12th**	6	9		1
NatWest Bank Trophy	Lost to Sussex (Final)				
Benson and Hedges Cup	Failed to qualify for Quarter-Final				

BRITANNIC ASSURANCE CHAMPIONSHIP AVERAGES

BATTING AND FIELDING

Cap		M	I	NO	HS	Runs	Avge	100	50	Ct/St
1969	C.H. Lloyd	6	7	0	128	328	46.85	1	2	—
1985	N.H. Fairbrother	21	32	7	131	1158	46.32	3	7	10
1986	G.D. Mendis	22	36	3	108	1265	38.33	2	9	—
1981	G. Fowler	19	30	1	180	1110	38.27	1	9	7
1982	J. Abrahams	23	37	7	189*	1134	37.80	2	6	12
—	D.W. Varey	6	10	2	83	271	33.87	—	2	5/1
1986	C. Maynard	19	26	5	132*	662	31.52	1	5	29/3
1981	P.J.W. Allott	17	19	5	65	382	27.28	—	1	9
1985	S.J. O'Shaughnessy	10	14	3	74	291	26.45	—	2	5
1971	J. Simmons	13	17	5	61	300	25.00	—	1	7
—	M.R. Chadwick	10	18	0	61	423	23.50	—	2	6
—	M. Watkinson	20	24	3	58*	377	17.95	—	1	14
—	D.J. Makinson	14	13	6	43	96	13.71	—	—	6
—	A.N. Hayhurst	9	12	0	31	146	12.16	—	—	2
—	I. Folley	16	19	2	20*	159	9.35	—	—	8
—	B.P. Patterson	17	15	5	12*	54	5.40	—	—	3

Also batted: K.A. Hayes (1 match) 17; W.K. Hegg (2 matches) 0,4 (2 ct, 2 st); S. Henriksen (2 matches) 6*,1 (1 ct); A.J. Murphy (4 matches) 1*,0*,1* (2 ct); J. Stanworth (2 matches) 2,11* (4 ct).

BOWLING

	O	M	R	W	Avge	Best	5 wI	10 wM
J. Simmons	230.5	52	762	36	21.16	7-79	2	1
P.J.W. Allott	405.1	106	1053	43	24.48	5-32	2	—
B.P. Patterson	356	61	1222	40	30.55	6-46	1	1
D.J. Makinson	285.1	55	963	30	32.10	4-69	—	—
I. Folley	327	90	1009	26	38.80	4-42	—	—
M. Watkinson	454.4	69	1632	30	54.40	5-90	1	—

Also bowled: J. Abrahams 37.5-4-161-1; M.R. Chadwick 5-0-51-0; N.H. Fairbrother 22-8-48-0; G. Fowler 4-0-34-2; A.N. Hayhurst 106.1-8-418-8; S. Henriksen 17-2-61-1; A.J. Murphy 64-13-203-7; S.J. O'Shaughnessy 97-18-363-5.

The First-Class Averages (pp. 167–182) give the records of Lancashire players in all first-class county matches (their other opponents being Oxford U.), with the exception of A.J. Murphy whose full county figures are as above.

LEICESTERSHIRE

Formation of Present Club: 25 March 1879
Colours: Dark Green and Scarlet
Badge: Gold Running Fox on Green Ground
Championships: (1) 1975
NatWest Trophy/Gillette Cup Winners: (0) Semi-Finalists 1977
Benson and Hedges Cup Winners: (3) 1972, 1975, 1985
John Player League Champions: (2) 1974, 1977
Match Awards: NWT 23; BHC 45

Secretary/Manager: F.M. Turner, County Ground, Grace Road, Leicester LE2 8AD
Captain: P. Willey
Scorer: G.R. Blackburn
Scores/Prospects: ☎ Leicester (0533) 836236

AGNEW, Jonathan Philip (Uppingham S), b Macclesfield, Cheshire 4 Apr 1960. 6'3½". RHB, RF. Debut 1978. Cap 1984. **Tests:** 3 (1984 to 1985); HS 5; BB 2-51 v WI (Oval) 1984. LOI: 3. Tours: Ind 1984-85; SL 1985-86 (Eng B); Zim 1980-81 (Leics). HS 56 v Worcs (Worcester) 1982. BB 9-70 v Kent (Leicester) 1985. **NWT:** HS 5*. BB 2-36 v Derbys (Leicester) 1984. **BHC:** 23* and BB 5-43 v Warwicks (Leicester) 1984. **JPL:** HS 13* v Sussex (Hove) 1985. BB 3-36 v Glam (Leicester) 1985.
BALDERSTONE, John Christopher (Paddock Council S, Huddersfield), b Longwood, Huddersfield, Yorks 16 Nov 1940. 6'0½". RHB, SLA. Yorkshire 1961-69. Leicestershire debut 1971. Cap 1973. Testimonial 1984. **Tests:** 2 (1976); HS 35 v WI (Leeds) 1976; BB 1-80. Tour: Zim 1980-81 (Leics). 1000 runs (11); most – 1482 (1982). HS 181* v Glos (Leicester) 1984. BB 6-25 v Hants (Southampton) 1978. Awards: NWT 3; BHC 10. Soccer for Huddersfield Town, Carlisle United, Doncaster Rovers and Queen of the South. **NWT:** HS 119* v Somerset (Taunton) 1973. BB 4-33 v Herts (Leicester) 1977. **BHC:** HS 113* v Glos (Leicester) 1977. BB 2-13 v Warwicks (Leicester) 1972. **JPL:** HS 96 v Northants (Leicester) 1976. BB 3-29 v Worcs (Leicester) 1971.
BENJAMIN, Winston Keithroy Matthew (All Saints S, Antigua), b St John's Antigua 31 Dec 1964. 6'3". RHB, RF. Debut Rest of the World XI 1985. Leicestershire debut 1986. Leeward Islands 1985-86. Cheshire 1985. LOI (WI): 9. Tours (WI): Aus 1986-87; Pak 1986-87. HS 95* v Indians (Leicester) 1986. BB 6-33 v Notts (Leicester) 1986. **NWT:** HS 5. BB 3-28 v Glos (Bristol) 1986. **BHC:** HS 19* and BB 5-17 v Minor C (Leicester) 1986. **JPL:** HS 19* v Glam (Swansea) 1986. BB 4-19 v Lancs (Leicester) 1986.
BILLINGTON, David James (Kendal GS; Leeds U; Loughborough U), b Leyland, Lancs 6 Dec 1965. 5'7". RHB. Debut 1985. HS 19 v Warwicks (Hinckley) 1985.
BLACKETT, Mark (Edmonton County S), b Edmonton, London 3 Feb 1964. 5'8". RHB. Debut 1985. HS 28* v Worcs (Leicester) 1985. **JPL:** HS 21* v Worcs (Leicester) 1985.
BOON, Timothy James (Edlington CS, Doncaster), b Doncaster, Yorks 1 Nov 1961. 6'0". RHB, RM. Debut 1980. Cap 1986. Tour: Zim 1980-81 (Leics). 1000 runs (2); most – 1233 (1984). HS 144 v Glos (Leicester) 1984. BB 3-40 v Yorks (Leicester) 1986. **NWT:** HS 22* v Derbys (Leicester) 1984. **BHC:** HS 43 v Warwicks (Leicester) 1986. **JPL:** HS 49* v Sussex (Leicester) 1986.

BOWLER, Peter Duncan (Educated at Canberra, Australia), b Plymouth, Devon 30 Jul 1963. 6'1". RHB, OB. Debut 1986 scoring 100* and 62 v Hants at Leicester – first to score hundred on f-c debut for Leics. Tasmania 1986–87. HS 100* (on debut). **JPL:** HS 55 v Sussex (Leicester) 1986.
BRIERS, Nigel Edwin (Lutterworth GS; Borough Road CE), b Leicester 15 Jan 1955. 6'0". RHB, RM. Debut 1971 – youngest player at 16 years 103 days to represent Leicestershire. Cap 1981. Tour: Zim 1980-81 (Leics). 1000 runs (3); most – 1289 (1983). HS 201* v Warwicks (Birmingham) 1983. BB 4-29 v Derbys (Leicester) 1985. Award: BHC 1. **NWT:** HS 59 v Wilts (Swindon) 1984. BB 2-6 v Worcs (Leicester) 1979. **BHC:** HS 71* v Hants (Southampton) 1979. BB 1-26. **JPL:** HS 119* v Hants (Bournemouth) 1981. BB 3-29 v Middx (Leicester) 1984.
BUTCHER, Ian Paul (John Ruskin HS), b Farnborough, Kent 1 Jul 1962. 6'0". RHB, RM. Brother of A.R. and M.S. (Surrey). Debut 1980. Cap 1984. 1000 runs (2); most – 1349 (1984). HS 139 v Notts (Leicester) 1983. BB 1-2. **NWT:** HS 81 v Northants (Northampton) 1984. BB 1-6. **BHC:** HS 103* v Minor C (Leicester) 1986. **JPL:** HS 71 v Northants (Leics) 1982.
CLIFT, Patrick Bernard (**'Paddy'**) (St George's C, Salisbury), b Salisbury, Rhodesia 14 Jul 1953. 6'1". RHB, RM. Rhodesia 1971-80. Leicestershire debut 1975. Cap 1976. Natal 1980-85; captain 1984-85. HS 106 v Essex (Chelmsford) 1985. BB 8-17 v MCC (Lord's) 1976. Award: BHC 1. **NWT:** HS 48* and BB 3-36 v Worcs (Leicester) 1979. **BHC:** HS 91 v Notts (Leicester) 1980. BB 4-13 v Minor C (E) (Chesham) 1978. **JPL:** HS 51* v Somerset (Leicester) 1979. BB 4-14 v Lancs (Leicester) 1978.
COBB, Russell Alan (Trent C), b Leicester 18 May 1961. 5'11". RHB, SLA. Debut 1980. Cap 1986. Tours: NZ 1979-80 (DHR); Zim 1980-81 (Leics). 1000 runs (1): 1092 (1986). HS 91 v Northants (Leicester) 1986. **NWT:** HS 26 v Ireland (Leicester) 1986. **BHC:** HS 22 v Warwicks (Leicester) 1986. **JPL:** HS 24 v Worcs (Leicester) 1981.
DEFREITAS, Phillip Anthony Jason (Willesden HS, London), b Scotts Head, Dominica 18 Feb 1966. 6'0". RHB, RFM. UK resident since 1976. Debut 1985. Cap 1986. **Tests:** 4 (1986-87): HS 40 and BB 3-62 v Aus (Brisbane) 1986-87. LOI: 3. Tour: Aus 1986-87. HS 106 v Kent (Canterbury) 1986. BB 7-44 (13-86 match) v Essex (Southend) 1986. **NWT:** HS 69 v Lancs (Leicester) 1986. BB 3-28 v Warwicks (Leicester) 1986. **JPL:** HS 32 v Hants (Southampton) 1986. BB 4-20 v Middx and 4-20 v Worcs (Leicester) 1986.
FERRIS, George John Fitzgerald (Jennings SS, Antigua), b Urlings Village, Antigua 18 Oct 1964. 6'3". RHB, RF. Leeward Is 1982-86. Leicestershire debut 1983. Tour: Zim 1983-84 (Young WI). HS 26 Leeward Is v Guyana (Nevis) 1982-83. BB 7-42 v Glam (Hinckley) 1983. **BHC:** HS 0*. BB 4-31 v Lancs (Manchester) 1985. **JPL:** HS 9*. BB 3-40 v Worcs (Leicester) 1985.
GILL, Paul (Saddleworth S; Grange S), b Greenfield, Manchester 31 May 1963. 5'7". RHB, WK. Debut 1986. HS 17 v Essex (Southend) 1986.
GOWER, David Ivon (Kings S, Canterbury; London U), b Tunbridge Wells, Kent 1 Apr 1957. 6'0". LHB, OB. Debut 1975. Cap 1977. *Wisden* 1978. YC 1978. Captain 1984-86. Benefit 1987. **Tests:** 91 (1978 to 1986-87, 26 as captain); HS 215 v Aus (Birmingham) 1985; BB 1-1. LOI: 89. Tours (C = Captain): Aus 1978-79, 1979-80, 1982-83, 1986-87; WI 1980-81, 1985-86C; NZ 1983-84; Ind 1979-80, 1981-82, 1984-85C; Pak 1983-84; SL 1977-78 (DHR), 1981-82, 1984-85C. 1000 runs (6); most – 1530 (1982). HS 215 (Tests). BB 3-47 v Essex (Leicester) 1977. Awards: NWT 4; BHC 1. **NWT:** HS 156 v Derbys (Leicester) 1984. **BHC:** HS 114* v Derbys (Derby) 1980. **JPL:** HS 135* v Warwicks (Leicester) 1977.
HARRIS, Gordon Andrew Robert (Merchant Taylors' S, Northwood; Uxbridge TC; Leicester Polytechnic), b Tottenham, London 11 Jan 1964. 6'2½. RHB, RFM. Debut 1986. HS 6. **JPL:** BB 1-27.
POTTER, Laurie (Kelmscott HS, Perth, Aus), b Bexleyheath, Kent 7 Nov 1962. 6'1". RHB, SLA. Kent 1981-85. GW 1984-86 (captain 1985-86). Leicestershire debut 1986. HS 165* GW v Border (East London) 1984-85. Leics HS 81* v Glos (Leicester)

1986. BB 4-52 GW v Boland (Stellenbosch) 1985-86. Leics BB 3-37 v Glam (Leicester) 1986. Award: BHC 1. **NWT:** HS 45 Kent v Essex (Chelmsford) 1982. BB 1-28. **BHC:** HS 112 and BB 2-70 v Minor C (Leicester) 1986. **JPL:** HS 105 v Derbys (Leicester) 1986. BB 4-9 Kent v Derbys (Folkestone) 1985.

TAYLOR, Leslie Brian (Heathfield HS), b Earl Shilton 25 Oct 1953. 6'3½". RHB, RFM. Debut 1977. Cap 1981. Natal 1981-84. **Tests:** 2 (1985); HS 1* and BB 2-34 v Aus (Oval). LOI: 2. Tours: SA 1981-82 (SAB); WI 1985-86; Zim 1980-81 (Leics). HS 47 v Derbys (Derby) 1983. BB 7-28 v Derbys (Leicester) 1981. Award: NWT 1. **NWT:** HS 6*. BB 4-14 v Norfolk (Norwich) 1985. **BHC:** HS 5. BB 6-35 v Worcs (Worcester) 1982. **JPL:** HS 15* v Somerset (Taunton) 1980. BB 5-23 v Notts (Nottingham) 1978.

TENNANT, Lloyd (Shellfield CS), b Walsall, Staffs 9 Apr 1968. 5'11". RHB, RM. Debut 1986. HS 12* v Sussex (Leicester) 1986. England YC v Sri Lanka 1986 and to Sri Lanka 1987.

WHITAKER, John **James** (Uppingham S), b Skipton, Yorks 5 May 1962. 5'10". RHB, OB. Debut 1983. Cap 1986. *Wisden* 1986. YC 1986. **Test:** 1 (1986-87); HS 11 v Aus (Adelaide) 1986-87. Tour: Aus 1986-87. 1000 runs (3); most – 1526 (1986). HS 200* v Notts (Leicester) 1986. BB 1-41. Awards: NWT 1; BHC 1. **NWT:** HS 155 v Wilts (Swindon) 1984. **BHC:** HS 73* v Warwicks (Birmingham) 1985. **JPL:** HS 132 v Glam (Swansea) 1984.

WHITTICASE, Philip (Crestwood CS, Kingswinford), b Marston Green, Solihull 15 Mar 1965. 5'11". RHB, WK. Debut 1984. HS 67* v Somerset (Leicester) 1986. **NWT:** HS 32 v Lancs (Leicester) 1986. **BHC:** HS 19* v Northants (Northampton) 1986. **JPL:** HS 5*.

WILLEY, Peter (Seaham SS) b Sedgefield, Co. Durham 6 Dec 1949. 6'1". RHB, OB. Northamptonshire 1966-83; cap 1971. Benefit 1981. Leicestershire debut/cap 1984. Captain 1987. Eastern Province 1982-85. **Tests:** 26 (1976-86); HS 102* v WI (St John's) 1980-81; BB 2-73 v WI (Lord's) 1980. LOI: 26. Tours: Aus 1979-80; SA 1972-73 (DHR), 1981-82 (SAB); WI 1980-81, 1985-86; Ind 1979-80; SL 1977-78 (DHR). 1000 runs (7); most – 1783 (1982). HS 227 Northants v Somerset (Northampton) 1976. Leics HS 172* v Hants (Leicester) 1986. BB 7-37 Northants v OU (Oxford) 1975. Leics BB 6-43 v Hants (Leicester) 1985. Awards: NWT 5; BHC 6. **NWT:** HS 101 v Ireland (Leicester) 1986. BB 3-33 v Derbys (Leicester) 1984. **BHC:** HS 88* v Northants (Leicester) 1984. BB 3-12 Northants v Minor C (E) (Horton) 1977. **JPL:** HS 107 Northants v Warwicks 1975 and 107 Northants v Hants 1976. BB 4-37 Somerset (Leicester) 1986.

SALVETE

BENSON, Justin David Ramsey, b Dublin, Ireland 1 Mar 1967. RHB, RM. Cambridgeshire 1984-86. Award: NWT 1.

LEWIS, Clairmont **Christopher**, b in Guyana. RHB, RMF.

SUCH, Peter Mark (Harry Carlton CS, East Leake, Notts), b Helensburgh, Dunbartonshire 12 Jun 1964. 5'11". RHB, OB. Nottinghamshire 1982-86. HS 16 v Middx (Lord's) 1984. BB 6-123 v Kent (Nottingham) 1983. **BHC:** BB 3-50 v Scotland (Glasgow) 1985. **JPL:** HS 0*. BB 2-50 v Glos (Bristol) 1985.

LEICESTERSHIRE RECORDS

FIRST-CLASS CRICKET

Highest Total	For	701-4d		v	Worcs	Worcester	1906
	V	739-7d		by	Notts	Nottingham	1903
Lowest Total	For	25		v	Kent	Leicester	1912
	V	24		by	Glamorgan	Leicester	1971
		24		by	Oxford U	Oxford	1985
Highest Innings	For	252*	S. Coe	v	Northants	Leicester	1914
	V	341	G.H. Hirst	for	Yorks	Leicester	1905

Highest Partnerships

Wkt						
1st	390	B. Dudleston/J.F. Steele	v	Derbyshire	Leicester	1979
2nd	289*	J.C. Balderstone/D.I. Gower	v	Essex	Leicester	1981
3rd	316*	W. Watson/A. Wharton	v	Somerset	Taunton	1961
4th	290*	P. Willey/T.J. Boon	v	Warwicks	Leicester	1984
5th	233	N.E. Briers/R.W. Tolchard	v	Somerset	Leicester	1979
6th	262	A.T. Sharpe/G.H.S. Fowke	v	Derbyshire	Chesterfield	1911
7th	206	B. Dudleston/J. Birkenshaw	v	Kent	Canterbury	1969
8th	164	M.R. Hallam/C.T. Spencer	v	Essex	Leicester	1964
9th	160	W.W. Odell/R.T. Crawford	v	Worcs	Leicester	1902
10th	228	R. Illingworth/K. Higgs	v	Northants	Leicester	1977

Best Bowling (Innings)	For	10-18	G. Geary	v	Glamorgan	Pontypridd	1929
	V	10-32	H. Pickett	for	Essex	Leyton	1895
Best Bowling (Match)	For	16-96	G. Geary	v	Glamorgan	Pontypridd	1929
	V	16-102	C. Blythe	for	Kent	Leicester	1909

Most Runs – Season	2,446	L.G. Berry	(av 52.04)	1937
Most Runs – Career	30,143	L.G. Berry	(av 30.32)	1924-1951
Most 100s – Season	7	L.G. Berry		1937
	7	W. Watson		1959
	7	B.F. Davison		1982
Most 100s – Career	45	L.G. Berry		1924-1951
Most Wkts – Season	170	J.E. Walsh	(av 18.96)	1948
Most Wkts – Career	2,130	W.E. Astill	(av 23.19)	1906-1939

LIMITED-OVERS CRICKET

Highest Total	NWT	354-7		v	Wiltshire	Swindon	1984
	BHC	327-4		v	Warwicks	Coventry	1972
	JPL	291-5		v	Glamorgan	Swansea	1984
Lowest Total	NWT	56		v	Northants	Leicester	1964
	BHC	56		v	Minor C	Wellington	1982
	JPL	36		v	Sussex	Leicester	1973
Highest Innings	NWT	156	D.I. Gower	v	Derbyshire	Leicester	1984
	BHC	158*	B.F. Davison	v	Warwicks	Coventry	1972
	JPL	152	B. Dudleston	v	Lancashire	Manchester	1975
Best Bowling	NWT	6-20	K. Higgs	v	Staffs	Longton	1975
	BHC	6-35	L.B. Taylor	v	Worcs	Worcester	1982
	JPL	6-17	K. Higgs	v	Glamorgan	Leicester	1973

LEICESTERSHIRE 1986

RESULTS SUMMARY

	Place	Won	Lost	Drew	Abandoned
Britannic Assurance Championship	**7th**	5	7	12	
All First-class Matches		5	7	14	
John Player League	**15th**	5	10		1
NatWest Bank Trophy	Lost to Lancashire (Quarter-Final)				
Benson and Hedges Cup	Failed to qualify for Quarter-Final				

BRITANNIC ASSURANCE CHAMPIONSHIP AVERAGES

BATTING AND FIELDING

Cap		*M*	*I*	*NO*	*HS*	*Runs*	*Avge*	*100*	*50*	*Ct/St*
1986	J.J. Whitaker	19	28	8	200*	1382	69.10	5	7	14
1984	P. Willey	16	27	5	172*	1019	46.31	4	3	5
1981	N.E. Briers	5	6	1	83	220	44.00	—	2	1
1986	T.J. Boon	21	33	9	117	933	38.87	1	4	12
1977	D.I. Gower	9	14	2	83	436	36.33	—	4	6/1
—	P. Whitticase	17	20	4	67*	554	34.62	—	5	23/1
—	W.K.M. Benjamin	18	18	9	57*	309	34.33	—	2	8
1986	R.A. Cobb	23	38	3	91	982	28.05	—	7	8
—	P.D. Bowler	8	11	1	100*	249	24.90	1	1	2
1986	P.A.J. DeFreitas	24	28	2	106	630	24.23	1	3	6
1976	P.B. Clift	13	14	0	49	311	22.21	—	—	12
1973	J.C. Balderstone	14	23	1	115	410	18.63	1	—	3
—	L. Potter	18	27	3	81*	444	18.50	—	4	17
—	G.J.F. Ferris	5	6	1	17*	67	13.40	—	—	4
1984	J.P. Agnew	17	18	5	35*	158	12.15	—	—	2
1984	I.P. Butcher	10	16	1	39	175	11.66	—	—	8
—	P. Gill	7	10	4	17	60	10.00	—	—	23
1981	L.B. Taylor	15	15	6	13	48	5.33	—	—	3

Also batted: G.A.R. Harris (1 match) 6,0*; K. Higgs (2 matches – cap 1972) 3*,8 (1 ct); L. Tennant (2 matches) 12*,1.

BOWLING

	O	*M*	*R*	*W*	*Avge*	*Best*	*5 wI*	*10 wM*
P.A.J. DeFreitas	675.1	123	1977	89	22.21	7-44	7	1
P.B. Clift	384.2	113	901	39	23.10	4-35	—	—
J.P. Agnew	486.5	114	1397	53	26.35	5-27	1	—
G.J.F. Ferris	104	20	356	13	27.38	4-54	—	—
L.B. Taylor	280.3	66	809	27	29.96	4-106	—	—
L. Potter	112	30	318	10	31.80	3-37	—	—
W.K.M. Benjamin	438.3	83	1449	42	34.50	6-33	3	—

Also bowled: J.C. Balderstone 45-9-143-2; T.J. Boon 30.3-2-170-5; P.D. Bowler 25.4-10-57-0; N.E. Briers 13-0-60-2; I.P. Butcher 2-0-4-0; R.A. Cobb 10-3-41-0; G.A.R. Harris 8-1-34-0; K. Higgs 36-10-71-5; L. Tennant 8-1-35-0; J.J. Whitaker 5.2-0-47-1; P. Willey 165.5-48-372-6.

The First-Class Averages (pp. 167–182) give the records of Leicestershire players in all first-class county matches (their other opponents being the Indians, and Cambridge U.), with the exception of D.I. Gower, whose full county figures are as above, and: P.A.J. DeFreitas 26-30-2-106-645-23.03-1-3-6 ct. 704.3-129-2073-91-22.78-7/44-7-1. J.J. Whitaker 21-31-9-200*-1504-68.36-5-8-15 ct. 5.2-0-47-1-47.00-1/41. P. Willey 17-28-5-172*-1031-44.82-4-3-6 ct. 176.2-49-418-7-59.71-2/25.

MIDDLESEX

Formation of Present Club: 2 February 1864
Colours: Blue
Badge: Three Seaxes
Championships (since 1890): (8) 1903, 1920, 1921, 1947, 1976, 1980, 1982, 1985.
Joint Championships: (2) 1949, 1977
NatWest Trophy/Gillette Cup Winners: (3) 1977, 1980, 1984
Benson and Hedges Cup Winners: (2) 1983, 1986
John Player League Champions: (0) Second 1982
Match Awards: NWT 36; BHC 39

Secretary/General Manager: T.M. Lamb, Lord's Cricket Ground, London NW8 8QN
Captain: M.W. Gatting
Scorer: H.P.H. Sharp
Scores/Prospects: ☎ London (01) 286 8011

BROWN, Keith Robert (Chace S, Enfield), b Edmonton 18 Mar 1963. 5'11". RHB, WK. Debut 1984. HS 102 v Aus (Lord's) 1985. **JPL:** HS 33 v Warwicks (Birmingham) 1985.
BROWN, Gary Kevin (Chace S, Enfield), b Welling, Kent 16 Jun 1965. Brother of K.R. 5'11". RHB, RM. Debut 1986. HS 14 v Notts (Nottingham) 1986.
BUTCHER, Roland Orlando (Shephalbury SS, Stevenage), b East Point, Barbados 14 Oct 1953. 5'8". UK resident since 1967. RHB, RM. Debut 1974. Barbados 1974-75, Tasmania 1982-83. Cap 1979. **Tests:** 3 (1980-81); HS 32 v WI (Kingston) 1980-81. LOI: 3. Tours: WI 1980-81, 1982-83 (Int XI); Pak 1981-82 (Int XI); Zim 1980-81 (Middx). 1000 runs (4); most – 1326 (1984). HS 197 v Yorks (Lord's) 1982. BB 2-37 v Glos (Cheltenham) 1986. Awards: BHC 2. **NWT:** HS 59 v Cumberland (Uxbridge) 1985. BB 1-18. **BHC:** HS 85 v Surrey (Oval) 1983. **JPL:** HS 100 v Glos (Lord's) 1983.
CARR, John Donald (Repton S; Worcester C, OU), b St John's Wood, London 15 Jun 1963. 5'11". RHB, OB. Son of D.B. (Derbyshire, OU and England 1945-63). OU and Middlesex debuts 1983. Blue 1983-84-85. Hertfordshire 1982-84. HS 123 OU v Lancs (Oxford) 1984. Middx HS 84* v Worcs (Worcester) 1986. BB 6-61 v Glos (Lord's) 1985. **BHC:** HS 67 Comb Us v Essex (Chelmsford) 1985. BB 3-22 Comb Us v Glos (Bristol) 1984. **JPL:** HS 45* and BB 2-10 v Glam (Cardiff) 1986.
COWANS, Norman George (Park High SS, Stanmore), b Enfield St Mary, Jamaica 17 Apr 1961. 6'3". RHB, RF. Debut 1980. YC 1982. Cap 1984. **Tests:** 19 (1982-83 to 1985); HS 36 v Aus (Perth) 1982-83; BB 6-77 v Aus (Melbourne) 1982-83. LOI: 23. Tours: Aus 1982-83; NZ 1983-84; Ind 1984-85; Pak 1983-84; SL 1984-85, 1985-86 (Eng B); Zim 1980-81 (Middx). HS 66 v Surrey (Lord's) 1984. BB 6-31 v Leics (Leicester) 1985. Awards: NWT 1; BHC 1. **NWT:** HS 12* v Lancs (Lord's) 1984. BB 4-24 v Yorks (Leeds) 1986. **BHC:** HS 6. BB 4-33 v Lancs (Lord's) 1983. **JPL:** HS 20 v Notts (Nottingham) 1985. BB 4-44 v Sussex (Hove) 1982.
DANIEL, Wayne Wendell (Princess Margaret S), b St Philip, Barbados 16 Jan 1956. 6'1". RHB, RF. Barbados 1975-85. Middlesex debut/cap 1977. W Australia 1981-82. Benefit 1985. **Tests** (WI): 10 (1975-76 to 1983-84); HS 11 v Ind (Kingston) 1975-76; BB 5-39 v Ind (Ahmedabad) 1983-84. LOI: 18. Tours: Eng 1976; Ind 1983-84; Zim 1981-82 (Young WI). HS 53* Barbados v Jamaica (Bridgetown) 1979-80, 53* v Yorks (Lord's) 1981. BB 9-61 v Glam (Swansea) 1982. Awards: NWT 2; BHC 2. **NWT:** HS 14 v Lancs (Manchester) 1978. BB 6-15 v Sussex (Hove) 1980. **BHC:** HS 20* v Derbys (Derby) 1978. BB 7-12 v Minor C (E) (Ipswich) 1978. **JPL:** HS 14 v Kent (Lord's) 1980. BB 5-27 v Lancs (Lord's) 1982.

DOWNTON, Paul Rupert (Sevenoaks S; Exeter U), b Farnborough, Kent 4 Apr 1957. 5'10". RHB, WK, OB. Son of G.C. (Kent 1948). Kent 1977-79 (cap 1979). Middlesex debut 1980. Cap 1981. **Tests:** 27 (1980-81 to 1986); HS 74 v Ind (Delhi) 1984-85. LOI: 17. Tours: WI 1980-81, 1985-86; NZ 1977-78; Ind/SL 1984-85; Pak 1977-78; Zim 1980-81 (Middx). HS 126* v OU (Oxford) 1986. **NWT:** HS 62 v Notts (Nottingham) 1984. **BHC:** HS 53* v Kent (Canterbury) 1986. **JPL:** HS 70 v Notts (Nottingham) 1985.

EDMONDS, Philippe Henri (Gilbert Rennie HS, Lusaka; Skinners S, Tunbridge Wells; Cranbrook S; Fitzwilliam C, Cambridge), b Lusaka, N Rhodesia 8 Mar 1951. 6'1½". RHB, SLA. Cambridge U and Middlesex debuts 1971. CU 1971-73; blue 1971-72-73 (capt 1973). Cap 1974. YC 1974. Eastern Province 1975-76. Benefit 1983. **Tests:** 46 (1975 to 1986-87); HS 64 v Ind (Lord's) 1982; BB 7-66 v Pak (Karachi) 1977-78. LOI: 27. Tours: Aus 1978-79, 1986-87; SA 1975-76 (Int Wand); WI 1985-86; NZ 1977-78; Ind/SL 1984-85; Pak 1977-78. HS 142 v Glam (Swansea) 1984. BB 8-53 v Hants (Bournemouth) 1984. Awards: NWT 1; BHC 3. **NWT:** HS 63* v Somerset (Lord's) 1979. BB 5-12 v Cheshire (Enfield) 1982. **BHC:** HS 44* v Notts (Newark) 1976. BB 5-43 v Comb Us (Cambridge) 1985. **JPL:** HS 52 v Somerset (Taunton) 1980. BB 3-19 v Leics (Lord's) 1973.

EMBUREY, John Ernest (Peckham Manor SS), b Peckham, London 20 Aug 1952. 6'2". RHB, OB. Debut 1973. Cap 1977. *Wisden* 1983. Western Province 1982-84. Benefit 1986. **Tests:** 42 (1978 to 1986-87); HS 75 v NZ (Nottingham) 1986; BB 7-78 v Aus (Sydney) 1986-87. LOI: 20. Tours: Aus 1978-79, 1979-80, 1986-87; SA 1981-82 (SAB); WI 1980-81, 1985-86; Ind 1979-80, 1981-82; SL 1977-78 (DHR), 1981-82; Zim 1980-81 (Middx). 100 wickets (1): 103 (1983). HS 133 v Essex (Chelmsford) 1983. BB 7-36 v CU (Cambridge) 1977. Awards: NWT 1; BHC 5. **NWT:** HS 36* v Lancs (Manchester) 1978. BB 3-20 v Northumb (Jesmond) 1984. **BHC:** HS 50 v Kent (Lord's) 1984. BB 4-22 v Notts (Lord's) 1986. **JPL:** HS 49 v Notts (Lord's) 1986. BB 5-36 v Warwicks (Lord's) 1983.

FRASER, Alastair Gregory James (Gayton HS, John Lyon S, Harrow; Harrow Weald SFC), b Edgware 17 Oct 1967. Brother of A.R.C. 6'1". RHB, RFM. Debut 1986. HS 19* v Warwicks (Uxbridge) 1986. BB 3-46 v NZ (Lord's) 1986. **JPL:** HS 2*. BB 1-19. England YC v Sri Lanka 1986 and to Sri Lanka 1987.

FRASER, Angus Robert Charles (Gayton HS, Harrow), b Billinge, Lancs 8 Aug 1965. Brother of A.G.J. 6'5". RHB, RFM. Debut 1984. HS 13 v Worcs (Worcester) 1986. BB 4-48 v CU (Cambridge) 1985. **BHC:** HS 2. BB 1-31. **JPL:** HS 9*. BB 3-46 v Yorks (Bradford) 1985.

GATTING, Michael William (John Kelly HS), b Kingsbury 6 Jun 1957. 5'10". RHB, RM. Debut 1975. Cap 1977. Captain 1983-. *Wisden* 1983. YC 1981. **Tests:** 53 (1977-78 to 1986-87, 10 as captain); HS 207 v Ind (Madras) 1984-85; BB 1-14. LOI: 51. Tours: Aus 1986-87 (capt); WI 1980-81, 1985-86; NZ 1977-78, 1983-84; Ind/SL 1981-82, 1984-85; Pak 1977-78, 1983-84; Zim 1980-81 (Middx). 1000 runs (8+1); most – 2257 (1984). HS 258 v Somerset (Bath) 1984. BB 5-34 v Glam (Swansea) 1982. Awards: NWT 2; BHC 7. **NWT:** HS 118* v Northants (Northampton) 1986. BB 2-14 v Ire 1980 and 2-14 v Lancs 1984. **BHC:** HS 143* v Sussex (Hove) 1985. BB 4-49 v Sussex (Lord's) 1984. **JPL:** HS 109 v Leics (Leicester) 1984. BB 4-32 v Kent (Lord's) 1978.

HUGHES, Simon Peter (Latymer Upper S, Hammersmith; Durham U), b Kingston upon Thames 20 Dec 1959. 5'10". RHB, RFM. Debut 1980. Cap 1981. N Transvaal 1982-83. Tours: Ind 1980-81 (Overseas XI); Zim 1980-81 (Middx). HS 47 v Warwicks (Uxbridge) 1986. BB 7-35 v Surrey (Oval) 1986. Award: NWT 1. **NWT:** HS 6. BB 3-23 v Worcs (Worcester) 1980. **BHC:** HS 8*. BB 2-35 v Kent (Lord's) 1986. **JPL:** HS 22* v Surrey (Lord's) 1985. BB 3-31 v Kent (Canterbury) 1985.

METSON, Colin Peter (Enfield GS; Stanborough S, Welwyn Garden City), b Goffs Oak, Herts 2 Jul 1963. 5'5½". RHB, WK. Debut 1981. HS 96 v Glos (Uxbridge) 1984. **JPL:** HS 15* v Sussex (Hove) 1984.

MILLER, Andrew John Trevor (Haileybury C; St Edmund Hall, OU), b Chesham, Bucks 30 May 1963. 5'11". LHB, RM. OU debut 1982 (blue 1983-84-85, captain 1985). Middlesex debut 1983. 1000 runs (1): 1002 (1983). HS 128* OU v CU (Lord's) 1984. Middx HS 111* v Hants (Lord's) 1986. BB 1-4. Awards: BHC 2. **NWT:** HS 35 v Northants (Northampton) 1986. **BHC:** HS 101 Comb Us v Glos (Bristol) 1984. BB 1-30. **JPL:** HS 69 v Yorks (Lord's) 1986.
RADLEY, Clive Thornton (King Edward VI GS, Norwich), b Hertford 13 May 1944. 5'8". RHB, LB. Debut 1964. Cap 1967. Benefit 1977. 2nd Benefit 1987. *Wisden* 1978. Norfolk 1961. **Tests:** 8 (1977-78 and 1978); HS 158 v NZ (Auckland) 1977-78. LOI: 4. Tours: Aus 1978-79; SA 1972-73 (DHR), 1974-75 (DHR); NZ 1977-78; Zim 1980-81 (Middx). 1000 runs (16); most – 1491 (1980). HS 200 v Northants (Uxbridge) 1985. BB 2-38 v Glam (Cardiff) 1985. Awards: NWT 3; BHC 4. **NWT:** HS 105* v Worcs (Worcester) 1975. **BHC:** HS 121* v Minor C (E) (Lord's) 1976. **JPL:** HS 133* v Glam (Lord's) 1969. BB 1-2.
ROSEBERRY, Michael Anthony (Durham S), b Houghton-le-Spring, Co Durham 28 Nov 1966. 6'1". RHB, RM. Debut 1986. HS 70* v Northants (Northampton) 1986. Captained England YC v Sri Lanka 1986. **JPL:** HS 23 v Essex (Lord's) 1986.
SLACK, Wilfred Norris (Troumaca Govt S; Wellesbourne SS, High Wycombe), b Troumaca, St Vincent 12 Dec 1954. 5'11". LHB, RM. Debut 1977. Cap 1981. Windward Is 1981-83. Buckinghamshire 1976. **Tests:** 3 (1985-86 and 1986); HS 52 v WI (St John's) 1985-86. LOI: 2. Tours: Aus 1986-87; WI 1985-86; Pak 1981-82 (Int XI); SL 1985-86 (Eng B); Zim 1980-81 (Middx). 1000 runs (6); most – 1900 (1985). HS 248* v Worcs (Lord's) 1981. BB 3-17 v Leics (Uxbridge) 1982. Awards: NWT 2. **NWT:** HS 98 v Cumberland (Uxbridge) 1985. BB 3-37 v Northants (Northampton) 1983. **BHC:** HS 65 v Notts (Lord's) 1986. **JPL:** HS 101* v Yorks (Lord's) 1986. BB 5-32 v Leics (Lord's) 1983.
SYKES, James Frederick **('Jamie')** (Bow CS), b Shoreditch, London 30 Dec 1965. 6'1". RHB, OB. Debut 1983. HS 126 v CU (Cambridge) 1985. BB 4-102 v Essex (Chelmsford) 1986. **JPL:** HS 25 v Kent (Canterbury) 1985. BB 2-49 v Sussex (Hove) 1986.
TUFNELL, Philip Clive Roderick (Highgate S), b Barnet, Herts 29 Apr 1966. 6'0". RHB, SLA. Debut 1986. HS 9. BB 2-47 v Warwicks (Uxbridge) 1986.
WILLIAMS, Neil FitzGerald (Acland Burghley CS), b Hope Well, St Vincent 2 Jul 1962. 5'11". RHB, RFM. Debut 1982. Windward Is 1982-83. Tasmania 1983-84. Cap 1984. Tour: Zim 1984-85 (Eng Co). HS 67 v CU (Cambridge) 1985. BB 7-55 Eng Co XI v Zimbabwe (Harare) 1984-85. Middx BB 5-15 v Essex (Lord's) 1985. Award: BHC 1. **NWT:** HS 10 v Northumb (Jesmond) 1984. BB 4-36 v Derbys (Derby) 1983. **BHC:** HS 29* v Surrey (Lord's) 1985. BB 3-16 v Comb Us (Cambridge) 1982. **JPL:** HS 31* v Notts (Cleethorpes) 1983. BB 4-40 v Derbys (Chesterfield) 1983.

SALVETE

HUTCHINSON, Ian James Frederick (Shrewsbury S), b Welshpool, Montgomerys 31 Oct 1964. 6'1". RHB, RMF. Shropshire 1984-86. MCC staff 1984-86. Fielded for Eng v NZ (Lord's) 1986. Scored 204 off 124 balls (14 sixes) before lunch for Cross Arrows 1985.
MACLAURIN, Neil Ralph Charter (Malvern C), b Welwyn Garden City, Herts 22 Mar 1966. RHB, RM. **JPL:** HS 3.
NEEDHAM, Andrew (Ecclesbourne GS; Paisley GS; Watford GS), b Calow, Derbys 23 Mar 1957. 5'9". RHB, OB. Surrey 1977-86 (cap 1985). 1000 (1): 1223 (1985). HS 138 v Warwicks (Oval) 1985. BB 6-30 v OU (Oval) 1983. **NWT:** HS 26 v Kent (Canterbury) 1985. BB 4-32 v Derbys (Derby) 1986. **BHC:** HS 30 v Glos (Oval) 1984. **JPL:** HS 55 v Essex (Southend) 1982. BB 3-41 v Lancs (Manchester) 1982.
RAMPRAKASH, Mark Ravin (Gayton HS; Harrow Weald SFC), b Bushey, Herts 5 Sep 1969. 5'9". RHB, RM. England YC v Sri Lanka 1986 and to Sri Lanka 1987.

 VALETE – see p. 211.

MIDDLESEX RECORDS

FIRST-CLASS CRICKET

Highest Total	For	642-3d		v	Hampshire	Southampton	1923
	V	665		by	W Indians	Lord's	1939
Lowest Total	For	20		v	MCC	Lord's	1864
	V	31		by	Glos	Bristol	1924
Highest Innings	For	331*	J.D.B. Robertson	v	Worcester	Worcester	1949
	V	316*	J.B. Hobbs	for	Surrey	Lord's	1926

Highest Partnerships

Wkt						
1st	367*	G.D. Barlow/W.N. Slack	v	Kent	Lord's	1981
2nd	380	F.A. Tarrant/J.W. Hearne	v	Lancashire	Lord's	1914
3rd	424*	W.J. Edrich/D.C.S. Compton	v	Somerset	Lord's	1948
4th	325	J.W. Hearne/E.H. Hendren	v	Hampshire	Lord's	1919
5th	338	R.S. Lucas/T.C. O'Brien	v	Sussex	Hove	1895
6th	227	C.T. Radley/F.J. Titmus	v	S Africans	Lord's	1965
7th	271*	E.H. Hendren/F.T. Mann	v	Notts	Nottingham	1925
8th	182*	M.H.C. Doll/H.R. Murrell	v	Notts	Lord's	1913
9th	160*	E.H. Hendren/T.J. Durston	v	Essex	Leyton	1927
10th	230	R.W. Nicholls/W. Roche	v	Kent	Lord's	1899

Best Bowling (Innings)	For	10-40	G.O.B. Allen	v	Lancashire	Lord's	1929
	V	9-38	R.C. Glasgow†	for	Somerset	Lord's	1924
Best Bowling (Match)	For	16-114	G. Burton	v	Yorkshire	Sheffield	1888
		16-114	J.T. Hearne	v	Lancashire	Manchester	1898
	V	16-109	C.W.L. Parker	for	Glos	Cheltenham	1930

Most Runs – Season	2,669	E.H. Hendren	(av 83.41)	1923
Most Runs – Career	40,302	E.H. Hendren	(av 48.81)	1907-1937
Most 100s – Season	13	D.C.S. Compton		1947
Most 100s – Career	119	E.H. Hendren		1907-1937
Most Wkts – Season	158	F.J. Titmus	(av 14.63)	1955
Most Wkts – Career	2,361	F.J. Titmus	(av 21.27)	1949-1982

LIMITED-OVERS CRICKET

Highest Total	**NWT**	283-9		v	Cumberland	Uxbridge	1985
	BHC	303-7		v	Northants	Northampton	1977
	JPL	270-5		v	Glos	Lord's	1983
Lowest Total	**NWT**	41		v	Essex	Westcliff	1972
	BHC	73		v	Essex	Lord's	1985
	JPL	23		v	Yorkshire	Leeds	1974
Highest Innings	**NWT**	158	G.D. Barlow	v	Lancashire	Lord's	1984
	BHC	143*	M.W. Gatting	v	Sussex	Hove	1985
	JPL	133*	C.T. Radley	v	Glamorgan	Lord's	1969
Best Bowling	**NWT**	6-15	W.W. Daniel	v	Sussex	Hove	1980
	BHC	7-12	W.W. Daniel	v	Minor C (E)	Ipswich	1978
	JPL	6-6	R.W. Hooker	v	Surrey	Lord's	1969

† R.C. Robertson-Glasgow

MIDDLESEX 1986

RESULTS SUMMARY

	Place	Won	Lost	Drew	Tied	Aban
Britannic Assurance Championship	**12th**	4	9	11		
All First-class Matches		5	9	12		1
John Player League	**9th**	5	7		1	3
NatWest Bank Trophy	Lost to Yorkshire (2nd Round)					
Benson and Hedges Cup .	**Winners**					

BRITANNIC ASSURANCE CHAMPIONSHIP AVERAGES

BATTING AND FIELDING

Cap		*M*	*I*	*NO*	*HS*	*Runs*	*Avge*	*100*	*50*	*Ct/St*
1977	M.W. Gatting	10	10	1	158	452	50.22	1	2	6
1976	G.D. Barlow	4	5	1	107	190	47.50	1	1	1
1981	W.N. Slack	20	30	2	106	1136	40.57	3	6	13
—	J.D. Carr	17	26	3	84*	782	34.00	—	5	11
1981	P.R. Downton	21	25	3	104	668	30.36	1	4	35/5
—	A.J.T. Miller	22	34	4	111*	907	30.23	1	4	11
1979	R.O. Butcher	24	34	3	171	933	30.09	1	7	14
1967	C.T. Radley	23	31	6	113*	738	29.52	2	3	14
—	K.R. Brown	10	16	2	66	367	26.21	—	2	9
—	M.A. Roseberry	5	8	1	70*	174	24.85	—	2	1
—	J.F. Sykes	3	4	1	26	63	21.00	—	—	—
1977	J.E. Emburey	11	10	1	49	163	18.11	—	—	9
1984	N.G. Cowans	19	19	7	44*	195	16.25	—	—	4
—	G.D. Rose	5	6	1	52	74	14.80	—	1	—
1977	W.W. Daniel	16	16	6	33	140	14.00	—	—	3
1974	P.H. Edmonds	11	10	3	25	94	13.42	—	—	13
1981	S.P. Hughes	21	24	2	47	255	11.59	—	—	3
—	A.R.C. Fraser	5	6	1	13	39	7.80	—	—	—
—	C.P. Metson	3	4	0	15	29	7.25	—	—	3
—	P.C.R. Tufnell	6	7	1	9	32	5.33	—	—	1

Also batted: G.K. Brown (1 match) 14,3 (1 ct); A.G.J. Fraser (3 matches) 19*,11*; N.F. Williams (4 matches – cap 1984) 1,11.

BOWLING

	O	*M*	*R*	*W*	*Avge*	*Best*	*5 wI*	*10 wM*
J.E. Emburey	251	79	505	24	21.04	5-51	1	—
W.W. Daniel	402.1	52	1387	62	22.37	4-27	—	—
N.G. Cowans	396.2	85	1265	52	24.32	5-61	1	—
S.P. Hughes	478.3	109	1522	54	28.18	7-35	1	—
P.H. Edmonds	293.4	90	623	20	31.15	4-67	—	—

Also bowled: K.R. Brown 0.4-0-10-0; R.O. Butcher 13.4-2-49-2; J.D. Carr 93.2-17-284-1; A.G.J. Fraser 36.4-12-82-5; A.R.C. Fraser 131-32-327-8; M.W. Gatting 42-18-99-5; A.J.T. Miller 1-0-5-0; G.D. Rose 64-10-277-7; W.N. Slack 17-3-75-1; J.F. Sykes 43.3-5-161-5; P.C.R. Tufnell 148-32-479-5; N.F. Williams 59.3-7-214-8.

The First-Class Averages (pp. 167–182) give the records of Middlesex players in all first-class county matches (their other opponents being the New Zealanders and Oxford U.), with the exception of: P.R. Downton 23-27-5-126*-872-39.63-2-5-42 ct/5 st. P.H. Edmonds 12-11-3-31-124-15.50-0-0-13 ct. 343-103-721-23-31.34-4/67. J.E. Emburey 13-13-1-49-188-15.66-0-0-12 ct. 316.5-109-590-31-19.03-5/51-1-0. M.W. Gatting 12-12-1-158-628-57.09-2-2-8 ct. 72-24-186-8-23.25-2/8. W.N. Slack 22-33-3-106-1205-40.16-3-7-15 ct. 17-3-75-1-75.00-1/14.

NORTHAMPTONSHIRE

Formation of Present Club: 31 July 1878
Colours: Maroon
Badge: Tudor Rose
Championships: (0) Runners-up 1912, 1957, 1965, 1976
NatWest Trophy/Gillette Cup Winners: (1) 1976
Benson and Hedges Cup Winners: (1) 1980
John Player League Champions: (0) Fourth 1974
Match Awards: NWT 27; BHC 27

Secretary: S.P. Coverdale, County Ground, Wantage Road, Northampton, NN1 4TJ
Captain: G. Cook
Scorer: B.H. Clarke
Scores/Prospects: ☎ Northampton (0604) 37040

BAILEY, Robert John (Biddulph HS), b Biddulph, Staffs 28 Oct 1963. 6'3". RHB, OB. Debut 1982. YC 1984. Cap 1985. Staffs 1980. LOI: 1. 1000 runs (3); most – 1915 (1986). HS 224* v Glam (Swansea) 1986. BB 3-33 v CU (Cambridge) 1983. Awards: BHC 2. **NWT:** HS 56* v Middx (Lord's) 1984. BB 1-2. **BHC:** HS 86 v Warwicks (Birmingham) 1986. BB 1-22. **JPL:** HS 118* v Worcs (Northampton) 1986.

BOYD-MOSS, Robin James (Bedford S; Magdalene C, Cambridge), b Hatton, Ceylon 16 Dec 1959. 5'10½". RHB, SLA. Cambridge U and Northamptonshire debuts 1980. CU 1980-83; blue 1980-81-82-83 (achieved unique feat of a hundred in each innings in 1983 Varsity Match). Cap 1984. Bedfordshire 1977-79. 1000 runs (3); most – 1602 (1982). HS 155 v Lancs (Northampton) 1986. BB 5-27 CU v OU (Lord's) 1983. Northants BB 3-39 v Warwicks (Birmingham) 1986. Award: NWT 1. **NWT:** HS 88* v Leics (Northampton) 1984. BB 3-47 v Shropshire (Telford) 1985. **BHC:** HS 58 Comb Us v Northants (Northampton) 1980 and 58 v Warwicks (Birmingham) 1986. **JPL:** HS 99 v Glos (Bristol) 1984.

CAPEL, David John (Roade CS), b Northampton 6 Feb 1963. 5'11". RHB, RM. Debut 1981. Cap 1986. E Province 1985-87. HS 111 v Leics (Northampton) 1986. BB 7-62 v Lancs (Lytham) 1985. **NWT:** HS 27 v Middx (Northampton) 1983. BB 2-74 v Glos (Bristol) 1985. **BHC:** HS 43* v Leics (Northampton) 1986. BB 4-29 v Warwicks (Birmingham) 1986. **JPL:** HS 79 v Kent (Northampton) 1982. BB 4-30 v Yorks (Middlesbrough) 1982.

COOK, Geoffrey (Middlesbrough HS), b Middlesbrough 9 Oct 1951. 6'0". RHB, SLA. Debut 1971. Cap 1975. E Province 1978-81. Captain 1981-. Benefit 1985. **Tests:** 7 (1981-82 to 1982-83); HS 66 v Ind (Manchester) 1982. LOI: 6. Tours: Aus 1982-83; Ind/SL 1981-82. 1000 runs (11); most – 1759 (1981). HS 183 v Lancs (Northampton) 1986. BB 3-47 England XI v S Australia (Adelaide) 1982-83. Awards: NWT 5; BHC 3. **NWT:** HS 130 v Shropshire (Telford) 1985. **BHC:** HS 96 v Minor C (E) (Northampton) 1978. **JPL:** HS 98 v Lancs (Northampton) 1985.

COOK, Nicholas Grant Billson (Lutterworth GS), b Broughton Astley, Leics 17 June 1956. 6'0". RHB, SLA. Leicestershire 1978-85; cap 1982. Northamptonshire debut 1986. **Tests:** 9 (1983-84); HS 26 v NZ (Nottingham) 1983; BB 6-65 (11-83 match) v Pak (Karachi) 1983-84. LOI: 1. Tours: NZ 1979-80 (DHR), 1983-84; Pak

1983-84; SL 1985-86 (Eng B); Zim 1980-81 (Leics), 1984-85 (Eng Co). HS 75 Leics v Somerset (Taunton) 1980. Northants HS 45 v Yorks (Scarborough) 1986. BB 7-63 Leics v Somerset (Taunton) 1982. Northants BB 6-72 v Worcs (Northampton) 1986. **NWT:** HS 13 v Middx (Northampton) 1986. BB 2-33 Leics v Wilts (Swindon) 1984. **BHC:** HS 23 Leics v Warwicks (Leicester) 1984. BB 1-18. **JPL:** HS 13* (thrice). BB 3-23 v Sussex (Hastings) 1986.

FORDHAM, Alan (Bedford Modern S; Durham U), b Bedford 9 Nov 1964. 6'1". RHB, RM. Debut 1986. Bedfordshire 1982-85. HS 17 v Notts (Nottingham) 1986.

GOULDSTONE, Mark Roger (Newport GS; Braintree CFE), b Bishop's Stortford, Herts 3 Feb 1963. 5'11". RHB, RM. Debut 1986. HS 35 v NZ (Northampton) 1986. **JPL:** HS 4*.

HARPER, Roger Andrew (Queen's College HS, Georgetown), b Georgetown, British Guiana 17 Mar 1963. 6'5". RHB, OB. Brother of M.A. (Guyana). Demerara 1979-83. Guyana 1979-86. Northants debut 1985. Cap 1986. **Tests** (WI): 19 (1983-84 to 1986-87); HS 60 v Eng (St John's) 1985-86; BB 6-57 v Eng (Manchester) 1984. LOI (WI): 40. Tours (WI): Eng 1984; Aus 1984-85, 1986-87; Ind 1983-84; Pak 1986-87. HS 234 v Glos (Northampton) 1986. BB 6-57 (Tests). Northants BB 5-84 v Leics (Northampton) 1986. **NWT:** HS 1. BB 1-56. **BHC:** HS 56 v Warwicks (Birmingham) 1986. BB 3-48 v Notts (Nottingham) 1985. **JPL:** HS 57* v Kent (Northampton) 1986. BB 4-17 v Sussex (Hastings) 1986.

LAMB, Allan Joseph (Wynberg HS; Abbots C) b Langebaanweg, Cape Province, SA 20 Jun 1954. 5'8". RHB, RM. W Province 1972-82. Northants debut/cap 1978. *Wisden* 1980. **Tests:** 51 (1982 to 1986-87); HS 137* v NZ (Nottingham) 1983; BB 1-6. LOI: 55. Tours: Aus 1982-83, 1986-87; WI 1985-86; NZ 1983-84; Ind/SL 1984-85; Pak 1983-84. 1000 runs (7); most – 2049 (1981). HS 178 v Leics (Leicester) 1979. BB 1-1. Awards: NWT 1; BHC 6. **NWT:** HS 101 v Sussex (Hove) 1979. BB 1-4. **BHC:** HS 106* v Leics (Leicester) 1983. **JPL:** HS 132* v Surrey (Guildford) 1985.

LARKINS, Wayne (Bushmead SS, Eaton Socon), b Roxton, Beds 22 Nov 1953. 5'11". RHB, RM. Debut 1972. Cap 1976. E Province 1982-84. Benefit 1986. **Tests:** 6 (1979-80 to 1981); HS 34 v Aus (Oval) 1981. LOI: 6. Tours: Aus 1979-80; SA 1981-82 (SAB); Ind 1979-80, 1980-81 (Overseas XI). 1000 runs (8); most – 1863 (1982). HS 252 v Glam (Cardiff) 1983. BB 5-59 v Worcs (Worcester) 1984. Awards: NWT 1; BHC 5. **NWT:** HS 92* v Leics (Northampton) 1979. BB 2-38 v Glos (Bristol) 1985. **BHC:** HS 132 v Warwicks (Birmingham) 1982. BB 4-37 v Comb Us (Northampton) 1980. **JPL:** HS 172* v Warwicks (Luton) 1983. BB 5-32 v Essex (Ilford) 1978.

RIPLEY, David (Royds SS, Leeds), b Leeds, Yorks 13 Sep 1966. 5'9". RHB, WK. Debut 1984. HS 134* v Yorks (Scarborough) 1986. **NWT:** HS 27* v Durham (Darlington) 1984. **BHC:** HS 26 v Derbys (Northampton) 1986. **JPL:** HS 36* v Hants (Southampton) 1984.

SMITH, Gareth (Boldon CS; South Tyneside C), b Jarrow, Co Durham 20 Jul 1966. 6'1". RHB, LFM. Debut 1986 (dismissing S.M. Gavaskar with his second ball). HS 4. BB 1-38.

WALKER, Alan (Shelley HS), b Emley, Yorks 7 Jul 1962. 5'11". LHB, RFM. Debut 1983. HS 40* v Indians (Northampton) 1986. BB 6-50 v Lancs (Northampton) 1986. **NWT:** HS 3*. BB 2-33 v Leics (Northampton) 1984. **BHC:** HS 3*. BB 4-46 v Glos (Northampton) 1985. **JPL:** HS 13 v Yorks (Tring) 1983. BB 4-21 v Worcs (Worcester) 1985.

WATERTON, Stuart Nicholas Varney (Gravesend S; LSE), b Dartford, Kent 6 Dec 1960. 5'11½". RHB, WK. Kent 1980-85. Northamptonshire debut 1986. HS 58* v Worcs (Northampton) 1986. **NWT:** HS 4*. **JPL:** HS 28 v Essex (Colchester) 1986.

WILD, Duncan James (Northampton GS), b Northampton 28 Nov 1962. 5'11½". LHB, RM. Son of John Wild (Northamptonshire 1953-61). Debut 1980. Cap 1986. HS 144 v Lancs (Southport) 1984. BB 4-4 v CU (Cambridge) 1986. **NWT:** HS 11 v Middx (Lord's) 1984. BB 3-47 v Leics (Northampton) 1984. **BHC:** HS 48 v Warwicks (Northampton) 1984. BB 3-40 v Leics (Northampton) 1986. **JPL:** HS 63* v Glos (Northampton) 1985. BB 5-7 v Derbys (Finedon) 1986.

WILLIAMS, Richard Grenville (Ellesmere Port GS), b Bangor, Caernarvonshire 10 Aug 1957. 5'6½". RHB, OB. Debut 1974. Cap 1979. Tours: NZ 1979-80 (DHR); Zim 1984-85 (Eng Co). 1000 runs (6); most – 1262 (1980). HS 175* v Leics (Leicester) 1980. BB 7-73 v CU (Cambridge) 1980. Awards: NWT 1; BHC 3. **NWT:** HS 94 v Worcs (Northampton) 1984. BB 3-15 v Leics (Northampton) 1979. **BHC:** HS 83 v Yorks (Bradford) 1980. BB 2-11 v Worcs (Worcester) 1981. **JPL:** HS 82 v Glos (Bristol) 1982. BB 5-30 v Warwicks (Luton) 1983.

SALVETE

BROWN, Simon John (Boldon CS), b Cleadon, Co Durham 29 Jun 1969. 6'3". RHB, LFM. England YC to Sri Lanka 1987.

DAVIS, Winston Walter (Emmanuel HS, St Vincent), b Sion Hill, St Vincent 18 Sep 1958. RHB, RF. Combined Is/Windward Is 1979-86. Glamorgan 1982-84. Tasmania 1985-86. **Tests** (WI): 11 (1982-83 to 1984-85); HS 77 v Eng (Manchester) 1984; BB 4-19 v NZ (Kingston) 1984-85. LOI (WI): 32; BB 7-51 v Aus (Leeds) 1983 – LOI world record. Tours (WI): Eng 1984; Aus 1984-85; Ind 1983-84; Zim 1981-82 (Young WI). HS 77 (Tests). BB 7-70 Glam v Notts (Ebbw Vale) 1983. Award: BHC 1. **NWT:** HS 5. BB 3-26 Glam v Norfolk (Norwich) 1983. **BHC:** HS 8. BB 5-29 Glam v Middx (Cardiff) 1984. **JPL:** HS 5. BB 4-24 Glam v Derbys (Derby) 1982.

ROBINSON, Mark Andrew, b Hull, Yorks 23 Nov 1966. RHB, RFM.

STEVENSON, Graham Barry (Minsthorpe HS), b Ackworth 16 Dec 1955. 5'11". RHB, RMF. Yorkshire 1973-86 (cap 1978). **Tests:** 2 (1979-80 and 1980-81); HS 27* v Ind (Bombay) 1979-80; BB 3-111 v WI (St John's) 1980-81. LOI: 4. Tours: Aus 1979-80; WI 1980-81; Ind 1979-80. HS 115* (batting number 11) v Warwicks (Birmingham) 1982. BB 8-57 v Northants (Leeds) 1980. Awards: NWT 1; BHC 1. **NWT:** HS 34 v Northants (Leeds) 1983. BB 5-27 v Berks (Reading) 1983. **BHC:** HS 36 v Warwicks (Leeds) 1984. BB 5-28 v Kent (Canterbury) 1978. **JPL:** HS 81* v Somerset (Middlesbrough) 1984. BB 5-41 v Leics (Leicester) 1976.

VALETE

GRIFFITHS, Brian **James** (Irthlingborough & Finedon SS), b Wellingborough 13 Jun 1949. 6'3". RHB, RFM. Debut 1974. Cap 1978. Testimonial 1987. Joins Lincolnshire 1987. HS 16 v Glos (Bristol) 1982. BB 8-50 v Glam (Northampton) 1981. Award: NWT 1.

MALLENDER, N.A. – see SOMERSET.

STORIE, A.C. – see WARWICKSHIRE.

NORTHAMPTONSHIRE RECORDS

FIRST-CLASS CRICKET

Highest Total	For	557-6d		v	Sussex	Hove	1914
	V	670-9d		by	Sussex	Hove	1921
Lowest Total	For	12		v	Glos	Gloucester	1907
	V	33		by	Lancashire	Northampton	1977
Highest Innings	For	300	R. Subba Row	v	Surrey	The Oval	1958
	V	333	K.S. Duleepsinhji	for	Sussex	Hove	1930

Highest Partnerships

Wkt						
1st	361	N. Oldfield/V. Broderick	v	Scotland	Peterborough	1953
2nd	344	G. Cook/R.J. Boyd-Moss	v	Lancashire	Northampton	1986
3rd	320	L. Livingston/F. Jakeman	v	S Africans	Northampton	1951
4th	370	R.T. Virgin/P. Willey	v	Somerset	Northampton	1976
5th	347	D. Brookes/D.W. Barrick	v	Essex	Northampton	1952
6th	376	R. Subba Row/A. Lightfoot	v	Surrey	The Oval	1958
7th	229	W.W. Timms/F.A. Walden	v	Warwicks	Northampton	1926
8th	155	F.R. Brown/A.E. Nutter	v	Glamorgan	Northampton	1952
9th	156	R. Subba Row/S. Starkie	v	Lancashire	Northampton	1955
10th	148	B.W. Bellamy/J.V. Murdin	v	Glamorgan	Northampton	1925

Best Bowling (Innings)	For	10-127	V.W.C. Jupp	v	Kent	Tunbridge W	1932
	V	10-30	C. Blythe	for	Kent	Northampton	1907
Best Bowling (Match)	For	15-31	G.E. Tribe	v	Yorkshire	Northampton	1958
	V	17-48	C. Blythe	for	Kent	Northampton	1907

Most Runs – Season	2,198	D. Brookes	(av 51.11)	1952
Most Runs – Career	28,980	D. Brookes	(av 36.13)	1934-1959
Most 100s – Season	8	R.A. Haywood		1921
Most 100s – Career	67	D. Brookes		1934-1959
Most Wkts – Season	175	G.E. Tribe	(av 18.70)	1955
Most Wkts – Career	1,097	E.W. Clark	(av 21.31)	1922-1947

LIMITED-OVERS CRICKET

Highest Total	NWT	285-6		v	Wiltshire	Swindon	1983
	BHC	283-5		v	Warwicks	Birmingham	1986
	JPL	306-2		v	Surrey	Guildford	1985
Lowest Total	NWT	62		v	Leics	Leicester	1974
	BHC	85		v	Sussex	Northampton	1978
	JPL	41		v	Middlesex	Northampton	1972
Highest Innings	NWT	130	G. Cook	v	Shropshire	Telford	1985
	BHC	132	W. Larkins	v	Warwicks	Birmingham	1982
	JPL	172*	W. Larkins	v	Warwicks	Luton	1983
Best Bowling	NWT	7-37	N.A. Mallender	v	Worcs	Northampton	1984
	BHC	5-21	Sarfraz Nawaz	v	Middlesex	Lord's	1980
	JPL	7-39	A. Hodgson	v	Somerset	Northampton	1976

NORTHAMPTONSHIRE 1986

RESULTS SUMMARY

	Place	Won	Lost	Drew	Abandoned
Britannic Assurance Championship	**9th**	5	3	16	
All First-class Matches		5	3	19	
John Player League	**5th**	9	5		2
NatWest Bank Trophy	Lost to Middlesex (1st Round)				
Benson and Hedges Cup	Lost to Worcestershire (Quarter-Final)				

BRITANNIC ASSURANCE CHAMPIONSHIP AVERAGES

BATTING AND FIELDING

Cap		*M*	*I*	*NO*	*HS*	*Runs*	*Avge*	*100*	*50*	*Ct/St*
1978	A.J. Lamb	14	20	4	160*	1261	78.81	4	8	12
1985	R.J. Bailey	24	36	7	224*	1562	53.86	4	7	20
1975	G. Cook	20	29	4	183	1057	42.28	3	3	16
1986	R.A. Harper	24	29	4	234	921	36.84	1	2	32
—	D. Ripley	11	12	3	134*	286	31.77	1	—	11/4
1984	R.J. Boyd-Moss	24	37	3	155	1033	30.38	2	6	7
1986	D.J. Wild	11	16	1	85	448	29.86	—	4	2
1976	W. Larkins	17	29	4	86	664	26.56	—	2	13
1986	D.J. Capel	24	30	4	111	685	26.34	2	2	11
—	S.N.V. Waterton	13	16	4	58*	314	26.16	—	1	29/4
—	A.C. Storie	6	7	0	38	152	21.71	—	—	3
—	N.G.B. Cook	24	25	3	45	343	15.59	—	—	18
1984	N.A. Mallender	21	19	9	37	116	11.60	—	—	4
—	A. Walker	17	14	9	13*	47	9.40	—	—	6
1979	R.G. Williams	3	4	0	18	35	8.75	—	—	—
1978	B.J. Griffiths	9	6	3	7	18	6.00	—	—	2

Also batted: A. Fordham (1 match) 5,17; G. Smith (1 match) 3 (1 ct).

BOWLING

	O	*M*	*R*	*W*	*Avge*	*Best*	*5 wI*	*10 wM*
R.A. Harper	815.2	273	1670	62	26.93	5-84	1	—
N.G.B. Cook	807.2	264	1746	61	28.62	6-72	2	—
D.J. Capel	549.4	109	1774	52	34.11	7-86	2	—
B.J. Griffiths	208.3	40	666	19	35.05	4-59	—	—
N.A. Mallender	585	128	1636	45	36.35	5-110	1	—
A. Walker	394	72	1224	32	38.25	6-50	1	—

Also bowled: R.J. Bailey 11.5-6-12-2; R.J. Boyd-Moss 75.3-18-212-7; G. Cook 17-4-38-1; A.J. Lamb 2-2-0-0; G. Smith 23-4-94-1; D.J. Wild 87-5-329-7; R.G. Williams 36-7-111-3.

The First-Class Averages (pp. 167–182) give the records of Northamptonshire players in all first-class county matches (their other opponents being the Indians, the New Zealanders and Cambridge U.), with the exception of: R.J. Bailey 27-41-8-224*-1805-54.69-4-9-22 ct. 15.5-7-47-2-23.50-1/2. D.J. Capel 27-35-6-111-847-29.20-2-3-11 ct. 592.4-120-1907-57-33.45-7/86-2-0. A.J. Lamb 15-22-4-160*-1294-71.88-4-8-12 ct. 2-2-0-0.

NOTTINGHAMSHIRE

Formation of Present Club: March/April 1841
Substantial Reorganisation: 11 December 1866
Colours: Green and Gold
Badge: County Badge of Nottinghamshire
Championships (since 1890): (3) 1907, 1929, 1981
NatWest Trophy/Gillette Cup Winners: (0) Finalists 1985
Benson and Hedges Cup Winners: (0) Finalists 1982
John Player League Champions: (0) Second 1984
Match Awards: NWT 23; BHC 39

Secretary: B. Robson, Trent Bridge, Nottingham NG2 6AG
Captain: C.E.B. Rice
Scorers: L. Beaumont and L. Tomlinson
Scores/Prospects: ☎ Nottingham (0602) 822753

AFFORD, John Andrew (Spalding GS; Stamford CFE), b Crowland, Lincs 12 May 1964. 6′1½″. RHB, SLA. Debut 1984. HS 9*. BB 6-81 v Kent (Nottingham) 1986. **JPL:** BB 1-27.

BIRCH, John Dennis (William Crane Bilateral S), b Nottingham 18 Jun 1955. 5′11″. RHB, RM. Debut 1973. Cap 1981. 1000 runs (2); most – 1086 (1983). HS 125 v Leics (Nottingham) 1982. BB 6-64 v Hants (Bournemouth) 1975. Award: BHC 1. **NWT:** HS 32 v Yorks (Bradford) 1978. BB 1-58. **BHC:** HS 85 v Minor C (N) (Nottingham) 1979. BB 2-14 v Minor C (N) (Newark) 1975. **JPL:** HS 92 v Sussex (Nottingham) 1983. BB 3-29 v Glam (Swansea) 1976.

BROAD, Brian **Christopher** (Colston's S, Bristol; St Paul's C, Cheltenham), b Bristol 29 Sep 1957. 6′4″. LHB, RM. Gloucestershire 1979-83 (cap 1981). Nottinghamshire debut/cap 1984. OFS 1985-86 (captain). **Tests:** 10 (1984 to 1986-87); HS 162 v Aus (Perth) 1986-87. LOI: 4. Tours: Aus 1986-87; Zim 1984-85 (Eng Co). 1000 runs (6); most – 1786 (1985). HS 171 v Derbys (Derby) 1985. BB 2-14 Glos v WI (Bristol) 1980. Awards: NWT 2; BHC 1. **NWT:** HS 98 Glos v Middx (Bristol) 1982. **BHC:** HS 122 v Derbys (Derby) 1984. BB 2-73 v Lancs (Nottingham) 1984. **JPL:** HS 104* v Derbys (Nottingham) 1986. BB 3-46 Glos v Worcs (Bristol) 1982.

COOPER, Kevin Edwin (Hucknall National SS), b Hucknall 27 Dec 1957. 6′1″. LHB, RFM. Debut 1976. Cap 1980. HS 46 v Middx (Nottingham) 1985. BB 8-44 v Middx (Lord's) 1984. **NWT:** HS 11 v Glos (Nottingham) 1982. BB 4-49 v Warwicks (Nottingham) 1985. **BHC:** HS 25* v Lancs (Manchester) 1983. BB 4-23 v Kent (Canterbury) 1979. **JPL:** HS 31 v Glos (Nottingham) 1984. BB 4-25 v Hants (Nottingham) 1976.

EVANS, Kevin Paul (Colonel Frank Seely S) b Calverton 10 Sep 1963. 6′2″. RHB, RMF. Brother of R.J. Debut 1984. HS 42 and BB 2-31 v CU (Nottingham) 1984. **NWT:** HS 10 v Devon (Exmouth) 1986. BB 4-30 v Kent (Nottingham) 1986. **BHC:** HS 20 v Glos (Bristol) 1985. BB 1-47. **JPL:** HS 28 v Glos 1985 and 28 v Kent 1985. BB 3-36 v Middx (Nottingham) 1985.

EVANS, Russell John (Colonel Frank Seely S), b Calverton 1 Oct 1965. 6'0". RHB, RM. Brother of K.P. Played in one JPL match 1985. Awaiting f-c debut. **JPL:** HS 20 v Hants (Nottingham) 1985.

FRASER-DARLING, Callum **David** (The Edinburgh Academy), b Sheffield, Yorks 30 Sep 1963. 6'5". RHB, RFM. Debut 1984. HS 61 v Northants (Northampton) 1986. BB 5-84 v Northants (Northampton) 1986. **JPL:** HS 7. BB 1-24.

FRENCH, Bruce Nicholas (The Meden CS), b Warsop 13 Aug 1959. 5'6". RHB, WK. Debut 1976 aged 16 years 287 days. Cap 1980. **Tests:** 5 (1986); HS 21 v NZ (Nottingham) 1986. LOI: 3. Tours: Aus 1986-87; WI 1985-86; Ind/SL 1984-85. HS 98 v Lancs (Nottingham) 1984. Award: BHC 1. **NWT:** HS 49 v Staffs (Nottingham) 1985. **BHC:** HS 48* v Worcs (Nottingham) 1984. **JPL:** HS 37 v Glos (Bristol) 1985.

HADLEE, Richard John (Christchurch BHS), b Christchurch, NZ 3 Jul 1951. 6'1". LHB, RFM. Fourth son of W.A. (Canterbury, Otago and NZ); brother of D.R. (Canterbury and NZ), and B.G. (Canterbury); wife Karen (NZ). Canterbury 1971-85. Nottinghamshire debut/cap 1978. Tasmania 1979-80. MBE 1980. *Wisden* 1981. **Tests** (NZ): 66 (1972-73 to 1986); HS 103 v WI (Christchurch) 1979-80; BB 9-52 v Aus (Brisbane) 1985-86. LOI (NZ): 91. Tours: Eng 1973, 1978, 1983, 1986; Aus 1972-73, 1973-74, 1980-81, 1985-86; WI 1984-85; Ind/Pak 1976-77; SL 1983-84. 1000 runs (1): 1179 (1984). 100 wickets (2); most – 117 (1984). Double 1984 (first since 1967). HS 210* v Middx (Lord's) 1984. BB 9-52 (Tests). Notts BB 8-41 v Lancs (Nottingham) 1985. Awards: NWT 2; BHC 7. **NWT:** HS 56 v Warwicks (Nottingham) 1985. BB 5-17 v Surrey (Oval) 1986. **BHC:** HS 70 v Warwicks (Nottingham) 1982. BB 4-13 v Derbys (Nottingham) 1980. **JPL:** HS 100* v Glos (Cheltenham) 1982. BB 6-12 v Lancs (Nottingham) 1980.

HEMMINGS, Edward Ernest (Campion S), b Leamington Spa, Warwicks 20 Feb 1949. 5'10". RHB, OB. Warwickshire 1966-1978 (cap 1974). Nottinghamshire debut 1979. Cap 1980. Benefit 1987. **Tests:** 5 (1982 and 1982-83); HS 95 and BB 3-68 v Aus (Sydney) 1982-83. LOI: 5. Tours: Aus 1982-83; SA 1974-75 (DHR); WI 1982-83 (Int XI); Pak 1981-82 (Int XI). HS 127* v Yorks (Worksop) 1982. BB 10-175 Int XI v West Indies XI (Kingston) 1982-83. Notts BB 7-23 v Lancs (Nottingham) 1983. **NWT:** HS 31* v Staffs (Nottingham) 1985. BB 3-27 v Warwicks (Nottingham) 1985. **BHC:** HS 61* Warwicks v Leics (Birmingham) 1974. BB 3-12 v Surrey (Nottingham) 1984. **JPL:** HS 44* Warwicks v Kent (Birmingham) 1971. BB 5-22 Warwicks v Notts (Birmingham) 1974.

JOHNSON, Paul (Grove CS, Balderton), b Newark 24 Apr 1965. 5'7". RHB, RM. Debut 1982. Cap 1986. 1000 runs (1): 1250 (1986). HS 133 v Kent (Folkestone) 1984. BB 1-9. Award: NWT 1. **NWT:** HS 101* v Staffs (Nottingham) 1985. **BHC:** HS 22 v Essex (Chelmsford) 1986. **JPL:** HS 90 v Leics (Leicester) 1986.

MARTINDALE, Duncan John Richardson (Lymm GS; Trent Polytechnic), b Harrogate, Yorks 13 Dec 1963. 5'11". RHB, OB. Debut 1985. HS 104* v Lancs (Manchester) 1985. **NWT:** HS 20* v Essex (Lord's) 1985. **JPL:** HS 33 v Essex (Nottingham) 1985.

NEWELL, Michael (West Bridgford CS), b Blackburn, Lancs 25 Feb 1965. 5'8". RHB, LB. Debut 1984. HS 112* v OU (Oxford) 1986. BB 1-38.

PICK, Robert **Andrew** (Alderman Derbyshire CS; High Pavement SFC), b Nottingham 19 Nov 1963. 5'10". LHB, RMF. Debut 1983. HS 63 v Warwicks (Nuneaton) 1985. BB 6-68 v Yorks (Worksop) 1986. **NWT:** HS 34* v Sussex (Hove) 1983. BB 2-23 v Devon (Exmouth) 1986. **BHC:** HS 3*. BB 3-41 v Scotland (Nottingham) 1986. **JPL:** HS 24 v Yorks (Hull) 1986. BB 4-36 v Leics (Leicester) 1984.

RANDALL, Derek William (Sir Frederick Milner SS), b Retford 24 Feb 1951. 5'9". RHB, RM. Debut 1972. Cap 1973. *Wisden* 1979. Benefit 1983. **Tests:** 47 (1976-77 to 1984); HS 174 v Aus (Melbourne) 1976-77. LOI: 49. Tours: Aus 1976-77, 1978-79, 1979-80, 1982-83; SA 1975-76 (DHR); NZ 1977-78, 1983-84; Ind/SL 1976-77; Pak 1977-78, 1983-84; Zim 1985-86 (Eng B). 1000 runs (10); most – 2151 (1985). HS 209 v Middx (Nottingham) 1979. BB 3-15 v MCC (Lord's) 1982. Awards: NWT 2; BHC 4. **NWT:** HS 75 v Sussex (Hove) 1979. **BHC:** HS 103* v Minor C (N) (Nottingham) 1979. **JPL:** HS 107* v Middx (Lord's) 1976.

RICE, Clive Edward Butler (Sandringham S; St John's C; Damelin C; Natal U), b Johannesburg, SA 23 Jul 1949. 6'0". RHB, RMF. Grandson of P.S.S. Bower (Oxford U 1919). Transvaal 1969-87 (capt 1981-87). Nottinghamshire debut/cap 1975. Captain 1979-. Wisden 1980. Benefit 1985. 1000 runs (12); most – 1871 (1978). HS 246 v Sussex (Hove) 1976. BB 7-62 Transvaal v W Province (Johannesburg) 1975-76. Notts BB 6-16 v Worcs (Worcester) 1977. Awards: NWT 2; BHC 9. **NWT:** HS 71 v Yorks (Bradford) 1978. BB 6-18 v Sussex (Hove) 1982. **BHC:** HS 130* v Scotland (Glasgow) 1982. BB 6-22 v Northants (Northampton) 1981. **JPL:** HS 120* v Glam (Swansea) 1978. BB 4-15 v Hants (Nottingham) 1980.

ROBINSON, Robert **Timothy** (Dunstable GS; High Pavement SFC; Sheffield U), b Sutton-in-Ashfield 21 Nov 1958. 6'0". RHB, RM. Debut 1978. Cap 1983. *Wisden* 1985. **Tests:** 16 (1984-85 to 1986); HS 175 v Aus (Leeds) 1985. LOI: 10. Tours: WI 1985-86; Ind/SL 1984-85. 1000 runs (4); most – 2032 (1984). HS 207 v Warwicks (Nottingham) 1983. BB 1-22. Awards: NWT 3; BHC 2. **NWT:** HS 139 v Worcs (Worcester) 1985. **BHC:** HS 120 v Scotland (Glasgow) 1985. **JPL:** HS 97* v Worcs (Worcester) 1984.

SAXELBY, Kevin (Magnus GS), b Worksop 23 Feb 1959. 6'2". RHB, RMF. Debut 1978. Cap 1984. HS 59* v Derbys (Chesterfield) 1982. BB 6-64 v Kent (Tunbridge Wells) 1985. **NWT:** HS 12 v Worcs (Worcester) 1983. BB 4-28 v Middx (Nottingham) 1984. **BHC:** HS 13* v Lancs (Nottingham) 1982. BB 3-12 v Surrey (Nottingham) 1984. **JPL:** HS 23* v Middx (Cleethorpes) 1983. BB 4-29 v Warwicks (Birmingham) 1983.

SCOTT, Christopher Wilmot (Robert Pattinson CS), b Thorpe-on-the-Hill, Lincs 23 Jan 1964. 5'8". RHB, WK. Debut 1981. HS 78 v CU (Cambridge) 1983. **JPL:** HS 10 v Yorks (Hull) 1986.

SALVE

MILLNS, David James, b Mansfield 27 Feb 1965. LHB, RFM.

VALE

SUCH, P.M. – see LEICESTERSHIRE.

NOTTINGHAMSHIRE RECORDS

FIRST-CLASS CRICKET

Highest Total	For	739-7d		v	Leics	Nottingham	1903
	V	706-4d		by	Surrey	Nottingham	1947
Lowest Total	For	13		v	Yorkshire	Nottingham	1901
	V	{ 16		by	Derbyshire	Nottingham	1879
		{ 16		by	Surrey	The Oval	1880
Highest Innings	For	312*	W.W. Keeton	v	Middlesex	The Oval	1939
	V	345	C.G. Macartney	for	Australians	Nottingham	1921

Highest Partnerships

Wkt						
1st	391	A.O. Jones/A. Shrewsbury	v	Glos	Bristol	1899
2nd	398	W. Gunn/A. Shrewsbury	v	Sussex	Nottingham	1890
3rd	369	W. Gunn/J.R. Gunn	v	Leics	Nottingham	1903
4th	361	A.O. Jones/J.R. Gunn	v	Essex	Leyton	1905
5th	266	A. Shrewsbury/W. Gunn	v	Sussex	Hove	1884
6th	303*	F. H. Winrow/P.F. Harvey	v	Derbyshire	Nottingham	1947
7th	204	M.J. Smedley/R.A. White	v	Surrey	The Oval	1967
8th	220	G.F.H. Heane/R. Winrow	v	Somerset	Nottingham	1935
9th	165	W. McIntyre/G. Wootton	v	Kent	Nottingham	1869
10th	152	E.B. Alletson/W. Riley	v	Sussex	Hove	1911

Best Bowling	For	10-66	K. Smales	v	Glos	Stroud	1956
(Innings)	V	10-10	H. Verity	for	Yorkshire	Leeds	1932
Best Bowling	For	17-89	F.C. Matthews	v	Northants	Nottingham	1923
(Match)	V	17-89	W.G. Grace	for	Glos	Cheltenham	1877

Most Runs – Season	2,620	W.W. Whysall	(av 53.46)	1929
Most Runs – Career	31,592	G. Gunn	(av 35.69)	1902-1932
Most 100s – Season	{ 9	W.W. Whysall		1928
	{ 9	M.J. Harris		1971
Most 100s – Career	65	J. Hardstaff, jr		1930-1955
Most Wkts – Season	181	B. Dooland	(av 14.96)	1954
Most Wkts – Career	1,653	T.G. Wass	(av 20.34)	1896-1920

LIMITED-OVERS CRICKET

Highest Total	**NWT**	287-8		v	Glos	Bristol	1985
	BHC	282-4		v	Derbyshire	Derby	1984
	JPL	260-5		v	Warwicks	Birmingham	1976
Lowest Total	**NWT**	123		v	Yorkshire	Scarborough	1969
	BHC	94		v	Lancashire	Nottingham	1975
	JPL	66		v	Yorkshire	Bradford	1969
Highest Innings	**NWT**	139	R.T. Robinson	v	Worcs	Worcester	1985
	BHC	130*	C.E.B. Rice	v	Scotland	Glasgow	1982
	JPL	{ 120*	C.E.B. Rice	v	Glamorgan	Swansea	1978
		{ 120*	B. Hassan	v	Warwicks	Birmingham	1981
Best Bowling	**NWT**	6-18	C.E.B. Rice	v	Sussex	Hove	1982
	BHC	{ 6-22	M.K. Bore	v	Leics	Leicester	1980
		{ 6-22	C.E.B. Rice	v	Northants	Northampton	1981
	JPL	6-12	R.J. Hadlee	v	Lancashire	Nottingham	1980

NOTTINGHAMSHIRE 1986

RESULTS SUMMARY

	Place	Won	Lost	Drew	Abandoned
Britannic Assurance Championship	**4th**	7	2	15	
All First-class Matches		8	2	16	
John Player League	**3rd**	10	5		1
NatWest Bank Trophy	Lost to Surrey (Quarter-Final)				
Benson and Hedges Cup	Lost to Middlesex (Semi-Final)				

BRITANNIC ASSURANCE CHAMPIONSHIP AVERAGES

BATTING AND FIELDING

Cap		*M*	*I*	*NO*	*HS*	*Runs*	*Avge*	*100*	*50*	*Ct/St*
1978	R.J. Hadlee	14	18	5	129*	720	55.38	2	3	6
1983	R.T. Robinson	19	30	5	159*	1319	52.76	4	7	13
1975	C.E.B. Rice	22	31	6	156*	1118	44.72	2	5	28
—	C.W. Scott	9	8	3	69*	220	44.00	—	1	22/1
1986	P. Johnson	24	34	5	128	1156	39.86	3	4	24
1984	B.C. Broad	24	40	2	122	1476	38.84	6	6	17
—	C.D. Fraser-Darling	5	4	0	61	142	35.50	—	1	3
—	M. Newell	17	27	8	80	671	35.31	—	4	14/1
1981	J.D. Birch	19	25	6	79*	636	33.47	—	4	21
1984	K. Saxelby	9	7	4	34	99	33.00	—	—	2
1980	B.N. French	14	14	2	58	269	22.41	—	1	30/4
1973	D.W. Randall	13	21	0	60	392	18.66	—	1	13
1980	E.E. Hemmings	20	21	3	54*	300	16.66	—	1	7
1980	K.E. Cooper	16	12	5	19	105	15.00	—	—	4
—	R.A. Pick	17	15	1	55	180	12.85	—	1	4
—	J.A. Afford	14	12	7	9*	19	3.80	—	—	4
—	P.M. Such	4	4	0	6	9	2.25	—	—	2

Also batted: K.P. Evans (2 matches) 1 (1 ct); D.J.R. Martindale (2 matches) 9,4,14.

BOWLING

	O	*M*	*R*	*W*	*Avge*	*Best*	*5 wI*	*10 wM*
R.J. Hadlee	393.4	108	825	57	14.47	6-31	5	1
K.E. Cooper	374.5	98	940	41	22.93	5-102	1	—
C.E.B. Rice	413.2	115	1111	44	25.25	4-54	—	—
E.E. Hemmings	780.3	244	2014	71	28.36	7-102	5	2
K. Saxelby	240	45	763	24	31.79	4-47	—	—
R.A. Pick	419.2	75	1455	42	34.64	6-68	1	—
J.A. Afford	466.4	119	1426	41	34.78	6-81	3	1
P.M. Such	132	33	382	10	38.20	3-39	—	—
C.D. Fraser-Darling	120	16	461	12	38.41	5-84	1	—

Also bowled: J.D. Birch 11-1-24-1; B.C. Broad 7-1-41-0; K.P. Evans 15-2-73-0; P. Johnson 19-2-113-0; M. Newell 2-0-19-0; D.W. Randall 3-0-17-0; R.T. Robinson 2-0-18-0.

The First-Class Averages (pp. 167–182) give the records of Nottinghamshire players in all first-class county matches (their other opponents being the New Zealanders and Oxford U.), with the exception of R.J. Hadlee, whose full county figures are as above, and: B.N. French 15-16-3-58-306-23.53-0-1-32 ct/4 st. R.T. Robinson 20-32-5-159*-1352-50.07-4-7-15 ct. 2-0-18-0. P.M. Such 5-4-0-6-9-2.25-0-0-3 ct. 170.3-53-438-19-23.05-5/36-1-0.

SOMERSET

Formation of Present Club: 18 August 1875
Colours: Black, White and Maroon
Badge: Wessex Wyvern
Championships: (0) Third in 1892, 1958, 1963, 1966, 1981
NatWest Trophy/Gillette Cup Winners: (2) 1979, 1983
Benson and Hedges Cup Winners: (2) 1981, 1982
John Player League Champions: (1) 1979
Match Awards: NWT 35; BHC 38

Secretary: A.S. Brown, The County Ground, St. James Street, Taunton TA1 1JT
Captain: P.M. Roebuck
Scorer: D.A. Oldam
Scores/Prospects: ☎ Taunton (0823) 70007

ATKINSON, Jonathon Colin Mark (Millfield S), b Butleigh 10 July 1968. 6'3". RHB, RMF. Debut 1985. HS 79 v Northants (Weston) 1985 – on debut. BB 2-80 v Indians (Taunton) 1986. **NWT:** BB 1-16.

BAIL, Paul Andrew Clayton (Millfield S; Downing C, CU), b Burnham-on-Sea 23 Jun 1965. 5'10". RHB, OB. Debut 1985. CU debut/blue 1986. HS 174 CU v OU (Lord's) 1986. Somerset HS 78* v Kent (Canterbury) 1985. **BHC:** HS 59 Comb Us v Hants (Oxford) 1986. BB 1-20. **JPL:** HS 18 v Derbys (Taunton) 1986.

BARTLETT, Richard James (Taunton S), b Ash Priors 8 Oct 1966. 5'9". RHB. Debut 1985 scoring 117* v OU (Oxford). England YC v Sri Lanka YC 1986. HS 117* (above). **BHC:** HS 4.

CROWE, Martin David (Auckland GS), b Henderson, Auckland, NZ, 22 Sep 1962. Son of D.W. (Wellington and Canterbury); brother of J.J. (Auckland and S Australia). 6'1½". RHB, RMF. Auckland 1979-83. Central Districts 1983-87. MCC staff 1981. Somerset debut/cap 1984. **Tests** (NZ): 32 (1981-82 to 1986); HS 188 v WI (Georgetown) 1984-85 and 188 v Aus (Brisbane) 1985-86; BB 2-25 v WI (Bridgetown) 1984-85. LOI (NZ): 56. Tours (NZ): Eng 1983, 1986; Aus 1982-83, 1985-86; WI 1984-85; Pak 1984-85; SL 1983-84. 1000 runs (1+1); most 1870 (1984). HS 242* NZ v S Australia (Adelaide) 1985-86. Somerset HS 190 v Leics (Taunton) 1984. BB 5-18 Central Districts v Auckland (Auckland) 1983-84. Somerset BB 5-66 v Leics (Leicester) 1984. Awards: NWT 1; BHC 1; **NWT:** HS 114 v Sussex (Hove) 1984. BB 3-33 v Kent (Taunton) 1984. **BHC:** HS 89 v Warwicks (Birmingham) 1984. BB 4-24 v Kent (Canterbury) 1984. **JPL:** HS 78 v Kent (Bath) 1984. BB 2-14 v Derbys (Taunton) 1984.

DAVIS, Mark Richard (West Somerset S; Bridgwater C), b Kilve, Somerset 26 Feb 1962. 6'1". LHB, LFM. Debut 1982. HS 60* v Glam (Taunton) 1984. BB 7-55 v Northants (Northampton) 1984. Award: BHC 1. **NWT:** HS 6. BB 1-31. **BHC:** HS 28 v Glam (Taunton) 1985. BB 3-21 v Minor C (Shrewsbury) 1985. **JPL:** HS 11 v Middx 1982 and 11 v Glam 1985. BB 3-30 v Essex (Chelmsford) 1984.

DREDGE, Colin Herbert (Oakfield SS, Frome) b Frome 4 Aug 1954. 6'5". LHB, RMF. Debut 1976, Cap 1978. Benefit 1987. HS: 56* v Yorks (Harrogate) 1977. BB 6-37 v Glos (Bristol) 1981. Award: NWT 1. **NWT:** HS 9. BB 4-23 v Kent (Canterbury) 1978. **BHC:** HS 25* v Essex (Taunton) 1986. BB 4-10 v Hants (Bournemouth) 1980. **JPL:** HS 28* v Glam (Cardiff) 1986. BB 5-35 v Middx (Lord's) 1981.

FELTON, Nigel Alfred (Millfield S; Loughborough U), b Guildford, Surrey 24 Oct 1960. 5'8". LHB. Debut 1982. Cap 1986. 1000 runs (1): 1030 (1986). HS 173* v Kent (Taunton) 1983. Award: NWT 1. **NWT:** HS 87 v Kent (Taunton) 1984. **BHC:** HS 3. **JPL:** HS 96 v Essex (Chelmsford) 1986.

FOSTER, Daren Joseph (Somerset S; Southgate TS), b Tottenham, London 14 Mar 1966. 5'9". RHB, RFM. Debut 1986. HS 0.
GARD, Trevor (Huish Episcopi CS), b West Lambrook 2 Jun 1957. 5'7". RHB, WK. Debut 1976. Cap 1983. HS 51* v Indians (Taunton) 1979. Award: NWT 1. **NWT:** HS 17 v Shropshire (Wellington) 1983. **BHC:** HS 34 v Sussex (Hove) 1986. **JPL:** HS 19 v Hants (Taunton) 1986.
HARDEN, Richard John (King's C, Taunton), b Bridgwater 16 Aug 1965. 5'11". RHB, LM. Debut 1985. 1000 runs (1): 1093 (1986). HS 108 v Sussex (Taunton) 1986. **BHC:** HS 24 v Glam (Taunton) 1986. **JPL:** HS 71 v Notts (Bath) 1986.
HARDY, Jonathan James Ean (Canford S), b Nakaru, Kenya 2 Oct 1960. 6'3½". LHB. Hampshire 1984-85. Somerset debut 1986. HS 107* Hants v Essex (Southampton) 1985. Somerset HS 79 v Yorks (Taunton) 1986. **NWT:** HS 53 v Lancs (Taunton) 1986. **BHC:** HS 25 v Glam (Taunton) 1986. **JPL:** HS 58 Hants v Northants (Southampton) 1984.
HARMAN, Mark David (Frome C; Loughborough U), b Aylesbury, Bucks 30 June 1964. 5'11". RHB, OB. Debut 1986. HS 15 v Lancs (Manchester) 1986. BB 1-88.
MARKS, Victor James (Blundell's S; St. John's C, Oxford), b Middle Chinnock 25 Jun 1955. 5'9". RHB, OB. Oxford U/Somerset debuts 1975. Blue 1975-76-77-78; captain 1976-77. Cap 1979. W Australia 1986–87. **Tests:** 6 (1982 to 1983-84); HS 83 v Pak (Faisalabad) 1983-84; BB 3-78 v NZ (Oval) 1983. LOI: 33. Tours: Aus 1982-83; NZ 1983-84; Ind/SL 1984-85; Pak 1983-84. 1000 runs (2): most 1262 (1984). HS 134 v Worcs (Weston) 1984. BB 8-17 v Lancs (Bath) 1985. Awards: NWT 2; BHC 3. **NWT:** HS 55 v Warwicks (Taunton) 1982. BB 3-15 v Herts (St Albans) 1984. **BHC:** HS 81* v Hants (Bournemouth) 1980. BB 3-25 v Sussex (Taunton) 1982. **JPL:** HS 72 v Worcs (Taunton) 1982. BB 4-11 v Surrey (Weston) 1984.
PALMER, Gary Vincent (Queen's C), b Taunton 1 Nov 1965. 6'1". RHB, RMF. Son of K.E. (Somerset and England 1955-69) – see 1987 Umpires. Debut 1982. HS 78 v Glos (Bristol) 1983. BB 5-38 v Warwicks (Taunton) 1983. **NWT:** BB 1-47. **BHC:** HS 53 and BB 2-20 v Sussex (Hove) 1986. **JPL:** HS 33 v Worcs (Weston) 1986. BB 5-34 v Kent (Canterbury) 1985.
PRINGLE, Nicholas John (Taunton S), b Weymouth, Dorset 20 Sep 1966. 5'10½". RHB, RMF. MCC Staff. Debut 1986. HS 11 v Worcs (Worcester) 1986.
ROEBUCK, Peter Michael (Millfield S; Emmanuel C, Cambridge), b Oxford 6 Mar 1956. 6'0". RHB, LB. Brother of P.G.P. (CU and Glos 1983-85). Debut 1974. CU 1975-77; blue 1975-76-77. Cap 1978. Captain 1986. 2nd XI debut 1969 (aged 13). 1000 runs (6); most – 1702 (1984). HS 221* v Notts (Nottingham) 1986. BB 6-50 CU v Kent (Canterbury) 1977. Award: BHC 1. **NWT:** HS 98 v Sussex (Hove) 1984. **BHC:** HS 53* v Notts (Lord's) 1982. BB 2-13 v Comb Us (Taunton) 1982. **JPL:** HS 105 v Glos (Bath) 1983. BB 2-4 v Warwicks (Birmingham) 1982.
ROSE, Brian Charles (Weston-super-Mare GS; Borough Road CE, Isleworth), b Dartford, Kent 4 Jun 1950. 6'1½". LHB. LM. Debut 1969. Cap 1975. Captain 1978-83. *Wisden* 1979. Benefit 1983. **Tests:** 9 (1977-78 to 1980-81); HS 70 v WI (Manchester) 1980. LOI: 2. Tours: WI 1980-81; NZ 1977-78; Pak 1977-78. 1000 runs (8); most – 1624 (1976). HS 205 v Northants (Weston) 1977. BB 3-9 v Glos (Taunton) 1975. Awards: NWT 2; BHC 2. **NWT:** HS 128 v Derbys (Ilkeston) 1977. **BHC:** HS 137* v Kent (Canterbury) 1980. **JPL:** HS 112* v Essex (Ilford) 1980. BB 3-25 v Lancs (Manchester) 1975.
TAYLOR, Nicholas Simon (Gresham's S, Holt), b Holmfirth, Yorks 2 Jun 1963. 6'3". RHB, RFM. Son of Kenneth (Yorkshire and England). Yorkshire 1982–83. Surrey 1984-85. HS 24* v Glos (Taunton) 1986. BB 7-44 Surrey v CU (Cambridge) 1985. Somerset BB 4-40 v Essex (Taunton) 1986. **NWT:** HS 1*. BB 3-47 v Lancs (Taunton) 1986. **BHC:** HS 9. BB 5-51 v Glam (Taunton) 1986. **JPL:** HS 28 and BB 3-39 v Leics (Leicester) 1986.
WYATT, Julian George (Wells Cathedral S), b Paulton 19 Jun 1963. 5'10". RHB, RM. Debut 1983. HS 145 v OU (Oxford) 1985. BB 1-0. **NWT:** HS 3. **BHC:** HS 22 v Kent (Taunton) 1985. **JPL:** HS 48* v Middx (Taunton) 1986.

SALVETE

BURNS, Neil David (Moulsham HS, Chelmsford 19 Sep 1965. 5'10". LHB, WK. W Province B 1985-86. Essex 1986. HS 29 v Middx (Chelmsford) 1986.
JONES, Adrian Nicholas (Seaford C), b Woking, Surrey 22 Jul 1961. 6'2". LHB, RFM. Sussex 1981-86 (Cap 1986). Border 1981-82. HS 35 v Middx (Hove) 1984. BB 5-29 v Glos (Hove) 1984. Award: BHC 1. **NWT:** HS 3*. BB 4-26 v Yorks (Leeds) 1986. **BHC:** HS 20 v Middx (Lord's) 1986. BB 4-32 v Somerset (Hove) 1986. **JPL:** HS 17* and BB 7-41 v Notts (Nottingham) 1986.
MALLENDER, Neil Alan (Beverley GS), b Kirk Sandall, Yorks 13 Aug 1961. 6'0". RHB, RFM. Northamptonshire 1980-86. Cap 1984. Otago 1983-87. HS 88 Otago v Central Districts (Oamaru) 1984-85. BB 7-27 Otago v Auckland (Auckland) 1984-85. Awards: NWT 1. **NWT:** HS 11* v Yorks (Leeds) 1983. BB 7–37 v Worcs (Northampton) 1984. **BHC:** HS 7. BB 5-53 v Leics (Northampton) 1986. **JPL:** HS 22 v Warwicks 1981 and 22 v Somerset 1983. BB 5-34 v Middlesex (Tring) 1981.
PHILLIPS, Alan Russell (Millfield S), b Weston-super-Mare 4 Oct 1968. RHB, RMF.
ROSE, Graham David (Northumberland Park S, Tottenham), b Tottenham, London 12 Apr 1964. 6'4". RHB, RM. Middlesex 1985–86. HS 52 v Warwicks (Uxbridge) 1986. BB 6-41 v Worcs (Worcester) 1985 – on debut. **BHC:** HS 3. **JPL:** HS 33 v Notts (Cleethorpes) 1983. BB 2-31 v Derbys (Derby) 1986.
TRUMP, Harvey Russell John (Millfield S), Taunton 11 Oct 1968. 6'0". RHB, OB. England YC to Sri Lanka 1987.

VALETE

BLITZ, Rayner John (Gaynes S, Upminster), b Watford, Herts, 25 Mar 1968. 5'4". RHB, WK. Debut 1986. HS 18 v Hants (Bournemouth) 1986.
BOTHAM, I.T. see WORCESTERSHIRE.
COOMBS, R.V.J. see SUSSEX.
GARNER, Joel (Boys' Foundation S, Christ Church), b Christ Church, Barbados 16 Dec 1952. 6'8". RHB, RF. Barbados 1975-86. Somerset debut 1977. Cap 1979. *Wisden* 1979. S Australia 1982-83. MBE 1985. **Tests** (WI): 56 (1976-77 to 1985-86); HS 60 v Aus (Brisbane) 1979-80; BB 6-56 v NZ (Auckland) 1979-80. LOI: 87. Tours (WI): Eng 1980, 1984; Aus 1979-80, 1981-82, 1984-85, 1986-87; NZ 1979–80; Pak 1980-81. HS 104 WI v Glos (Bristol) 1980. Somerset HS 90 v Glos (Bath) 1981. BB 8-31 v Glam (Cardiff) 1977. Awards: NWT 2; BHC 2.
RICHARDS, Isaac **Vivian** Alexander (Antigua GS), b St John's, Antigua 7 Mar 1952. 5'11". RHB, OB. Leeward Islands 1971-86. Somerset debut/cap 1974. *Wisden* 1976. Queensland 1976-77. Benefit 1982. **Tests** (WI): 85 (1974-75 to 1986-87, 14 as captain); HS 291 v Eng (Oval) 1976; BB 2-20 v Pak (Lahore) 1980-81. LOI (WI): 120. Tours (WI) (C=Captain): Eng 1976, 1980, 1984; Aus 1975-76, 1979-80, 1981-82, 1984-85, 1986-87C; Ind 1974-75, 1983-84; Pak 1974-75, 1980-81, 1986-87C; SL 1974-75. 1000 runs (12+3); most – 2161 (1977). HS 322 v Warwicks (Taunton) 1985. BB 5-88 WI v Queensland (Brisbane) 1981-82. Somerset BB 4-55 v Glam (Taunton) 1981. Awards: NWT 4; BHC 6.
TURNER, Murray Stewart (Richard Huish GS), b Shaftesbury 27 Jan 1964. 6'2". RHB, RFM. Somerset debut 1984. HS 24* and BB 4-74 v Warwicks (Taunton) 1985.

SOMERSET RECORDS

FIRST-CLASS CRICKET

Highest Total	For	675-9d		v	Hampshire	Bath	1924
	V	811		by	Surrey	The Oval	1899
Lowest Total	For	25		v	Glos	Bristol	1947
	V	22		by	Glos	Bristol	1920
Highest Innings	For	322	I.V.A. Richards	v	Warwicks	Taunton	1985
	V	424	A.C. MacLaren	for	Lancashire	Taunton	1895

Highest Partnerships

Wkt						
1st	346	H.T. Hewett/L.C.H. Parlairet	v	Yorkshire	Taunton	1892
2nd	290	J.C.W. MacBryan/M.D. Lyon	v	Derbyshire	Buxton	1924
3rd	319	P.M. Roebuck/M.D. Crowe	v	Leics	Taunton	1984
4th	310	P.W. Denning/I.T. Botham	v	Glos	Taunton	1980
5th	235	J.C. White/C.C.C. Case	v	Glos	Taunton	1927
6th	265	W.E. Alley/K.E. Palmer	v	Northants	Northampton	1961
7th	240	S.M.J. Woods/V.T. Hill	v	Kent	Taunton	1898
8th	172	I.V.A. Richards/I.T. Botham	v	Leics	Leicester	1983
9th	183	C.H.M. Greetham/ H.W. Stephenson	v	Leics	Weston-s-Mare	1963
10th	143	J.J. Bridges/A.H.D. Gibbs	v	Essex	Weston-s-Mare	1919

Best Bowling (Innings)	For	10-49	E.J. Tyler	v	Surrey	Taunton	1895
	V	10-35	A. Drake	for	Yorkshire	Weston-s-Mare	1914
Best Bowling (Match)	For	16-83	J.C. White	v	Worcs	Bath	1919
	V	17-137	W. Brearley	for	Lancashire	Manchester	1905

Most Runs – Season	2,761	W.E. Alley	(av 58.74)	1961
Most Runs – Career	21,142	H. Gimblett	(av 36.96)	1935-1954
Most 100s – Season	10	W.E. Alley		1961
Most 100s – Career	49	H. Gimblett		1935-1954
Most Wkts – Season	169	A.W. Wellard	(av 19.24)	1938
Most Wkts – Career	2,166	J.C. White	(av 18.02)	1909-1937

LIMITED-OVERS CRICKET

Highest Total	NWT	330-4		v	Glamorgan	Cardiff	1978
	BHC	307-6		v	Glos	Taunton	1982
	JPL	286-7		v	Hampshire	Taunton	1981
Lowest Total	NWT	59		v	Middlesex	Lord's	1977
	BHC	98		v	Middlesex	Lord's	1982
	JPL	58		v	Essex	Chelmsford	1977
Highest Innings	NWT	145	P.W. Denning	v	Glamorgan	Cardiff	1978
	BHC	137*	B.C. Rose	v	Kent	Canterbury	1980
	JPL	175*	I.T. Botham	v	Northants	Wellingborough	1986
Best Bowling	NWT	6-29	J. Garner	v	Northants	Lord's	1979
	BHC	5-14	J. Garner	v	Surrey	Lord's	1981
	JPL	6-24	I.V.A. Richards	v	Lancashire	Manchester	1983

SOMERSET 1986

RESULTS SUMMARY

	Place	Won	Lost	Drew	Abandoned
Britannic Assurance Championship	**16th**	3	7	13	1
All First-class Matches		3	7	15	1
John Player League	**6th**	8	6		2
NatWest Bank Trophy	Lost to Lancashire (2nd Round)				
Benson and Hedges Cup	Failed to qualify for Quarter-Final				

BRITANNIC ASSURANCE CHAMPIONSHIP AVERAGES

BATTING AND FIELDING

Cap		M	I	NO	HS	Runs	Avge	100	50	Ct/St
1978	P.M. Roebuck	20	32	8	221*	1261	52.54	4	5	10
1979	V.J. Marks	23	33	11	110	1029	46.77	1	7	9
1975	B.C. Rose	13	22	5	129	784	46.11	2	3	3
1976	I.T. Botham	12	19	1	139	804	44.66	2	4	8
1974	I.V.A. Richards	18	28	1	136	1174	43.48	4	5	19
—	R.J. Bartlett	4	6	1	43	171	34.20	—	—	2
—	R.J. Harden	21	34	3	108	1053	33.96	2	6	12
—	J.J.E. Hardy	17	26	0	79	779	29.96	—	8	12
1986	N.A. Felton	21	34	3	156*	898	28.96	2	5	8
—	M.R. Davis	8	7	4	21*	60	20.00	—	—	2
1979	J. Garner	18	15	4	47	182	16.54	—	—	8
—	J.C.M. Atkinson	3	4	1	16*	49	16.33	—	—	—
—	R.V.J. Coombs	8	5	3	18	30	15.00	—	—	3
1983	T. Gard	19	24	6	36	228	12.66	—	—	29/5
1978	C.H. Dredge	16	20	2	40	215	11.94	—	—	7
—	M.D. Harman	3	5	2	15	27	9.00	—	—	1
—	R.J. Blitz	4	4	0	18	33	8.25	—	—	8
—	J.G. Wyatt	3	5	0	20	41	8.20	—	—	—
—	N.S. Taylor	14	16	5	24*	87	7.90	—	—	2
—	G.V. Palmer	3	5	0	17	29	5.80	—	—	1

Also batted: P.A.C. Bail (2 matches) 55,47,0; D.J. Foster (1 match) 0; N.J. Pringle (1 match) 10,11; M.S. Turner (1 match) did not bat.

BOWLING

	O	M	R	W	Avge	Best	5 wI	10 wM
J. Garner	419	95	1091	47	23.21	5-56	1	—
C.H. Dredge	385	81	1146	34	33.70	3-10	—	—
V.J. Marks	719.5	191	2046	57	35.89	8-100	2	1
N.S. Taylor	314.2	57	1141	28	40.75	4-40	—	—
I.T. Botham	285.1	61	961	22	43.68	6-125	1	—
R.V.J. Coombs	247.5	56	807	16	50.43	3-60	—	—
M.R. Davis	163.3	18	630	10	63.00	2-43	—	—

Also bowled: J.C.M. Atkinson 10-1-52-0; N.A. Felton 1-0-3-0; D.J. Foster 5-0-29-0; R.J. Harden 39-3-153-2; J.J.E. Hardy 1-0-5-0; M.D. Harman 60.3-12-149-1; G.V. Palmer 63-7-231-4; N.J. Pringle 10-0-48-0; I.V.A. Richards 161-32-500-9; P.M. Roebuck 24-3-120-1; B.C. Rose 11-0-57-2; M.S. Turner 15-3-55-2.

The First-Class Averages (pp. 167–182) give the records of Somerset players in all first-class county matches (their other opponents being the Indians and Oxford U.), with the exception of P.A.C. Bail and I.T. Botham whose full county figures are as above.

SURREY

Formation of Present Club: 22 August 1845
Colours: Chocolate
Badge: Prince of Wales' Feathers
Championships (since 1890): (15) 1890, 1891, 1892, 1894, 1895, 1899, 1914, 1952, 1953, 1954, 1955, 1956, 1957, 1958, 1971.
Joint Championships: (1) 1950
NatWest Trophy/Gillette Cup Winners: (1) 1982
Benson and Hedges Cup Winners: (1) 1974
John Player League Champions: (0) Fifth 1969, 1980
Match Awards: NWT 27; BHC 37

Secretary: I.F.B. Scott-Browne, Kennington Oval, London SE11 5SS
Captain: I.A. Greig
Scorer: T. Billson
Scores/Prospects: ☎ London (01) 735 4911

BICKNELL, Martin Paul (Robert Haining SS), b Guildford 14 Jan 1969. 6'3". RHB, RFM. Debut 1986. England YC v Sri Lanka YC 1986 and to Sri Lanka 1987. HS 9*. BB 3-27 v Leics (Oval) 1986. **NWT:** HS 2 and BB 2-36 v Cheshire (Birkenhead) 1986. **JPL:** HS 13 v Northants (Tring) 1986. BB 2-19 v Hants (Oval) 1986.

BROWN, Graham Elliott (Spencer Park S, Wandsworth; South London C), b Balham, London 11 Oct 1966. 5'7". RHB, WK. Debut 1986. HS 2*.

BULLEN, Christopher Keith (Rutlish S, Merton) b Clapham 5 Nov 1962. 6'4½". RHB, OB. Debut 1982. HS 19 v Glos (Oval) 1985. BB 2-36 v CU (Cambridge) 1985. **JPL:** HS 10 v Kent (Oval) 1985. BB 2-18 v Essex (Chelmsford) 1986.

CLARKE, Sylvester Theophilus (St Bartholomew's BS), b Christ Church, Barbados 11 Dec 1954. 6'1". RHB, RF. Barbados 1977-1982. Surrey debut 1979. Cap 1980. Benefit 1987. Transvaal 1983-86. **Tests** (WI): 11 (1977-78 to 1981-82); HS 35* v Pak (Faisalabad) 1980-81; BB 5-126 v Ind (Bangalore) 1978-79. LOI (WI): 10. Tours (WI): Aus 1981-82; SA (WI XI) 1982-83, 1983-84; Ind/SL 1978-79; Pak 1980-81. HS 100* v Glam (Swansea) 1981. BB 7-34 WI XI v SA XI (Johannesburg) 1982-83. Surrey BB 7-53 v Warwicks (Oval) 1983. Awards: NWT 1; BHC 2. **NWT:** HS 45* v Leics (Oval) 1981. BB 4-21 v Lancs (Oval) 1986. **BHC:** HS 39 v Hants (Southampton) 1982. BB 5-23 v Kent (Oval) 1980. **JPL:** HS 34* v Hants (Oval) 1980. BB 3-18 v Somerset (Weston) 1984.

CLINTON, Grahame Selvey (Chislehurst and Sidcup GS), b Sidcup 5 May 1953. 5'10". LHB, RM. Kent 1974-78. Surrey debut 1979. Cap 1980. Rhodesia 1979-80. 1000 runs (5); most – 1240 (1980). HS 192 v Yorks (Oval) 1984. BB 2-8 Kent v Pak (Canterbury) 1978. Awards: BHC 3. **NWT:** HS 146 v Kent (Canterbury) 1985. **BHC:** HS 106* v Middx (Lord's) 1985. **JPL:** HS 105* v Yorks (Scarborough) 1981.

FALKNER, Nicholas James (Reigate GS), b Redhill 30 Sep 1962. 5'10". RHB, RM. Debut 1984 scoring 101* v CU (Banstead). HS 102 v Middx (Uxbridge) 1986. BB 1-3. **NWT:** HS 36 v Derbys (Derby) 1986. **BHC:** HS 2. **JPL:** HS 44 v Glos (Oval) 1985.

FELTHAM, Mark Andrew (Tiffin S), b St John's Wood, London 26 Jun 1963. 6'2½". RHB, RM. Debut 1983. HS 76 v Glos (Oval) 1986. BB 5-62 v Warwicks (Birmingham) 1984. **NWT:** HS 12 v Lancs (Oval) 1986. BB 2-27 v Cheshire (Birkenhead) 1986. **BHC:** HS 22* v Hants (Oval) 1984. BB 3-25 v Glos (Oval) 1984. **JPL:** HS 37 and BB 4-35 v Sussex (Guildford) 1986.

GRAY, Anthony Hollis (Malick SS), b Port-of-Spain, Trinidad 23 May 1963. 6'7". RHB, RF. Debut (N/E Trinidad in Beaumont Cup) 1983-84. Trinidad 1984-86 Surrey debut/cap 1985. **Tests** (WI): 3 (1986-87); HS 12* and BB 4-39 v Pak (Faisalabad) 1986-87. LOI (WI): 12. Tours (WI): Aus 1986-87; Pak 1986-87. HS 54* Trinidad v Leeward Is (Basseterre) 1985-86. Surrey HS 28 v Kent (Oval) 1986. BB 8-40 v Yorks (Sheffield) 1985. **NWT:** HS 3 and BB 3-23 v Cheshire (Birkenhead) 1986. **JPL:** HS 24* v Essex (Chelmsford) 1986. BB 4-21 v Leics (Oval) 1986.

JESTY, Trevor Edward (Privet County SS, Gosport), b Gosport 2 Jun 1948. 5'8½". RHB, RM. Hampshire 1966-84 (Cap 1971; benefit 1982). Border 1973-74. GW 1974-76, 1980-81. Canterbury 1979-80. *Wisden* 1982. Surrey debut/cap 1985. Captain 1985. LOI: 10. Tours: WI 1982-83 (Int XI); Aus/NZ 1982-83 (no f-c matches). 1000 runs (8); most – 1645 (1982). HS 248 Hants v CU (Cambridge) 1984. Surrey HS 221 v Essex (Oval) 1986. BB 7-75 Hants v Worcs (Southampton) 1976. Surrey BB 2-32 v Kent (Canterbury) 1985. Awards: NWT 6; BHC 9. **NWT:** HS 118 Hants v Derbys (Derby) 1980. BB 6-46 Hants v Glos (Bristol) 1979. **BHC:** HS 105 Hants v Glam (Swansea) 1977. BB 4-22 Hants v Minor C (Southampton) 1981. **JPL:** HS 166* Hants v Surrey (Portsmouth) 1983. BB 6-20 Hants v Glam (Cardiff) 1976.

LYNCH, Monte Alan (Ryden's S, Walton-on-Thames), b Georgetown, British Guiana 21 May 1958. 5'8". RHB, RM/OB. Debut 1977. Cap 1982. Guyana 1982-83. Tours: SA 1983-84 (WI XI); Pak 1981-82 (Int XI). 1000 runs (5); most – 1714 (1985). HS 152 v Notts (Oval) 1986. BB 3-6 v Glam (Swansea) 1981. Awards: NWT 1; BHC 1. **NWT:** HS 129 v Durham (Oval) 1982. BB 1-25. **BHC:** HS 85 v Comb Us (Oxford) 1984. **JPL:** HS 136 v Yorks (Bradford) 1985.

MEDLYCOTT, Keith Thomas (Parmiters GS, Wandsworth), b Whitechapel, London 12 May 1965. 5'11". RHB, SLA. Debut 1984 scoring 117* v CU (Banstead). BB 6-63 v Kent (Oval) 1986.

RICHARDS, Clifton James (**'Jack'**) (Humphrey Davy GS, Penzance) b Penzance, Cornwall 10 Aug 1958. 5'11". RHB, WK, OB. Debut 1976. Cap 1978. OFS 1983-84. **Tests:** 5 (1986-87); HS 133 v Aus (Perth) 1986-87. LOI: 9. Tours: Aus 1986-87; WI 1982-83 (Int XI); NZ 1979-80 (DHR); Ind/SL 1981-82. 1000 runs (1): 1006 (1986). HS 117* v Notts (Oval) 1982. BB 2-42 v Somerset (Oval) 1985. Awards: NWT 2. **NWT:** HS 105* v Lincs (Sleaford) 1983. **BHC:** HS 45 v Kent (Canterbury) 1986. **JPL:** HS 55* v Glos (Bristol) 1986.

STEWART, Alec James (Tiffin S) b Merton 8 Apr 1963. 5'11". RHB, WK. Son of M.J. (Surrey and England 1954-72). Debut 1981. Cap 1985. 1000 runs (2): most 1665 (1986). HS 166 v Kent (Oval) 1986. Award: BHC 1. **NWT:** HS 37 v Kent (Canterbury) 1985. **BHC:** HS 63* v Comb Us (Oval) 1986. **JPL:** HS 86 v Warwicks (Oval) 1985.

THOMAS, David James (Licensed Victuallers' S, Slough), b Solihull 30 Jun 1959. 6'0". LHB, LFM. Debut 1977. Cap 1982. N Transvaal 1980-81. Natal 1983-84. HS 119 v Notts (Oval) 1983. BB 6-36 v Somerset (Oval) 1984. Award: NWT 1. **NWT:** HS 65 v Notts (Oval) 1986. BB 3-16 v Durham (Oval) 1982. **BHC:** HS 19 v Notts (Nottingham) 1984. BB 3-30 v Leics (Oval) 1981. **JPL:** HS 72 v Glam (Swansea) 1983. BB 4-13 v Sussex (Oval) 1978.

WARD, David Mark (Haling Manor HS), b Croydon 10 Feb 1961. 6'1". RHB, OB. Debut 1985. HS 143 v Derbys (Derby) 1985. **JPL:** HS 59* v Worcs (Oval) 1984.

SALVETE

ATKINS, Paul David (Aylesbury GS), b Aylesbury, Bucks 11 Jun 1966. RHB.

BICKNELL, Darren John, b Guildford 24 Jun 1967. Brother of M.P. LHB, LM.

GREIG, Ian Alexander (Queen's S, Queenstown; Downing C, Cambridge), b Queenstown, S Africa 8 Dec 1955. 5'11½". RHB, RMF. Brother of A.W. (Border, Sussex, E Province and England 1965-78). Border 1974-75, 1979-80. Griqualand West 1975-76. Cambridge U 1977-79 (blue 1977-78-79; Captain 1979). Sussex 1980-85 (Cap 1981). Surrey captain 1987. Tests: 2 (1982); HS 14 and BB 4-53 v Pak (Birmingham). HS 147* v OU (Oxford) 1983. BB 7-43 v CU (Cambridge) 1981. Awards: NWT 1; BHC 1.

KENDRICK, Neil Michael, b Bromley, Kent 11 Nov 1967. RHB, SLA.

ROBINSON, Jonathan David (Lancing C; Chichester CE), b Epsom 3 Aug 1966. LHB, RM.

SADIQ, Zahid Asa (Rutlish S), Nairobi, Kenya 6 May 1965. 5'10". RHB.

VALETE

DOUGHTY, Richard James (Scarborough C), b Bridlington, Yorks 17 Nov 1960. 6'0". RHB, RFM. Gloucestershire 1981-84. Surrey debut 1985. HS 65 v Derbys (Derby) 1985. BB 6-33 v Warwicks (Oval) 1985.

MONKHOUSE, Graham (Penrith Queen Elizabeth GS; Notts C of Agriculture), b Langwathby, Cumberland 26 Apr 1955. 6'1". RHB, RMF. Debut 1981. Cap 1984. Cumberland 1973-79. Tour: Zim 1984-85 (Eng Co). HS 100* v Kent (Oval) 1984. BB 7-51 v Notts (Oval) 1983. Soccer: Carlisle United and Workington Town.

POCOCK, Patrick Ian ('Percy') (Merton SS; Wimbledon TC), b Bangor, Caernarvonshire 24 Sep 1946. 6'1". RHB, OB. Debut 1964. Cap 1967. Benefit 1977. Testimonial 1986. Captain 1986. N Transvaal 1971-72. **Tests:** 25 (1967-68 to 1984-85); HS 33 v Pak (Hyderabad) 1972-73; BB 6-79 v Aus (Manchester) 1968. LOI: 1. Tours: WI 1967-68, 1973-74; Ind 1972-73, 1984-85; Pak 1966-67 (MCC U-25), 1968-69, 1970-71 (RW), 1972-73; SL 1968-69, 1969-70, 1972-73, 1984-85. 100 wickets (1): 112 (1967). Set world records v Sussex (Eastbourne) 1972 by taking 6 wickets in 9 balls and 7 in 11 (including 4 in 4 and 5 in 6). HS 75* v Notts (Oval) 1968. BB 9-57 v Glam (Cardiff) 1979. Awards: BHC 2.

NEEDHAM, A. – see MIDDLESEX.

WINTERBORNE, Gary (George Abbot S, Guildford), b Hammersmith, London 26 June 1967. 6'0". RHB, RM. Debut 1986 (did not bat).

SURREY RECORDS

FIRST-CLASS CRICKET

Highest Total	For	811		v	Somerset	The Oval	1899
	V	705-8d		by	Sussex	Hastings	1902
Lowest Total	For	14		v	Essex	Chelmsford	1983
	V	16		by	MCC	Lord's	1872
Highest Innings	For	357*	R. Abel	v	Somerset	The Oval	1899
	V	300*	F.B. Watson	for	Lancashire	Manchester	1928
		300	R. Subba Row	for	Northants	The Oval	1958

Highest Partnerships

Wkt						
1st	428	J.B. Hobbs/A. Sandham	v	Oxford U	The Oval	1926
2nd	371	J.B. Hobbs/E.G. Hayes	v	Hampshire	The Oval	1909
3rd	353	A. Ducat/E.G. Hayes	v	Hampshire	Southampton	1919
4th	448	R. Abel/T.W. Hayward	v	Yorkshire	The Oval	1899
5th	308	J.N. Crawford/F.C. Holland	v	Somerset	The Oval	1908
6th	298	A. Sandham/H.S. Harrison	v	Sussex	The Oval	1913
7th	200	T.F. Shepherd/J.W. Hitch	v	Kent	Blackheath	1921
8th	204	T.W. Hayward/L.C. Braund	v	Lancashire	The Oval	1898
9th	168	E.R.T. Holmes/E.W.J. Brooks	v	Hampshire	The Oval	1936
10th	173	A. Ducat/A. Sandham	v	Essex	Leyton	1921

Best Bowling (Innings)	For	10-43	T. Rushby	v	Somerset	Taunton	1921
	V	10-28	W.P. Howell	for	Australians	The Oval	1899
Best Bowling (Match)	For	16-83	G.A.R. Lock	v	Kent	Blackheath	1956
	V	15-57	W.P. Howell	for	Australians	The Oval	1899

Most Runs – Season	3,246	T.W. Hayward	(av 72.13)	1906
Most Runs – Career	43,554	J.B. Hobbs	(av 49.72)	1905-1934
Most 100s – Season	13	T.W. Hayward		1906
	13	J.B. Hobbs		1925
Most 100s – Career	144	J.B. Hobbs		1905-1934
Most Wkts – Season	252	T. Richardson	(av 13.94)	1895
Most Wkts – Career	1,775	T. Richardson	(av 17.87)	1892-1904

LIMITED-OVERS CRICKET

Highest Total	**NWT**	297-6		v	Lincs	Sleaford	1983
	BHC	276-6		v	Essex	The Oval	1982
	JPL	304-6		v	Warwicks	The Oval	1985
Lowest Total	**NWT**	74		v	Kent	The Oval	1967
	BHC	89		v	Notts	Nottingham	1984
	JPL	64		v	Worcs	Worcester	1978
Highest Innings	**NWT**	146	G.S. Clinton	v	Kent	Canterbury	1985
	BHC	115	G.R.J. Roope	v	Essex	Chelmsford	1973
	JPL	136	M.A. Lynch	v	Yorkshire	Bradford	1985
Best Bowling	**NWT**	7-33	R.D. Jackman	v	Yorkshire	Harrogate	1970
	BHC	5-21	P.H.L. Wilson	v	Comb Univs	The Oval	1979
	JPL	6-25	Intikhab Alam	v	Derbyshire	The Oval	1974

SURREY 1986

RESULTS SUMMARY

	Place	Won	Lost	Drew	Tied	Aban
Britannic Assurance Championship	**3rd**	8	6	10		
All First-class Matches		8	6	11		
John Player League	**12th**	5	8		1	2
NatWest Bank Trophy	Lost to Lancashire (Semi-Final)					
Benson and Hedges Cup	Failed to qualify for Quarter-Final					

BRITANNIC ASSURANCE CHAMPIONSHIP AVERAGES

BATTING AND FIELDING

Cap		*M*	*I*	*NO*	*HS*	*Runs*	*Avge*	*100*	*50*	*Ct/St*
1985	A.J. Stewart	24	38	3	166	1629	46.54	3	14	15
1978	C.J. Richards	23	34	9	115	1006	40.24	2	5	39/5
—	N.J. Falkner	11	18	2	102	567	35.43	1	2	7
1982	M.A. Lynch	24	38	3	152	1201	34.31	3	5	38
1985	T.E. Jesty	19	29	1	221	955	34.10	2	4	9
1980	G.S. Clinton	22	34	4	117	1004	33.46	1	6	10
1982	D.J. Thomas	9	12	4	47*	222	27.75	—	—	1
—	M.A. Feltham	11	13	4	76	217	24.11	—	1	1
—	R.J. Doughty	14	18	2	61	366	22.87	—	1	10
1984	G. Monkhouse	10	12	4	51	162	20.25	—	1	6
—	D.M. Ward	4	6	1	34	100	20.00	—	—	1
1975	A.R. Butcher	15	24	0	71	477	19.87	—	3	5
1985	A. Needham	10	16	2	52	256	18.28	—	1	5
1980	S.T. Clarke	13	12	3	32*	156	17.33	—	—	7
—	K.T. Medlycott	13	14	2	61	170	14.16	—	1	8
1985	A.H. Gray	11	14	2	28	108	9.00	—	—	4
1967	P.I. Pocock	21	20	9	16*	93	8.45	—	—	6
—	M.P. Bicknell	9	10	2	9*	21	2.62	—	—	4

Also batted: G.E. Brown (1 match) 0*,2* (4 ct, 1 st).

BOWLING

	O	*M*	*R*	*W*	*Avge*	*Best*	*5 wI*	*10 wM*
S.T. Clarke	341.3	95	806	48	16.79	5-31	3	—
A.H. Gray	342.3	69	966	51	18.94	7-23	3	1
M.P. Bicknell	196	43	600	27	22.22	3-27	—	—
K.T. Medlycott	309.4	71	1077	36	29.91	6-63	3	1
M.A. Feltham	191	32	741	23	32.21	4-47	—	—
R.J. Doughty	279	46	1056	31	34.06	4-52	—	—
P.I. Pocock	394.5	107	1095	30	36.50	4-45	—	—
G. Monkhouse	233.1	69	589	14	42.07	4-37	—	—
D.J. Thomas	166.3	29	588	12	49.00	2-44	—	—

Also bowled: A.R. Butcher 68-12-249-6; G.S. Clinton 3-1-12-0; N.J. Falkner 4-1-9-1; T.E. Jesty 59-21-155-5; M.A. Lynch 23.2-2-119-2; A. Needham 67-21-163-0; C.J. Richards 5-0-34-1; A.J. Stewart 5-0-55-0.

The First-Class Averages (pp. 167–182) give the records of Surrey players in all first-class county matches, their other opponents being Cambridge U.

SUSSEX

Formation of Present Club: 1 March 1839
Substantial Reorganisation: August 1857
Colours: Dark Blue, Light Blue and Gold
Badge: County Arms of Six Martlets
Championships: (0) Runners up 1902, 1903, 1932, 1933, 1934, 1953, 1981
NatWest Trophy/Gillette Cup Winners: (4) 1963, 1964, 1978, 1986
Benson and Hedges Cup Winners: (0) Semi-Finalists 1982
John Player League Champions: (1) 1982
Match Awards: NWT 39; BHC 34

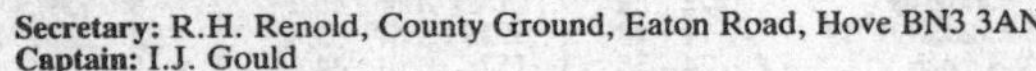

Secretary: R.H. Renold, County Ground, Eaton Road, Hove BN3 3AN
Captain: I.J. Gould
Scorer: L.V. Chandler
Scores/Prospects: ☎ Brighton (0273) 772766

ALIKHAN, Rehan Iqbal (**'Ray'**) (KCS, Wimbledon), b Westminster Hospital, London 28 Dec 1962. 6'1½". RHB. Debut 1986. HS 72 v Derbys (Eastbourne) 1986. **NWT:** HS 41 v Worcs (Worcester) 1986. **JPL:** HS 10 v Northants (Hastings) 1986.

BABINGTON, Andrew Mark (Reigate GS; Borough Road PE College), b Middlesex Hospital, London 22 Jul 1963. 6'2". LHB, RFM. Debut 1986. HS 1. BB 4-18 (including hat-trick) v Glos (Bristol) 1986. **NWT:** HS 4*. BB 2-9 v Suffolk (Hove) 1986. **JPL:** BB 1-39.

GOULD, Ian James (Westgate SS, Cippenham), b Slough, Bucks 19 Aug 1957. 5'8". LHB, WK. Middlesex 1975-80 (cap 1977). Auckland 1979-80. Sussex debut/cap 1981. Captain 1987. LOI: 18. Tours: Aus 1982-83; Pak 1980-81 (Int XI); Zim 1980-81 (Middx). HS 128 Middx v Worcs (Worcester) 1978. Sussex HS 101 v Leics (Hove) 1985. BB 2-67 v Derbys (Eastbourne) 1986. Awards: NWT 1; BHC 2. **NWT:** HS 88 v Yorks (Leeds) 1986. **BHC:** HS 72 v Kent (Hove) 1982. **JPL:** HS 69* v Hants (Basingstoke) 1981.

GREEN, Allan Michael (Knoll S, Hove; Brighton SFC), b Pulborough 28 May 1960. 5'11". RHB, RM. Debut 1980. Cap 1985. OFS 1984-87. 1000 runs (3); most – 1646 (1985). HS 179 v Glam (Cardiff) 1986. BB 4-59 OFS v N Transvaal (Bloemfontein) 1986–87. Sussex BB 2-20 Glamorgan (Hove) 1985. Award: NWT 1. **NWT:** HS 102 v Glam (Hove) 1986. **BHC:** HS 50 v Essex (Hove) 1986. BB 1-4. **JPL:** HS 83 v Derbys (Heanor) 1984.

IMRAN KHAN NIAZI (Aitchison C, and Cathedral S, Lahore; Worcester RGS; Keble C, Oxford), b Lahore, Pakistan 25 Nov 1952. 6'0". RHB, RF. Lahore, Dawood Industries, and PIA since 1969-70. Worcestershire 1971-76 (cap 1976). Oxford U 1973-75 (blue 1973-74-75; captain 1974). Sussex debut 1977. Cap 1978. *Wisden* 1982. Benefit 1987. **Tests** (Pak): 60 (1971 to 1986-87, 20 as captain); HS 123 v WI (Lahore) 1980-81; BB 8-58 (14-116 match) v SL (Faisalabad) 1981-82. LOI (Pak): 83. Tours (Pak) (C = captain): Eng 1971, 1974, 1982C; Aus 1976-77, 1978-79, 1981-82, 1983-84C; WI 1976-77; NZ 1978-79; Ind 1979-80, 1986–87C; SL 1975-76; 1985-86C. 1000 runs (4); most – 1339 (1978). HS 170 OU v Northants

(Oxford) 1974. Sussex HS 167 v Glos (Hove) 1978. BB 8-34 v Middx (Lord's) 1986. Awards: NWT 7; BHC 8. **NWT:** HS 114* v Notts (Hove) 1983. BB 4-27 v Staffs (Stone) 1978. **BHC:** HS 112* v Essex (Hove) 1986. BB 5-8 v Northants (Northampton) 1978. **JPL:** HS 104* v Hants (Hove) 1985. BB 5-29 Worcs v Leics (Leicester) 1973.

LENHAM, Neil John (Brighton C), b Worthing 17 Dec 1965. 5'11". RHB, RMF. Son of L.J. (Sussex 1956-70). Debut 1984. HS 89 v Kent (Canterbury) 1985. BB 4-85 v Leics (Leicester) 1986. Award: BHC 1. **NWT:** HS 6. BB 1-48. **BHC:** HS 82 v Somerset (Hove) 1986. **JPL:** HS 7*.

LE ROUX, Garth Stirling (Wynberg BHS; Stellenbosch U), b Kenilworth, Cape Town, SA 4 Sep 1955. 6'3". RHB, RFM. Western Province 1975-87. Sussex debut 1978. Cap 1981. HS 86 W Province v Border (Cape Town) 1986-87. Sussex HS 83 v Surrey (Hove) 1982. BB 8-107 v Somerset (Taunton) 1981. Awards: BHC 2. **NWT:** HS 39* v Yorks (Leeds) 1986. BB 5-7 (including hat-trick) v Ireland (Hove) 1985. **BHC:** HS 50 v Yorks (Hove) 1984. BB 4-22 v Hants (Hove) 1983. **JPL:** HS 88 v Glam (Hastings) 1982. BB 4-18 v Notts (Hove) 1982.

MAYS, Christopher Sean (Lancing C; Middlesex Hospital Medical S), b Brighton 11 May 1966. 5'9". RHB, OB. Debut 1986. HS 8*. BB 3-77 v NZ (Hove) 1986. England YC to West Indies 1985.

MOORES, Peter (King Edward VI S, Macclesfield), b Macclesfield, Cheshire 18 Dec 1962. 6'0". RHB, WK. Worcestershire 1983-84. Sussex debut 1985. HS 45 Worcs v Somerset (Weston) 1984. **JPL:** HS 14* Worcs v Northants (Wellingborough) 1984.

PARKER, Paul William Giles (Collyer's GS; St Catharine's C, Cambridge), b Bulawayo, Rhodesia 15 Jan 1956. 5'10". RHB, RM. CU and Sussex debuts 1976. Blue 1976-77-78. Cap 1979. YC 1979. Benefit 1988. **Tests:** 1 (1981); HS 13 v Aus (Oval). 1000 runs (7); most – 1692 (1984). HS 215 CU v Essex (Cambridge) 1976. Sussex HS 181 v Sri Lankans (Hove) 1981. BB 2-21 v Surrey (Guildford) 1984. Awards: NWT 3; BHC 3. **NWT:** HS 109 v Ireland (Hove) 1985. BB 1-10. **BHC:** HS 77 v Hants (Bournemouth) 1982. **JPL:** HS 121* v Northants (Hastings) 1983. BB 1-2.

PIGOTT, Anthony Charles Shackleton (Harrow S), b London 4 Jun 1958. 6'1". RHB, RFM. Debut 1978. Cap 1982. Tour: NZ 1979-80 (DHR). Wellington 1982-84. **Tests:** 1 (1983-84); HS 8* and BB 2-75 v NZ (Christchurch) 1983-84. HS 104* v Warwicks (Birmingham) 1986. BB 7-74 v Northants (Eastbourne) 1982. **NWT:** HS 30 v Northants (Hove) 1979. BB 3-4 v Ireland (Hove) 1985. **BHC:** HS 21 v Somerset (Hove) 1986. BB 3-33 v Hants 1982 and 3-33 v Somerset 1986. **JPL:** HS 49 v Warwicks (Hove) 1979. BB 5-24 v Lancs (Manchester) 1986.

REEVE, Dermot Alexander (King George V S, Kowloon), b Kowloon, Hong Kong 2 Apr 1963. 6'0". RHB, RMF. Debut 1983. Cap 1986. Hong Kong 1982 (ICC Trophy). HS 119 v Surrey (Guildford) 1984. BB 5-22 v CU (Cambridge) 1984. Awards: NWT 2. **NWT:** HS 16* v Ireland (Dublin) 1983. BB 4-20 v Lancs (Lord's) 1986. **BHC:** HS 21* v Somerset (Hove) 1986. BB 3-34 v Glam (Hove) 1984. **JPL:** HS 19 v Leics (Hove) 1985. BB 4-22 v Glos (Hove) 1986.

SCOTT, Alastair Martin Gordon (Seaford Head CS; Queens C, CU), b Guildford 31 Mar 1966. 5'10". RHB, LM. Cambridge U blue 1985-86. Sussex debut 1986. HS 8. BB 5–68 CU v Notts (Cambridge) 1985. **BHC:** HS 2*. BB 1-26.

SPEIGHT, Martin Peter (Hurstpierpoint C; Durham U), b Walsall, Staffs 24 Oct 1967. 5'9". RHB, WK. Debut 1986. HS 17 v Notts (Hove) 1986. England YC to Sri Lanka 1987.

STANDING, David Kevin (Tideway CS, Newhaven; Brighton and Hove GS), b Brighton 21 Oct 1963. 5'7". RHB, OB. Debut 1983. HS 65 v Warwicks (Birmingham) 1986. BB 2-28 v NZ (Hove) 1986. **NWT:** HS 1* and BB 2-27 v Suffolk (Hove) 1986. **JPL:** HS 8*. BB 1-16.

WARING, Ian Charles (Tupton Hall S), b Chesterfield, Derbys 6 Dec 1963. 6'1". LHB, RFM. Debut 1985. BB 1-16.

WELLS, Alan Peter (Tideway CS, Newhaven), b Newhaven 2 Oct 1961. 6'0". RHB, RM. Brother of C.M. Debut 1981. Border 1981-82. 1000 runs (1): 1045 (1984). HS 150* v Notts (Hove) 1986. BB 1-42. **NWT:** HS 24 v Somerset (Hove) 1984. **BHC:** HS 62 v Surrey (Hove) 1985. BB 1-17. **JPL:** HS 71* v Hants (Southampton) 1984. BB 1-7.

WELLS, Colin Mark (Tideway CS, Newhaven), b Newhaven 3 Mar 1960. 5'11". RHB, RM. Brother of A.P. Debut 1979. Cap 1982. Border 1980-81. W Province 1984-85. LOI: 2. 1000 runs (4); most – 1389 (1984). HS 203 v Hants (Hove) 1984. BB 5-25 v Kent (Hastings) 1984. Award: BHC 1. **NWT:** HS 76 v Ireland (Hove) 1985. BB 2-20 v Suffolk (Hove) 1979. **BHC:** HS 80 v Kent (Hove) 1982. BB 4-21 v Middx (Lord's) 1980. **JPL:** HS 104* v Warwicks (Hove) 1983. BB 4-15 v Worcs (Worcester) 1983.

SALVETE

BOARER, Paul Vincent, b Haslemere, Surrey 19 Jul 1967. RHB, RFM.

COOMBS, Robert Vincent Jerome (King's C, Taunton; St Luke's C, Exeter), b Barnet, Herts 20 July 1959. 6'4". RHB, SLA. Somerset 1985–86. Dorset 1979–85. HS 18 v Glos (Bristol) 1986. BB 5-58 v Middx (Weston) 1985 – on debut.

MYLES, Simon David, b Mansfield, Notts 2 Jun 1966. RHB, LB.

PUGH, Andrew Joseph, b Paignton, Devon 26 May 1969. RHB.

VALETE

BARCLAY, John Robert Troutbeck (Eton C), b Bonn, West Germany 22 Jan 1954. 5'11". RHB, OB. Debut 1970 aged 16 years 205 days. Cap 1976. Captain 1981-86. OFS 1978-79. 1000 runs (4); most – 1093 (1979). HS 119 v Leics (Hove) 1980. BB 6-61 v Sri Lankans (Hove) 1979. Awards: NWT 1; BHC 3.

BREDIN, Andrew Michael (KCS, Wimbledon), b Wimbledon, London 12 Jan 1962. 5'10". RHB, SLA. Debut 1986. HS 8*. BB 2-50 v Essex (Ilford) 1986.

JONES, A.N. – see SOMERSET.

PHILLIPSON, Christopher **Paul** (Ardingly C; Loughborough C), b Brindaban, India 10 Feb 1952. 6'1". RHB, RM. Debut 1970. Cap 1980. Benefit 1985. HS 87 v Hants (Hove) 1980. BB 6-56 v Notts (Hove) 1972. Awards: BHC 2.

SUSSEX RECORDS

FIRST-CLASS CRICKET

Highest Total	For	705-8d		v	Surrey	Hastings	1902
	V	726		by	Notts	Nottingham	1895
Lowest Total	For	19		v	Surrey	Godalming	1830
		19		v	Notts	Hove	1873
	V	18		by	Kent	Gravesend	1867
Highest Innings	For	333	K.S. Duleepsinhji	v	Northants	Hove	1930
	V	322	E. Paynter	for	Lancashire	Hove	1937

Highest Partnerships

Wkt						
1st	490	E.H. Bowley/J.G. Langridge	v	Middlesex	Hove	1933
2nd	385	E.H. Bowley/M.W. Tate	v	Northants	Hove	1921
3rd	298	K.S. Ranjitsinhji/E.H. Killick	v	Lancashire	Hove	1901
4th	326*	J. Langridge/G. Cox	v	Yorkshire	Leeds	1949
5th	297	J.H. Parks/H.W. Parks	v	Hampshire	Portsmouth	1937
6th	255	K.S. Duleepsinhji/M.W. Tate	v	Northants	Hove	1930
7th	344	K.S. Ranjitsinhji/W. Newham	v	Essex	Leyton	1902
8th	229*	C.L.A. Smith/G. Brann	v	Kent	Hove	1902
9th	178	H.W. Parks/A.F. Wensley	v	Derbyshire	Horsham	1930
10th	156	G.R. Cox/H.R. Butt	v	Cambridge U	Cambridge	1908

Best Bowling (Innings)	For	10-48	C.H.G. Bland	v	Kent	Tonbridge	1899
	V	9-11	A.P. Freeman	for	Kent	Hove	1922
Best Bowling (Match)	For	17-106	G.R. Cox	v	Warwicks	Horsham	1926
	V	17-67	A.P. Freeman	for	Kent	Hove	1922

Most Runs – Season	2,850	J.G. Langridge	(av 64.77)	1949
Most Runs – Career	34,152	J.G. Langridge	(av 37.69)	1928-1955
Most 100s – Season	12	J.G. Langridge		1949
Most 100s – Career	76	J.G. Langridge		1928-1955
Most Wkts – Season	198	M.W. Tate	(av 13.47)	1925
Most Wkts – Career	2,211	M.W. Tate	(av 17.41)	1912-1937

LIMITED-OVERS CRICKET

Highest Total	**NWT**	314-7		v	Kent	Tunbridge W	1963
	BHC	305-6		v	Kent	Hove	1982
	JPL	293-4		v	Worcs	Horsham	1980
Lowest Total	**NWT**	49		v	Derbyshire	Chesterfield	1969
	BHC	61		v	Middlesex	Hove	1978
	JPL	61		v	Derbyshire	Derby	1978
Highest Innings	**NWT**	141*	G.D. Mendis	v	Warwicks	Hove	1980
	BHC	117	R.D.V. Knight	v	Surrey	The Oval	1977
	JPL	129	A.W. Greig	v	Yorkshire	Scarborough	1976
Best Bowling	**NWT**	6-30	D.L. Bates	v	Glos	Hove	1968
	BHC	5-8	Imran Khan	v	Northants	Northampton	1978
	JPL	7-41	A.N. Jones	v	Notts	Nottingham	1986

SUSSEX 1986

RESULTS SUMMARY

	Place	*Won*	*Lost*	*Drew*	*Abandoned*
Britannic Assurance Championship	**14th**	4	7	12	1
All First-class Matches		4	7	14	1
John Player League	**4th**	10	6		
NatWest Bank Trophy	**Winners**				
Benson and Hedges Cup	Lost to Middlesex (Quarter-Final)				

BRITANNIC ASSURANCE CHAMPIONSHIP AVERAGES

BATTING AND FIELDING

Cap		*M*	*I*	*NO*	*HS*	*Runs*	*Avge*	*100*	*50*	*Ct/St*
1978	Imran Khan	10	17	3	135*	729	52.07	2	4	1
1982	A.C.S. Pigott	18	18	6	104*	572	47.66	1	2	4
1979	P.W.G. Parker	23	40	5	125	1459	41.68	5	8	18
1982	C.M. Wells	22	36	8	106	994	35.50	1	6	5
—	R.I. Alikhan	16	26	3	72	808	35.13	—	7	6
1986	A.P. Wells	21	32	6	150*	842	32.38	1	2	10
1981	I.J. Gould	18	23	5	78*	561	31.16	—	4	33
1981	G.S. Le Roux	14	16	6	72*	298	29.80	—	1	6
1985	A.M. Green	23	42	3	179	1106	28.35	2	3	11
1986	D.A. Reeve	18	21	9	51	307	25.58	—	1	9
—	N.J. Lenham	17	28	3	77	544	21.76	—	3	6
—	D.K. Standing	15	22	1	65	321	15.28	—	1	9
1986	A.N. Jones	11	10	3	13	55	7.85	—	—	5
—	A.M. Bredin	6	6	2	8*	26	6.50	—	—	1
—	C.S. Mays	7	6	2	8*	19	4.75	—	—	2

Also batted: A.M. Babington (5 matches) 1,0*,0 (2 ct); J.R.T. Barclay (2 matches – cap 1976) 4,28,4; C.P. Phillipson (1 match – cap 1980) 6 (2 ct); A.M.G. Scott (1 match) 0 (1 ct); M.P. Speight (5 matches) 4,17 (6 ct).

BOWLING

	O	*M*	*R*	*W*	*Avge*	*Best*	*5 wI*	*10 wM*
Imran Khan	294.3	62	825	33	25.00	8-34	2	—
D.A. Reeve	508.5	127	1368	51	26.82	5-32	1	—
A.C.S. Pigott	379	47	1327	48	27.64	5-50	3	—
A.N. Jones	171	26	620	21	29.52	3-36	—	—
C.M. Wells	415.2	93	1263	36	35.08	4-23	—	—
G.S. Le Roux	303.2	66	928	26	35.69	3-27	—	—

Also bowled: R.I. Alikhan 10-0-65-0; A.M. Babington 83.5-11-242-9; J.R.T. Barclay 13-2-65-0; A.M. Bredin 84-20-316-6; I.J. Gould 18.3-0-96-2; A.M. Green 170.1-25-574-7; N.J. Lenham 131-25-409-9; C.S. Mays 170.5-38-561-9; P.W.G. Parker 2-1-4-0; A.M.G. Scott 17-3-70-1; D.K. Standing 156-29-451-2; A.P. Wells 11-1-43-1.

The First-Class Averages (pp. 167–182) give the records of Sussex players in all first-class county matches, their other opponents being the New Zealanders and Cambridge U, with the exception of A.M.G. Scott whose full county figures are as above.

WARWICKSHIRE

Formation of Present Club: 8 April 1882
Substantial Reorganisation: 19 January 1884
Colours: Dark Blue, Gold and Silver
Badge: Bear and Ragged Staff
Championships: (3) 1911, 1951, 1972
NatWest Trophy/Gillette Cup Winners: (2) 1966, 1968
Benson and Hedges Cup Winners: (0) Finalists 1984
John Player League Champions: (1) 1980
Match Awards: NWT 31; BHC 36

Secretary: D.M.W. Heath, County Ground, Edgbaston, Birmingham B5 7QU
Captain: N. Gifford, MBE
Scorer: S.P. Austin
Scores/Prospects: ☎ Birmingham (021) 440 3624

AMISS, Dennis Leslie (Oldknow S), b Harborne, Birmingham 7 Apr 1943. 5′11″. RHB, SLA. Debut 1960. Cap 1965. *Wisden* 1974. Benefit 1975. Testimonial 1985. **Tests:** 50 (1966 to 1977); HS 262* v WI (Kingston) 1973-74. LOI: 18. Tours: Aus 1974-75, 1976-77; SA 1981-82 (SAB); WI 1973-74; NZ 1974-75; Ind/SL 1967-68 (Int XI), 1972-73, 1976-77; Pak 1966-67 (MCC U-25), 1967-68 (Int XI), 1970-71 (RW), 1972-73. 1000 runs (22+1); most – 2239 (1984). HS 262* (Tests). Wa HS 232* v Glos (Bristol) 1979. BB 3-21 v Middx (Lord's) 1970. Awards: NWT 4; BHC 5. **NWT:** HS 135 v Cambs (Birmingham) 1982. **BHC:** HS 115 v Leics (Leicester) 1984. **JPL:** HS 117* v Sussex (Horsham) 1981. BB 1-15.

ASIF DIN, Mohamed (Ladywood CS, Birmingham), b Kampala, Uganda 21 Sep 1960. 5′9½″. RHB, LB. Debut 1981. HS 102 v Middlesex (Coventry) 1982. BB 5-100 v Glam (Birmingham) 1982. **NWT:** HS 45 v Surrey (Lord's) 1982. BB 1-5. **BHC:** HS 61 v Notts (Nottingham) 1982. **JPL:** HS 108 v Essex (Chelmsford) 1986. BB 1-11.

GIFFORD, Norman (Ulverston SS), b Ulverston, Lancs 30 Mar 1940. 5′10½″. LHB, SLA. Worcestershire 1960-82 (cap 1961; captain 1971-80; benefit 1974; testimonial 1981). *Wisden* 1974. MBE 1978. England selector 1982. Warwickshire debut/cap 1983. Captain 1985-. **Tests:** 15 (1964 to 1973); HS 25* v NZ (Nottingham) 1973; BB 5-55 v Pak (Karachi) 1972-73. LOI: 2. Tours: Aus 1971-72 (RW); Rhod/Zim 1961-62 (Int XI), 1964-65 (Worcs), 1972-73 (IW); Ind 1972-73; Pak 1961-62 (Int XI), 1970-71 (RW), 1972-73; SL 1985-86 (Eng B). 100 wkts (4); most – 133 (1961). HS 89 Worcs v OU (Oxford) 1963. BB 8-28 Worcs v Yorks (Sheffield) 1968. Awards: NWT 1; BHC 2. **NWT:** HS 38 Worcs v Wa (Lord's) 1966. BB 4-7 Worcs v Surrey (Worcester) 1972. **BHC:** HS 33 Worcs v Kent (Lord's) 1973. BB 6-8 Worcs v Minor C (S) (High Wycombe) 1979. **JPL:** HS 32* v Northants (Luton) 1983. BB 6-20 v Northants (Birmingham) 1985.

HUMPAGE, Geoffrey William (Golden Hillock CS), b Sparkhill, Birmingham 24 Apr 1954. 5′9″. RHB, WK, RM. Debut 1974. Cap 1976. Benefit 1987. OFS 1981-82. *Wisden* 1984. LOI: 3. Tour: SA 1981-82 (SAB). 1000 runs (9); most – 1891 (1984). HS 254 v Lancs (Southport) 1982, adding 470 with A.I. Kallicharran (English 4th wicket record). BB 2-13 v Glos (Birmingham) 1980. Awards: NWT 1; BHC 2. **NWT:** HS 77 v Shropshire (Birmingham) 1984. **BHC:** HS 100* v Scotland (Birmingham) 1984. BB 2-43 v Worcs (Worcester) 1980. **JPL:** HS 109* v Glos (Birmingham) 1984. BB 4-53 v Glos (Moreton) 1979.

KALLICHARRAN, Alvin Isaac (Port Mourant CS), b Paidama, British Guiana 21 Mar 1949. 5'4". LHB, OB. Brother of D.I. (Trinidad). Guyana 1966-81. Warwickshire debut 1971. Cap 1972. Queensland 1977-78. Transvaal 1981-84. OFS 1984-85 (captain) and 1986-87. *Wisden* 1982. Benefit 1983. **Tests** (WI): 66 (1971-72 to 1980-81, 9 as captain); scored 100* and 101 in first two innings (v NZ); HS 187 v Ind (Bombay) 1979-80; BB 2-16 v NZ (Christchurch) 1979-80. LOI (WI): 31. Tours: Eng 1973, 1976, 1980; Aus 1975-76, 1979-80; SA (WI XI) 1982-83, 1983-84; NZ 1979-80; Ind/SL 1974-75, 1978-79 (capt); Pak 1973-74 (RW), 1974-75, 1980-81. 1000 runs (12+1); most – 2301 (1984). HS 243* v Glam (Birmingham) 1983. BB 5-45 Transvaal v W. Province (Cape Town) 1982-83. Wa BB 4-48 v Derbys (Birmingham) 1978. Awards: NWT 4; BHC 3. **NWT:** HS 206 and BB 6-32 v Oxfordshire (Birmingham) 1984. **BHC:** HS 122* v Northants (Northampton) 1984. **JPL:** HS 102* v Notts (Birmingham) 1981. BB 3-32 v Lancs (Birmingham) 1985.
LLOYD, Timothy **Andrew** (Oswestry HS; Dorset CHE), b Oswestry, Shropshire 5 Nov 1956. 5'10". LHB, RM. Debut 1977. Cap 1980. Orange Free State 1978-80. Shropshire 1975. **Tests:** 1 (1984); HS 10* (rtd hurt) v WI (Birmingham). LOI: 3. Tour: Zim 1984-85 (Eng Co). 1000 runs (5); most – 1673 (1983). HS 208* v Glos (Birmingham) 1983. BB 3-62 v Surrey (Birmingham) 1985. Awards: NWT 2; BHC 2. **NWT:** HS 81 v Devon (Birmingham) 1980. BB 1-4. **BHC:** HS 137* v Lancs (Birmingham) 1985. **JPL:** HS 90 v Kent (Birmingham) 1980. BB 1-42.
MOLES, Andrew James (Finham Park CS; Butts CHE), b Solihull 12 Feb 1961. 5'10". RHB, RM. Debut 1986. GW 1986–87. HS 102 v Somerset (Weston) 1986. BB 2-57 v Sussex (Birmingham) 1986. **JPL:** HS 85 v Glos (Birmingham) 1986. BB 1-25.
MUNTON, Timothy Alan (Sarson HS; King Edward HS), b Melton Mowbray, Leics 30 Jul 1965. 6'5". RHB, RFM. Debut 1985. HS 19 v Hants (Portsmouth) 1986. BB 4-60 v Kent (Birmingham) 1986. **BHC:** HS 0*. BB 2-25 v Minor C (Walsall) 1986. **JPL:** HS 5*. BB 2-27 v Leics (Birmingham) 1986.
PARSONS, Gordon James (Woodside County SS, Slough), b Slough, Bucks 17 Oct 1959. 6'1". LHB, RMF. Leicestershire 1978-85; cap 1984. Boland 1983-85. GW 1985-87. Warwickshire debut 1986. Buckinghamshire 1977. Tours: NZ 1979-80 (DHR); Zim 1980-81 (Leics). HS 76 Boland v W. Province B (Cape Town) 1984-85. BB 9-72 Boland v Transvaal B (Johannesburg) 1984-85. Award: BHC 1. **NWT:** HS 23 Leics v Northants (Northampton) 1984. BB 2-11 Leics v Wilts (Swindon) 1984. **BHC:** HS 29* Leics v Northants (Leics) 1983. BB 4-33 Leics v Worcs (Leics) 1981. **JPL:** HS 24* Leics v Som (Taunton) 1985. BB 4-19 Leics v Essex (Harlow) 1982.
PIERSON, Adrian Roger Kirshaw (Kent C, Canterbury; Hatfield Polytechnic), b Enfield, Middx 21 Jul 1963. 6'4". RHB, OB. Debut 1985. HS 42* v Northants (Northampton) 1986. BB 3-92 v OU (Oxford) 1985. **NWT:** HS 1*. **BHC:** HS 11 and BB 1-25 v Minor C (Walsall) 1986. **JPL:** HS 5*. BB 1-29.
SMALL, Gladstone Cleophas (Moseley S; Hall Green TC), b St. George, Barbados 18 Oct 1961. 5'11". RHB, RFM. Debut 1979-80 (DHR XI in NZ). Warwickshire debut 1980. Cap 1982. S Australia 1985-86. **Tests:** 4 (1986 and 1986-87); HS 21* and BB 5-48 v Aus (Melbourne) 1986-87. LOI: 4. Tours: Aus 1986–87; NZ 1979-80 (DHR); Pak 1981-82 (Int XI). HS 57* v OU (Oxford) 1982. BB 7-42 S Australia v NSW (Adelaide) 1985-86. Warwicks BB 7-68 v Yorks (Birmingham) 1982. **NWT:** HS 33 v Surrey (Lord's) 1982. BB 3-22 v Glam (Cardiff) 1982. **BHC:** HS 19* v Yorks (Birmingham) 1981. BB 3-41 v Leics (Leicester) 1984. **JPL:** HS 40* v Essex (Ilford) 1984. BB 5-29 v Surrey (Birmingham) 1980.
SMITH, Paul Andrew (Heaton GS), b Jesmond, Newcastle upon Tyne 15 Apr 1964. 6'2". RHB, RFM. Son of K.D. sr (Leics 1950-51) and brother of K.D. jr (Warwicks 1973-85). Debut 1982. Cap 1986. 1000 runs (2): most 1508 (1986). HS 119 v Worcs (Birmingham) 1986. BB 4-25 v Lancs (Birmingham) 1985. **NWT:** HS 79 v Durham (Birmingham) 1986. BB 3-10 v Shropshire (Birmingham) 1984. **BHC:** HS 37 v Somerset (Birmingham) 1984. BB 2-30 v Lancs (Birmingham) 1985. **JPL:** HS 50* v Sussex (Hove) 1985. BB 4-23 v Notts (Birmingham) 1983.

TEDSTONE, Geoffrey Alan (Warwick S; St. Paul's C, Cheltenham), b Southport, Lancs 19 Jan 1961. 5'7". RHB, WK. Debut 1982. HS 67* v CU (Cambridge) 1983. **JPL:** HS 23 v Middx (Birmingham) 1982.
THORNE, David Anthony (Coventry S; Keble C, OU), b Coventry 12 Dec 1964. 5'11". RHB, LM. Warwickshire debut 1983. Oxford U/blue 1984-85-86; captain 1986. HS 124 OU v Zimbabweans (Oxford) 1985. Warwicks HS 58 v Derbys (Birmingham) 1986. BB 5-39 OU v CU (Lord's) 1984. Warwicks BB 1-21. **NWT:** HS 21 v Essex (Birmingham) 1986. **BHC:** HS 36* Comb Us v Middx (Lord's) 1986. BB 1-67. **JPL:** HS 42 v Glos (Moreton) 1983. BB 3-48 v Kent (Canterbury) 1985.

SALVETE

MERRICK, Tyrone **Anthony,** b Antigua 10 Jun 1963. RHB, RFM. Leeward Is 1982-86. HS 62* and BB 5-54 v Jamaica (Kingston) 1983-84. WIYC to England 1982.
MILBURN, Edward Thomas, b Nuneaton 15 Sep 1967. RHB, RM.
SMITH, Neil Michael Knight (Warwick S), b Birmingham 27 July 1967. Son of M.J.K. (Leicestershire, Warwickshire and England). 6'0". RHB, OB.
STORIE, Alastair Caleb (St Stithians C, Johannesburg), b Bishopbriggs, Glasgow 25 Jul 1965. 5'9". RHB, RM. Northamptonshire 1985–86. HS 106 v Hampshire (Northampton) 1985 – on debut.
WEIR, Robert Stephen, b Coventry 4 Dec 1966. RHB, RMF.

VALETE

DYER, Robin Ian Henry Benbow (Wellington C; Durham U), b Hertford 22 Dec 1958. 6'4". RHB, RM. Debut 1981. 1000 runs (2); most – 1242 (1985). HS 109* v Zimbabweans (Birmingham) 1985. Award: NWT 1.
FERREIRA, Anthonie Michal (**'Anton'**) (Hillview HS; Pretoria U), b Pretoria, SA 13 Apr 1955. 6'3". RHB, RMF. Northern Transvaal 1974-86. Warwickshire debut 1979. Cap 1983. HS 112* v Indians (Birmingham) 1982. BB 8-38 N Transvaal v Transvaal B (Pretoria) 1977-78. Wa BB 6-70 v Leics (Birmingham) 1984.
KERR, Kevin John (Sandown HS, SA; Witwatersrand U, SA), b Airdrie, Scotland 11 Sept 1961. 5'11". RHB, OB. Transvaal B 1978-86. Warwickshire debut 1986. HS 74 v W Province B (Pietermaritzburg) 1985-86. Warwicks HS 45* v Glos (Nuneaton) 1986. BB 5-27 Transvaal B v Natal B (Durban) 1978-79 – on debut. Warwicks BB 5-47 v Glam (Swansea) 1986. Chartered accountant.
LORD, Gordon John (Warwick S; Durham U), b Edgbaston, Birmingham 25 Apr 1961. 5'10". LHB, SLA. Debut 1983. HS 199 v Yorks (Birmingham) 1985.
McMILLAN, Brian Mervin (Carleton Jones HS; Witwatersrand U), b Welkom, OFS, SA 22 Dec 1963. 6'4". RHB, RMF. Transvaal 1984-87. Warwicks debut 1986. HS 136 v Notts (Nottingham) 1986. BB 4-53 Transvaal B v Boland (Johannesburg) 1984-85. Warwicks BB 3-47 v Somerset (Weston) 1986. Awards: BHC 2.
MONKHOUSE, S. – see GLAMORGAN.

WARWICKSHIRE RECORDS

FIRST-CLASS CRICKET

Highest Total	For	657-6d		v	Hampshire	Birmingham	1899
	V	887		by	Yorkshire	Birmingham	1896
Lowest Total	For	16		v	Kent	Tonbridge	1913
	V	15		by	Hampshire	Birmingham	1922
Highest Innings	For	305*	F.R. Foster	v	Worcs	Dudley	1914
	V	322	I.V.A. Richards	for	Somerset	Taunton	1985

Highest Partnerships

Wkt						
1st	377*	N.F. Horner/K. Ibadulla	v	Surrey	The Oval	1960
2nd	465*	J.A. Jameson/R.B. Kanhai	v	Glos	Birmingham	1974
3rd	327	S.P. Kinneir/W.G. Quaife	v	Lancashire	Birmingham	1901
4th	470	A.I. Kallicharran/G.W. Humpage	v	Lancashire	Southport	1982
5th	268	W. Quaife/W.G. Quaife	v	Essex	Leyton	1900
6th	220	H.E. Dollery/J. Buckingham	v	Derbyshire	Derby	1938
7th	250	H.E. Dollery/J.S. Ord	v	Kent	Maidstone	1953
8th	228	A.J.W. Croom/R.E.S. Wyatt	v	Worcs	Dudley	1925
9th	154	G.W. Stephens/A.J.W. Croom	v	Derbyshire	Birmingham	1925
10th	128	F.R. Santall/W. Sanders	v	Yorkshire	Birmingham	1930

Best Bowling	For	10-41	J.D. Bannister	v	Comb Servs	Birmingham	1959
(Innings)	V	10-36	H. Verity	for	Yorkshire	Leeds	1931
Best Bowling	For	15-76	S. Hargreave	v	Surrey	The Oval	1903
(Match)	V	17-92	A.P. Freeman	for	Kent	Folkestone	1932

Most Runs – Season	2,417	M.J.K. Smith	(av 60.42)	1959
Most Runs – Career	33,862	W.G. Quaife	(av 36.17)	1894-1928
Most 100s – Season	9	A.I. Kallicharran		1984
Most 100s – Career	76	D.L. Amiss		1960-1986
Most Wkts – Season	180	W.E. Hollies	(av 15.13)	1946
Most Wkts – Career	2,201	W.E. Hollies	(av 20.45)	1932-1957

LIMITED-OVERS CRICKET

Highest Total	**NWT**	392-5		v	Oxfordshire	Birmingham	1984
	BHC	291-5		v	Lancashire	Manchester	1981
	JPL	301-6		v	Essex	Colchester	1982
Lowest Total	**NWT**	109		v	Kent	Canterbury	1971
	BHC	96		v	Leics	Leicester	1972
	JPL	65		v	Kent	Maidstone	1979
Highest Innings	**NWT**	206	A.I. Kallicharran	v	Oxfordshire	Birmingham	1984
	BHC	137*	T.A. Lloyd	v	Lancashire	Birmingham	1985
	JPL	123*	J.A. Jameson	v	Notts	Nottingham	1973
Best Bowling	**NWT**	6-32	K. Ibadulla	v	Hampshire	Birmingham	1965
		6-32	A.I. Kallicharran	v	Oxfordshire	Birmingham	1984
	BHC	7-32	R.G.D. Willis	v	Yorkshire	Birmingham	1981
	JPL	6-20	N. Gifford	v	Northants	Birmingham	1985

WARWICKSHIRE 1986

RESULTS SUMMARY

	Place	Won	Lost	Drew	Tied	Aban
Britannic Assurance Championship	**12th**	4	5	15		
All First-class Matches		5	5	16		
John Player League	**9th**	5	7		2	2
NatWest Bank Trophy	Lost to Worcestershire (Quarter-Final)					
Benson and Hedges Cup	Failed to qualify for Quarter-Final					

BRITANNIC ASSURANCE CHAMPIONSHIP AVERAGES

BATTING AND FIELDING

Cap		*M*	*I*	*NO*	*HS*	*Runs*	*Avge*	*100*	*50*	*Ct/St*
—	B.M. McMillan	11	19	4	136	895	59.66	3	5	10
1972	A.I. Kallicharran	13	22	5	163*	884	52.00	4	2	12
—	A.J. Moles	11	18	3	102	738	49.20	2	5	4
1983	A.M. Ferreira	10	13	5	69*	354	44.25	—	3	8
1965	D.L. Amiss	24	42	5	110	1418	38.32	4	6	10
1986	P.A. Smith	24	42	4	119	1431	37.65	1	12	7
—	Asif Din	23	36	14	69*	750	34.09	—	5	10
1976	G.W. Humpage	24	39	3	130	1216	33.77	1	6	37/8
1980	T.A. Lloyd	15	26	0	100	791	30.42	1	6	6
—	D.A. Thorne	6	8	3	58	107	21.40	—	1	—
—	G.J. Parsons	19	23	5	58*	309	17.16	—	1	3
1982	G.C. Small	21	23	6	45*	280	16.47	—	—	4
—	K.J. Kerr	13	11	4	45*	87	12.42	—	—	6
—	R.I.H.B. Dyer	4	8	1	28	69	9.85	—	—	4
—	G.J. Lord	2	4	0	17	38	9.50	—	—	2
—	T.A. Munton	17	13	5	19	44	5.50	—	—	—
1983	N. Gifford	24	14	6	8	27	3.37	—	—	2

Also batted: S. Monkhouse (1 match) 0; A.R.K. Pierson (2 matches) 42*,0*.

BOWLING

	O	*M*	*R*	*W*	*Avge*	*Best*	*5 wI*	*10 wM*
G.C. Small	537.3	126	1573	68	23.13	5-35	2	—
N. Gifford	542.3	148	1377	58	23.74	6-27	2	—
T.A. Munton	246.4	51	803	25	32.12	4-60	—	—
K.J. Kerr	296	46	913	24	38.04	5-47	1	—
B.M. McMillan	207	34	752	17	44.23	3-47	—	—
G.J. Parsons	316.4	58	1028	23	44.69	5-75	1	—
P.A. Smith	156	18	725	13	55.76	3-36	—	—

Also bowled: Asif Din 87-8-358-4; A.M. Ferreira 125-31-391-8; A.I. Kallicharran 9-0-65-2; T.A. Lloyd 15-0-109-0; A.J. Moles 64.3-10-198-5; S. Monkhouse 10-4-34-1; A.R.K. Pierson 36-5-133-2; D.A. Thorne 53-6-174-1.

The First-Class Averages (pp. 167–182) give the records of Warwickshire players in all first-class county matches (their other opponents being the New Zealanders and Cambridge U.), with the exception of: G.C. Small 23-24-6-45*-290-16.11-0-0-4 ct. 575.3-138-1647-73-22.56-5/35-2-0. D.A. Thorne 7-10-3-58-127-18.14-0-1-1 ct. 60-8-198-1-198.00-1/44.

WORCESTERSHIRE

Formation of Present Club: 11 March 1865
Colours: Dark Green and Black
Badge: Shield Argent bearing Fess between Three Pears Sable
Championships: (3) 1964, 1965, 1974
NatWest Trophy/Gillette Cup Winners: (0) Finalists 1963, 1966
Benson and Hedges Cup Winners: (0) Finalists 1973, 1976
John Player League Champions: (1) 1971
Match Awards: NWT 24; BHC 35

Secretary: M.D. Vockins, County Ground, New Road, Worcester WR2 4QQ
Captain: P.A. Neale
Scorer: J.W. Sewter
Scores/Prospects: ☎ Worcester (0905) 422011

BARRETT, Brian Joseph, b Auckland, New Zealand 16 Nov 1966. 6′2″. RHB, RFM. Debut 1985. Auckland 1985-86. Tour (NZ): Eng 1986. HS 5*. BB 4-51 Auckland v Otago (Dunedin) 1985-86. **JPL:** HS 5*.
BENT, Paul (Worcester RGS), b Worcester 1 May 1965. 6′0″. RHB, OB. Debut 1985. MCC staff. HS 14 v CU (Cambridge) 1985.
CURTIS, Timothy Stephen (Worcester RGS; Durham U; Magdalene C, Cambridge), b Chislehurst, Kent 15 Jan 1960. 5′11″. RHB, LB. Debut 1979. Cambridge U; blue 1983. Cap 1984. 1000 runs (3); most – 1498 (1986). HS 153 v Somerset (Worcester) 1986. BB 2-58 CU v Notts (Cambridge) 1983. Awards: NWT 2; BHC 1. **NWT:** HS 94 v Hants (Southampton) 1986. **BHC:** HS 75 v Warwicks (Worcester) 1985. **JPL:** HS 102 v Glam (Worcester) 1986.
D'OLIVEIRA, Damian Basil (Blessed Edward Oldcorne SS), b Cape Town SA 19 Oct 1960. 5′9″. RHB, OB. Son of B.L. (Worcs and England 1964-80). Debut 1982. Cap 1985. Tour: Zim 1984-85 (Eng Co). 1000 runs (2): most 1244 (1985). HS 146* v Glos (Bristol) 1986. BB 2-17 v Glos (Bristol) 1986. Awards: NWT 2; BHC 2. **NWT:** HS 99 v Oxon (Worcester) 1986. BB 2-28 v Notts (Worcester) 1983. **BHC:** HS 66 v Yorks (Leeds) 1986. BB 3-12 v Scotland (Glasgow) 1986. **JPL:** HS 103 v Surrey (Worcester) 1985. BB 3-23 v Derbys (Derby) 1983.
ELLCOCK, Ricardo McDonald (Combermere S, Barbados; Malvern C), b Bridgetown, Barbados 17 Jun 1965. 5′11″. RHB, RF. Debut 1982. Barbados 1983-84. HS 45* v Essex (Worcester) 1984. BB 4-34 v Glam (Worcester) 1984. **NWT:** HS 6. BB 3-49 v Notts (Worcester) 1983. **BHC:** HS 12 and BB 2-45 v Notts (Nottingham) 1984. **JPL:** HS 5*. BB 4-43 v Kent (Canterbury) 1983.
HICK, Graeme Ashley (Prince Edward HS, Salisbury), b Salisbury, Rhodesia 23 May 1966. 6′3″. RHB, OB. Debut (Zimbabwe) 1983-84. Worcestershire debut 1984. Cap 1986. *Wisden* 1986. Tours (Zim): Eng 1985; SL 1983-84. 1000 runs (2): most 2004 (1984 – youngest to score 2000). HS 230 Zimbabweans v OU (Oxford) 1985. Worcs HS 227* v Notts (Worcester) 1986. BB 3-39 Zimbabweans v Sri Lanka Board President's XI (Moratuwa) 1983-84. Awards: BHC 2. **NWT:** HS 27 v Oxon (Worcester) 1986. BB 1-21. **BHC:** HS 103* v Notts and 103* v Northants – (Worcester) 1986. BB 2-25 v Lancs (Worcester) 1986. **JPL:** HS 90 v Glos (Moreton) 1985. BB 2-36 v Warwicks (Worcester) 1985.
ILLINGWORTH, Richard Keith (Salts GS), b Bradford 23 Aug 1963. 5′11″. RHB, SLA. Debut 1982. Cap 1986. HS 55 v Leics (Hereford) 1983. BB 7-50 v OU (Oxford)

1985. **NWT:** HS 22 v Northants (Northampton) 1984. BB 2-14 v Notts (Worcester) 1983. **BHC:** HS 11* v Leics (Worcester) 1983. BB 4-36 v Yorks (Bradford) 1985. **JPL:** HS 21 v Middx (Worcester) 1982. BB 5-24 v Somerset (Worcester) 1983.

LAMPITT, Stuart Richard (Kingswinford S; Dudley TC), b Wolverhampton 29 Jul 1966. 5'11". RHB, RM. Debut 1985. HS 11* v Sussex (Hove) 1986.

McEWAN, Steven Michael (Worcester RGS), b Worcester 5 May 1962. 6'1". RHB, RFM. Debut 1985. HS 13* v OU (Oxford) 1985. BB 3-33 v Leics (Worcester) 1986. **JPL:** HS 7*. BB 4-35 v Derbys (Worcester) 1986.

NEALE, Phillip Anthony (Frederick Gough CS; John Leggott SFC; Leeds U), b Scunthorpe, Lincs 5 Jun 1954. 5'11". RHB, RM. Debut 1975. Cap 1978. Captain 1982. Lincolnshire 1972. 1000 runs (7); most – 1706 (1984). HS 163* v Notts (Worcester) 1979. BB 1-15. Award: BHC 1. Soccer: Lincoln City. **NWT:** HS 81 v Lancs (Manchester) 1985. **BHC:** HS 128 v Lancs (Manchester) 1980. **JPL:** HS 102 v Northants (Luton) 1982. BB 2-46 v Warwicks (Worcester) 1976.

NEWPORT, Philip John (High Wycombe RGS; Portsmouth Polytechnic), b High Wycombe, Bucks 11 Oct 1962. 6'3". RHB, RFM. Debut 1982. Cap 1986. Buckinghamshire 1981-82. HS 68 v Derbys (Derby) 1986. BB 6-48 v Hants (Southampton) 1986. **NWT:** HS 15 and BB 1-39 v Lancs (Worcester) 1986. **JPL:** HS 24 v Northants (Wellingborough) 1984. BB 3-20 v Somerset (Taunton) 1984.

PRIDGEON, Alan **Paul** (Summerhill SS, Kingswinford), b Wall Heath, Staffs 22 Feb 1954. 6'3". RHB, RM. Debut 1972. Cap 1980. HS 67 v Warwicks (Worcester) 1984. BB 7-35 v OU (Oxford) 1976. **NWT:** HS 13* and BB 3-25 v Somerset (Taunton) 1980. **BHC:** HS 13* v Leics (Worcester) 1982. BB 3-57 v Warwicks 1976 and 3-57 v Yorks 1986. **JPL:** HS 17 v Kent (Worcester) 1982. BB 6-26 v Surrey (Worcester) 1978.

RADFORD Neal Victor (Athlone BHS, Johannesburg), b Luanshya, Northern Rhodesia 7 Jun 1957. 5'11". RHB, RFM. Brother of W.R. (OFS). Transvaal 1978-86. Lancashire 1980-84. Worcestershire debut/cap 1985. *Wisden* 1985. **Tests:** 2 (1986); HS 12* v NZ (Lord's); BB 2-131 v Ind (Birmingham). 100 wickets (1); 101 (1985). HS 76* Lancs v Derbys (Blackpool) 1981. BB 9-70 v Somerset (Worcester) 1986. **NWT:** HS 16 v Notts (Worcester) 1985. BB 3-20 Lancs v Middx 1981 and 3-20 v Sussex 1986. **BHC:** HS 29* v Kent (Worcester) 1986. BB 2-27 Lancs v Middx (Lord's) 1983. **JPL:** HS 48* Lancs v Glam (Cardiff) 1981. BB 4-24 v Warwicks (Worcester) 1985.

RHODES, Steven John (Lapage Middle S; Carlton-Bolling S, Bradford), b Bradford 17 Jun 1964. 5'7". RHB, WK. Son of W.E. (Nottinghamshire 1961-64). Yorkshire 1981-84. Worcestershire debut 1985. Cap 1986. Tour: SL 1985-86 (Eng B). HS 77* v Surrey (Worcester) 1986. **NWT:** HS 32* v Hants (Southampton) 1986. **BHC:** HS 27* v Leics (Leicester) 1985. **JPL:** HS 46 v Northants (Northampton) 1986.

SMITH, Lawrence Kilner, b Mirfield, Yorkshire 6 Jan 1964. 5'10". RHB. Son of D.H.K. (Derbyshire 1965-70 and OFS 1976-78). Debut 1985. HS 28 v CU (Cambridge) 1985. **JPL:** HS 3.

WESTON, Martin John (Samuel Southall SS), b Worcester 8 Apr 1959. 6'1". RHB, RM. Debut 1979. Cap 1986. 1000 runs (1): 1061 (1984). HS 145* v Northants (Worcester) 1984. BB 4-44 v Northants (Wellingborough) 1984. **NWT:** HS 44* v Oxon (Worcester) 1986. BB 4-30 v Suffolk (Worcester) 1984. **BHC:** HS 56 v Scotland (Aberdeen) 1983. BB 2-27 v Yorks (Bradford) 1985. **JPL:** HS 109 v Somerset (Taunton) 1982. BB 4-24 v Kent (Worcester) 1984.

SALVETE

BOTHAM, Ian Terence (Buckler's Mead SS, Yeovil), b Heswall, Cheshire 24 Nov 1955. 6'1". RHB, RFM. Somerset 1974-86 (Cap 1976; Captain 1984-85), Benefit 1984. *Wisden* 1977. YC 1977. **Tests:** 89 (1977 to 1986-87, 12 as captain); HS 208 v India (Oval) 1982; BB 8-34 v Pak (Lord's) 1978. LOI: 82. Tours: Aus 1978-79,

1979-80, 1982-83, 1986-87; WI 1980-81 (capt), 1985-86; NZ 1977-78, 1983-84; Ind 1979-80, 1981-82; Pak 1977-78, 1983-84; SL 1981-82. 1000 runs (4); most – 1530 (1985) Hit 80 sixes 1985 (f-c record). 100 wickets (1): 100 (1978). HS 228 v Glos (Taunton) 1980. BB 8-34 (Tests). Awards: NWT 2; BHC 6. **NWT:** HS 96* v Middx (Lord's) 1983. BB 4-20 v Sussex (Hove) 1983. **BHC:** HS 126* v Glam (Taunton) 1986. BB 4-16 v Comb Us (Taunton) 1978. **JPL:** HS 175* v Northants (Wellingborough) 1986. BB 4-10 v Yorks (Scarborough) 1979.
DILLEY, Graham Roy (Dartford West SS), b Dartford 18 May 1959. 6'3". LHB, RF. Debut 1977. Cap 1980. YC 1980. Natal 1985-86. **Tests:** 26 (1979-80 to 1986-87); HS 56 v Aus (Leeds) 1981; BB 5-68 v Aus (Brisbane) 1986–87. LOI: 25. Tours: Aus 1979-80, 1986-87; WI 1980-81; NZ 1983-84; Ind 1979-80, 1981-82; Pak 1983-84; SL 1981-82. HS 81 v Northants (Northampton) 1979. BB 7-63 Natal v Transvaal (Johannesburg) 1985-86. Kent BB 6-57 v Lancs (Canterbury) 1986. Awards: NWT 1; BHC 1. **NWT:** HS 19 v Somerset 1983 and 19 v Essex 1985. BB 5-29 v Scotland (Edinburgh) 1986. **BHC:** HS 37* v Hants (Canterbury) 1983. BB 4-14 v Comb Us (Canterbury) 1981. **JPL:** HS 33 v Northants (Northampton) 1982. BB 4-20 v Glos (Canterbury) 1980.
GARNHAM, Michael Anthony (Camberwell GS, Melbourne; Scotch C, Perth; Barnstaple GS; N Devon SFC; East Anglia U), b Johannesburg, SA 20 Aug 1960. 5'10". RHB, WK. Gloucestershire 1979. Leicestershire 1980-85. Registered for Worcs 1986 – no appearances. Cambridgeshire 1986. HS 100 v OU (Oxford) 1985. Award: BHC 1. **NWT:** HS 29* v Norfolk (Norwich) 1985. **BHC:** HS 55 v Derbys (Leicester) 1982. **JPL:** HS 79* v Lancs (Leicester) 1982.
LEATHERDALE, David Anthony, b Bradford, Yorkshire 26 Nov 1967. RHB, RM.
TOLLEY, Christopher Mark (King Edward VI C, Stourbridge), b Kidderminster 30 Dec 1967. RHB, LMF.
WRIGHT, Jonathon, b Sheffield, Yorkshire 4 Jun 1965. RHB, RFM.

VALETE

INCHMORE, John Darling (Ashington GS: St Peter's CE, Birmingham), b Ashington, Northumberland 22 Feb 1949. 6'2½". RHB, RFM. Debut 1973. Cap 1976. Northumberland 1970. N Transvaal 1976-77. Benefit 1985. HS 113 v Essex (Worcester) 1974. BB 8-58 v Yorks (Worcester) 1977. Awards: NWT 1; BHC 3.
PATEL, Dipak Narshibhai (George Salter CS, West Bromwich), b Nairobi, Kenya 25 Oct 1958. 5'11". RHB, OB. Debut 1976. Cap 1979. Auckland 1985-86. Tour: NZ 1979-80 (DHR). 1000 runs (6); most – 1615 (1983). HS 197 v CU (Worcester) 1984. BB 7-46 v Lancs (Worcester) 1982. Awards: BHC 2. **NWT:** HS 54 v Glam (Swansea) 1985. BB 4-22 v Suffolk (Worcester) 1984. **BHC:** HS 90* v Lancs (Manchester) 1984. BB 3-42 v Yorks (Worcester) 1980. **JPL:** HS 125 v Hants (Southampton) 1982. BB 5-27 v Northants (Worcester) 1983.
SMITH, David Mark (Battersea GS), b Balham, London 9 Jan 1956. 6'4". LHB, RM. Surrey 1973-83 (cap 1980). Worcestershire debut/cap 1984. **Tests:** 2 (1985-86); HS 47 v WI (P-of-S). LOI: 1. Tour: WI 1985-86. 1000 runs (4); most – 1113 (1985). HS 189* v Kent (Worcester) 1984. BB 3-40 Surrey v Sussex (Oval) 1976. Awards: NWT 2; BHC 2.

WORCESTERSHIRE RECORDS

FIRST-CLASS CRICKET

Highest Total	For	633	v	Warwicks	Worcester	1906
	V	701-4d	by	Leics	Worcester	1906
Lowest Total	For	24	v	Yorkshire	Huddersfield	1903
	V	30	by	Hampshire	Worcester	1903
Highest Innings	For	311* G.M. Turner	v	Warwicks	Worcester	1982
	V	331* J.D.B. Robertson	for	Middlesex	Worcester	1949

Highest Partnerships

Wkt						
1st	309	F.L. Bowley/H.K. Foster	v	Derbyshire	Derby	1901
2nd	287*	T.S. Curtis/G.A. Hick	v	Glamorgan	Neath	1986
3rd	314	M.J. Horton/T.W. Graveney	v	Somerset	Worcester	1962
4th	281	J.A. Ormrod/Younis Ahmed	v	Notts	Nottingham	1979
5th	393	E.G. Arnold/W.B. Burns	v	Warwicks	Birmingham	1909
6th	227	E.J.O. Hemsley/D.N. Patel	v	Oxford U	Oxford	1976
7th	197	H.H.I. Gibbons/R. Howorth	v	Surrey	The Oval	1938
8th	145*	F. Chester/W.H. Taylor	v	Essex	Worcester	1914
9th	181	J.A. Cuffe/R.D. Burrows	v	Glos	Worcester	1907
10th	119	W.B. Burns/G.A. Wilson	v	Somerset	Worcester	1906

Best Bowling	For	9-23	C.F. Root	v	Lancashire	Worcester	1931
(Innings)	V	10-51	J. Mercer	for	Glamorgan	Worcester	1936
Best Bowling	For	15-87	A.J. Conway	v	Glos	Moreton-in-M	1914
(Match)	V	17-212	J.C. Clay	for	Glamorgan	Swansea	1937

Most Runs – Season	2,654	H.H.I. Gibbons	(av 52.03)	1934
Most Runs – Career	33,490	D. Kenyon	(av 33.19)	1946-1967
Most 100s – Season	10	G.M. Turner		1970
Most 100s – Career	72	G.M. Turner		1967-1982
Most Wkts – Season	207	C.F. Root	(av 17.52)	1925
Most Wkts – Career	2,143	R.T.D. Perks	(av 23.73)	1930-1955

LIMITED-OVERS CRICKET

Highest Total	**NWT**	312-5		v	Lancashire	Manchester	1985
	BHC	314-5		v	Lancashire	Manchester	1980
	JPL	307-4		v	Derbyshire	Worcester	1975
Lowest Total	**NWT**	98		v	Durham	Chester-le-St	1968
	BHC	92		v	Comb Univs	Cambridge	1975
	JPL	86		v	Yorkshire	Leeds	1969
Highest Innings	**NWT**	117*	G.M. Turner	v	Lancashire	Worcester	1971
	BHC	143*	G.M. Turner	v	Warwicks	Birmingham	1976
	JPL	147	G.M. Turner	v	Sussex	Horsham	1980
Best Bowling	**NWT**	6-14	J.A. Flavell	v	Lancashire	Worcester	1963
	BHC	6-8	N. Gifford	v	Minor C (S)	High Wycombe	1979
	JPL	6-26	A.P. Pridgeon	v	Surrey	Worcester	1978

WORCESTERSHIRE 1986

RESULTS SUMMARY

	Place	Won	Lost	Drew	Abandoned
Britannic Assurance Championship	**5th**	7	5	12	
All First-class Matches		7	5	13	
John Player League	**16th**	5	11		
NatWest Bank Trophy	Lost to Sussex (Semi-Final)				
Benson and Hedges Cup	Lost to Kent (Semi-Final)				

BRITANNIC ASSURANCE CHAMPIONSHIP AVERAGES

BATTING AND FIELDING

Cap		M	I	NO	HS	Runs	Avge	100	50	Ct/St
1986	G.A. Hick	23	36	6	227*	1934	64.46	6	10	29
1984	T.S. Curtis	23	38	9	153	1451	50.03	2	10	9
1979	D.N. Patel	23	29	9	132*	991	49.55	3	2	5
1984	D.M. Smith	20	28	4	165*	1041	43.37	3	5	9
1978	P.A. Neale	24	33	7	118*	979	37.65	1	6	7
1986	S.J. Rhodes	24	26	10	77*	506	31.62	—	3	57/8
1985	D.B. D'Oliveira	24	39	2	146*	1054	28.48	1	3	11
1986	P.J. Newport	22	16	4	68	281	23.41	—	1	8
1986	R.K. Illingworth	17	14	3	39	185	16.81	—	—	9
1985	N.V. Radford	17	12	2	30	144	14.40	—	—	12
1986	M.J. Weston	7	11	2	30	118	13.11	—	—	2
1976	J.D. Inchmore	9	8	2	23*	55	9.16	—	—	3
1980	A.P. Pridgeon	20	10	3	10*	44	6.28	—	—	9

Also batted: R.M. Ellcock (1 match) 4*; S.R. Lampitt (1 match) 11*; S.M. McEwan (8 matches) 5*,1*,7 (7 ct); L.K. Smith (1 match) 2,2 (1 ct).

BOWLING

	O	M	R	W	Avge	Best	5 wI	10 wM
A.P. Pridgeon	535	134	1396	59	23.66	6-52	1	—
N.V. Radford	584.4	122	1882	76	24.76	9-70	6	3
P.J. Newport	617.3	88	2081	83	25.07	6-48	5	1
S.M. McEwan	180.1	31	638	16	39.87	3-33	—	—
J.D. Inchmore	221.1	49	562	13	43.23	2-41	—	—
D.N. Patel	451	115	1251	28	44.67	5-88	1	—
R.K. Illingworth	551.2	188	1310	27	48.51	5-64	1	—

Also bowled: D.B. D'Oliveira 27.4-6-118-5; R.M. Ellcock 15-1-40-1; G.A. Hick 28.4-5-109-3; S.R. Lampitt 7-1-21-0; D.M. Smith 11-3-35-2; M.J. Weston 126-36-354-5.

The First-Class Averages (pp. 167–182) give the records of Worcestershire players in all first-class county matches (their other opponents being the Indians), with the exception of: N.V. Radford 18-13-2-30-165-15.00-0-0-11 ct. 602.4-125-1945-78-24.93-9/70-6-3.

YORKSHIRE

Formation of Present Club: 8 January 1863
Substantial Reorganisation: 10 December 1891
Colours: Oxford Blue, Light Blue and Gold
Badge: White Rose
Championships (since 1890): (29) 1893, 1896, 1898, 1900, 1901, 1902, 1905, 1908, 1912, 1919, 1922, 1923, 1924, 1925, 1931, 1932, 1933, 1935, 1937, 1938, 1939, 1946, 1959, 1960, 1962, 1963, 1966, 1967, 1968.
Joint Championships: (1) 1949
NatWest Trophy/Gillette Cup Winners: (2) 1965, 1969
Benson and Hedges Cup Winners. (0) Finalists 1972
John Player League Champions: (1) 1983
Match Awards: NWT 19; BHC 38

Secretary: J. Lister, Headingley Cricket Ground, Leeds LS6 3BU
Captain: P. Carrick
Scorer: E.I. Lester
Scores/Prospects: ☎ Leeds (0532) 787394

BAIRSTOW, David Leslie (Hanson GS, Bradford), b Bradford 1 Sep 1951. 5'9½". RHB, WK, RM. Debut 1970. Cap 1973. Captain 1984-86. GW 1976-78 (capt 1977-78). Benefit 1982. **Tests:** 4 (1979 to 1980-81); HS 59 v Ind (Oval) on debut. LOI: 21. Tours: Aus 1978-79, 1979-80; WI 1980-81. 1000 runs (3); most – 1181 (1985). HS 145 v Middx (Scarborough) 1980. BB 3-82 GW v Transvaal B (Johannesburg) 1976-77. Held 11 catches v Derbys (Scarborough) 1982 to equal world record for a first-class match. Awards: NWT 1; BHC 6. Soccer: Bradford City. **NWT:** HS 92 v Worcs (Leeds) 1982. **BHC:** HS 103* v Derbys (Derby) 1981. **JPL:** HS 83* v Surrey (Oval) 1986.

BERRY, Philip John (Saltscar CS; Longlands CFE, Redcar), b Saltburn 28 Dec 1966. 6'0". RHB, OB. Debut 1986. HS 4*. BB 1-10. England YC v Sri Lanka 1986.

BLAKEY, Richard John (Rastrick GS), b Huddersfield 15 Jan 1967. 5'9". RHB, WK. Debut 1985. HS 90 v Somerset (Leeds) 1985. BB 1-68. **JPL:** HS 3.

BOOTH, Paul Antony (Hanley HS), b Huddersfield 5 Sep 1965. 5'10". LHB, SLA. Debut 1982. HS 26 v Worcs (Scarborough) 1984. BB 3-22 v Northants (Northampton) 1984. **NWT:** HS 6*. **BHC:** HS 1. BB 2-28 v Worcs (Bradford) 1985. **JPL:** BB 1-57.

BYAS, David (Scarborough C), b Kilham 26 Aug 1963. 6'4". LHB, RM. Debut 1986. HS 0. **BHC:** HS 2. **JPL:** HS 15 v Leics (Leicester) 1985.

CARRICK, Phillip (Bramley SS; Intake SS; Park Lane CPE), b Armley 16 Jul 1952. 5'11½". RHB, SLA. Debut 1970. Cap 1976. Captain 1987. E. Province 1976-77. N. Transvaal 1982-83. Benefit 1985. Tours: SA 1975-76 (DHR); SL 1977-78 (DHR). HS 131* v Northants (Northampton) 1980. BB 8-33 v CU (Cambridge) 1973. Award: BHC 1. **NWT:** HS 54 v Sussex (Leeds) 1986. BB 3-27 v Northants (Leeds) 1983. **BHC:** HS 53 v Warwicks (Leeds) 1985. BB 3-40 v Warwicks (Birmingham) 1984. **JPL:** HS 43* v Surrey (Oval) 1984. BB 4-13 v Derbys (Bradford) 1983.

DENNIS, Simon John (Scarborough C), b Scarborough 18 Oct 1960. 6'1". RHB, LFM. Nephew of F. Dennis (Yorkshire 1928-33) and Sir Leonard Hutton (Yorkshire and England 1934-55). Debut 1980. Cap 1983. OFS 1982-83. HS 53* v Notts (Nottingham) 1984. BB 5-35 v Somerset (Sheffield) 1981. **NWT:** HS 14 v Salop (Telford) 1984. BB 2-45 v Northants (Leeds) 1983. **BHC:** HS 10 v Warwicks (Birmingham) 1984. BB 3-41 v Northants (Bradford) 1984. **JPL:** HS 16* v Glam, 16* v Derbys 1983. BB 3-19 v Hants (Middlesbrough) 1981.

FLETCHER, Stuart David (Reins Wood SS), b Keighley 8 Jun 1964. 5'10". RHB, RMF. Debut 1983. HS 28* v Kent (Tunbridge Wells) 1984. BB 5-90 v Middx (Leeds) 1986. **NWT:** HS 2*. BB 3-34 v Somerset (Leeds) 1985. **BHC:** HS 0*. BB 2-42 v Sussex (Hove) 1984. **JPL:** HS 8. BB 4-32 v Glam (Scarborough) 1986.

HARTLEY, Peter John (Greenhead GS; Bradford C), b Keighley 18 Apr 1960. 6'0". RHB, RMF. Warwickshire 1982. Yorkshire debut 1985. HS 87* v Essex (Chelmsford) 1986. BB 6-68 v Notts (Sheffield) 1986. Award: BHC 1. **NWT:** HS 23 and BB 3-47 v Sussex (Leeds) 1986. **BHC:** HS 29* v Notts (Nottingham) 1986. BB 5-43 v Scotland (Leeds) 1986. **JPL:** HS 35 v Derbys (Chesterfield) 1986. BB 3-47 v Northants (Luton) 1986.

HARTLEY, Stuart **Neil** (Beckfoot GS, Bingley; Cannington HS, Perth, WA), b Shipley 18 Mar 1956. 6'0". RHB, RM. Debut 1978. Cap 1981. OFS 1981-83. HS 114 v Glos (Bradford) 1982. BB 4-51 v Surrey (Oval) 1985. Awards: BHC 1. **NWT:** HS 69 v Somerset (Leeds) 1985. BB 1-41. **BHC:** HS 65* v Warwicks (Birmingham) 1984. BB 4-39 v Scotland (Perth) 1984. **JPL:** HS 73 v Warwicks (Scarborough) 1984. BB 3-31 v Notts (Scarborough) 1980.

JARVIS, Paul William (Bydales CS, Marske), b Redcar 29 Jun 1965. 5'10". RHB, RFM. Debut 1981 aged 16 years 75 days (youngest Yorkshire player). Cap 1986. HS 47 v Essex (Chelmsford) 1986. BB 7-55 v Surrey (Leeds) 1986. **NWT:** HS 16 v Somerset (Leeds) 1985. BB 3-32 v Middx (Leeds) 1986. **BHC:** HS 20 v Worcs (Bradford) 1985. BB 3-31 v Warwicks (Leeds) 1985. **JPL:** HS 27* v Essex (Sheffield) 1986. BB 4-13 v Worcs (Leeds) 1986.

LOVE, James Derek (Brudenell SS), b Leeds 22 Apr 1955. 6'2½". RHB, RM. Debut 1975. Cap 1980. LOI: 3. 1000 runs (2); most – 1203 (1981). HS 170* v Worcs (Worcester) 1979. BB 1-8. Awards: BHC 2. **NWT:** HS 61* v Hants (Southampton) 1980. **BHC:** HS 118* v Scotland (Bradford) 1981. **JPL:** HS 104* v Notts (Hull) 1986. BB 1-6.

METCALFE, Ashley Anthony (Bradford GS; University C, London), b Horsforth 25 Dec 1963. 5'8". RHB, OB. Debut 1983 scoring 122 v Notts (Bradford). Cap 1986. YC 1986. 1000 runs (1): 1803 (1986). HS 151 v Lancs (Manchester) 1986. **NWT:** HS 33 v Somerset (Leeds) 1985. **BHC:** HS 31 v Scotland (Leeds) 1986. **JPL:** HS 115* v Glos (Scarborough) 1984.

MOXON, Martyn Douglas (Holgate GS, Barnsley), b Barnsley 4 May 1960. 6'0". RHB, RM. Debut 1981 scoring 5 and 116 v Essex (Leeds). Cap 1984. GW 1982-84. **Tests:** 2 (1986); HS 74 v NZ (Lord's) on debut. Tours: Ind 1984-85; SL 1984-85, 1985-86 (Eng B). 1000 runs (2); most – 1447 (1985). HS 168 v Worcs (Worcester) 1985. BB 3-26 D.B. Close's XI v Sri Lankans (Scarborough) 1984. Awards: NWT 3; BHC 2. **NWT:** HS 82* v Cheshire (Birkenhead) 1985. **BHC:** HS 106* v Lancs (Manchester) 1986. BB 1-23. **JPL:** HS 86 v Somerset (Bath) 1985. BB 1-16.

OLDHAM, Stephen (Crossfield High Green S), b High Green, Sheffield 27 Jul 1948. 6'1". RHB, RFM. Yorkshire 1974-79 and 1984-. Derbyshire 1980-83 (cap 1980). HS 50 v Sussex (Hove) 1979. BB 7-78 Derbys v Warwicks (Birmingham) 1982. Award: BHC 1. **NWT:** HS 19 v Salop (Telford) 1984. BB 3-29 Derbys v Notts (Derby) 1981. **BHC:** HS 4*. BB 5-32 v Minor C (N) (Scunthorpe) 1975. **JPL:** HS 38* v Glam (Cardiff) 1977. BB 5-37 Derbys v Lancs (Derby) 1982.

PICKLES, Christopher Stephen (Whitcliffe Mount CS), b Mirfield 30 Jan 1966. 6'1". RHB, RM. Debut 1985. HS 31* v Leics (Bradford) 1985. BB 2-31 v Kent (Scarborough) 1985. **JPL:** HS 16* v Glam (Scarborough) 1986. BB 2-28 v Somerset (Bath) 1985.

ROBINSON, Phillip Edward (Greenhead GS, Keighley), b Keighley 3 Aug 1963. 5'9". RHB, LM. Debut 1984. HS 104* v Kent (Scarborough) 1986. **NWT:** HS 66 v Middx (Leeds) 1986. **BHC:** HS 42 v Leics (Leicester) 1985. **JPL:** HS 78* v Leics (Leicester) 1985.
SHARP, Kevin (Abbey Grange HS, Leeds), b Leeds 6 Apr 1959. 5'9". LHB, OB. Debut 1976. Cap 1982. GW 1981-84. Tour: NZ 1979-80 (DHR). 1000 runs (1): 1445 (1984). HS 181 v Glos (Harrogate) 1986. BB 2-13 v Glam (Bradford) 1984. **NWT:** HS 33* v Cambs (Leeds) 1986. **BHC:** HS 105* v Scotland (Leeds) 1986. **JPL:** HS 114 v Essex (Chelmsford) 1985.
SHAW, Christopher (Crofton HS), b Hemsworth 17 Feb 1964. 6'1". RHB, RFM. Debut 1984. HS 21 v Leics (Middlesbrough) 1986. BB 5-38 v Northants (Scarborough) 1986. **NWT:** HS 6*. BB 2-56 v Sussex (Leeds) 1986. **JPL:** HS 26 v Glam (Leeds) 1984. BB 5-41 v Hants (Bournemouth) 1984.
SIDEBOTTOM, Arnold (Broadway GS, Barnsley), b Barnsley 1 Apr 1954. 6'1". RHB, RMF. Debut 1973. Cap 1980. OFS 1981-84. **Tests:** 1 (1985); HS 2 and BB 1-65 v Aus (Nottingham). Tours: SA 1981-82 (SAB). HS 124 v Glam (Cardiff) 1977. BB 8-72 v Leics (Middlesbrough) 1986. Award: BHC 1. Soccer: Manchester United, Huddersfield Town and Halifax Town. **NWT:** HS 45 v Hants (Bournemouth) 1977. BB 4-35 v Kent (Leeds) 1980. **BHC:** HS 32 v Notts (Leeds) 1983. BB 5-27 v Worcs (Bradford) 1985. **JPL:** HS 52* v Northants (Middlesbrough) 1982. BB 4-24 v Surrey (Scarborough) 1975.
SWALLOW, Ian Geoffrey (Hoyland Kirk CS, Balk), b Barnsley 18 Dec 1962. 5'7½". RHB, OB. Debut 1983. HS 43* v Hants (Bournemouth) 1986. BB 4-52 v Kent (Tunbridge W) 1984. **BHC:** HS 10* v Worcs (Bradford) 1985. BB 1-40. **JPL:** HS 2.

SALVE

ANDREW, Christopher **Robert** (Barnard Castle S; St John's C Cambridge), b Richmond, Yorks 18 Feb 1963. 5'10". LHB, OB. Debut 1984. Blue 1984–85. Captain 1985. HS 101* v Notts (Nottingham) 1984. BB 3-77 v Leics (Cambridge) 1984. Rugby for CU and England (fly half); kicked all 21 points in defeat of Wales 1985-86. **BHC:** HS 82* Comb Us v Essex (Chelmsford) 1985. BB 1-15.

VALETE

BOYCOTT, Geoffrey (Hemsworth GS), b Fitzwilliam 21 Oct 1940. 5'10". RHB, RM. Yorkshire debut 1962. Cap 1963. *Wisden* 1964. YC 1964. Captain 1971-78. N Transvaal 1971-72. Benefit 1974. OBE 1980. Testimonial 1984. **Tests:** 108 (1964 to 1981-82, 4 as captain); HS 246* v Ind (Leeds) 1967; BB 3-47 v SA (Cape Town) 1964-65. LOI: 36. Tours: Aus 1965-66, 1970-71, 1978-79, 1979-80; SA 1964-65, 1981-82 (SAB); WI 1967-68, 1973-74, 1980-81; NZ 1965-66, 1977-78 (capt); Ind 1979-80, 1981-82; Pak 1977-78; SL 1969-70. 1000 runs (23+3); most – 2503 (1971). HS 261* MCC v WIBC President's XI (Bridgetown) 1973-74. Yorks HS 260* v Essex (Colchester) 1970. BB 4-14 v Lancs (Leeds) 1979. Awards: NWT 2; BHC 9.
STEVENSON, G.B. – see NORTHAMPTONSHIRE.

YORKSHIRE RECORDS

FIRST-CLASS CRICKET

Highest Total	For	887		v	Warwicks	Birmingham	1896
	V	630		by	Somerset	Leeds	1901
Lowest Total	For	23		v	Hampshire	Middlesbrough	1965
	V	13		by	Notts	Nottingham	1901
Highest Innings	For	341	G.H. Hirst	v	Leics	Leicester	1905
	V	318*	W.G. Grace	for	Glos	Cheltenham	1876

Highest Partnerships

Wkt						
1st	555	P. Holmes/H. Sutcliffe	v	Essex	Leyton	1932
2nd	346	W. Barber/M. Leyland	v	Middlesex	Sheffield	1932
3rd	323*	H. Sutcliffe/M. Leyland	v	Glamorgan	Huddersfield	1928
4th	312	D. Denton/G.H. Hirst	v	Hampshire	Southampton	1914
5th	340	E. Wainwright/G.H. Hirst	v	Surrey	The Oval	1899
6th	276	M. Leyland/E. Robinson	v	Glamorgan	Swansea	1926
7th	254	W. Rhodes/D.C.F. Burton	v	Hampshire	Dewsbury	1919
8th	292	R. Peel/Lord Hawke	v	Warwicks	Birmingham	1896
9th	192	G.H. Hirst/S. Haigh	v	Surrey	Bradford	1898
10th	149	G. Boycott/G.B. Stevenson	v	Warwicks	Birmingham	1982

Best Bowling	For	10-10	H. Verity	v	Notts	Leeds	1932
(Innings)	V	10-37	C.V. Grimmett	for	Australians	Sheffield	1930
Best Bowling	For	17-91	H. Verity	v	Essex	Leyton	1933
(Match)	V	17-91	H. Dean	for	Lancashire	Liverpool	1913

Most Runs – Season	2,883	H. Sutcliffe	(av 80.08)	1932
Most Runs – Career	38,561	H. Sutcliffe	(av 50.20)	1919-1945
Most 100s – Season	12	H. Sutcliffe		1932
Most 100s – Career	112	H. Sutcliffe		1919-1945
Most Wkts – Season	240	W. Rhodes	(av 12.72)	1900
Most Wkts – Career	3,608	W. Rhodes	(av 16.00)	1898-1930

LIMITED-OVERS CRICKET

Highest Total	**NWT**	317-4		v	Surrey	Lord's	1965
	BHC	317-5		v	Scotland	Leeds	1986
	JPL	263-8		v	Surrey	Bradford	1985
Lowest Total	**NWT**	76		v	Surrey	Harrogate	1970
	BHC	114		v	Kent	Canterbury	1978
	JPL	74		v	Warwicks	Birmingham	1972
Highest Innings	**NWT**	146	G. Boycott	v	Surrey	Lord's	1965
	BHC	142	G. Boycott	v	Worcs	Worcester	1980
	JPL	119	J.H. Hampshire	v	Leics	Hull	1971
Best Bowling	**NWT**	6-15	F.S. Trueman	v	Somerset	Taunton	1965
	BHC	6-27	A.G. Nicholson	v	Minor C (N)	Middlesbrough	1972
	JPL	7-15	R.A. Hutton	v	Worcs	Leeds	1969

YORKSHIRE 1986

RESULTS SUMMARY

	Place	Won	Lost	Drew	Tied	Aban
Britannic Assurance Championship	**10th**	4	5	15		
All First-class Matches		4	6	15		
John Player League	**8th**	7	6		1	2
NatWest Bank Trophy	Lost to Sussex (Quarter-Final)					
Benson and Hedges Cup	Failed to qualify for Quarter-Final					

BRITANNIC ASSURANCE CHAMPIONSHIP AVERAGES

BATTING AND FIELDING

Cap		*M*	*I*	*NO*	*HS*	*Runs*	*Avge*	*100*	*50*	*Ct/St*
1963	G. Boycott	12	18	1	135*	890	52.35	2	7	3
1986	A.A. Metcalfe	24	37	0	151	1582	42.75	6	5	10
—	P.E. Robinson	7	11	2	104*	373	41.44	1	3	5
1982	K. Sharp	18	29	6	181	948	41.21	2	5	9
1980	J.D. Love	21	29	5	109	831	34.62	1	4	7
—	P.J. Hartley	15	17	4	87*	441	33.92	—	4	7
—	I.G. Swallow	8	9	4	43*	141	28.20	—	—	—
1973	D.L. Bairstow	24	33	4	88	796	27.44	—	3	41/3
1984	M.D. Moxon	17	27	3	147	636	26.50	1	3	12
1982	S.N. Hartley	20	28	2	78	676	26.00	—	3	5
1976	P. Carrick	24	32	6	51	613	23.57	—	3	9
—	R.J. Blakey	3	5	0	46	99	19.80	—	—	4
1986	P.W. Jarvis	15	17	7	47	183	18.30	—	—	10
1983	S.J. Dennis	15	12	4	18*	82	10.25	—	—	3
—	S.D. Fletcher	14	10	3	24	67	9.57	—	—	1
—	C. Shaw	13	10	4	21	57	9.50	—	—	2
1980	A. Sidebottom	10	9	2	18	65	9.28	—	—	2

Also batted: P.J. Berry (1 match) 4* (2 ct); D. Byas (1 match) 0 (1 ct); G.B. Stevenson (2 matches – cap 1978) 58*.

BOWLING

	O	*M*	*R*	*W*	*Avge*	*Best*	*5 wI*	*10 wM*
P.W. Jarvis	428.4	82	1332	60	22.20	7-55	5	2
C. Shaw	281.1	60	773	29	26.65	5-38	1	—
P.J. Hartley	321.1	49	1095	41	26.70	6-68	1	—
A. Sidebottom	226.1	37	671	25	26.84	8-72	1	—
S.J. Dennis	384.3	75	1230	42	29.28	5-71	1	—
S.D. Fletcher	389	79	1172	29	40.41	5-90	1	—
P. Carrick	590.3	185	1412	31	45.54	4-111	—	—

Also bowled: D.L. Bairstow 5-3-7-0; P.J. Berry 39-13-83-1; R.J. Blakey 10.3-1-68-1; D. Byas 2-0-15-0; S.N. Hartley 45.4-8-195-4; J.D. Love 39.2-7-146-0; A.A. Metcalfe 18.1-4-75-0; M.D. Moxon 27.4-9-90-2; P.E. Robinson 11-0-115-0; K. Sharp 29-4-192-3; G.B. Stevenson 29-8-75-2; I.G. Swallow 142-36-386-5.

The First-Class Averages (pp. 167–182) give the records of Yorkshire players in all first-class county matches (their other opponents being the Indians), with the exception of G. Boycott, whose full county figures are as above, and: A.A. Metcalfe 25-39-0-151-1674-42.92-6-6-10 ct. 18.1-4-75-0. M.D. Moxon 18-29-4-147-871-34.84-3-3-12 ct. 35.4-10-113-2-56.50-1/18.

Congratulations to Sussex on winning the 1986 NatWest Trophy.
NatWest
The Action Bank

OXFORD v CAMBRIDGE
142ND UNIVERSITY MATCH

At Lord's on 2, 3, 4 July, 1986. Cambridge won by 5 wickets. Toss: Cambridge.

OXFORD UNIVERSITY

D.A. Hagan c Lea b Davidson	12	c Lea b Ellison	31
A.A.G. Mee c Brown b Ellison	41	c Bail b Davidson	0
M.J. Kilborn c Brown b Ellison	28	c Brown b Scott	59
*D.A. Thorne b Davidson	61	not out	104
C.D.M. Tooley c Bail b Golding	2	b Davidson	31
R.S. Rutnagur b Golding	5	b Golding	5
N.V. Salvi run out	7	c Browne b Davidson	10
R.A. Rydon c Bail b Davidson	2	c Browne b Golding	2
†J.E.B. Cope lbw b Davidson	1	c Lea b Golding	0
T.A.J. Dawson not out	1	c Brown b Davidson	0
M.P. Lawrence b Davidson	0	lbw b Scott	0
Extras (LB6, NB1)	7	(B3, LB16, W4, NB3)	26
Total	167		268

CAMBRIDGE UNIVERSITY

P.A.C. Bail lbw b Rydon	174	c Tooley b Thorne	7
M.S. Ahluwalia lbw b Thorne	9		
D.J. Fell b Rutnagur	22	c Lawrence b Rutnagur	20
D.W. Browne c Cope b Rutnagur	2	(6) not out	13
*D.G. Price lbw b Thorne	0	c Kilborn b Rutnagur	7
A.E. Lea c Lawrence b Dawson	19	(2) b Rutnagur	19
A.K. Golding b Dawson	47	not out	0
†A.D. Brown b Dawson	4		
J.E. Davidson not out	41	(4) run out	26
A.M.G. Scott not out	1		
C.C. Ellison did not bat			
Extras (LB7, W3, NB1)	11	(B1, LB12, W1)	14
Total (8 wickets declared)	330	(5 wickets)	106

CAMBRIDGE	*O*	*M*	*R*	*W*	*O*	*M*	*R*	*W*
Davidson	19.1	3	58	5	30	4	92	4
Scott	15	4	36	0	17.5	6	43	2
Ellison	10	5	19	2	11	5	21	1
Golding	22	8	39	2	30	10	51	3
Lea	3	0	9	0	10	0	42	0
OXFORD								
Thorne	32	11	42	2	8	0	43	1
Rydon	21	4	89	1				
Rutnagur	26	3	69	2	8	0	50	3
Dawson	28	4	92	3				
Lawrence	10	2	31	0				

FALL OF WICKETS

Wkt	*OU 1st*	*CU 1st*	*OU 2nd*	*CU 2nd*
1st	26	37	2	12
2nd	72	93	84	52
3rd	97	97	121	55
4th	117	100	199	68
5th	123	171	218	102
6th	163	269	229	—
7th	165	280	245	—
8th	166	289	267	—
9th	167	—	267	—
10th	167	—	268	—

Umpires: M.J. Kitchen and D.O. Oslear

UNIVERSITY MATCH RESULTS

Played: 142 Wins: Cambridge 54; Oxford 46 Draws: 42

This, the oldest surviving first-class fixture, dates from 1827 and, wartime interruptions apart, it has been played annually since 1838. With the exception of five matches played in the area of Oxford (1829, 1843, 1846, 1848 and 1850), all the fixtures have been played at Lord's.

Year	Result
1827	Drawn
1829	Oxford
1836	Oxford
1838	Oxford
1839	Cambridge
1840	Cambridge
1841	Cambridge
1842	Cambridge
1843	Cambridge
1844	Drawn
1845	Cambridge
1846	Oxford
1847	Cambridge
1848	Oxford
1849	Cambridge
1850	Oxford
1851	Cambridge
1852	Oxford
1853	Oxford
1854	Oxford
1855	Oxford
1856	Cambridge
1857	Oxford
1858	Oxford
1859	Cambridge
1860	Cambridge
1861	Cambridge
1862	Cambridge
1863	Oxford
1864	Oxford
1865	Oxford
1866	Oxford
1867	Cambridge
1868	Cambridge
1869	Cambridge
1870	Cambridge
1871	Oxford
1872	Cambridge
1873	Oxford
1874	Oxford
1875	Oxford
1876	Cambridge
1877	Oxford
1878	Cambridge
1879	Cambridge
1880	Cambridge
1881	Oxford
1882	Cambridge
1883	Cambridge
1884	Oxford
1885	Cambridge
1886	Oxford
1887	Oxford
1888	Drawn
1889	Cambridge
1890	Cambridge
1891	Cambridge
1892	Oxford
1893	Cambridge
1894	Oxford
1895	Cambridge
1896	Oxford
1897	Cambridge
1898	Oxford
1899	Drawn
1900	Drawn
1901	Drawn
1902	Cambridge
1903	Oxford
1904	Drawn
1905	Cambridge
1906	Cambridge
1907	Cambridge
1908	Oxford
1909	Drawn
1910	Oxford
1911	Oxford
1912	Cambridge
1913	Cambridge
1914	Oxford
1919	Oxford
1920	Drawn
1921	Cambridge
1922	Cambridge
1923	Oxford
1924	Cambridge
1925	Drawn
1926	Cambridge
1927	Cambridge
1928	Drawn
1929	Drawn
1930	Cambridge
1931	Oxford
1932	Drawn
1933	Drawn
1934	Drawn
1935	Cambridge
1936	Cambridge
1937	Oxford
1938	Drawn
1939	Oxford
1946	Oxford
1947	Drawn
1948	Oxford
1949	Cambridge
1950	Drawn
1951	Oxford
1952	Drawn
1953	Cambridge
1954	Drawn
1955	Drawn
1956	Drawn
1957	Cambridge
1958	Cambridge
1959	Oxford
1960	Drawn
1961	Drawn
1962	Drawn
1963	Drawn
1964	Drawn
1965	Drawn
1966	Oxford
1967	Drawn
1968	Drawn
1969	Drawn
1970	Drawn
1971	Drawn
1972	Cambridge
1973	Drawn
1974	Drawn
1975	Drawn
1976	Oxford
1977	Drawn
1978	Drawn
1979	Cambridge
1980	Drawn
1981	Drawn
1982	Cambridge
1983	Drawn
1984	Oxford
1985	Drawn
1986	Cambridge

CAMBRIDGE UNIVERSITY

AHLUWALIA, Manraj Singh (**'Manny'**) (Latymer Upper S; Emmanuel), b Isleworth Middx 27 Dec 1965. 5'4½". RHB, OB. Debut 1985. Blue 1986. HS 36 v Sussex (Hove) 1986.

BAIL, Paul Andrew Clayton (Millfield S; Downing), b Burnham-on-Sea, Somerset 23 Jun 1965. 5'10". RHB. Somerset debut 1985. CU debut/blue 1986. HS 174 v OU (Lord's) 1986.

BROWN, Adrian Desmond (Clacton County HS; Magdalene), b Clacton on Sea, Essex 18 May 1962. 5'10½". RHB, WK. Debut/blue 1986. Suffolk debut 1984. HS 30 v Surrey (Cambridge) 1986.

BROWNE, David William (Stamford S; St Catharine's), b Stamford, Lincs 4 Apr 1964. 6'6". RHB. Debut 1985. Blue 1986. HS 61* v Sussex (Hove) 1986. BB 1-13.

DAVIDSON, John Edward (Penglais CS; Trinity), b Aberystwyth, Cardiganshire 23 Oct 1964. 6'3". RHB, RFM. Debut 1985. Blue 1985-86. HS 41* v OU (Lord's) 1986. BB 5-35 v Hants (Cambridge) 1986.

ELLISON, Charles Christopher (Tonbridge S; Homerton), b Pembury, Kent 11 Feb 1962. 6'2". RHB, RM. Brother of R.M. (Kent and England). Debut 1982. Blue 1982-83-85-86. Wiltshire 1984-85. HS 51* v Warwicks (Cambridge) 1986. BB 5-82 v Leics (Cambridge) 1986.

FELL, David John (The John Lyon S, Harrow; Trinity), b Stafford 27 Oct 1964. 5'9". RHB, LB. Debut 1985. Blue 1985-86. HS 114 v Sussex (Hove) 1986.

GOLDING, Andrew Kenneth (Colchester RGS; St Catharine's), b Colchester 5 Oct 1963. 5'9". RHB, SLA. Essex debut 1983, CU debut 1984. Blue 1986. HS 47 and BB 3-51 v OU (Lord's) 1986.

GORMAN, Shaun Rodney (St Peter's S, York; Emmanuel), b Middlesbrough 28 Apr 1965. 6'2". RHB, OB. Debut/blue 1985. HS 43 v OU (Lord's) 1985. BB 1-27.

HEAD, Timothy John (Lancing C; Queens), b Hammersmith, London 22 Sep 1957. RHB, WK. Sussex 1976-81. CU debut 1986. HS 52* Sussex v Australians (Hove) 1981.

HEATH, Stephen David (King Edward's S, Birmingham; Trinity), b Bristol 7 Jul 1967. 6'1". RHB, LB. Debut 1986. HS 10 v Hants (Cambridge) 1986.

LEA, Antony Edward (High Arcal S; Churchill), b Wolverhampton 29 Sep 1962. 6'0½". RHB, LB. Debut 1984. Blue 1984-85-86. HS 119 v Essex (Cambridge) 1984. BB 3-61 v Sussex (Hove) 1986.

LORD, Timothy Michael (Bedford Modern S; Christ's), b Cambridge 10 Feb 1966. 5'10". RHB. Debut 1986. HS 23 v Warwicks (Cambridge) 1986. Rugby blue 1986.

PRICE, David Gregory (Haberdashers' Aske's S; Homerton), b Luton 7 Feb 1965. 5'11". RHB, OB. Debut 1984. Blue 1984-85-86. **Captain 1986-87**. HS 60 v Northants (Cambridge) 1986.

SCOTT, Alastair Martin Gordon (Seaford Head CS; Queens), b Guildford 31 Mar 1966. 5'10". RHB, LM. Debut 1985. Blue 1985-86. Secretary 1987. Sussex debut 1986. HS 8. BB 5-68 v Notts (Cambridge) 1985.

TREMELLEN, Jonathan Michael (Whitland GS; Bradfield C; St Catharine's), b Pendine, Carmarthenshire 30 Oct 1965. 6'1". RHB, RM. Debut 1986. HS 4*.

CAMBRIDGE UNIVERSITY 1986

RESULTS SUMMARY

	Played	Won	Lost	Drawn
All First-Class Matches	8	1	1	6

FIRST-CLASS AVERAGES

BATTING AND FIELDING

	M	I	NO	HS	Runs	Avge	100	50	Ct/St
†D.J. Fell	8	15	2	114	379	29.15	1	—	1
†C.C. Ellison	5	3	1	51*	54	27.00	—	1	1
†D.W. Browne	7	13	4	61*	228	25.33	—	1	4
†P.A.C. Bail	8	15	0	174	379	25.26	1	—	5
†A.K. Golding	6	9	3	47	134	22.33	—	—	2
†J.E. Davidson	8	8	3	41*	103	20.60	—	—	2
†M.S. Ahluwalia	6	11	0	36	198	18.00	—	—	—
†A.M.G. Scott	7	6	5	5	17	17.00	—	—	3
†D.G. Price	7	13	1	60	187	15.58	—	1	3
T.J. Head	3	5	1	40*	62	15.50	—	—	1
S.R. Gorman	6	9	3	37	76	12.66	—	—	4
†A.E. Lea	5	8	0	19	79	9.87	—	—	6
†A.D. Brown	8	9	1	30	78	9.75	—	—	15/2
T.M. Lord	2	4	0	23	31	7.75	—	—	—

Played in one match: S.D. Heath 10,6; J.M. Tremellen 3,4*.

BOWLING

	O	M	R	W	Avge	Best	5 wI	10 wM
C.C. Ellison	127	41	325	14	23.21	5-82	1	—
J.E. Davidson	288	47	877	28	31.32	5-35	2	—
A.E. Lea	54	6	191	6	31.83	3-61	—	—
A.M.G. Scott	238	62	662	16	41.37	4-100	—	—
A.K. Golding	220	46	604	10	60.40	3-51	—	—

Also bowled: P.A.C. Bail 4-0-28-0; D.W. Browne 23-5-76-1; S.R. Gorman 49-10-184-2; S.D. Heath 7-0-39-0; D.G. Price 1.2-0-11-0; J.M. Tremellen 7-0-32-0.

The above figures do not include performances in the match between a Combined Oxford and Cambridge Universities XI against the New Zealanders.

† Blue 1986

CAMBRIDGE UNIVERSITY RECORDS

FIRST-CLASS CRICKET

Highest Total	For	703-9d		v	Sussex	Hove	1890
	V	703-3d		by	W Indians	Cambridge	1950
Lowest Total	For	30		v	Yorkshire	Cambridge	1928
	V	32		by	Oxford U	Lord's	1878
Highest Innings	For	254*	K.S. Duleepsinhji	v	Middlesex	Cambridge	1927
	V	304*	E. de C. Weekes	for	W Indians	Cambridge	1950

Highest Partnerships

Wkt						
1st	349	J.G. Dewes/D.S. Sheppard	v	Sussex	Hove	1950
2nd	429*	J.G. Dewes/G.H.G. Doggart	v	Essex	Cambridge	1949
3rd	284	E.T. Killick/G.C. Grant	v	Essex	Cambridge	1929
4th	275	R. de W.K. Winlaw/J.H. Human	v	Essex	Cambridge	1934
5th	220	R. Subba Row/F.C.M. Alexander	v	Notts	Nottingham	1953
6th	245	J.L. Bryan/C.T. Ashton	v	Surrey	The Oval	1921
7th	289	G. Goonesena/G.W. Cook	v	Oxford U	Lord's	1957
8th	145	H. Ashton/A.E.R. Gilligan	v	F Foresters	Cambridge	1920
9th	200	G.W. Cook/C.S. Smith	v	Lancashire	Liverpool	1957
10th	177	A.E.R. Gilligan/J.H. Naumann	v	Sussex	Hove	1919

Best Bowling (Innings)	For	10-69	S.M.J. Woods	v	C.I.T's XI†	Cambridge	1890
	V	10-38	S.E. Butler	for	Oxford U	Lord's	1871
Best Bowling (Match)	For	15-88	S.M.J. Woods	v	C.I.T's XI†	Cambridge	1890
	V	15-95	S.E. Butler	for	Oxford U	Lord's	1871

Most Runs – Season	1,581	D.S. Sheppard	(av 79.05)	1952
Most Runs – Career	4,310	J.M. Brearley	(av 38.48)	1961-1968
Most 100s – Season	7	D.S. Sheppard		1952
Most 100s – Career	14	D.S. Sheppard		1950-1952
Most Wkts – Season	80	O.S. Wheatley	(av 17.63)	1958
Most Wkts – Career	208	G. Goonesena	(av 21.82)	1954-1957

UNIVERSITY MATCH RECORDS

Highest Total	432-9d		1936
Lowest Total	39		1858
Highest Innings	211	G. Goonesena	1957
Best Bowling (Innings)	8-44	G.E. Jeffery	1873
Best Bowling (Match)	13-73	A.G. Steel	1878
Hat-Tricks	F.C. Cobden (1870), A.G. Steel (1879), P.H. Morton (1880), J.F. Ireland (1911), R.G.H. Lowe (1926)		
Match Double	No instance		

† C.I. Thornton's XI

OXFORD UNIVERSITY

COPE, James Edward Bailye (St John's S, Leatherhead; Keble), b Leigh on Sea, Essex 5 May 1966. 6'1". RHB, WK. Debut/blue 1986. HS 8*.
DAWSON, Timothy Andrew John (Mill Hill S; LSE; Linacre), b BMH Munster, West Germany 29 Jan 1963. Grandson of A.E. Alderman (Derbyshire 1928-48). 6'0". RHB, OB. Debut/blue 1986. HS 10*. BB 3-65 v Somerset (Oxford) 1986.
HAGAN, David Andrew (Trinity S, Leamington Spa; St Edmund Hall), b Wide Open, Northumberland 25 Jun 1966. 5'9". RHB, OB. Debut 1985. Blue 1986. Secretary 1987. HS 88 v Lancs (Oxford) 1986.
KILBORN, Michael John (Farrer HS; U of NSW; St John's), b Gunnedah, Australia 20 Sep 1962. 6'2". RHB, RM. Debut/blue 1986. HS 59 v CU (Lord's) 1986.
LAWRENCE, Mark Philip (Manchester GS; Merton), b Warrington, Cheshire 6 May 1962. 5'9". LHB, SLA. Debut 1982. Blue 1984-85-86. HS 18 v Middx (Oxford) 1982. BB 3-79 v Kent (Oxford) 1984.
MacLARNON, Patrick Craig (Loughborough GS; St Peter's), b Nottingham 24 Sep 1963. 6'2". RHB, RM. Debut/blue 1985. HS 56 v Warwicks (Oxford) 1985. BB 2-25 v Middx (Oxford) 1986.
MEE, Adrian Alexander Graham (St Alban's C, Pretoria; Merchant Taylors', Northwood, Oriel), b Johannesburg, SA 29 May 1963. 6'0". RHB. Debut 1984. Blue 1986. HS 51 v Middx (Oxford) 1986.
PATEL, Tikendra **('Tiku')** (Vandyke Upper S; Queen's), b Ahmedabad, India 9 Oct 1965. 5'8". RHB, OB. Debut 1985. Beds 1983. HS 47 v Hants (Oxford) 1985.
QUINLAN, Jeremy David (Sherborne S; St Peter's), b Watford, Herts 18 Apr 1965. 6'2". RHB, RM. Debut/blue 1985. HS 24* v Lancs (Oxford) 1986. BB 4-76 v Leics (Oxford) 1985.
RUTNAGUR, Richard Sohrab (Westminster S; New), b Bombay, India 9 Aug 1964. 5'9". Son of D.J. (Cricket Correspondent). RHB, RM. Debut 1985. Blue 1985-86. HS 66 v Kent (Oxford) 1985. BB 5-112 v Zimbabweans (Oxford) 1985.
RYDON, Robert Anthony (Sherborne S; Pembroke), b Greatham, Sussex 27 Nov 1964. 6'0". LHB, RM. Debut/blue 1986. HS 20 v Lancs (Oxford) 1986. BB 3-106 v Kent (Oxford) 1986. Rugby blue 1985 and 1986.
SALVI, Neil Vijay (Rossall S; Christ Church), b Gwalior, India 21 May 1965. 5'11". RHB, LB. Debut/blue 1986. HS 36 v Glam (Oxford) 1986.
SYGROVE, Malcolm Robert (Lutterworth GS; St John's), b Lutterworth, Leics 17 Feb 1966. 6'0". RHB, RM. Debut 1986. HS 6. BB 1-19.
TAYLOR, Darren Philip (Burnley GS; Christ Church), b Burnley, Lancs 15 Feb 1965. 5'9". RHB, WK. Debut 1985. HS 17 v Glam (Oxford) 1986.
THORNE, David Anthony (Coventry S; Keble), b Coventry 12 Dec 1964. 5'11". RHB, LM. Warwickshire debut 1983. OU debut 1984. Blue 1984-85-86. **Captain 1986**. HS 124 v Zimbabweans (Oxford) 1985. BB 5-39 v CU (Lord's) 1984.
TOOGOOD, Giles John (N Bromsgrove HS; Lincoln), b West Bromwich 19 Nov 1961. 5'11". RHB, RMF. Debut 1982. Blue 1982-83-84-85. Captain 1983. HS 149 and BB 8-52 (10-93 match) v CU (Lord's) 1985.
TOOLEY, Christopher Donald Michael (St Dunstan's C; Magdalen), b Bromley, Kent 19 Apr 1964. 6'1". RHB, RM. Debut 1985. Blue 1985-86. **Captain 1987**. HS 66 v Hants (Oxford) 1985. Award: BHC 1.
WEALE, Simon David (Westminster City S; Keble), b Knightsbridge, London 16 Sep 1967. 6'2". RHB, SLA. Debut 1986. HS 28 v Notts (Oxford) 1986.

OXFORD UNIVERSITY 1986

RESULTS SUMMARY

	Played	*Won*	*Lost*	*Drawn*
All First-Class Matches	8	0	5	3

FIRST-CLASS AVERAGES

BATTING AND FIELDING

	M	*I*	*NO*	*HS*	*Runs*	*Avge*	*100*	*50*	*Ct/St*
†D.A. Thorne	6	9	1	104*	334	41.75	1	2	3
†C.D.M. Tooley	5	8	1	60	196	28.00	—	1	3
†D.A. Hagan	8	14	1	88	334	25.69	—	2	2
†N.V. Salvi	4	7	1	36	126	21.00	—	—	1
†M.J. Kilborn	7	12	1	59	219	19.90	—	1	4
†A.A.G. Mee	8	14	1	51	183	14.07	—	1	3
J.D. Quinlan	5	5	1	24*	46	11.50	—	—	2
†R.A. Rydon	5	9	1	20	64	8.00	—	—	1
†R.S. Rutnagur	5	7	0	24	56	8.00	—	—	2
†T.A.J. Dawson	7	9	5	10*	32	8.00	—	—	2
T. Patel	6	8	0	18	63	7.87	—	—	1
D.P. Taylor	4	6	0	17	39	6.50	—	—	6
†J.E.B. Cope	4	5	2	8*	11	3.66	—	—	5
P.C. MacLarnon	4	5	1	4	9	2.25	—	—	—
†M.P. Lawrence	6	10	2	10*	12	1.50	—	—	2

Played in two matches: G.J. Toogood 1,11.
Played in one match: M.R. Sygrove 2,6; S.D. Weale 12,28.

BOWLING

	O	*M*	*R*	*W*	*Avge*	*Best*	*5 wI*	*10 wM*
R.S. Rutnagur	136	28	439	14	31.35	3-50	—	—
D.A. Thorne	156.3	56	330	9	36.66	3-42	—	—
T.A.J. Dawson	194	38	649	13	49.92	3-65	—	—
M.P. Lawrence	156	29	554	7	79.14	2-28	—	—
R.A. Rydon	119	21	471	5	94.20	3-106	—	—

Also bowled: D.A. Hagan 0.1-0-4-0; P.C. MacLarnon 26.5-5-89-2; T. Patel 2-0-12-0; J.D. Quinlan 103.3-14-369-4; M.R. Sygrove 17-0-85-2; G.J. Toogood 58-16-155-4.

The above figures do not include performances in the match between a Combined Oxford and Cambridge Universities XI against the New Zealanders.

† Blue 1986

OXFORD UNIVERSITY RECORDS

FIRST-CLASS CRICKET

Highest Total	For	651		v	Sussex	Hove	1895
	V	679-7d		by	Australians	Oxford	1938
Lowest Total	For	12		v	MCC	Oxford	1877
	V	24		by	MCC	Oxford	1846
Highest Innings	For	281	K.J. Key	v	Middlesex	Chiswick Park	1887
	V	338	W.W. Read	for	Surrey	The Oval	1888

Highest Partnerships

Wkt						
1st	338	T. Bowring/H. Teesdale	v	Gentlemen	Oxford	1908
2nd	226	W.G. Keighley/H.A. Pawson	v	Cambridge U	Lord's	1947
3rd	273	F.C. de Saram/N.S. M-Innes†	v	Glos	Oxford	1934
4th	276	P.G.T. Kingsley/N.M. Ford	v	Surrey	The Oval	1930
5th	256*	A.A. Baig/C.A. Fry	v	F Foresters	Oxford	1959
6th	270	D.R. Walsh/S.A. Westley	v	Warwicks	Oxford	1969
7th	340	K.J. Key/H. Philipson	v	Middlesex	Chiswick Park	1887
8th	160	H. Philipson/A.C.M. Croome	v	MCC	Lord's	1889
9th	157	H.M. Garland-Wells/ C.K.H. Hill-Wood	v	Kent	Oxford	1928
10th	149	F.H. Hollins/B.A. Collins	v	MCC	Oxford	1901

Best Bowling (Innings)	For	10-38	S.E. Butler	v	Cambridge U	Lord's	1871
	V	10-49	W.G. Grace	for	MCC	Oxford	1886
Best Bowling (Match)	For	15-65	B.J.T. Bosanquet	v	Sussex	Oxford	1900
	V	16-225	J.E. Walsh	for	Leics	Oxford	1953

Most Runs – Season	1,307	Nawab of Pataudi, sr	(av 93.35)	1931
Most Runs – Career	3,319	N.S. Mitchell-Innes	(av 47.41)	1934-1937
Most 100s – Season	6	Nawab of Pataudi, sr		1931
Most 100s – Career	9	A.M. Crawley		1927-1930
	9	Nawab of Pataudi, sr		1928-1931
	9	N.S. Mitchell-Innes		1934-1937
	9	M.P. Donnelly		1946-1947
Most Wkts – Season	70	I.A.R. Peebles	(av 18.15)	1930
Most Wkts – Career	182	R.H.B. Bettington	(av 19.38)	1920-1923

UNIVERSITY MATCH RECORDS

Highest Total	503		1900
Lowest Total	32		1878
Highest Innings	238*	Nawab of Pataudi, sr	1931
Best Bowling (Innings)	10-38	S.E. Butler	1871
Best Bowling (Match)	15-95	S.E. Butler	1871
Hat-Tricks	No instance		
Match Doubles	160 and 11-66	P.R. le Couteur	1910
	149 and 10-93	G.J. Toogood	1985

† N.S. Mitchell-Innes

1986 FIRST-CLASS AVERAGES

These averages include performances in all first-class matches played in the British Isles in 1986.

'Cap' denotes the season in which the player was awarded a 1st XI cap by the county he represented in 1986.

Team abbreviations: CU – Cambridge University; D – Derbyshire; DBC – D.B. Close's XI; Eng – England; Ex – Essex; Gm – Glamorgan; Gs – Gloucestershire; H – Hampshire; Ind – India; Ire – Ireland; K – Kent; La – Lancashire; Le – Leicestershire; M – Middlesex; MC – Minor Counties CA; NZ – New Zealand; Nh – Northamptonshire; Nt – Nottinghamshire; OU – Oxford University; Sc – Scotland; Sm – Somerset; Sy – Surrey; Sx – Sussex; TCCB – TCCB XI; Us – Combined Universities; Wa – Warwickshire; Wo – Worcestershire; Y – Yorkshire.

† Left-handed batsman.

BATTING AND FIELDING

	Cap	*M*	*I*	*NO*	*HS*	*Runs*	*Avge*	*100*	*50*	*Ct/St*
†Abrahams, J. (La)	1982	24	38	7	189*	1251	40.35	3	6	13
Acfield, D.L. (Ex)	1970	19	19	10	11	52	5.77	—	—	5
Afford, J.A. (Nt)	—	15	12	7	9*	19	3.80	—	—	4
Agnew, J.P. (Le)	1984	19	20	6	35*	181	12.92	—	—	2
Ahluwalia, M.S. (CU)	—	6	11	0	36	198	18.00	—	—	—
Alderman, T.M. (K)	1984	20	21	8	25	102	7.84	—	—	9
Alikhan, R.I. (Sx)	—	18	28	4	72	843	35.12	—	7	7
Alleyne, M.W. (Gs)	—	10	16	5	116*	336	30.54	1	1	4
Allott, P.J.W. (La)	1981	17	19	5	65	382	27.28	—	1	9
Amarnath, M. (Ind)	—	9	13	3	101	473	47.30	1	2	7
Amiss, D.L. (Wa)	1965	26	45	6	110	1450	37.17	4	6	12
Anderson, I.S. (D)	1985	13	23	1	93	449	20.40	—	2	6
Andrew, S.J.W. (H)	—	7	5	2	7	15	5.00	—	—	3
Asif Din (Wa)	—	24	38	14	69*	788	32.83	—	5	10
Ashley, D.J. (MC)	—	1	2	0	4	4	2.00	—	—	–/1
Aslett, D.G. (K)	1983	17	23	0	63	517	22.47	—	3	17
Athey, C.W.J. (Gs/Eng)	1985	19	31	1	171*	1233	41.10	1	7	21
Atkinson, J.C.M. (Sm)	—	4	6	2	16*	71	17.75	—	—	—
Azharuddin, M. (Ind)	—	10	14	3	142	596	54.18	2	3	12
†Babington, A.M. (Sx)	—	6	3	1	1	1	0.50	—	—	4
Bail, P.A.C. (Sm/CU/Us)	—	11	20	0	174	530	26.50	1	1	5
Bailey, R.J. (Nh/TCCB)	1985	28	43	9	224*	1915	56.32	4	10	23
Bainbridge, P. (Gs)	1981	26	43	4	105	1065	27.30	1	7	12
Bairstow, D.L. (Y)	1973	24	33	4	88	796	27.44	—	3	41/3
Bakker, P.J. (H)	—	3	2	1	3*	6	6.00	—	—	—
Balderstone, J.C. (Le)	1973	14	23	1	115	410	18.63	1	—	3
Baptiste, E.A.E. (K)	1983	7	8	0	113	273	34.12	1	1	1
Barclay, J.R.T. (Sx)	1976	2	3	0	28	36	12.00	—	—	1
†Barlow, G.D. (M)	1976	5	6	1	107	194	38.80	1	1	2
Barnett, K.J. (D/TCCB)	1982	26	45	3	143	1544	36.76	2	10	24
Barrett, B.J. (NZ)	—	8	4	3	5*	8	8.00	—	—	1
Bartlett, R.J. (Sm)	—	6	9	2	117*	307	43.85	1	—	4
Barwick, S.R. (Gm)	—	11	8	2	9	33	5.50	—	—	3
Base S.J. (Gm)	—	12	11	4	15*	53	7.57	—	—	3
Benjamin, W.K.M. (Le)	—	20	20	10	95*	404	40.40	—	3	9
†Benson, M.R. (K/Eng)	1981	23	39	2	128	1461	39.48	2	7	5
Berry, P.J. (Y)	—	1	1	1	4*	4	—	—	—	2

	Cap	M	I	NO	HS	Runs	Avge	100	50	Ct/St
Bicknell, M.P. (Sy)	—	9	10	2	9*	21	2.62	—	—	4
Binny, R.M.H. (Ind)	—	8	9	1	64	182	22.75	—	1	6
Birch, J.D. (Nt)	1981	21	28	7	79*	718	34.19	—	4	24
Blain, T.E. (NZ)	—	9	9	2	37	172	24.57	—	—	19/3
Blakey, R.J. (Y)	—	4	7	0	46	143	20.42	—	—	4
Blitz, R.J. (Sm)	—	5	5	0	18	33	6.60	—	—	8
Boon, T.J. (Le)	1986	23	36	10	117	1003	38.57	1	4	12
†Border, A.R. (Ex)	1986	20	32	4	150	1385	49.46	4	9	17
Botham, I.T. (Sm/Eng)	1976	13	20	2	139	863	47.94	2	5	8
Bowler, P.D. (Le)	—	8	11	1	100*	249	24.90	1	1	2
Boycott, G. (Y/DBC)	1963	13	20	1	135*	992	52.21	2	8	4
Boyd-Moss, R.J. (Nh)	1984	27	42	3	155	1192	30.56	2	8	7
Bracewell, J.G. (NZ)	—	12	11	6	110	386	77.20	2	—	2
Bredin, A.M. (Sx)	—	7	6	2	8*	26	6.50	—	—	1
Briers, N.E. (Le)	1981	6	7	1	83	223	37.16	—	2	1
†Broad, B.C. (Nt)	1984	25	42	2	122	1593	39.82	6	7	19
Brown, A. (Sc)	—	1	1	0	74	74	74.00	—	1	1
Brown, A.D. (CU/Us)	—	9	11	1	30	86	8.60	—	—	15/2
†Brown, A.M. (D)	—	2	3	1	23	53	26.50	—	—	1
Brown, G.E. (Sy)	—	1	2	2	2*	2	—	—	—	4/1
Brown, G.K. (M)	—	1	2	0	14	17	8.50	—	—	1
Brown, K.R. (M)	—	10	16	2	66	367	26.21	—	2	9
Browne, D.W. (CU)	—	7	13	4	61*	228	25.33	—	1	4
Burnett, N.W. (Sc)	—	1	1	0	4	4	4.00	—	—	—
†Burns, N.D. (Ex)	—	2	3	0	29	54	18.00	—	—	2/2
†Butcher, A.R. (Sy)	1975	16	25	0	157	634	25.36	1	3	5
Butcher, I.P. (Le)	1984	12	19	1	58	273	15.16	—	1	11
Butcher, R.O. (M)	1979	26	37	4	171	1016	30.78	1	7	15
†Byas, D. (Y)	—	1	1	0	0	0	0.00	—	—	1
†Cann, M.J. (Gm)	—	1	1	1	16*	16	—	—	—	1
Capel, D.J. (Nh/TCCB)	1986	28	36	7	111	853	29.41	2	3	11
Carr, J.D. (M)	—	17	26	3	84*	782	34.00	—	5	11
Carrick, P. (Y)	1976	25	33	7	51	637	24.50	—	3	11
Chadwick, M.R. (La)	—	10	18	0	61	423	23.50	—	2	6
Chatfield, E.J. (NZ)	—	7	2	1	5	5	5.00	—	—	3
†Childs, J.H. (Ex)	1986	22	23	7	34	214	13.37	—	—	4
Clarke, S.T. (Sy)	1980	14	13	4	32*	156	17.33	—	—	9
Clift, P.B. (Le)	1976	15	16	1	49	370	24.66	—	—	13
†Clinton, G.S. (Sy)	1980	23	35	4	117	1027	33.12	1	6	10
†Close, D.B. (DBC)	—	1	2	0	22	26	13.00	—	—	—
Cobb, R.A. (Le)	1986	25	41	3	91	1092	28.73	—	8	9
Cohen, M.F. (Ire)	—	1	2	0	29	39	19.50	—	—	—
Coney, J.V. (NZ)	—	13	17	5	140*	688	57.33	1	4	7
Connor, C.A. (H)	—	20	13	5	16	41	5.12	—	—	3
Cook, G. (Nh)	1975	22	30	4	183	1084	41.69	3	3	17
Cook, N.G.B. (Nh)	—	27	27	3	45	351	14.62	—	—	19
Coombs, R.V.J. (Sm)	—	9	6	3	18	31	10.33	—	—	3
†Cooper, K.E. (Nt)	1980	17	13	5	19	105	13.12	—	—	4
Cope, J.E.B. (OU)	—	4	5	2	8*	11	3.66	—	—	5
Corlett, S.C. (Ire)	—	1	2	1	44*	67	67.00	—	—	—
Cottey, P.A. (Gm)	—	4	5	1	9*	24	6.00	—	—	2
Cowans, N.G. (M)	1984	21	21	7	44*	223	15.92	—	—	4
Cowdrey, C.S. (K)	1979	22	33	3	100	873	29.10	1	5	32
Cowdrey, G.R. (K)	—	17	26	1	75	425	17.00	—	3	9

	Cap	M	I	NO	HS	Runs	Avge	100	50	Ct/St
Cowley, N.G. (H)	1978	19	21	7	78*	360	25.71	—	2	5
Crowe, J.J. (NZ)	—	13	19	2	159	624	36.70	1	4	11
Crowe, M.D. (NZ)	—	12	18	6	106	787	65.58	2	6	10
Curran, K.M. (Gs)	1985	26	39	8	117*	1353	43.64	4	7	29
Curtis, T.S. (Wo)	1984	24	40	10	153	1498	49.93	2	10	9
Dale, C.S. (K)	—	3	3	1	16	18	9.00	—	—	—
Daniel, W.W. (M.)	1977	16	16	6	33	140	14.00	—	—	3
Davidson, J.E. (CU/Us)	—	9	10	3	41*	108	15.42	—	—	2
Davies, T. (Gm)	1985	24	28	13	41	316	21.06	—	—	32/8
†Davis, M.R. (Sm)	—	9	8	4	21*	63	15.75	—	—	2
Davis, R.P. (K)	—	1	1	1	0*	0	—	—	—	1
Dawson, T.A.J. (OU)	—	7	9	5	10*	32	8.00	—	—	2
DeFreitas, P.A.J. (Le/TCCB)	1986	27	30	2	106	645	23.03	1	3	7
Dennis, S.J. (Y)	1983	16	12	4	18*	82	10.25	—	—	4
Derrick, J. (Gm)	—	18	24	8	78*	569	35.56	—	4	3
†Dilley, G.R. (K/Eng)	1980	18	26	8	30	218	12.11	—	—	7
D'Oliveira, D.B. (Wo)	1985	25	41	3	146*	1093	28.76	1	3	15
Donald, W.A. (Sc)	—	1	1	0	29	29	29.00	—	—	1
†Doshi, D.R. (DBC)	—	1	1	1	9*	9	—	—	—	—
Doughty, R.J. (Sy)	—	15	19	2	61	387	22.76	—	1	12
Downton, P.R. (M/Eng)	1981	24	29	5	126*	905	37.70	2	5	43/5
†Dredge, C.H. (Sm)	1978	17	21	3	40	227	12.61	—	—	7
Duthie, P.G. (Sc)	—	1	1	1	54*	54	—	—	1	—
Dyer, R.I.H.B. (Wa)	—	5	10	2	28	91	11.37	—	—	5
East, D.E. (Ex)	1982	25	40	4	100*	730	20.27	1	2	64/19
†Edgar, B.A. (NZ)	—	12	19	5	110*	590	42.14	1	3	5
Edmonds, P.H. (M/Eng)	1974	17	19	5	31	202	14.42	—	—	17
Ellcock, R.M. (Wo)	—	2	2	2	4*	4	—	—	—	—
Ellison, C.C. (CU)	—	5	3	1	51*	54	27.00	—	1	1
†Ellison, R.M. (K/Eng)	1983	20	29	6	62*	552	24.00	—	2	5
Emburey, J.E. (M/Eng)	1977	18	22	3	75	354	18.63	—	1	16
Estwick, R.O. (DBC)	—	1	1	0	2	2	2.00	—	—	—
Evans, K.P. (Nt)	—	4	3	0	14	15	5.00	—	—	1
†Fairbrother, N.H. (La)	1985	22	33	8	131	1217	48.68	3	8	11
Falkner, N.J. (Sy)	—	11	18	2	102	567	35.43	1	2	7
Fell, D.J. (CU/Us)	—	9	17	3	114	388	27.71	1	—	1
Feltham, M.A. (Sy)	—	12	14	5	76	237	26.33	—	1	1
†Felton, N.A. (Sm)	1986	23	37	3	156*	1030	30.29	3	5	8
Ferreira, A.M. (Wa)	1983	12	15	6	69*	413	45.88	—	3	8
Ferris G.J.F. (Le)	—	5	6	1	17*	67	13.40	—	—	4
Finney, R.J. (D)	1985	17	17	5	54	277	23.08	—	1	2
Fleming, D. (Sc)	—	1	—	—	—	—	—	—	—	3
Fletcher, K.W.R. (Ex)	1963	20	28	6	91	736	33.45	—	6	26
Fletcher, S.D. (Y)	—	15	10	3	24	67	9.57	—	—	3
Folley, I. (La)	—	17	19	2	20*	159	9.35	—	—	11
Fordham, A. (Nh)	—	2	3	0	17	26	8.66	—	—	—
Foster, D.J. (Sm)	—	1	1	0	0	0	0.00	—	—	—
Foster, N.A. (Ex/Eng)	1983	23	30	7	53*	458	19.91	—	2	12
†Fowler, G. (La)	1981	20	32	2	180	1163	38.76	1	9	9
Franklin, T.J. (NZ)	—	7	10	0	96	227	22.70	—	1	5
Fraser, A.G.J. (M)	—	4	3	2	19*	32	32.00	—	—	—
Fraser, A.R.C. (M)	—	6	7	1	13	41	6.83	—	—	—
Fraser-Darling, C.D. (Nt)	—	5	4	0	61	142	35.50	—	1	3

	Cap	M	I	NO	HS	Runs	Avge	100	50	Ct/St
French, B.N. (Nt/Eng)	1980	20	23	5	58	361	20.05	—	1	44/4
Gard, T. (Sm)	1983	20	25	6	36	228	12.00	—	—	30/6
Garner, J. (Sm)	1979	18	15	4	47	182	16.54	—	—	8
Garth, J.D. (Ire)	—	1	2	0	6	7	3.50	—	—	—
Gatting, M.W. (M/Eng)	1977	18	23	3	183*	1091	54.55	4	2	13
Gavaskar, S.M. (Ind)	—	8	12	1	136*	372	33.81	1	1	5
†Gifford, N. (Wa)	1983	25	14	6	8	27	3.37	—	—	2
Gill, P. (Le)	—	8	11	4	17	68	9.71	—	—	24
†Gladwin, C. (Ex)	1984	8	15	0	73	195	13.00	—	1	4
Golding, A.K. (CU/Us)	—	7	11	3	47	188	23.50	—	—	2
Gooch, G.A. (Ex/Eng)	1975	19	32	0	183	1221	38.15	3	5	22
Gorman, S.R. (CU)	—	6	9	3	37	76	12.66	—	—	4
†Gould, I.J. (Sx)	1981	20	24	6	78*	586	32.55	—	4	36/1
Gouldstone, M.R. (Nh)	—	1	1	0	35	35	35.00	—	—	—
†Gower, D.I. (Le/Eng)	1977	14	23	2	131	830	39.52	1	6	11/1
Graveney, D.A. (Gs)	1976	22	18	9	30*	94	10.44	—	—	20
Gray, A.H. (Sy)	1985	11	14	2	28	108	9.00	—	—	4
Gray, E.J. (NZ)	—	13	13	4	108*	467	51.88	1	4	9
Green, A.M. (Sx)	1985	25	46	3	179	1343	31.23	3	3	12
Greenidge, C.G. (H)	1972	20	34	4	222	2035	67.83	8	6	18
Greensword, S. (MC)	—	1	2	0	35	69	34.50	—	—	—
Griffiths, B.J. (Nh)	1978	10	6	3	7	18	6.00	—	—	2
†Hadlee, R.J. (Nt/NZ)	1978	17	21	5	129*	813	50.81	2	4	6
Hagan, D.A. (OU/Us)	—	9	16	1	88	364	24.26	—	2	2
Halliday, M. (Ire)	—	1	2	0	15	22	11.00	—	—	—
Harden, R.J. (Sm)	—	22	36	3	108	1093	33.12	2	6	12
Hardie, B.R. (Ex)	1974	22	35	5	113*	883	29.43	2	4	19
†Hardy, J.J.E. (Sm)	—	19	29	0	79	863	29.75	—	8	12
Harman, M.D. (Sm)	—	3	5	2	15	27	9.00	—	—	1
Harper, M.A. (DBC)	—	1	2	0	55	55	27.50	—	1	2
Harper, R.A. (Nh)	1986	25	30	4	234	933	35.88	1	2	32
Harris, G.A.R. (Le)	—	1	2	1	6	6	6.00	—	—	—
†Harrison, G.D. (Ire)	—	1	2	0	68	81	40.50	—	1	—
Hartley, P.J. (Y)	—	15	17	4	87*	441	33.92	—	4	7
Hartley, S.N. (Y)	1981	21	30	2	87	785	28.03	—	4	5
Hayes, K.A. (La)	—	1	1	0	17	17	17.00	—	—	—
Hayhurst, A.N. (La)	—	10	14	0	31	156	11.14	—	—	2
Head, T.J. (CU)	—	3	5	1	40*	62	15.50	—	—	1
Heath, S.D. (CU)	—	1	2	0	10	16	8.00	—	—	—
Hegg, W.K. (La)	—	2	2	0	4	4	2.00	—	—	2/2
Hemmings, E.E. (Nt)	1980	21	23	4	54*	330	17.36	—	1	7
Henriksen, S. (La)	—	2	2	1	6*	7	7.00	—	—	1
Herbert, R. (MC)	—	1	2	0	23	33	16.50	—	—	—
Hick, G.A.,(Wo)	1986	24	37	6	227*	2004	64.64	6	11	29
Hickey, D.J. (Gm)	—	13	9	5	9*	19	4.75	—	—	3
†Higgs, K. (Le)	1972	2	2	1	8	11	11.00	—	—	1
Hill, A. (D)	1976	24	40	6	172*	1438	42.29	3	7	9
†Hinks, S.G. (K)	1985	23	38	2	131	936	26.00	2	2	15
Holding, M.A. (D)	1983	14	20	2	36*	295	16.38	—	—	6
Holmes, G.C. (Gm)	1985	26	44	5	107	1106	28.35	1	6	18
Hopkins, J.A. (Gm)	1977	15	26	0	142	738	28.38	1	3	10
Hughes, S.P. (M)	1981	23	26	2	47	296	12.33	—	—	3
Humpage, G.W. (Wa)	1976	26	42	4	130	1462	38.47	3	6	41/8
Igglesden, A.P. (K)	—	5	5	2	8*	22	7.33	—	—	2

	Cap	M	I	NO	HS	Runs	Avge	100	50	Ct/St
Illingworth, R.K. (Wo)	1986	18	15	4	39	191	17.36	—	—	10
Imran Khan (Sx)	1978	11	18	3	135*	730	48.66	2	4	1
Inchmore, J.D. (Wo)	1976	9	8	2	23*	55	9.16	—	—	3
Jackson, P.B. (Ire)	—	1	1	0	2	2	2.00	—	—	1
†James, K.D. (H)	—	12	13	2	62	275	25.00	—	1	5
Jarvis, K.B.S. (K)	1977	7	6	4	4	9	4.50	—	—	2
Jarvis, P.W. (Y)	1986	15	17	7	47	183	18.30	—	—	10
Javed Miandad (DBC)	—	1	2	1	102*	143	143.00	1	—	—
Jean-Jacques, M. (D)	—	9	12	3	73	208	23.11	—	1	1
Jesty, T.E. (Sy)	1985	20	30	1	221	998	34.41	2	4	10
Johnson, P. (Nt)	1986	26	37	5	128	1250	39.06	3	5	24
†Jones, A.L. (Gm)	1983	13	21	4	50	429	25.23	—	1	7
†Jones, A.N. (Sx)	1986	11	10	3	13	55	7.85	—	—	5
†Kallicharran, A.I. (Wa)	1972	14	23	5	163*	1005	55.83	5	2	13
Kapil Dev (Ind)	—	6	9	4	115*	273	54.60	1	1	5
Ker, J.E. (Sc)	—	1	1	1	7*	7	—	—	—	—
Kerr, K.J. (Wa)	—	14	12	5	45*	120	17.14	—	—	6
Kilborn, M.J. (OU)	—	7	12	1	59	219	19.90	—	1	4
King, C.L. (DBC)	—	1	2	0	48	49	24.50	—	—	—
Lamb, A.J. (Nh/Eng)	1978	18	27	4	160*	1359	59.08	4	8	14
Lamba, R. (Ind)	—	5	7	0	116	301	43.00	1	2	1
Lampitt, S.R. (Wo)	—	1	1	1	11*	11	—	—	—	—
Larkins, W. (Nh)	1976	17	29	4	86	664	26.56	—	2	13
Lawrence, D.V. (Gs/TCCB)	1985	24	25	5	34*	198	9.90	—	—	5
†Lawrence, M.P. (OU/Us)	—	6	10	2	10*	12	1.50	—	—	2
Lea, A.E. (CU)	—	5	8	0	19	79	9.87	—	—	6
Lenham, N.J. (Sx)	—	18	29	4	77	544	21.76	—	3	6
Le Roux, G.S. (Sx)	1981	14	16	6	72*	298	29.80	—	1	6
Lever, J.K. (Ex/Eng)	1970	23	27	6	38	199	9.47	—	—	1
Lilley, A.W. (Ex)	1986	15	26	2	87	604	25.16	—	3	6
†Lloyd, C.H. (La)	1969	7	8	1	128	347	49.57	1	2	—
†Lloyd, T.A. (Wa)	1980	16	28	0	100	793	28.32	1	6	6
†Lloyds, J.W. (Gs)	1985	26	39	9	111	1295	43.16	1	8	22
†Lord, G.J. (Wa)	—	3	6	1	24*	63	12.60	—	—	2
Lord, T.M. (CU)	—	2	4	0	23	31	7.75	—	—	—
Love, J.D. (Y)	1980	21	29	5	109	831	34.62	1	4	7
Lynch, M.A. (Sy)	1982	25	39	3	152	1234	34.27	3	5	39
McBrine, A. (Ire)	—	1	1	0	0	0	0.00	—	—	—
McBrine, J. (Ire)	—	1	2	2	27*	29	—	—	—	1
McEwan, S.M. (Wo)	—	8	3	2	7	13	13.00	—	—	7
MacLarnon, P.C. (OU)	—	4	5	1	4	9	2.25	—	—	—
McMillan, B.M. (Wa)	—	12	21	4	136	999	58.76	3	6	11
Madan Lal (Ind)	—	1	2	0	22	42	21.00	—	—	—
Maher, B.J.M. (D)	—	14	24	5	126	752	39.57	1	5	23
Makinson, D.J. (La)	—	15	13	6	43	96	13.71	—	—	7
Malcolm, D.E. (D)	—	9	7	4	29*	37	12.33	—	—	2
Mallender, N.A. (Nh)	1984	22	20	10	37	119	11.90	—	—	4
Maninder Singh (Ind)	—	8	5	2	6*	16	5.33	—	—	3
Marks, V.J. (Sm)	1979	25	36	12	110	1057	44.04	1	7	9
Marples, C. (D)	—	15	24	3	57	466	22.19	—	2	31/4
Marsh, S.A. (K)	1986	26	36	8	70	857	30.60	—	6	48/3
Marshall, M.D. (H)	1981	23	23	2	51*	263	12.52	—	1	5
Martindale, D.J.R. (Nt)	—	3	4	0	88	115	28.75	—	1	—

	Cap	M	I	NO	HS	Runs	Avge	100	50	Ct/St
Maru, R.J. (H)	1986	17	10	6	23	116	29.00	—	—	13
Masood, M.A. (Ire)	—	1	2	0	12	12	6.00	—	—	—
Maynard, C. (La)	1986	19	26	5	132*	662	31.52	1	5	29/3
Maynard, M.P. (Gm)	—	22	34	4	148	1002	33.40	2	6	13
Mays, C.S. (Sx)	—	8	6	2	8*	19	4.75	—	—	2
Medlycott, K.T. (Sy)	—	14	15	2	61	197	15.15	—	1	9
Mee, A.A.G. (OU)	—	8	14	1	51	183	14.07	—	1	3
Mendis, G.D. (La)	1986	23	37	3	108	1363	40.08	2	10	2
Merry, W.G. (MC)	—	1	2	0	5	8	4.00	—	—	—
Metcalfe, A.A. (Y/TCCB)	1986	26	41	1	151	1803	45.07	6	8	10
Metson, C.P. (M)	—	3	4	0	15	29	7.25	—	—	3
Middleton, T.C. (H)	—	8	14	3	68*	316	28.72	—	1	7
†Miller, A.J.T. (M)	—	23	35	4	111*	963	31.06	1	5	13
Miller, G. (D)	1976	20	27	2	65	512	20.48	—	3	13
Moir, D.G. (Sc)	—	1	1	0	4	4	4.00	—	—	—
Moles, A.J. (Wa)	—	11	18	3	102	738	49.20	2	5	4
Monkhouse, G. (Sy)	1984	10	12	4	51	162	20.25	—	1	6
Monkhouse, S. (Wa)	—	1	1	0	0	0	0.00	—	—	—
More, K.S. (Ind)	—	7	8	2	52	228	38.00	—	1	22/1
†Morris, H. (Gm)	1986	26	44	2	128*	1522	36.23	2	11	9
Morris, J.E. (D/TCCB)	1986	26	40	3	191	1739	47.00	4	10	8
Mortensen, O.H. (D)	1986	16	17	9	31*	69	8.62	—	—	1
Moseley, E.A. (Gm)	1981	6	8	1	19	55	7.85	—	—	—
Moxon, M.D. (Y/Eng)	1984	20	33	4	147	982	33.86	3	4	13
Munton, T.A. (Wa)	—	19	15	6	19	58	6.44	—	—	1
Murphy, A.J. (La/MC)	—	5	5	3	6	8	4.00	—	—	2
Neale, P.A. (Wo)	1978	25	34	7	118*	987	36.55	1	6	7
Needham, A. (Sy)	1985	11	17	2	52	256	17.06	—	1	6
Newell, M. (Nt)	—	19	30	9	112*	862	41.04	1	5	15/1
Newman, P.G. (D)	1986	3	4	2	34	62	31.00	—	—	1
Newport, P.J. (Wo)	1986	23	17	4	68	285	21.92	—	1	8
Nicholas, M.C.J. (H/TCCB)	1982	24	32	2	55	564	18.80	—	2	13
North, P.D. (Gm)	—	5	5	2	17*	22	7.33	—	—	—
†Old, C.M. (DBC)	—	1	1	0	0	0	0.00	—	—	—
Ontong, R.C. (Gm)	1979	24	37	4	80*	744	22.54	—	6	8
O'Shaughnessy, S.J. (La)	1985	10	14	3	74	291	26.45	—	2	5
Palmer, G.V. (Sm)	—	4	6	0	17	31	5.16	—	—	1
Pandit, C.S. (Ind)	—	6	8	2	91	252	42.00	—	3	10
Parker. P.W.G. (Sx)	1979	25	43	7	125	1595	44.30	6	8	19
Parks, R.J. (H)	1982	25	23	5	80	420	23.33	—	3	73/8
†Parsons, G.J. (Wa)	—	21	24	5	58*	322	16.94	—	1	3
†Patel, A.S. (MC)	—	1	2	0	30	37	18.50	—	—	1
Patel, D.N. (Wo)	1979	24	30	9	132*	1005	47.85	3	2	6
Patel, T. (OU)	—	6	8	0	18	63	7.87	—	—	1
Patil, S.M. (Ind)	—	6	8	0	57	188	23.50	—	2	4
Patterson, B.P. (La)	—	18	15	5	12*	54	5.40	—	—	4
Pauline, D.B. (Gm)	—	12	20	0	97	455	22.75	—	3	4
Payne, I.R. (Gs)	—	11	12	4	30*	106	13.25	—	—	7
†Penn, C. (K)	—	6	7	2	84*	95	19.00	—	1	2
Philip, I.L. (Sc)	—	1	1	0	145	145	145.00	1	—	1
Phillipson, C.P. (Sx)	1980	1	1	0	6	6	6.00	—	—	1
†Pick, R.A. (Nt)	—	19	17	1	55	206	12.87	—	1	5
Pierson, A.R.K. (Wa)	—	2	2	2	42*	42	—	—	—	—

	Cap	M	I	NO	HS	Runs	Avge	100	50	Ct/St
Pigott, A.C.S. (Sx)	1982	19	18	6	104*	572	47.66	1	2	4
Plumb, S.G. (MC)	—	1	2	0	69	98	49.00	—	1	—
Pocock, P.I. (Sy)	1967	21	20	9	16*	93	8.45	—	—	6
Pont, I.L. (Ex)	—	3	6	3	43	73	24.33	—	—	1
Pont, K.R. (Ex)	1976	7	13	1	36	142	11.83	—	—	1
Potter, L. (Le)	—	20	30	3	81*	545	20.18	—	5	17
Prabhakar, M. (Ind)	—	6	6	1	33	77	15.40	—	—	1
Price, D.G. (CU/Us)	—	8	15	1	60	207	14.78	—	1	4
Prichard, P.J. (Ex)	1986	26	44	3	147*	1342	32.73	1	10	20
Pridgeon, A.P. (Wo)	1980	20	10	3	10*	44	6.28	—	—	9
Pringle, D.R. (Ex/Eng)	1982	20	32	4	97	611	21.82	—	3	13
Pringle, N.J. (Sm)	—	1	2	0	11	21	10.50	—	—	—
Prior, J.A. (Ire)	—	1	2	0	12	13	6.50	—	—	—
Quinlan, J.D. (OU)	—	5	5	1	24*	46	11.50	—	—	2
Radford, N.V. (Wo/Eng)	1985	20	16	3	30	178	13.69	—	—	12
Radley, C.T. (M)	1967	25	33	6	113*	792	29.33	2	3	16
Randall, D.W. (Nt)	1973	14	22	1	101*	493	23.47	1	1	14
Reeve, D.A. (Sx)	1986	19	21	9	51	307	25.58	—	1	10
Rhodes, S.J. (Wo)	1986	25	27	10	77*	509	29.94	—	3	58/8
Rice, C.E.B. (Nt)	1975	22	31	6	156*	1118	44.72	2	5	28
Richards, C.J. (Sy)	1978	23	34	9	115	1006	40.24	2	5	39/5
Richards, I.V.A. (Sm)	1974	18	28	1	136	1174	43.48	4	5	19
†Riddell, N.A. (MC)	—	1	2	0	20	27	13.50	—	—	2
Ripley, D. (Nh)	—	13	15	5	134*	301	30.10	1	—	12/4
Roberts, B. (D)	1986	25	37	3	124*	772	22.70	1	2	13/1
Roberts, M.L. (Gm)	—	2	1	0	8	8	8.00	—	—	2/1
Robinson, P.E. (Y)	—	8	13	2	104*	392	35.63	1	3	7
Robinson, R.T. (Nt/Eng)	1983	21	34	5	159*	1398	48.20	4	7	15
Roebuck, P.M. (Sm)	1978	22	35	8	221*	1288	47.70	4	5	12
Romaines, P.W. (Gs)	1983	15	27	4	67*	476	20.69	—	2	4
Roope, G.R.J. (MC)	—	1	2	0	15	18	9.00	—	—	—
†Rose, B.C. (Sm)	1975	14	23	5	129	784	43.55	2	3	3
Rose, G.D. (M)	—	5	6	1	52	74	14.80	—	1	—
Roseberry, M.A. (M)	—	5	8	1	70*	174	24.85	—	2	1
Rudd, C.F.B.P. (D)	—	1	1	0	1	1	1.00	—	—	—
Russell, A.B. (Sc)	—	1	1	0	24	24	24.00	—	—	2
†Russell, R.C. (Gs/TCCB)	1985	27	31	9	71	585	26.59	—	2	56/4
Rutherford, K.R. (NZ)	—	12	19	3	317	848	53.00	2	3	7
Rutnagur, R.S. (OU/Us)	—	6	9	0	26	88	9.77	—	—	2
†Rydon, R.A. (OU)	—	5	9	1	20	64	8.00	—	—	1
†Sadiq Mohammad (DBC)	—	1	2	0	77	114	57.00	—	1	1
Sainsbury, G.E. (Gs)	—	6	3	2	14*	28	28.00	—	—	—
Salvi, N.V. (OU)	—	4	7	1	36	126	21.00	—	—	1
Saxelby, K. (Nt)	1984	11	8	5	34	124	41.33	—	—	4
Scott, A.M.G. (Sx/CU/Us)	—	9	9	6	8	29	9.66	—	—	5
Scott, C.W. (Nt)	—	10	8	3	69*	220	44.00	—	1	22/1
Sharma, C. (Ind)	—	9	5	2	39	79	26.33	—	—	2
Sharma, R. (D)	—	15	17	6	71	321	29.18	—	2	14
†Sharp, K. (Y)	1982	19	31	6	181	958	38.32	2	5	10
Shastri, R.J. (Ind)	—	8	10	2	70*	220	27.50	—	2	4
Shaw, C. (Y)	—	14	10	4	21	57	9.50	—	—	2
Sidebottom, A. (Y)	1980	10	9	2	18	65	9.28	—	—	2
Simmons, J. (La)	1971	13	17	5	61	300	25.00	—	1	7
†Slack, W.N. (M/Eng)	1981	23	35	3	106	1224	38.25	3	7	17

	Cap	M	I	NO	HS	Runs	Avge	100	50	Ct/St
Small, G.C. (Wa/Eng)	1982	25	26	7	45*	304	16.00	—	—	4
Smith, C.L. (H/Eng)	1981	20	30	8	114*	1061	48.22	2	7	16
†Smith, D.M. (Wo)	1984	20	28	4	165*	1041	43.37	3	5	9
Smith, G. (Nh)	—	2	2	0	4	7	3.50	—	—	1
Smith, I. (Gm)	—	3	2	0	0	0	0.00	—	—	1
Smith, I.D.S. (NZ)	—	9	9	3	48	215	35.83	—	—	17/2
Smith, L.K. (Wo)	—	1	2	0	2	4	2.00	—	—	1
Smith, P.A. (Wa)	1986	25	44	4	119	1508	37.70	1	13	7
Smith, R.A. (H)	1985	25	38	8	128*	1237	41.23	2	8	21
Speight, M.P. (Sx)	—	5	2	0	17	21	10.50	—	—	6
Srikkanth, K. (Ind)	—	9	14	0	90	344	24.57	—	1	5
Standing, D.K. (Sx)	—	17	26	3	65	412	17.91	—	1	9
Stanworth, J. (La)	—	3	2	1	11*	13	13.00	—	—	4
Steele, J.F. (Gm)	1984	12	17	5	41*	282	23.50	—	—	9
Stephenson, F.D. (DBC)	—	1	2	1	33	55	55.00	—	—	—
Stephenson, J.P. (Ex)	—	14	25	1	85	647	26.95	—	4	6
Stevenson, A.W.J. (Sc)	—	1	—	—	—	—	—	—	—	—
Stevenson, G.B. (Y)	1978	2	1	1	58*	58	—	—	1	—
Stewart, A.J. (Sy)	1985	25	39	3	166	1665	46.25	3	14	15
Stirling, D.A. (NZ)	—	11	7	3	26	116	29.00	—	—	4
Storie, A.C. (Nh)	—	8	11	0	38	171	15.54	—	—	3
Stovold, A.W. (Gs)	1976	26	43	4	118	1123	28.79	1	7	9
Such, P.M. (Nt/TCCB)	—	6	4	0	6	9	2.25	—	—	3
Surridge, D. (MC)	—	1	2	2	1*	1	—	—	—	—
Swallow, I.G. (Y)	—	9	11	5	43*	152	25.33	—	—	—
Swan, R.G. (Sc)	—	1	1	0	30	30	30.00	—	—	1
Sygrove, M.R. (OU)	—	1	2	0	6	8	4.00	—	—	—
Sykes, J.F. (M)	—	3	4	1	26	63	21.00	—	—	—
Tavaré, C.J. (K)	1978	26	42	4	123	1267	33.34	2	6	21
Taylor, D.P. (OU)	—	4	6	0	17	39	6.50	—	—	6
†Taylor, J.P. (D)	—	4	5	2	9*	18	6.00	—	—	1
Taylor, L.B. (Le)	1981	15	15	6	13	48	5.33	—	—	3
Taylor, N.R. (K)	1982	26	42	5	106	1151	31.10	1	7	10
Taylor, N.S. (Sm)	—	16	18	6	24*	107	8.91	—	—	2
Taylor, R.W. (DBC)	—	1	1	0	21	21	21.00	—	—	2
Tennant, L. (Le)	—	2	2	1	12*	13	13.00	—	—	—
Terry, V.P. (H)	1983	23	36	4	80	896	28.00	—	7	17
†Thomas, D.J. (Sy)	1982	9	12	4	47*	222	27.75	—	—	1
Thomas, J.G. (Gm/Eng)	1986	22	27	6	70	523	24.90	—	2	7
Thorne, D.A. (Wa/OU/Us)	—	14	21	4	104*	490	28.82	1	3	4
Todd, P.A. (MC)	—	1	2	0	21	25	12.50	—	—	1
Tomlins, K.P. (Gs)	—	16	29	5	75	696	29.00	—	4	1
Toogood, G.J. (OU)	—	2	2	0	11	12	6.00	—	—	—
Tooley, C.D.M. (OU/Us)	—	6	10	1	60	221	24.55	—	1	4
Topley, T.D. (Ex)	—	9	11	2	45	113	12.55	—	—	8
Tremellen, J.M. (CU)	—	1	2	1	4*	7	7.00	—	—	—
Tremlett, T.M. (H)	1983	21	23	12	59*	322	29.27	—	2	2
Tufnell, P.C.R. (M)	—	6	7	1	9	32	5.33	—	—	1
†Turner, D.R. (H)	1970	10	14	1	96	472	36.30	—	3	2
Turner, M.S. (Sm)	—	1	—	—	—	—	—	—	—	—
Turner, S. (Ex)	1970	2	4	1	32	72	24.00	—	—	—
Twizell, P.H. (Gs)	—	1	1	0	0	0	0.00	—	—	—
Underwood, D.L. (K)	1964	24	26	5	29	243	11.57	—	—	2
Varey, D.W. (La)	—	6	10	2	83	271	33.87	—	2	5/1

	Cap	M	I	NO	HS	Runs	Avge	100	50	Ct/St
Vengsarkar, D.B. (Ind)	—	8	11	3	126*	536	67.00	2	3	3
†Walker, A. (Nh)	—	19	15	10	40*	87	17.40	—	—	6
Walsh, C.A. (Gs)	1985	23	24	6	52	221	12.27	—	1	7
Ward, D.M. (Sy)	—	4	6	1	34	100	20.00	—	—	1
Ward, T.R. (K)	—	1	2	0	29	41	20.50	—	—	—
†Waring, I.C. (Sx)	—	1	—	—	—	—	—	—	—	1
Warke, S.J.S. (Ire)	—	1	2	0	47	57	28.50	—	—	—
Warner, A.E. (D)	—	20	28	6	91	593	26.95	—	6	6
Waterton, S.N.V. (Nh)	—	14	17	4	58*	314	24.15	—	1	32/5
Watkin, S.L. (Gm)	—	1	—	—	—	—	—	—	—	—
Watkinson, M. (La)	—	21	25	4	58*	389	18.52	—	1	14
Watson, W. (NZ)	—	12	6	3	10	30	10.00	—	—	3
Weale, S.D. (OU)	—	1	2	0	28	40	20.00	—	—	—
Wells, A.P. (Sx)	1986	23	34	7	150*	891	33.00	1	2	11
Wells, C.M. (Sx)	1982	24	38	9	106	1098	37.86	1	7	5
Weston, M.J. (Wo)	1986	8	12	2	49	167	16.70	—	—	3
Whitaker, J.J. (Le/TCCB)	1986	22	32	9	200*	1526	66.34	5	8	18
Whitticase, P. (Le)	—	18	21	4	67*	554	32.58	—	5	23/1
†Wild, D.J. (Nh)	1986	14	21	3	101	608	33.77	1	4	2
Willey, P. (Le/Eng)	1984	18	30	5	172*	1117	44.68	4	3	6
Williams, N.F. (M)	1984	5	4	1	23*	51	17.00	—	—	—
Williams, R.G. (Nh)	1979	5	7	0	93	161	23.00	—	1	1
Winterborne, G. (Sy)	—	1	—	—	—	—	—	—	—	—
Wood, L.J. (D)	—	2	2	0	5	7	3.50	—	—	—
Wright, A.J. (Gs)	—	15	26	0	87	603	23.19	—	4	14
Wright, J.G. (D/NZ)	1977	14	22	1	119	682	32.47	1	5	5
Wyatt, J.G. (Sm)	—	4	6	0	40	81	13.50	—	—	—
Yadav, N.S. (Ind)	—	7	2	2	13*	22	—	—	—	3
†Younis Ahmed (Gm)	1985	15	23	2	105*	845	40.23	1	4	4

BOWLING

	Cat	O	M	R	W	Avge	Best	5 wI	10 wM
Abrahams, J. (La)	**OB**	44.5	5	175	3	58.33	2-14	—	—
Acfield, D.L. (Ex)	**OB**	401.1	107	912	33	27.63	5-38	1	—
Afford, J.A. (Nt)	**SLA**	492.4	131	1455	45	32.33	6-81	3	1
Agnew, J.P. (Le)	**RF**	522.5	118	1528	55	27.78	5-27	1	—
Alderman, T.M. (K)	**RFM**	610	139	1882	98	19.20	8-46	9	3
Alikhan, R.I. (Sx)		10	0	65	0	—	—	—	—
Allott, P.J.W. (La)	**RFM**	405.1	106	1053	43	24.48	5-32	2	—
Amarnath, M. (Ind)	**RM**	43.2	12	68	4	17.00	3-39	—	—
Andrew, S.J.W. (H)	**RMF**	141.2	32	419	14	29.92	3-25	—	—
Asif Din (Wa)	**LB**	103.4	13	409	5	81.80	2-93	—	—
Aslett, D.G. (K)	**LB**	35	3	187	4	46.75	1-10	—	—
Athey, C.W.J. (Gs/Eng)	**RM**	18	5	60	1	60.00	1-14	—	—
Atkinson, J.C.M. (Sm)	**RMF**	34	7	132	2	66.00	2-80	—	—
Azharuddin, M. (Ind)	**RM/LB**	20	1	68	0	—	—	—	—
Babington. A.M. (Sx)	**RFM**	117.5	16	348	15	23.20	4-18	—	—
Bail, P.A.C. (Sm/CU/Us)	**OB**	4	0	28	0	—	—	—	—
Bailey, R.J. (Nh/TCCB)	**OB**	15.5	7	47	2	23.50	1-2	—	—

	Cat	O	M	R	W	Avge	Best	5 wI	10 wM
Bainbridge, P. (Gs)	RM	414.1	89	1185	43	27.55	8-53	2	—
Bairstow, D.L. (Y)	RM	5	3	7	0	—	—	—	—
Bakker, P.J. (H)	RMF	66.5	20	220	6	36.66	2-15	—	—
Balderstone, J.C. (Le)	SLA	45	9	143	2	71.50	2-120	—	—
Baptiste, E.A.E. (K)	RFM	146	40	351	13	27.00	4-53	—	—
Barclay, J.R.T. (Sx)	OB	13	2	65	0	—	—	—	—
Barnett, K.J. (D/TCCB)	LB	117	29	403	6	67.16	1-8	—	—
Barrett, B.J. (NZ)	RFM	157.5	18	610	15	40.66	3-32	—	—
Barwick, S.R. (Gm)	RMF	292.4	61	964	26	37.07	3-25	—	—
Base. S.J. (Gm)	RMF	222.5	40	774	21	36.85	4-74	—	—
Benjamin, W.K.M. (Le)	RF	465.3	89	1541	46	33.50	6-33	3	—
Benson, M.R. (K/Eng)	OB	7	0	55	2	27.50	2-55	—	—
Berry, P.J. (Y)	OB	39	13	83	1	83.00	1-10	—	—
Bicknell, M.P. (Sy)	RFM	196	43	600	27	22.22	3-27	—	—
Binny, R.M.H. (Ind)	RM	182.2	29	637	16	39.81	5-40	1	—
Birch, J.D. (Nt)	RM	11	1	24	1	24.00	1-4	—	—
Blakey, R.J. (Y)		10.3	1	68	1	68.00	1-68	—	—
Boon, T.J. (Le)	RM	30.3	2	170	5	34.00	3-40	—	—
Border, A.R. (Ex)	SLA	26	3	120	1	120.00	1-8	—	—
Botham, I.T. (Sm/Eng)	RFM	311.1	65	1043	25	41.72	6-125	1	—
Bowler, P.D. (Le)	OB	25.4	10	57	0	—	—	—	—
Boyd-Moss, R.J. (Nh)	SLA	80.1	19	232	7	33.14	3-39	—	—
Bracewell, J.G. (NZ)	OB	411	122	1042	37	28.16	6-55	2	1
Bredin, A.M. (Sx)	SLA	115	25	385	7	55.00	2-50	—	—
Briers, N.E. (Le)	RM	13	0	60	2	30.00	2-54	—	—
Broad, B.C. (Nt)	RM	7	1	41	0	—	—	—	—
Brown, K.R. (M)		0.4	0	10	0	—	—	—	—
Browne, D.W. (CU)		23	5	76	1	76.00	1-13	—	—
Burnett, N.W. (Sc)		13	3	30	0	—	—	—	—
Butcher, A.R. (Sy)	LM	111	28	305	13	23.46	4-25	—	—
Butcher, I.P. (Le)	RM	2	0	4	0	—	—	—	—
Butcher, R.O. (M)	RM	13.4	2	49	2	24.50	2-37	—	—
Byas, D. (Y)	RM	2	0	15	0	—	—	—	—
Cann, M.J. (Gm)	OB	1	1	0	0	—	—	—	—
Capel, D.J. (Nh/TCCB)	RM	633.1	131	2044	63	32.44	7-86	2	—
Carr, J.D. (M)	OB	93.2	17	284	1	284.00	1-46	—	—
Carrick, P. (Y)	SLA	621.3	187	1550	36	43.05	4-111	—	—
Chadwick, M.R. (La)	RM	5	0	51	0	—	—	—	—
Chatfield, E.J. (NZ)	RFM	191.4	47	457	13	35.15	3-73	—	—
Childs, J.H. (Ex)	SLA	640.1	212	1449	89	16.28	8-58	5	3
Clarke, S.T. (Sy)	RF	341.3	95	806	48	16.79	5-31	3	—
Clift, P.B. (Le)	RM	413.3	120	1002	45	22.26	4-35	—	—
Clinton, G.S. (Sy)	RM	3	1	12	0	—	—	—	—
Close, D.B. (DBC)	OB	10	1	71	1	71.00	1-71	—	—
Cobb, R.A. (Le)	SLA	10	3	41	0	—	—	—	—
Coney, J.V. (NZ)	RM	75	23	194	7	27.71	2-14	—	—
Connor, C.A. (H)	RFM	541.4	123	1616	49	32.97	5-60	1	—
Cook, G. (Nh)	SLA	17	4	38	1	38.00	1-38	—	—
Cook, N.G.B. (Nh)	SLA	870.2	290	1890	64	29.53	6-72	2	—

	Cat	O	M	R	W	Avge	Best	5 wI	10 wM
Coombs. R.V.J. (Sm)	SLA	256.5	58	844	16	52.75	3-60	—	—
Cooper, K.E. (Nt)	RFM	410.5	106	1026	43	23.86	5-102	1	—
Corlett, S.C. (Ire)	RM	40	3	113	4	28.25	4-113	—	—
Cottey, P.A. (Gm)		—							
Cowans, N.G. (M)	RF	435.2	94	1380	58	23.79	5-61	1	—
Cowdrey, C.S. (K)	RM	266.2	45	905	27	33.51	5-69	1	—
Cowdrey, G.R. (K)	RM	10	3	27	1	27.00	1-17	—	—
Cowley, N.G. (H)	OB	385.2	78	1060	40	26.50	5-17	1	—
Crowe, M.D. (NZ)	RMF	49.5	8	190	2	95.00	1-37	—	—
Curran, K.M. (Gs)	RFM	33	8	83	0	—	—	—	—
Dale, C.S. (K)	OB	34	5	142	0	—	—	—	—
Daniel, W.W. (M)	RF	40[illegible].1	52	1387	62	22.37	4-27	—	—
Davidson, J.E. (CU/Us)	RMF	326	54	998	30	33.26	5-35	2	—
Davis, M.R. (Sm)	LFM	167.3	21	631	11	57.36	2-43	—	—
Davis, R.P. (K)	SLA	59.5	22	121	6	20.16	3-38	—	—
Dawson, T.A.J. (OU)	OB	194	38	649	13	49.92	3-65	—	—
DeFreitas, P.A.J. (Le/TCCB)	RFM	743.3	139	2171	94	23.09	7-44	7	1
Dennis, S.J. (Y)	LFM	407.3	79	1318	43	30.65	5-71	1	—
Derrick, J. (Gm)	RM	265.2	47	897	22	40.77	3-19	—	—
Dilley, G.R. (K/Eng)	RF	505.2	86	1634	63	25.93	6-57	3	1
D'Oliveira, D.B. (Wo)	OB	27.4	6	118	5	23.60	2-17	—	—
Donald, W.A. (Sc)	RM	32	17	37	3	12.33	3-17	—	—
Doshi, D.R. (DBC)	SLA	22	2	142	1	142.00	1-142	—	—
Doughty, R.J. (Sy)	RFM	300	50	1104	32	34.50	4-52	—	—
Dredge, C.H. (Sm)	RMF	389	83	1151	35	32.88	3-10	—	—
Duthie, P.G. (Sc)	RM	30	9	63	3	21.00	2-29	—	—
East, D.E. (Ex)		0.2	0	1	0	—	—	—	—
Edgar, B.A. (NZ)	RM	1	0	2	0	—	—	—	—
Edmonds, P.H. (M/Eng)	SLA	529	162	1111	38	29.23	4-31	—	—
Ellcock, R.M. (Wo)	RF	32	2	117	4	29.25	3-77	—	—
Ellison, C.C. (CU)	RMF	127	41	325	14	23.21	5-82	1	—
Ellison, R.M. (K/Eng)	RFM	385.4	90	1103	23	47.95	4-36	—	—
Emburey, J.E. (M/Eng)	OB	473.3	170	872	39	22.35	5-51	1	—
Estwick, R.O. (DBC)	RFM	23	4	95	3	31.66	3-95	—	—
Evans, K.P. (Nt)	RMF	51.2	8	218	1	218.00	1-19	—	—
Fairbrother, N.H. (La)	LM	23	9	48	0	—	—	—	—
Falkner, N.J. (Sy)	RM	4	1	9	1	9.00	1-3	—	—
Feltham, M.A. (Sy)	RM	224	48	781	26	30.03	4-47	—	—
Felton, N.A. (Sm)		1	0	3	0	—	—	—	—
Ferreira, A.M. (Wa)	RMF	178	47	532	10	53.20	2-61	—	—
Ferris, G.J.F. (Le)	RFM	104	20	356	13	27.38	4-54	—	—
Finney, R.J. (D)	LM	318.4	60	1057	28	37.75	7-54	1	—
Fletcher, S.D. (Y)	RMF	414	82	1273	31	41.06	5-90	1	—
Folley, I. (La)	SLA	349	98	1046	29	36.06	4-42	—	—
Foster, D.J. (Sm)	RFM	5	0	29	0	—	—	—	—
Foster, N.A. (Ex/Eng)	RFM	806.2	179	2349	105	22.37	6-57	10	2
Fowler, G. (La)	RM	4	0	34	2	17.00	2-34	—	—
Franklin, T.J. (NZ)	RM	1	0	5	0	—	—	—	—
Fraser, A.G.J. (M)	RFM	56.4	15	165	8	20.62	3-46	—	—
Fraser, A.R.C. (M)	RFM	156	40	370	10	37.00	3-19	—	—

	Cat	O	M	R	W	Avge	Best	5 wI	10 wM
Fraser-Darling, C.D. (Nt)	**RFM**	120	16	461	12	38.41	5-84	1	—
Gard, T. (Sm)		—							
Garner, J. (Sm)	**RF**	419	95	1091	47	23.21	5-56	1	—
Garth, J.D. (Ire)	**RM**	19	7	34	0	—	—	—	—
Gatting, M.W. (M/Eng)	**RM**	74	24	196	8	24.50	2-8	—	—
Gifford, N. (Wa)	**SLA**	564.4	157	1409	59	23.88	6-27	2	—
Golding, A.K. (CU/Us)	**SLA**	252	51	685	10	68.50	3-51	—	—
Gooch, G.A. (Ex/Eng)	**RM**	159.4	45	398	9	44.22	2-46	—	—
Gorman, S.R. (CU)	**OB**	49	10	184	2	92.00	1-28	—	—
Gould, I.J. (Sx)		22.3	0	110	2	55.00	2-67	—	—
Gower, D.I. (Le/Eng)	**OB**	1	0	5	0	—	—	—	—
Graveney, D.A. (Gs)	**SLA**	446	137	999	30	33.30	4-17	—	—
Gray, A.H. (Sy)	**RF**	342.3	69	966	51	18.94	7-23	3	1
Gray, E.J. (NZ)	**SLA**	438.2	144	1087	37	29.37	7-61	3	—
Green, A.M. (Sx)	**RM**	174.1	25	583	7	83.28	2-58	—	—
Greensword, S. (MC)	**RM**	13	4	33	1	33.00	1-33	—	—
Griffiths, B.J. (Nh)	**RFM**	237.3	49	741	21	35.28	4-59	—	—
Hadlee, R.J. (Nt/NZ)	**RFM**	547.3	150	1215	76	15.98	6-31	7	2
Hagan, D.A. (OU/Us)	**OB**	0.1	0	4	0	—	—	—	—
Halliday, M. (Ire)	**OB**	28	8	74	0	—	—	—	—
Harden, R.J. (Sm)	**LM**	54	5	208	4	52.00	2-24	—	—
Hardie, B.R. (Ex)	**RM**	12	0	58	0	—	—	—	—
Hardy, J.J.E. (Sm)		1	0	5	0	—	—	—	—
Harman, M.D. (Sm)	**OB**	60.3	12	149	1	149.00	1-88	—	—
Harper, R.A. (Nh)	**OB**	825.2	275	1700	62	27.41	5-84	1	—
Harris, G.A.R. (Le)	**RFM**	8	1	34	0	—	—	—	—
Harrison, G.D. (Ire)	**RFM**	12	2	27	0	—	—	—	—
Hartley, P.J. (Y)	**RMF**	321.1	49	1095	41	26.70	6-68	1	—
Hartley, S.N. (Y)	**RM**	48.4	9	206	4	51.50	3-59	—	—
Hayhurst, A.N. (La)	**RM**	114.1	13	429	10	42.90	4-69	—	—
Heath, S.D. (CU)	**LB**	7	0	39	0	—	—	—	—
Hemmings, E.E. (Nt)	**OB**	818.3	259	2134	73	29.23	7-102	5	2
Henriksen, S. (La)	**RFM**	17	2	61	1	61.00	1-26	—	—
Herbert, R. (MC)	**OB**	8	3	24	0	—	—	—	—
Hick, G.A. (Wo)	**OB**	28.4	5	109	3	36.33	2-24	—	—
Hickey, D.J. (Gm)	**RFM**	281.5	39	1102	24	45.91	5-57	1	—
Higgs, K. (Le)	**RMF**	36	10	71	5	14.20	5-22	1	—
Hill, A. (D)	**OB**	9	3	22	1	22.00	1-22	—	—
Hinks, S.G. (K)	**RM**	8	2	10	1	10.00	1-10	—	—
Holding, M.A. (D)	**RF**	388.1	110	1045	52	20.09	7-97	4	—
Holmes, G.C. (Gm)	**RM**	131	21	499	11	45.36	2-22	—	—
Hopkins, J.A. (Gm)		1.5	0	12	0	—	—	—	—
Hughes, S.P. (M)	**RFM**	529.4	123	1652	63	26.22	7-35	1	—
Igglesden, A.P. (K)	**RFM**	125	25	372	11	33.81	4-46	—	—
Illingworth, R.K. (Wo)	**SLA**	564.2	189	1361	28	48.60	5-64	1	—
Imran Khan (Sx)	**RF**	317.2	72	866	37	23.40	8-34	2	—
Inchmore, J.D. (Wo)	**RFM**	221.1	49	562	13	43.23	2-41	—	—
James, K.D. (H)	**LMF**	228.4	55	692	21	32.95	5-34	1	—
Jarvis, K.B.S. (K)	**RFM**	155.2	42	487	12	40.58	2-15	—	—
Jarvis, P.W. (Y)	**RFM**	428.4	82	1332	60	22.20	7-55	5	2
Jean-Jacques, M. (D)	**RMF**	159	16	599	22	27.22	8-77	1	1

	Cat	O	M	R	W	Avge	Best	5 wI	10 wM
Jesty, T.E. (Sy)	RM	59	21	155	5	31.00	2-14	—	—
Johnson, P. (Nt)	RM	19	2	113	0	—	—	—	—
Jones, A.N. (Sx)	RFM	171	26	620	21	29.52	3-36	—	—
Kallicharran, A.I. (Wa)	OB	9	0	65	2	32.50	2-65	—	—
Kapil Dev (Ind)	RFM	186.2	50	461	20	23.05	5-35	1	—
Ker, J.E. (Sc)	RM	20.4	7	25	1	25.00	1-15	—	—
Kerr, K.J. (Wa)	OB	316	52	955	24	39.79	5-47	1	—
King, C.L. (DBC)	RM	4	0	39	0	—	—	—	—
Lamb, A.J. (Nh/Eng)	RM	2	2	0	0	—	—	—	—
Lamba, R. (Ind)	RM	16	4	49	1	49.00	1-15	—	—
Lampitt, S.R. (Wo)	RM	7	1	21	0	—	—	—	—
Lawrence, D.V. (Gs/TCCB)	RF	588.1	85	2299	63	36.49	5-84	1	—
Lawrence, M.P. (OU/Us)	SLA	156	29	554	7	79.14	2-28	—	—
Lea, A.E. (CU)	LB	54	6	191	6	31.83	3-61	—	—
Lenham, N.J. (Sx)	RMF	131	25	409	9	45.44	4-85	—	—
Le Roux, G.S. (Sx)	RFM	303.2	66	928	26	35.69	3-27	—	—
Lever, J.K. (Ex/Eng)	LFM	638.1	154	1990	70	28.42	6-57	3	—
Lilley, A.W. (Ex)	RM	18.3	1	104	2	52.00	2-104	—	—
Lloyd, T.A. (Wa)	OB	16	0	113	0	—	—	—	—
Lloyds, J.W. (Gs)	OB	369.2	71	1221	37	33.00	5-111	2	—
Lord, G.J. (Wa)	SLA	1	0	6	0	—	—	—	—
Love, J.D. (Y)	RM	39.2	7	146	0	—	—	—	—
Lynch, M.A. (Sy)	RM/OB	24.2	3	119	2	59.50	1-18	—	—
McBrine, A. (Ire)	SLA	23	5	64	3	21.33	3-64	—	—
McBrine, J. (Ire)	RFM	27	4	67	0	—	—	—	—
McEwan, S.M. (Wo)	RFM	180.1	31	638	16	39.87	3-33	—	—
MacLarnon, P.C. (OU)	RM	26.5	5	89	2	44.50	2-25	—	—
McMillan, B.M. (Wa)	RMF	220	34	808	17	47.52	3-47	—	—
Madan Lal (Ind)	RMF	20.5	5	48	3	16.00	3-18	—	—
Maher, B.J.M. (D)		33	2	151	3	50.33	2-69	—	—
Makinson, D.J. (La)	LFM	322.1	66	1044	30	34.80	4-69	—	—
Malcolm, D.E. (D)	RF	216.2	38	765	28	27.32	5-42	1	—
Mallender, N.A. (Nh)	RFM	611	138	1693	47	36.02	5-110	1	—
Maninder Singh (Ind)	SLA	257.1	71	612	21	29.14	4-26	—	—
Marks, V.J. (Sm)	OB	744.5	198	2121	59	35.94	8-100	2	1
Marples, C. (D)		4	0	48	0	—	—	—	—
Marshall, M.D. (H)	RF	656.3	171	1508	100	15.08	6-51	5	—
Maru, R.J. (H)	SLA	497.5	146	1336	48	27.83	5-38	1	—
Maynard, M.P. (Gm)	RM	4	0	13	0	—	—	—	—
Mays, C.S. (Sx)	OB	212.5	45	706	13	54.30	3-77	—	—
Medlycott, K.T. (Sy)	SLA	356.2	86	1166	40	29.15	6-63	3	1
Merry, W.G. (MC)	RMF	20	5	47	1	47.00	1-47	—	—
Metcalfe, A.A. (Y/TCCB)	OB	18.1	4	75	0	—	—	—	—
Middleton, T.C. (H)	SLA	8	1	39	1	39.00	1-13	—	—
Miller, A.J.T. (M)	RM	2	0	6	0	—	—	—	—
Miller, G. (D)	OB	634.2	187	1406	33	42.60	5-37	2	—
Moir, D.G. (Sc)	SLA	52	9	117	7	16.71	4-53	—	—
Moles, A.J. (Wa)	RM	64.3	10	198	5	39.60	2-57	—	—
Monkhouse, G. (Sy)	RMF	233.1	69	589	14	42.07	4-37	—	—
Monkhouse, S. (Wa)	LFM	10	4	34	1	34.00	1-34	—	—

	Cat	O	M	R	W	Avge	Best	5 wI	10 wM
Morris, H. (Gm)	**RM**	11	4	44	0	—	—	—	—
Morris, J.E. (D/TCCB)	**RM**	44.4	5	245	1	245.00	1-103	—	—
Mortensen, O.H. (D)	**RFM**	416.2	111	1082	46	23.52	5-35	1	—
Moseley, E.A. (Gm)	**RFM**	124.3	14	447	11	40.63	4-70	—	—
Moxon, M.D. (Y/Eng)	**RM**	35.4	10	113	2	56.50	1-18	—	—
Munton, T.A. (Wa)	**RFM**	297.4	68	905	32	28.28	4-60	—	—
Murphy, A.J. (La/MC)	**RMF**	91	16	288	10	28.80	3-67	—	—
Needham, A. (Sy)	**OB**	109	39	227	1	227.00	1-47	—	—
Newell, M. (Nt)	**LB**	2	0	19	0	—	—	—	—
Newman, P.G. (D)	**RFM**	73.1	16	198	9	22.00	5-62	1	—
Newport, P.J. (Wo)	**RFM**	632.3	90	2146	85	25.24	6-48	5	1
Nicholas, M.C.J. (H/TCCB)	**RM**	64	13	198	3	66.00	1-27	—	—
North, P.D. (Gm)	**SLA**	60.4	13	149	4	37.25	4-49	—	—
Old, C.M. (DBC)	**RFM**	8	0	46	0	—	—	—	—
Ontong, R.C. (Gm)	**OB**	606.4	153	1774	64	27.71	8-101	2	1
O'Shaughnessy, S.J. (La)	**RM**	97	18	363	5	72.60	2-28	—	—
Palmer, G.V. (Sm)	**RMF**	81	9	290	5	58.00	4-77	—	—
Pandit, C.S. (Ind)		2.1	0	14	0	—	—	—	—
Parker, P.W.G. (Sx)	**RM**	3	1	13	0	—	—	—	—
Parks, R.J. (H)		23	1	110	0	—	—	—	—
Parsons, G.J. (Wa)	**RMF**	371.1	72	1179	31	38.03	5-24	2	—
Patel, A.S. (MC)	**SLA**	11	3	41	0	—	—	—	—
Patel, D.N. (Wo)	**OB**	453.2	115	1255	30	41.83	5-88	1	—
Patel, T. (OU)	**OB**	2	0	12	0	—	—	—	—
Patil, S.M. (Ind)	**RM**	38	6	122	2	61.00	1-19	—	—
Patterson, B.P. (La)	**RF**	391.4	69	1309	48	27.27	6-31	2	1
Pauline, D.B. (Gm)	**RM**	14	0	67	2	33.50	2-48	—	—
Payne, I.R. (Gs)	**RM**	215.1	58	576	15	38.40	3-48	—	—
Penn, C. (K)	**RFM**	117.3	24	407	14	29.07	5-65	1	—
Pick, R.A. (Nt)	**RMF**	469.1	88	1570	50	31.40	6-68	1	—
Pierson, A.R.K. (Wa)	**OB**	36	5	133	2	66.50	1-33	—	—
Pigott, A.C.S. (Sx)	**RFM**	390	48	1363	49	27.81	5-50	3	—
Plumb, S.G. (MC)	**RM**	9	1	33	1	33.00	1-33	—	—
Pocock, P.I. (Sy)	**OB**	394.5	107	1095	30	36.50	4-45	—	—
Pont, I.L. (Ex)	**RFM**	50.2	6	190	3	63.33	3-68	—	—
Pont, K.R. (Ex)	**RM**	35.5	8	102	4	25.50	4-63	—	—
Potter, L. (Le)	**SLA**	113	31	318	10	31.80	3-37	—	—
Prabhakar, M. (Ind)	**RMF**	119	25	353	9	39.22	3-42	—	—
Price, D.G. (CU/Us)	**OB**	1.2	0	11	0	—	—	—	—
Pridgeon, A.P. (Wo)	**RM**	535	134	1396	59	23.66	6-52	1	—
Pringle, D.R. (Ex/Eng)	**RMF**	506.3	128	1348	56	24.07	7-46	2	—
Pringle, N.J. (Sm)	**RM**	10	0	48	0	—	—	—	—
Quinlan, J.D. (OU)	**RM**	103.3	14	369	4	92.25	2-98	—	—
Radford, N.V. (Wo/Eng)	**RFM**	665.4	132	2164	81	26.71	9-70	6	3
Randall, D.W. (Nt)	**RM**	3	0	17	0	—	—	—	—
Reeve, D.A. (Sx)	**RM**	525.5	127	1411	52	27.13	5-32	1	—
Rice, C.E.B. (Nt)	**RMF**	413.2	115	1111	44	25.25	4-54	—	—

	Cat	O	M	R	W	Avge	Best	5 wI	10 wM
Richards, C.J. (Sy)	OB	5	0	34	1	34.00	1-34	—	—
Richards, I.V.A. (Sm)	OB	161	32	500	9	55.55	4-36	—	—
Riddell, N.A. (MC)	RM	1	0	5	0	—	—	—	—
Roberts, B. (D)	RM	22	5	53	2	26.50	1-11	—	—
Roberts, M.L. (Gm)		—							
Robinson, P.E. (Y)	LM	11	0	115	0	—	—	—	—
Robinson, R.T. (Nt/Eng)	RM	2	0	18	0	—	—	—	—
Roebuck, P.M. (Sm)	OB	24	3	120	1	120.00	1-30	—	—
Romaines, P.W. (Gs)		21.1	0	152	0	—	—	—	—
Roope, G.R.J. (MC)	RM	2	0	9	0	—	—	—	—
Rose, B.C. (Sm)	LM	11	0	57	2	28.50	2-28	—	—
Rose, G.D. (M)	RM	64	10	277	7	39.57	2-39	—	—
Rudd, C.F.B.P. (D)	OB	28.3	7	90	0	—	—	—	—
Rutherford, K.R. (NZ)	RM	5	0	25	0	—	—	—	—
Rutnagur, R.S. (OU/Us)	RM	164	34	528	14	37.71	3-50	—	—
Rydon, R.A. (OU)	RM	119	21	471	5	94.20	3-106	—	—
Sadiq Mohammad (DBC)	LB	4	0	21	1	21.00	1-21	—	—
Sainsbury, G.E. (Gs)	LMF	169.1	46	498	12	41.50	4-146	—	—
Saxelby, K. (Nt)	RMF	284	54	905	27	33.51	4-47	—	—
Scott, A.M.G. (Sx/CU/Us)	LM	283	71	814	18	45.22	4-100	—	—
Sharma, C. (Ind)	RFM	221.3	34	736	31	23.74	6-58	2	1
Sharma, R. (D)	RM/OB	140.5	33	407	11	37.00	3-72	—	—
Sharp, K. (Y)	OB	29	4	192	3	64.00	1-20	—	—
Shastri, R.J. (Ind)	SLA	217	57	494	12	41.16	3-44	—	—
Shaw, C. (Y)	RFM	300.1	64	848	31	27.35	5-38	1	—
Sidebottom, A. (Y)	RMF	226.1	37	671	25	26.84	8-72	1	—
Simmons, J. (La)	OB	230.5	52	762	36	21.16	7-79	2	1
Slack, W.N. (M/Eng)	RM	17	3	75	1	75.00	1-14	—	—
Small, G.C. (Wa/Eng)	RFM	639.3	158	1781	77	23.12	5-35	2	—
Smith, C.L. (H/Eng)	OB	40	7	177	1	177.00	1-54	—	—
Smith, D.M. (Wo)	RM	11	3	35	2	17.50	2-35	—	—
Smith, G. (Nh)	LFM	40	8	132	2	66.00	1-38	—	—
Smith, I. (Gm)	RM	24	3	111	1	111.00	1-18	—	—
Smith, I.D.S. (NZ)		2	0	8	0	—	—	—	—
Smith, P.A. (Wa)	RFM	159	19	743	13	57.15	3-36	—	—
Smith, R.A. (H)	LB	48.4	10	197	3	65.66	2-102	—	—
Srikkanth, K. (Ind)	RM	20	0	91	3	30.33	1-16	—	—
Standing, D.K. (Sx)	OB	195	37	536	4	134.00	2-28	—	—
Steele, J.F. (Gm)	SLA	156	27	583	9	64.77	2-21	—	—
Stephenson, F.D. (DBC)	RFM	23	3	90	1	90.00	1-90	—	—
Stephenson, J.P. (Ex)	RM	2	0	5	0	—	—	—	—
Stevenson, A.W.J. (Sc)	OB	27	7	77	2	38.50	1-26	—	—
Stevenson, G.B. (Y)	RMF	29	8	75	2	37.50	2-27	—	—
Stewart, A.J. (Sy)		5	0	55	0	—	—	—	—
Stirling, D.A. (NZ)	RFM	255	36	1025	28	36.60	5-98	1	—
Stovold, A.W. (Gs)		27	2	132	2	66.00	1-3	—	—
Such, P.M. (Nt/TCCB)	OB	231.3	69	566	22	25.72	5-36	1	—
Surridge, D. (MC)	RMF	19	5	61	2	30.50	2-61	—	—
Swallow, I.G. (Y)	OB	172	37	510	6	85.00	3-109	—	—

	Cat	O	M	R	W	Avge	Best	5 wI	10 wM
Sygrove, M.T. (OU)	RM	17	0	85	2	42.50	1-19	—	—
Sykes, J.F. (M)	OB	43.3	5	161	5	32.20	4-102	—	—
Tavaré, C.J. (K)	RM	27	6	107	2	53.50	1-3	—	—
Taylor, J.P. (D)	LFM	87	12	299	8	37.37	4-81	—	—
Taylor, L.B. (Le)	RFM	280.3	66	809	27	29.96	4-106	—	—
Taylor, N.R. (K)	OB	77.3	9	252	3	84.00	1-14	—	—
Taylor, N.S. (Sm)	RFM	342.2	62	1222	29	42.13	4-40	—	—
Tennant, L. (Le)	RM	8	1	35	0	—	—	—	—
Terry, V.P. (H)	RM	1	1	0	0	—	—	—	—
Thomas, D.J. (Sy)	LFM	166.3	29	588	12	49.00	2-44	—	—
Thomas, J.G. (Gm/Eng)	RF	478.5	70	1746	45	38.80	4-56	—	—
Thorne, D.A. (Wa/OU/Us)	LM	239.3	70	591	11	53.72	3-42	—	—
Todd, P.A. (MC)	OB	1	0	4	0	—	—	—	—
Tomlins, K.P. (Gs)	RM	6	0	34	0	—	—	—	—
Toogood, G.J. (OU)	RM	58	16	155	4	38.75	2-56	—	—
Topley, T.D. (Ex)	RMF	249.4	60	744	32	23.25	5-52	2	—
Tremellen, J.M. (CU)	RM	7	0	32	0	—	—	—	—
Tremlett, T.M. (H)	RMF	453.4	110	1263	43	29.37	5-46	1	—
Tufnell, P.C.R. (M)	SLA	148	32	479	5	95.80	2-47	—	—
Turner, D.R. (H)	RM	3	1	6	0	—	—	—	—
Turner, M.S. (Sm)	RFM	15	3	55	2	27.50	2-55	—	—
Turner, S. (Ex)	RMF	40	11	138	2	69.00	1-66	—	—
Twizell, P.H. (Gs)	RFM	11.1	3	38	0	—	—	—	—
Underwood, D.L. (K)	LM	638.1	259	1371	52	26.36	7-11	1	—
Walker, A. (Nh)	RFM	422	76	1314	33	39.81	6-50	1	—
Walsh, C.A. (Gs)	RF	789.5	193	2145	118	18.17	9-72	12	4
Waring, I.C. (Sx)	RFM	22	6	45	1	45.00	1-16	—	—
Warner, A.E. (D)	RFM	349.1	67	1200	28	42.85	4-38	—	—
Watkin, S.L. (Gm)		16	1	82	2	41.00	2-74	—	—
Watkinson, M. (La)	RMF	504.4	86	1753	35	50.08	5-90	1	—
Watson, W. (NZ)	RMF	308.1	60	963	26	37.03	4-31	—	—
Wells, A.P. (Sx)	RM	13	2	44	1	44.00	1-42	—	—
Wells, C.M. (Sx)	RM	458.2	103	1373	37	37.10	4-23	—	—
Weston, M.J. (Wo)	RM	135	37	376	5	75.20	2-29	—	—
Whitaker, J.J. (Le/TCCB)	OB	5.2	0	47	1	47.00	1-41	—	—
Wild, D.J. (Nh)	RM	132.3	17	429	15	28.60	4-4	—	—
Willey, P. (Le/Eng)	OB	176.2	49	418	7	59.71	2-25	—	—
Williams, N.F. (M)	RFM	79.3	9	264	10	26.40	3-44	—	—
Williams, R.G. (Nh)	OB	74	22	190	3	63.33	2-59	—	—
Winterborne, G. (Sy)	RM	20	5	47	0	—	—	—	—
Wood, L.J. (D)	SLA	39	10	95	2	47.50	2-82	—	—
Wright, A.J. (Gs)	RM	1	0	10	0	—	—	—	—
Wright, J.G. (D/NZ)	RM	4	1	13	0	—	—	—	—
Yadav, N.S. (Ind)	OB	188.4	39	534	15	35.60	6-30	1	—
Younis Ahmed (Gm)	SLA	20	4	82	0	—	—	—	—

LEADING CURRENT PLAYERS

These career records list in order of success in each department of the game the leading current players who are available for first-class county cricket in 1987. All figures are to the end of the 1986 English season.

BATTING AND BOWLING

An order of merit based on the highest career averages, with batting and bowling qualifications of 100 innings and 100 wickets respectively.

BATSMAN	*Runs*	*Avge*	BOWLER	*Wkts*	*Avge*
I.V.A. Richards	28533	49.97	M.D. Marshall	1017	17.87
M.D. Crowe	8270	49.52	R.J. Hadlee	1221	18.48
C.H. Lloyd	31232	49.26	H.A. Page	133	18.71
A.J. Lamb	18199	47.64	D.L. Underwood	2420	20.12
M.W. Gatting	16920	46.86	S.T. Clarke	758	20.12
C.G. Greenidge	31074	45.76	G.S. Le Roux	729	21.18
A.I. Kallicharran	30775	45.25	W.W. Daniel	833	21.82
D.L. Amiss	42123	43.42	C.A. Walsh	388	22.19
G.A. Gooch	22835	43.00	A.H. Gray	200	22.20
R.J. Bailey	4624	42.42	C.E.B. Rice	800	22.22
J.J. Whitaker	4031	41.98	M.A. Holding	612	22.97
C.L. Smith	10404	41.78	N. Gifford	2001	23.30
C.E.B. Rice	22571	41.03	T.M. Alderman	579	23.52
R.T. Robinson	10354	40.76	P.A.J. DeFreitas	121	23.75
J.G. Wright	17783	40.50	J.K. Lever	1619	23.97
D.I. Gower	16867	40.06	J.E. Emburey	953	24.01
W.N. Slack	10902	38.93	L.B. Taylor	501	24.41
R.J. Shastri	4653	38.45	A. Sidebottom	415	24.41
N.H. Fairbrother	4572	38.42	T.M. Tremlett	337	24.56
M.R. Benson	7802	38.24	K.M. Curran	114	24.57
K.W.R. Fletcher	36437	38.19	P.B. Clift	816	24.79
R.A. Smith	5108	38.11	N.A. Foster	384	24.85
C.J. Tavaré	15952	37.62	P.H. Edmonds	1185	25.24
D.W. Randall	21304	37.44	N.G. Cowans	353	25.25
G.W. Humpage	14701	37.12	P.J.W. Allott	436	25.38

WICKET-KEEPING AND FIELDING

The following wicket-keepers and fielders have most dismissals and catches in the field respectively:

WICKET-KEEPERS	*Total*	*Ct*	*St*	FIELDERS	*Ct*
D.L. Bairstow	988	856	132	K.W.R. Fletcher	623
G.W. Humpage	577	513	64	C.T. Radley	513
B.N. French	560	505	55	C.G. Greenidge	441
P.R. Downton	543	477	66	J.F. Steele	413
I.J. Gould	521	454	67	D.L. Amiss	410
C.J. Richards	505	443	62	G. Cook	384
R.J. Parks	429	382	47	C.H. Lloyd	377
D.E. East	404	361	43	I.V.A. Richards	354

FIRST-CLASS CAREER RECORDS

Compiled by Geoffrey Saulez

The following career records are for all players who appeared in first-class cricket during the 1986 season. Some players who did not appear for their counties in 1986, but may do so in 1987, are also included.

BATTING AND FIELDING

'1000' denotes instances of 1000 or more runs in a season. Where such aggregates have been achieved outside the United Kingdom they are shown after a 'plus' sign.

	M	*I*	*NO*	*HS*	*Runs*	*Avge*	*100*	*1000*	*Ct/St*
Abrahams, J.	240	371	51	201*	9476	29.61	13	4	155
Acfield, D.L.	420	417	212	42	1677	8.18	—	—	137
Afford, J.A.	21	13	7	9*	21	3.50	—	—	7
Agnew, J.P.	123	119	24	56	924	9.72	—	—	28
Ahluwalia, M.S.	10	18	1	36	253	14.88	—	—	3
Alderman, T.M.	146	166	76	52*	773	8.58	—	—	124
Alikhan, R.I.	18	28	4	72	843	35.12	—	—	7
Alleyne, M.W.	10	16	5	116*	336	30.54	1	—	4
Allott, P.J.W.	158	161	43	78	1953	16.55	—	—	52
Amarnath, M.	220	344	59	207	12646	44.37	28	0+3	143
Amiss, D.L.	633	1093	123	262*	42123	43.42	100	22+1	410
Anderson, I.S.	125	204	25	112	4319	24.12	2	1	100
Andrew, S.J.W.	26	16	10	7	36	6.00	—	—	9
Ashley, D.J.	1	2	0	4	4	2.00	—	—	0/1
Asif Din	95	150	27	102	3356	27.28	1	—	50
Aslett, D.G.	94	159	12	221*	5159	35.09	11	2	69
Athey, C.W.J.	239	400	34	184	11741	32.07	22	5	236/2
Atkinson, J.C.M.	10	11	3	79	238	29.75	—	—	—
Azharuddin, M.	46	70	12	151	3080	53.10	11	—	42
Babington, A.M.	6	3	1	1	1	0.50	—	—	4
Bail, P.A.C.	16	29	2	174	657	24.33	1	—	5
Bailey, R.J.	84	134	25	224*	4624	42.42	9	3	49
Bainbridge, P.	174	298	47	151*	8234	32.80	12	6	84
Bairstow, D.L.	407	576	111	145	12262	26.36	7	3	856/132
Bakker, P.J.	3	2	1	3*	6	6.00	—	—	—
Balderstone, J.C.	390	619	61	181*	19034	34.11	32	11	210
Baptiste, E.A.E.	108	154	23	136*	3725	28.43	3	—	54
Barclay, J.R.T.	274	434	44	119	9677	24.81	9	4	214
Barlow, G.D.	251	404	59	177	12387	35.90	26	7	136
Barnett, K.J.	191	303	29	144	9415	34.36	17	4	121
Barrett, B.J.	12	5	4	5*	8	8.00	—	—	1
Bartlett, R.J.	6	9	2	117*	307	43.85	1	—	4
Barwick, S.R.	80	71	30	29	372	9.07	—	—	21
Base, S.J.	14	13	5	15*	55	6.87	—	—	3
Benjamin, W.K.M.	26	29	12	95*	515	30.29	—	—	11
Benson, M.R.	130	224	20	162	7802	38.24	17	5	60
Bent, P.	1	1	0	14	14	14.00	—	—	—
Berry, P.J.	1	1	1	4*	4	—	—	—	2

	M	I	NO	HS	Runs	Avge	100	1000	Ct/St
Bicknell, M.P.	9	10	2	9*	21	2.62	—	—	4
Binny, R.M.H.	106	170	16	211*	5093	33.07	10	—	63
Birch, J.D.	203	303	52	125	6983	27.82	5	2	158
Blackett, M.	2	4	2	28*	41	20.50	—	—	—
Blain, T.E.	30	48	8	129	1440	36.00	2	—	52/11
Blakey, R.J.	18	29	2	90	661	24.48	—	—	16
Blitz, R.J.	5	5	0	18	33	6.60	—	—	8
Boon, T.J.	82	136	22	144	3386	29.70	5	2	31
Booth, P.A.	16	18	4	26	82	5.85	—	—	4
Border, A.R.	194	324	48	200	14820	53.69	45	2+5	180
Botham, I.T.	290	450	33	228	14679	35.20	31	4	260
Bowler, P.D.	8	11	1	100*	249	24.90	1	—	2
Boycott, G.	609	1014	162	261*	48426	56.83	151	23+3	264
Boyd-Moss, R.J.	145	244	19	155	6850	30.44	13	3	58
Bracewell, J.G.	96	136	26	110	2741	24.91	3	—	79
Brassington, A.J.	127	155	46	35	881	8.08	—	—	215/48
Bredin, A.M.	7	6	2	8*	26	6.50	—	—	1
Briers, N.E.	194	301	31	201*	7471	27.67	10	3	75
Broad, B.C.	171	304	21	171	10297	36.38	18	6	88
Brown, A.	8	11	0	74	241	21.90	—	—	11/3
Brown, A.D.	9	11	1	30	86	8.60	—	—	15/2
Brown, A.M.	4	6	1	74	146	29.20	—	—	4
Brown, G.E.	1	2	2	2*	2	—	—	—	4/1
Brown, G.K.	1	2	0	14	17	8.50	—	—	1
Brown, K.R.	19	28	4	102	671	27.95	1	—	18
Browne, D.W.	8	14	4	61*	238	23.80	—	—	5
Bullen, C.K.	4	4	0	19	53	13.25	—	—	2
Burnett, N.W.	1	1	0	4	4	4.00	—	—	—
Burns, N.D.	5	8	0	29	84	10.50	—	—	10/2
Butcher, A.R.	290	490	43	216*	14734	32.96	29	7	131
Butcher, I.P.	86	141	9	139	4025	30.49	9	2	72
Butcher, R.O.	228	353	35	197	10043	31.58	14	4	244/1
Byas, D.	1	1	0	0	0	0.00	—	—	1
Cann, M.J.	1	1	1	16*	16	—	—	—	1
Capel, D.J.	105	151	28	111	3452	28.06	3	—	48
Carr, J.D.	46	66	8	123	1791	30.87	4	—	31
Carrick, P.	312	391	73	131*	7003	22.02	3	—	159
Chadwick, M.R.	30	51	1	132	1128	22.56	1	—	14
Chatfield, E.J.	121	110	55	24*	513	9.32	—	—	44
Childs, J.H.	193	178	80	34*	766	7.81	—	—	68
Chivers, I.J.	1	—	—	—	—	—	—	—	—
Clarke, S.T.	196	215	40	100*	2694	15.39	1	—	110
Clift, P.B.	295	414	87	106	7671	23.45	2	—	152
Clinton, G.S.	191	319	39	192	9054	32.33	15	5	69
Close, D.B.	786	1225	173	198	34994	33.26	52	20	813/1
Cobb, R.A.	85	132	8	91	3028	24.41	—	1	46
Cohen, M.F.	4	6	0	29	70	11.66	—	—	1
Coney, J.V.	155	256	46	174*	7528	35.84	8	—	183
Connor, C.A.	58	45	18	36	171	6.33	—	—	19
Cook, G.	388	674	51	183	19997	32.09	30	11	384/3
Cook, N.G.B.	206	208	56	75	1874	12.32	—	—	123
Coombs, R.V.J.	13	9	3	18	32	5.33	—	—	3
Cooper, K.E.	198	186	45	46	1357	9.62	—	—	61

	M	I	NO	HS	Runs	Avge	100	1000	Ct/St
Cope, J.E.B.	4	5	2	8*	11	3.66	—	—	5
Corlett, S.C.	32	45	8	60	613	16.56	—	—	24
Cottey, P.A.	4	5	1	9*	24	6.00	—	—	2
Cowans, N.G.	125	121	25	66	885	9.21	—	—	42
Cowdrey, C.S.	211	314	44	159	8326	30.83	11	3	206
Cowdrey, G.R.	24	36	3	75	674	20.42	—	—	15
Cowley, N.G.	240	337	53	109*	6340	22.32	2	1	90
Crowe, J.J.	105	177	18	159	5355	33.67	9	0+1	116
Crowe, M.D.	121	198	31	242*	8270	49.52	25	1+1	127
Curran, K.M.	73	106	17	117*	2785	31.29	4	1	43
Curtis, T.S.	110	189	26	153	5672	34.79	6	3	52
Dale, C.S.	11	11	3	49	118	14.75	—	—	1
Daniel, W.W.	248	227	98	53*	1520	11.78	—	—	58
Davidson, I.C.	1	2	0	13	13	6.50	—	—	2
Davidson, J.E.	13	14	5	41*	133	14.77	—	—	4
Davies, T.	100	121	36	75	1775	20.88	—	—	165/27
Davis, M.R.	69	71	23	60*	746	15.54	—	—	25
Davis, R.P.	1	1	1	0*	0	—	—	—	1
Dawson, T.A.J.	7	9	5	10*	32	8.00	—	—	2
DeFreitas, P.A.J.	36	42	5	106	762	20.59	1	—	9
Dennis, S.J.	65	63	24	53*	395	10.12	—	—	17
Derrick, J.	47	59	20	78*	1132	29.02	—	—	15
Dilley, G.R.	155	173	57	81	1644	14.17	—	—	62
D'Oliveira, D.B.	101	167	11	146*	4198	26.91	4	2	68
Donald, W.A.	8	13	2	45	221	20.09	—	—	4
Doshi, D.R.	238	253	70	44	1442	7.87	—	—	62
Doughty, R.J.	40	50	11	65	840	21.53	—	—	22
Downton, P.R.	226	278	55	126*	5188	23.26	3	—	477/66
Dredge, C.H.	191	218	68	56*	2100	14.00	—	—	84
Duthie, P.G.	3	4	1	54*	119	39.66	—	—	2
Dyer, R.I.H.B.	65	116	11	109*	2843	27.07	3	2	39
East, D.E.	141	190	27	131	3433	21.06	3	—	361/43
Edgar, B.A.	141	248	21	203	8554	37.68	16	—	79/1
Edmonds, P.H.	365	467	83	142	7348	19.13	3	—	332
Ellcock, R.M.	28	36	10	45*	344	13.23	—	—	4
Ellison, C.C.	23	22	7	51*	268	17.86	—	—	7
Ellison, R.M.	109	151	36	108	2805	24.39	1	—	40
Emburey, J.E.	296	355	75	133	5803	20.72	2	—	262
Estwick, R.O.	19	30	6	34*	177	7.37	—	—	9
Evans, K.P.	10	10	0	42	87	8.70	—	—	5
Fairbrother, N.H.	87	137	18	164*	4572	38.42	7	3	50
Falkner, N.J.	12	19	3	102	668	41.75	2	—	7
Fell, D.J.	18	33	4	114	720	24.82	2	—	5
Feltham, M.A.	26	31	10	76	478	22.76	—	—	6
Felton, N.A.	70	112	5	173*	3173	29.65	6	1	21
Ferreira, A.M.	206	316	63	112*	7114	28.11	4	—	108
Ferris, G.J.F.	39	42	22	26	230	11.50	—	—	7
Finney, R.J.	87	127	22	82	1954	18.60	—	—	15
Fleming, D.	1	—	—	—	—	—	—	—	3
Fletcher, K.W.R.	694	1118	164	228*	36437	38.19	62	20	623
Fletcher, S.D.	40	29	13	28*	152	9.50	—	—	6
Folley, I.	84	98	27	69	871	12.26	—	—	32
Fordham, A.	2	3	0	17	26	8.66	—	—	—

	M	I	NO	HS	Runs	Avge	100	1000	Ct/St
Foster, D.J.	1	1	0	0	0	0.00	—	—	—
Foster, N.A.	100	119	31	63	1567	17.80	—	—	43
Fowler, G.	155	255	11	226	8866	36.33	22	5	72/5
Franklin, T.J.	71	125	11	181	3880	34.03	7	—	45
Fraser, A.G.J.	4	3	2	19*	32	32.00	—	—	—
Fraser, A.R.C.	9	8	1	13	42	6.00	—	—	—
Fraser-Darling, C.D.	8	8	1	61	175	25.00	—	—	8
French, B.N.	221	286	57	98	4175	18.23	—	—	505/55
Gard, T.	110	124	25	51*	1349	13.62	—	—	176/39
Garner, J.	203	217	54	104	2802	17.19	1	—	122
Garth, J.D.	1	2	0	6	7	3.50	—	—	—
Gatting, M.W.	281	430	69	258	16920	46.86	40	8+1	254
Gavaskar, S.M.	333	544	61	340	24749	51.24	78	2+10	280
Gifford, N.	667	755	241	89	6812	13.25	—	—	315
Gill, P.	8	11	4	17	68	9.71	—	—	24
Gladwin, C.	57	97	5	162	2614	28.41	1	1	26
Golding, A.K.	16	26	5	47	385	18.33	—	—	4
Gooch, G.A.	341	576	45	227	22835	43.00	57	10+1	329
Gorman, S.R.	15	24	8	43	253	15.81	—	—	7
Gould, I.J.	227	294	48	128	5984	24.32	2	—	454/67
Gouldstone, M.R.	1	1	0	35	35	35.00	—	—	—
Gower, D.I.	290	461	40	215	16867	40.06	35	6	184/1
Graveney, D.A.	311	408	115	119	5447	18.59	2	—	171
Gray, A.H.	50	52	8	54*	486	11.04	—	—	18
Gray, E.J.	109	166	31	128*	4123	30.54	6	—	81
Green, A.M.	119	211	13	179	6049	30.55	7	3	62
Greenidge, C.G.	435	743	64	273*	31074	45.76	73	15+1	441
Greensword, S.	42	73	8	84*	1094	16.83	—	—	29
Griffiths, B.J.	177	138	51	16	290	3.33	—	—	36
Hadlee, R.J.	287	398	74	210*	9806	30.26	11	1	165
Hagan, D.A.	14	26	2	88	512	21.33	—	—	6
Halliday, M.	12	12	4	47	144	18.00	—	—	5
Harden, R.J.	34	53	8	108	1459	32.42	3	1	21
Hardie, B.R.	309	501	63	162	14836	33.87	20	10	282
Hardy, J.J.E.	48	74	10	107*	2118	33.09	1	—	25
Harman, M.D.	3	5	2	15	27	9.00	—	—	1
Harper, M.A.	32	53	5	149*	1674	34.87	4	—	29
Harper, R.A.	113	144	19	234	3332	26.65	2	—	132
Harris, G.A.R.	1	2	1	6	6	6.00	—	—	—
Harrison, G.D.	4	6	1	86	230	46.00	—	—	—
Hartley, P.J.	30	32	8	87*	631	26.29	—	—	9
Hartley, S.N.	130	194	25	114	4309	25.49	4	—	49
Hayes, K.A.	44	71	4	152	1595	23.80	2	—	15
Hayhurst, A.N.	11	15	0	31	173	11.53	—	—	2
Head, T.J.	25	31	7	52*	397	16.54	—	—	55/6
Heath, S.D.	1	2	0	10	16	8.00	—	—	—
Hegg, W.K.	2	2	0	4	4	2.00	—	—	2/2
Hemmings, E.E.	364	481	104	127*	7475	19.82	1	—	164
Henriksen, S.	3	4	3	10*	17	17.00	—	—	2
Herbert, R.	8	12	1	43	138	12.54	—	—	6
Hick, G.A.	57	91	11	230	4262	53.27	12	2	62
Hickey, D.J.	17	11	6	9*	27	5.40	—	—	4
Higgs, K.	511	530	207	98	3648	11.29		—	312

	M	I	NO	HS	Runs	Avge	100	1000	Ct/St
Hill, A.	258	447	47	172*	12356	30.89	18	5	97
Hinks, S.G.	65	114	6	131	2922	27.05	3	1	44
Holding, M.A.	168	214	28	80	2900	15.59	—	—	75
Holmes, G.C.	128	206	32	112	4670	26.83	4	3	58
Hopkins, J.A.	277	486	29	230	12837	28.08	18	7	191/1
Hughes, D.P.	354	463	84	153	8612	22.72	8	2	242
Hughes, S.P.	100	101	37	47	664	10.37	—	—	25
Humpage, G.W.	274	451	55	254	14701	37.12	28	9	513/64
Hussain, M.	1	1	0	4	4	4.00	—	—	—
Igglesden, A.P.	5	5	2	8*	22	7.33	—	—	2
Illingworth, R.K.	95	106	29	55	1166	15.14	—	—	40
Imran Khan	328	508	82	170	15349	36.03	24	4	104
Inchmore, J.D.	218	246	53	113	3137	16.25	1	—	72
Jackson, P.B.	6	7	1	46	136	22.66	—	—	12/1
James, K.D.	41	46	12	124	880	25.88	1	—	14
James, S.P.	1	—	—	—	—	—	—	—	—
Jarvis, K.B.S.	231	174	74	19	325	3.25	—	—	56
Jarvis, P.W.	50	55	18	47	520	14.05	—	—	23
Javed Miandad	324	518	84	311	23133	53.30	65	5+8	295/3
Jean-Jacques, M.	9	12	3	73	208	23.11	—	—	1
Jesty, T.E.	410	650	84	248	18184	32.12	33	8	242/1
Johnson, P.	77	120	13	133	3532	33.00	7	1	53/1
Jones, A.L.	160	278	24	132	6548	25.77	5	2	104
Jones, A.N.	49	46	20	35	284	10.92	—	—	10
Kallicharran, A.I.	462	762	82	243*	30775	45.25	83	12+1	299
Kapil Dev	192	280	32	193	7884	31.79	10	—	138
Ker, J.E.	10	14	6	50	158	19.75	—	—	3
Kerr, K.J.	53	53	16	74	535	14.45	—	—	47
Kilborn, M.J.	7	12	1	59	219	19.90	—	—	4
King, C.L.	119	192	24	163	6620	39.40	14	1	97
Lamb, A.J.	272	457	75	178	18199	47.64	45	7	203
Lamba, R.	47	74	6	231	2952	43.41	8	—	26
Lampitt, S.R.	2	2	1	11*	11	11.00	—	—	—
Larkins, W.	304	523	31	252	16878	34.30	37	8	161
Lawrence, D.V.	83	90	19	41	677	9.53	—	—	20
Lawrence, M.P.	30	35	10	18	101	4.04	—	—	9
Lea, A.E.	22	41	2	119	772	19.79	1	—	11
Lenham, N.J.	30	46	6	89	1048	26.20	—	—	11
Le Roux, G.S.	206	248	69	86	4563	25.49	—	—	72
Lever, J.K.	492	509	189	91	3509	10.96	—	—	178
Lilley, A.W.	62	100	6	100*	2295	24.41	1	—	29
Lloyd, C.H.	490	730	96	242*	31232	49.26	79	10+4	377
Lloyd, T.A.	181	322	32	208*	10445	36.01	18	5	98
Lloyds, J.W.	152	235	36	132*	6163	30.96	7	1	132
Lord, G.J.	18	26	2	199	508	21.16	1	—	6
Lord, T.M.	2	4	0	23	31	7.75	—	—	—
Love, J.D.	200	316	48	170*	8637	32.22	13	2	100
Lynch, M.A.	190	317	35	152	9837	34.88	24	5	175
McBrine, A.	2	2	0	24	24	12.00	—	—	—
McBrine, J.	1	2	2	27*	29	—	—	—	1
McEwan, S.M.	18	11	7	13*	38	9.50	—	—	8
MacLarnon, P.C.	11	15	2	56	177	13.61	—	—	3
McMillan, B.M.	23	40	5	136	1531	43.74	4	—	23

	M	I	NO	HS	Runs	Avge	100	1000	Ct/St
Madan Lal	204	299	86	223	9373	44.00	20	—	127
Maher, B.J.M.	55	79	21	126	1253	21.60	1	—	91/7
Makinson, D.J.	34	39	17	58*	486	22.09	—	—	9
Malcolm, D.E.	17	16	5	29*	77	7.00	—	—	6
Mallender, N.A.	158	174	55	88	1628	13.68	—	—	56
Maninder Singh	71	66	32	61*	340	10.00	—	—	33
Marks, V.J.	266	396	68	134	9873	30.10	5	2	112
Marples, C.	26	39	8	57	580	18.70	—	—	54/5
Marsh, S.A.	37	50	11	70	1037	26.58	—	—	74/6
Marshall, M.D.	229	287	32	116*	5542	21.73	4	—	92
Martindale, D.J.R.	12	18	3	104*	432	28.80	1	—	6
Maru, R.J.	73	65	22	62	736	17.11	—	—	64
Masood, M.A.	24	41	3	114	1069	28.13	1	—	19
Maynard, C.	117	150	27	132*	2541	20.65	1	—	186/28
Maynard, M.P.	26	37	4	148	1200	36.36	3	1	14
Mays, C.S.	8	6	2	8*	19	4.75	—	—	2
Medlycott, K.P.	22	24	8	117*	336	21.00	1	—	9
Mee, A.A.G.	9	15	1	51	185	13.21	—	—	4
Mendis, G.D.	229	400	36	209*	12984	35.67	25	7	93/1
Merry, W.G.	29	19	11	14*	50	6.25	—	—	6
Merrick, T.A.	18	24	3	62*	342	16.28	—	—	10
Metcalfe, A.A.	42	68	1	151	2405	35.89	8	1	17
Metson, C.P.	24	31	9	96	426	19.36	—	—	50/2
Middleton, T.C.	9	16	3	68*	331	25.46	—	—	7
Miller, A.J.T.	59	98	12	128*	2744	31.90	3	1	19
Miller, G.	317	469	74	130	10700	27.08	2	—	244
Moir, D.G.	73	87	11	107	1172	15.42	1	—	64
Moles, A.J.	11	18	3	102	738	49.20	2	—	4
Monkhouse, G.	75	86	33	100*	1158	21.84	1	—	35
Monkhouse, S.	2	3	1	5	7	3.50	—	—	—
Moores, P.	12	15	3	45	215	17.91	—	—	19/6
More, K.S.	42	55	14	181*	1205	29.39	2	—	91/25
Morris, H.	66	104	16	128*	2901	32.96	3	1	23
Morris, J.E.	70	117	6	191	3788	34.12	8	1	21
Mortensen, O.H.	55	63	35	40*	247	8.82	—	—	14
Moseley, E.A.	56	71	14	70*	1048	18.38	—	—	15
Moxon, M.D.	103	174	9	168	5905	35.78	14	2	68
Munton, T.A.	20	15	6	19	58	6.44	—	—	1
Murphy, A.J.	10	12	5	6	12	1.71	—	—	2
Neale, P.A.	248	417	58	163*	12912	35.96	20	7	92
Needham, A.	91	132	17	138	2620	22.78	4	1	42
Newell, M.	30	50	10	112*	1280	32.00	1	—	25/1
Newman, P.G.	86	102	18	115	1315	15.65	1	—	19
Newport, P.J.	58	63	21	68	920	21.90	—	—	13
Nicholas, M.C.J.	178	293	33	206*	8297	31.91	16	4	115
North, P.D.	6	6	3	17*	22	7.33	—	—	—
Old, C.M.	379	463	91	116	7756	20.84	6	—	214
Ontong, R.C.	305	507	62	204*	12983	29.17	18	5	142
O'Shaughnessy, S.J.	91	145	23	159*	3292	26.98	5	1	37
Page, H.A.	38	52	13	57	816	20.92	—	—	10
Palmer, G.V.	39	52	7	78	646	14.35	—	—	26
Pandit, C.S.	36	54	12	157	2117	50.40	5	—	93/16
Parker, P.W.G.	245	414	59	215	12664	35.67	31	7	166

	M	I	NO	HS	Runs	Avge	100	1000	Ct/St
Parks, R.J.	157	170	41	89	2342	18.15	—	—	382/47
Parsons, G.J.	159	201	44	76	2974	18.94	—	—	44
Patel, A.S.	3	5	1	30	93	23.25	—	—	2
Patel, D.N.	246	381	32	197	10379	29.73	18	6	136
Patel, T.	15	25	4	47	222	10.57	—	—	6
Patil, S.M.	105	161	11	210	6151	41.00	16	—	58
Patterson, B.P.	57	57	19	22	155	4.07	—	—	14
Pauline, D.B.	61	96	6	115	2258	25.08	1	—	22
Payne, I.R.	47	55	10	43	550	12.22	—	—	41
Penn, C.	35	38	10	115	592	21.14	1	—	24
Philip, I.L.	1	1	0	145	145	145.00	1	—	1
Phillipson, C.P.	168	226	61	87	3052	18.49	—	—	137
Pick, R.A.	50	50	13	63	636	17.18	—	—	11
Pickles, C.S.	6	3	1	31*	52	26.00	—	—	3
Pierson, A.R.K.	14	16	9	42*	132	18.85	—	—	3
Pigott, A.C.S.	117	124	29	104*	1810	19.05	1	—	46
Plumb, S.G.	5	8	1	69	216	30.85	—	—	2
Pocock, P.I.	554	585	156	75*	4867	11.34	—	—	186
Pont, I.L.	14	20	6	43	169	12.07	—	—	2
Pont, K.R.	198	305	44	125*	6558	25.12	7	—	92
Potter, L.	80	131	11	165*	3259	27.15	4	—	63
Prabhakar, M.	33	43	7	122	1351	37.52	4	—	11
Price, D.G.	21	35	2	60	506	15.33	—	—	8
Prichard, P.J.	67	107	9	147*	3009	30.70	2	1	44
Pridgeon, A.P.	208	195	78	67	1076	9.19	—	—	71
Pringle, D.R.	162	239	46	127*	5335	27.64	7	—	91
Pringle, N.J.	1	2	0	11	21	10.50	—	—	—
Prior, J.A.	6	10	1	87	232	25.77	—	—	3
Quinlan, J.D.	12	11	3	24*	80	10.00	—	—	3
Radford, N.V.	126	136	34	76*	1763	17.28	—	—	55
Radley, C.T.	550	867	131	200	26068	35.41	46	16	513
Randall, D.W.	368	626	57	209	21304	37.44	38	10	274
Reeve, D.A.	74	78	23	119	1155	21.00	1	—	37
Rhodes, S.J.	61	73	28	77*	1380	30.66	—	—	124/14
Rice, C.E.B.	408	652	102	246	22571	41.03	42	12	339
Richards, C.J.	235	303	75	117*	6035	26.46	5	1	443/62
Richards, I.V.A.	386	611	40	322	28533	49.97	92	12+3	354/1
Riddell, N.A.	3	5	0	23	84	16.80	—	—	4
Ripley, D.	41	50	12	134*	665	17.50	1	—	59/20
Roberts, B.	91	148	15	124*	3763	28.29	3	1	68/1
Roberts, M.L.	3	2	0	8	8	4.00	—	—	2/1
Robinson, P.E.	36	53	8	104*	1598	35.51	1	—	16
Robinson, R.T.	168	290	36	207	10354	40.76	22	4	88
Roebuck, P.M.	250	410	62	221*	12533	36.01	19	6	122
Romaines, P.W.	110	199	16	186	5400	29.50	10	2	42
Roope, G.R.J.	403	647	129	171	19116	36.90	26	8	602/2
Rose, B.C.	267	444	50	205	13176	33.44	25	8	123
Rose, G.D.	7	8	1	52	93	13.28	—	—	—
Roseberry, M.A.	5	8	1	70*	174	24.85	—	—	1
Rudd, C.F.B.P.	1	1	0	1	1	1.00	—	—	—
Russell, A.B.	2	2	0	51	75	37.50	—	—	2
Russell, R.C.	100	120	30	71	1940	21.55	—	—	198/39
Rutherford, K.R.	47	78	8	317	2765	39.50	7	—	32

	M	I	NO	HS	Runs	Avge	100	1000	Ct/St
Rutnagur, R.S.	17	24	2	66	334	15.18	—	—	5
Rydon, R.A.	5	9	1	20	64	8.00	—	—	1
Sadiq Mohammad	387	684	40	203	24160	37.51	50	7+3	326
Sainsbury, G.E.	60	53	30	14*	151	6.56	—	—	11
Salvi, N.V.	4	7	1	36	126	21.00	—	—	1
Saxelby, K.	92	92	28	59*	873	13.64	—	—	15
Scott, A.M.G.	18	16	10	8	41	6.83	—	—	7
Scott, C.W.	19	17	6	78	410	37.27	—	—	40/3
Sharma, C.	46	51	19	72*	1024	32.00	—	—	24
Sharma, R.	22	29	8	71	530	25.23	—	—	20
Sharp, K.	165	276	25	181	7953	31.68	13	1	82
Shastri, R.J.	100	144	23	200*	4653	38.45	10	0+1	57
Shaw, C.	34	28	11	21	146	8.58	—	—	7
Sidebottom, A.	168	187	45	124	3248	22.87	1	—	40
Simmons, J.	399	501	126	112	8738	23.30	6	—	309
Slack, W.N.	188	315	35	248*	10902	38.93	19	6	144
Small, G.C.	148	180	43	57*	1820	13.28	—	—	38
Smith, C.L.	164	283	34	193	10404	41.78	28	5	98
Smith, D.M.	202	312	62	189*	8662	34.64	16	4	129
Smith, G.	2	2	0	4	7	3.50	—	—	1
Smith, I.	9	7	0	12	27	3.85	—	—	2
Smith, I.D.S.	109	160	23	145	3424	24.99	4	—	249/23
Smith, L.K.	2	3	0	28	32	10.66	—	—	1
Smith, P.A.	95	155	15	119	4204	30.02	2	2	34
Smith, R.A.	96	161	27	140*	5108	38.11	10	2	54
Speight, M.P.	5	2	0	17	21	10.50	—	—	6
Srikkanth, K.	73	120	1	172	4373	36.74	7	—	42
Standing, D.K.	24	38	7	65	674	21.74	—	—	12
Stanworth, J.	22	28	8	50*	191	9.55	—	—	28/4
Steele, J.F.	379	605	85	195	15054	28.95	21	6	413
Stephenson, F.D.	31	47	5	165	973	23.16	1	—	19
Stephenson, J.P.	15	27	1	85	661	25.42	—	—	7
Stevenson, A.W.J.	2	1	0	9	9	9.00	—	—	—
Stevenson, G.B.	187	227	34	115*	3963	20.53	2	—	73
Stewart, A.J.	75	117	14	166	3804	36.93	5	2	80/2
Stirling, D.A.	59	75	24	51*	1057	20.72	—	—	15
Storie, A.C.	15	23	2	106	578	27.52	1	—	6
Stovold, A.W.	297	530	30	212*	15109	30.21	18	7	267/45
Such, P.M.	53	50	17	16	72	2.18	—	—	29
Surridge, D.	35	30	18	14*	104	8.66	—	—	7
Swallow, I.G.	32	34	12	43*	408	18.54	—	—	14
Swan, R.G.	7	12	1	66	235	21.36	—	—	4
Sygrove, M.R.	1	2	0	6	8	4.00	—	—	—
Sykes, J.F.	15	18	4	126	342	24.42	1	—	10
Tavaré, C.J.	280	474	50	168*	15952	37.62	30	10	270
Taylor, D.P.	8	12	2	17	44	4.40	—	—	7/2
Taylor, J.P.	7	7	2	11	29	5.80	—	—	3
Taylor, L.B.	177	156	69	47	824	9.47	—	—	44
Taylor, N.R.	132	226	33	155*	6609	34.24	15	4	70
Taylor, N.S.	34	33	11	24*	180	8.18	—	—	7
Taylor, R.W.	638	879	167	100	12061	16.93	1	—	1473/175
Tedstone, G.A.	18	23	6	67*	310	18.23	—	—	29/7
Tennant, L.	2	2	1	12*	13	13.00	—	—	—

	M	I	NO	HS	Runs	Avge	100	1000	Ct/St
Terry, V.P.	105	171	20	175*	5130	33.97	11	3	94
Thomas, D.J.	130	172	36	119	2724	20.02	2	—	44
Thomas, J.G.	101	130	25	84	1757	16.73	—	—	44
Thorne, D.A.	40	64	13	124	1707	33.47	2	—	22
Todd, P.A.	157	278	16	178	7193	27.45	8	3	106
Tomlins, K.P.	100	152	19	146	3579	26.90	4	—	64
Toogood, G.J.	33	56	6	149	1384	27.68	2	—	11
Tooley, C.D.M.	17	26	1	66	478	19.12	—	—	6
Topley, T.D.	14	15	4	45	128	11.63	—	—	10
Tremellen, J.M.	1	2	1	4*	7	7.00	—	—	—
Tremlett, T.M.	161	209	52	102*	3337	21.25	1	—	62
Tufnell, P.C.R.	6	7	1	9	32	5.33	—	—	1
Turner, D.R.	369	604	56	181*	16109	29.39	24	7	176
Turner, M.S.	12	14	6	24*	144	18.00	—	—	2
Turner, S.	361	513	101	121	9411	22.84	4	—	217
Twizell, P.H.	2	1	0	0	0	0.00	—	—	—
Underwood, D.L.	653	690	191	111	4997	10.01	1	—	258
Varey, D.W.	58	100	11	156*	2437	27.38	2	—	24/1
Vengsarkar, D.B.	190	294	35	210	12583	48.58	36	0+4	135
Walker, A.	50	48	25	40*	252	10.95	—	—	19
Walsh, C.A.	93	107	30	52	814	10.57	—	—	27
Ward, D.M.	10	16	4	143	379	31.58	1	—	3
Ward, T.R.	1	2	0	29	41	20.50	—	—	—
Waring, I.C.	2	—	—	—	—	—	—	—	1
Warke, S.J.S.	5	8	1	144*	432	61.71	1	—	3
Warner, A.E.	63	87	17	91	1387	19.81	—	—	18
Waterton, S.N.V.	39	45	9	58*	700	19.44	—	—	75/15
Watkin, S.L.	1	—	—	—	—	—	—	—	—
Watkinson, M.	73	103	15	106	1917	21.78	1	—	29
Watson, W.	25	14	8	10	44	7.33	—	—	8
Weale, S.D.	1	2	0	28	40	20.00	—	—	—
Wells, A.P.	94	146	28	150*	3512	29.76	4	1	47
Wells, C.M.	166	259	42	203	7216	33.25	12	4	44
Weston, M.J.	97	162	9	145*	3776	24.67	3	1	41
Whitaker, J.J.	76	114	18	200*	4031	41.98	10	3	48
Whitticase, P.	29	35	7	67*	738	26.35	—	—	50/1
Wild, D.J.	66	98	14	144	2391	28.46	3	—	15
Willey, P.	452	743	104	227	19747	30.90	38	7	186
Williams, N.F.	96	102	24	67	1573	20.16	—	—	24
Williams, R.G.	210	338	40	175*	9092	30.51	15	6	76
Winterborne, G.	1	—	—	—	—	—	—	—	—
Wood, L.J.	4	4	0	5	12	3.00	—	—	—
Wright, A.J.	66	117	10	139	2602	24.31	1	—	35
Wright, J.G.	273	471	32	190	17783	40.50	41	6+1	158
Wyatt, J.G.	43	72	2	145	1915	27.35	3	—	16
Yadav, N.S.	82	82	24	50	1067	18.39	—	—	36
Younis Ahmed	450	746	114	221*	25388	40.17	44	13	239

BOWLING

'100wS' denotes instances of 100 or more wickets in a season.

	Runs	*Wkts*	*Avge*	*Best*	*5wI*	*10wM*	*100wS*
Abrahams, J.	2746	54	50.85	3-27	—	—	—
Acfield, D.L.	26800	950	28.21	8-55	34	4	—
Afford, J.A.	1788	54	33.11	6-81	3	1	—
Agnew, J.P.	10149	343	29.58	9-70	12	2	—
Alderman, T.M.	13623	579	23.52	8-46	34	7	—
Alikhan, R.I.	65	0	—	—	—	—	—
Allott, P.J.W.	11068	436	25.38	8-48	23	—	—
Amarnath, M.	8723	268	32.54	7-27	8	1	—
Amiss, D.L.	718	18	39.88	3-21	—	—	—
Anderson, I.S.	1290	20	64.50	4-35	—	—	—
Andrew, S.J.W.	1941	55	35.29	6-43	1	—	—
Asif Din	2261	39	57.97	5-100	1	—	—
Aslett, D.G.	918	15	61.20	4-119	—	—	—
Athey, C.W.J.	1437	33	43.54	3-3	—	—	—
Atkinson, J.C.M.	382	4	95.50	2-80	—	—	—
Azharuddin, M.	162	1	162.00	1-35	—	—	—
Babington, A.M.	348	15	23.20	4-18	—	—	—
Bail, P.A.C.	32	0	—	—	—	—	—
Bailey, R.J.	143	6	23.83	3-33	—	—	—
Bainbridge, P.	6671	184	36.25	8-53	5	—	—
Bairstow, D.L.	254	6	42.33	3-82	—	—	—
Bakker, P.J.	220	6	36.66	2-15	—	—	—
Balderstone, J.C.	8160	310	26.32	6-25	5	—	—
Baptiste, E.A.E.	7312	268	27.28	6-42	7	—	—
Barclay, J.R.T.	9936	324	30.66	6-61	9	1	—
Barlow, G.D.	68	3	22.66	1-6	—	—	—
Barnett, K.J.	2587	46	56.23	6-115	1	—	—
Barrett, B.J.	860	26	33.07	4-51	—	—	—
Barwick, S.R.	5285	162	32.62	8-42	5	—	—
Base, S.J.	835	26	32.11	4-74	—	—	—
Benjamin, W.K.M.	2002	69	29.01	6-33	4	—	—
Benson, M.R.	265	3	88.33	2-55	—	—	—
Berry, P.J.	83	1	83.00	1-10	—	—	—
Bicknell, M.P.	600	27	22.22	3-27	—	—	—
Binny, R.M.H.	6215	172	36.13	8-22	4	—	—
Birch, J.D.	1927	39	49.41	6-64	1	—	—
Blain, T.E.	21	1	21.00	1-12	—	—	—
Blakey, R.J.	68	1	68.00	1-68	—	—	—
Boon, T.J.	227	5	45.40	3-40	—	—	—
Booth, P.A.	1109	23	48.21	3-22	—	—	—
Border, A.R.	2013	55	36.60	4-61	—	—	—
Botham, I.T.	24671	936	26.35	8-34	52	7	1
Bowler, P.D.	57	0	—	—	—	—	—
Boycott, G.	1459	45	32.42	4-14	—	—	—
Boyd-Moss, R.J.	2111	50	42.22	5-27	1	—	—
Bracewell, J.G.	8652	346	25.00	7-9	22	5	—
Brassington, A.J.	10	0	—	—	—	—	—
Bredin, A.M.	385	7	55.00	2-50	—	—	—
Briers, N.E.	970	32	30.31	4-29	—	—	—
Broad, B.C.	1002	16	62.62	2-14	—	—	—

	Runs	Wkts	Avge	Best	5wI	10wM	100wS
Brown, K.R.	10	0	—	—	—	—	—
Browne, D.W.	76	1	76.00	1-13	—	—	—
Bullen, C.K.	104	2	52.00	2-36	—	—	—
Burnett, N.W.	30	0	—	—	—	—	—
Butcher, A.R.	4808	126	38.15	6-48	1	—	—
Butcher, I.P.	24	1	24.00	1-2	—	—	—
Butcher, R.O.	171	4	42.75	2-37	—	—	—
Byas, D.	15	0	—	—	—	—	—
Cann, M.J.	0	0	—	—	—	—	—
Capel, D.J.	4904	133	36.87	7-62	4	—	—
Carr, J.D.	2261	49	46.14	6-61	3	—	—
Carrick, P.	22780	756	30.13	8-33	35	5	—
Chadwick, M.R.	71	0	—	—	—	—	—
Chatfield, E.J.	10373	481	21.56	8-24	23	8	—
Childs, J.H.	15445	515	29.99	9-56	26	5	—
Chivers, I.J.	72	1	72.00	1-5	—	—	—
Clarke, S.T.	15254	758	20.12	7-34	46	6	—
Clift, P.B.	20236	816	24.79	8-17	23	2	—
Clinton, G.S.	185	4	46.25	2-8	—	—	—
Close, D.B.	30947	1171	26.42	8-41	43	3	2
Cobb, R.A.	46	0	—	—	—	—	—
Coney, J.V.	3241	108	30.00	6-17	1	—	—
Connor, C.A.	5032	146	34.46	7-37	2	—	—
Cook, G.	713	15	47.53	3-47	—	—	—
Cook, N.G.B.	16269	555	29.31	7-63	22	3	—
Coombs, R.V.J.	1112	32	34.75	5-58	1	—	—
Cooper, K.E.	12893	475	27.14	8-44	15	—	—
Corlett, S.C.	2295	78	29.42	7-82	4	—	—
Cowans, N.G.	8916	353	25.25	6-31	16	—	—
Cowdrey, C.S.	4878	124	39.33	5-69	1	—	—
Cowdrey, G.R.	49	2	24.50	1-17	—	—	—
Cowley, N.G.	12851	392	32.78	6-48	5	—	—
Crowe, J.J.	48	1	48.00	1-10	—	—	—
Crowe, M.D.	3244	102	31.80	5-18	4	—	—
Curran, K.M.	2802	114	24.57	5-35	2	—	—
Curtis, T.S.	194	4	48.50	2-58	—	—	—
Dale, C.S.	609	7	87.00	3-10	—	—	—
Daniel, W.W.	18178	833	21.82	9-61	31	7	—
Davidson, I.C.	24	2	12.00	2-24	—	—	—
Davidson, J.E.	1252	34	36.82	5-35	2	—	—
Davis, M.R.	4803	138	34.80	7-55	4	1	—
Davis, R.P.	121	6	20.16	3-38	—	—	—
Dawson, T.A.J.	649	13	49.92	3-65	—	—	—
DeFreitas, P.A.J.	2874	121	23.75	7-44	8	1	—
Dennis, S.J.	5556	182	30.52	5-35	5	—	—
Derrick, J.	2075	44	47.15	4-60	—	—	—
Dilley, G.R.	10917	395	27.63	7-63	15	2	—
D'Oliveira, D.B.	776	20	38.80	2-17	—	—	—
Donald, W.A.	164	5	32.80	3-17	—	—	—
Doshi, D.R.	23874	898	26.58	7-29	43	6	1
Doughty, R.J.	2910	89	32.69	6-33	2	—	—
Downton, P.R.	5	0	—	—	—	—	—
Dredge, C.H.	13113	440	29.80	6-37	12	—	—

	Runs	Wkts	Avge	Best	5wI	10wM	100wS
Duthie, P.G.	208	6	34.66	2-29	—	—	—
Dyer, R.I.H.B.	41	0	—	—	—	—	—
East, D.E.	12	0	—	—	—	—	—
Edgar, B.A.	47	1	47.00	1-17	—	—	—
Edmonds, P.H.	29910	1185	25.24	8-53	47	9	—
Ellcock, R.M.	2128	67	31.76	4-34	—	—	—
Ellison, C.C.	1383	39	35.46	5-82	1	—	—
Ellison, R.M.	6675	247	27.02	7-87	8	2	—
Emburey, J.E.	22891	953	24.01	7-36	47	8	1
Estwick, R.O.	1722	63	27.33	6-68	3	—	—
Evans, K.P.	460	4	115.00	2-31	—	—	—
Fairbrother, N.H.	144	2	72.00	1-3	—	—	—
Falkner, N.J.	9	1	9.00	1-3	—	—	—
Feltham, M.A.	1911	60	31.85	5-62	1	—	—
Felton, N.A.	7	0	—	—	—	—	—
Ferreira, A.M.	16283	538	30.26	8-38	18	2	—
Ferris, G.J.F.	3090	104	29.71	7-42	3	1	—
Finney, R.J.	5290	174	30.40	7-54	8	—	—
Fletcher, K.W.R.	2287	51	44.84	5-41	1	—	—
Fletcher, S.D.	3183	79	40.29	5-90	1	—	—
Folley, I.	4627	138	33.52	6-8	3	—	—
Foster, D.J.	29	0	—	—	—	—	—
Foster, N.A.	9544	384	24.85	6-30	24	3	1
Fowler, G.	128	4	32.00	2-34	—	—	—
Franklin, T.J.	41	1	41.00	1-21	—	—	—
Fraser, A.G.J.	165	8	20.62	3-46	—	—	—
Fraser, A.R.C.	613	19	32.26	4-48	—	—	—
Fraser-Darling, C.D.	604	15	40.26	5-84	1	—	—
French, B.N.	22	0	—	—	—	—	—
Gard, T.	8	0	—	—	—	—	—
Garner, J.	15465	835	18.52	8.31	46	7	—
Garth, J.D.	34	0	—	—	—	—	—
Gatting, M.W.	3236	124	26.09	5-34	2	—	—
Gavaskar, S.M.	1221	22	55.50	3-43	—	—	—
Gifford, N.	46634	2001	23.30	8-28	91	14	4
Gladwin, C.	71	0	—	—	—	—	—
Golding, A.K.	1604	18	89.11	3-51	—	—	—
Gooch, G.A.	5776	179	32.26	7-14	3	—	—
Gorman, S.R.	649	5	129.80	1-27	—	—	—
Gould, I.J.	220	2	110.00	2-67	—	—	—
Gower, D.I.	214	4	53.50	3-47	—	—	—
Graveney, D.A.	19158	665	28.80	8-85	28	4	—
Gray, A.H.	4440	200	22.20	8-40	14	3	—
Gray, E.J.	8187	323	25.34	8-37	14	2	—
Green, A.M.	1533	32	47.90	4-59	—	—	—
Greenidge, C.G.	472	17	27.76	5-49	1	—	—
Greensword, S.	950	29	32.75	3-22	—	—	—
Griffiths, B.J.	12899	444	29.05	8-50	13	—	—
Hadlee, R.J.	22566	1221	18.48	9-52	74	12	2
Hagan, D.A.	10	0	—	—	—	—	—
Halliday, M.	732	31	23.61	5-39	1	—	—
Harden, R.J.	241	6	40.16	2-24	—	—	—
Hardie, B.R.	173	3	57.66	2-39	—	—	—

	Runs	Wkts	Avge	Best	5wI	10wM	100wS
Hardy, J.J.E.	8	0	—	—	—	—	—
Harman, M.D.	149	1	149.00	1-88	—	—	—
Harper, M.A.	267	6	44.50	2-10	—	—	—
Harper, R.A.	8956	326	27.47	6-57	14	1	—
Harris, G.A.R.	34	0	—	—	—	—	—
Harrison, G.D.	92	2	46.00	2-30	—	—	—
Hartley, P.J.	2485	74	33.58	6-68	3	—	—
Hartley, S.N.	2107	46	45.80	4-51	—	—	—
Hayes, K.A.	537	17	31.58	6-58	1	—	—
Hayhurst, A.N.	466	13	35.84	4-69	—	—	—
Heath, S.D.	39	0	—	—	—	—	—
Hemmings, E.E.	30872	1060	29.12	10-175	52	13	—
Henriksen, S.	105	2	52.50	1-26	—	—	—
Herbert, R.	262	6	43.66	3-64	—	—	—
Hick, G.A.	1161	21	55.28	3-39	—	—	—
Hickey, D.J.	1465	41	35.73	7-81	3	1	—
Higgs, K.	36267	1536	23.61	7-19	50	5	5
Hill, A.	365	9	40.55	3-5	—	—	—
Hinks, S.G.	188	4	47.00	1-10	—	—	—
Holding, M.A.	14063	612	22.97	8-92	33	4	—
Holmes, G.C.	2828	67	42.20	5-86	1	—	—
Hopkins, J.A.	102	0	—	—	—	—	—
Hughes, D.P.	18254	610	29.92	7-24	20	2	—
Hughes, S.P.	7573	271	27.94	7-35	8	—	—
Humpage, G.W.	444	10	44.40	2-13	—	—	—
Igglesden, A.P.	372	11	33.81	4-46	—	—	—
Illingworth, R.K.	6920	188	36.80	7-50	6	1	—
Imran Khan	25011	1145	21.84	8-34	62	11	—
Inchmore, J.D.	14777	510	28.97	8-58	18	1	—
James, K.D.	2277	72	31.62	6-22	3	—	—
Jarvis, K.B.S.	17879	606	29.50	8-97	18	3	—
Jarvis, P.W.	4440	147	30.20	7-55	10	2	—
Javed Miandad	6363	191	33.31	7-39	6	—	—
Jean-Jacques, M.	599	22	27.22	8-77	1	1	—
Jesty, T.E.	15737	574	27.41	7-75	18	—	—
Johnson, P.	288	3	96.00	1-9	—	—	—
Jones, A.L.	152	1	152.00	1-60	—	—	—
Jones, A.N.	2953	95	31.08	5-29	2	—	—
Kallicharran, A.I.	3508	77	45.55	5-45	1	—	—
Kapil Dev	16414	619	26.51	9-83	31	3	—
Ker, J.E.	373	13	28.69	3-45	—	—	—
Kerr, K.J.	3467	118	29.38	5-27	4	—	—
King, C.L.	4189	125	33.51	5-91	1	—	—
Lamb, A.J.	123	5	24.60	1-1	—	—	—
Lamba, R.	336	6	56.00	2-9	—	—	—
Lampitt, S.R.	22	0	—	—	—	—	—
Larkins, W.	1644	39	42.15	5-59	1	—	—
Lawrence, D.V.	7221	205	35.22	7-48	9	—	—
Lawrence, M.P.	2979	42	70.92	3-79	—	—	—
Lea, A.E.	292	8	36.50	3-61	—	—	—
Lenham, N.J.	409	9	45.44	4-85	—	—	—
Le Roux, G.S.	15444	729	21.18	8-107	32	3	—
Lever, J.K.	38817	1619	23.97	8-37	82	12	4

	Runs	Wkts	Avge	Best	5wI	10wM	100wS
Lilley, A.W.	309	7	44.14	3-116	—	—	—
Lloyd, C.H.	4104	114	36.00	4-48	—	—	—
Lloyd, T.A.	980	13	75.38	3-62	—	—	—
Lloyds, J.W.	6463	193	33.48	7-88	9	1	—
Lord, G.J.	37	0	—	—	—	—	—
Love, J.D.	387	2	193.50	1-8	—	—	—
Lynch, M.A.	828	17	48.70	3-6	—	—	—
McBrine, A.	92	3	30.66	3-64	—	—	—
McBrine, J.	67	0	—	—	—	—	—
McEwan, S.M.	1273	32	39.78	3-33	—	—	—
MacLarnon, P.C.	318	3	106.00	2-25	—	—	—
McMillan, B.M.	1520	41	37.07	4-53	—	—	—
Madan Lal	13988	556	25.15	9-31	26	5	—
Maher, B.J.M.	151	3	50.33	2-69	—	—	—
Makinson, D.J.	2436	69	35.30	5-60	1	—	—
Malcolm, D.E.	1521	47	32.36	5-42	1	—	—
Mallender, N.A.	11575	389	29.75	7-27	9	1	—
Maninder Singh	6912	291	23.75	8-48	20	7	—
Marks, V.J.	21015	636	33.04	8-17	30	4	—
Marples, C.	48	0	—	—	—	—	—
Marshall, M.D.	18174	1017	17.87	8-71	62	9	2
Martindale, D.J.R.	8	0	—	—	—	—	—
Maru, R.J.	5689	191	29.78	7-79	6	—	—
Masood, M.A.	72	2	36.00	1-4	—	—	—
Maynard, C.	8	0	—	—	—	—	—
Maynard, M.P.	17	0	—	—	—	—	—
Mays, C.S.	706	13	54.30	3-77	—	—	—
Medlycott, K.T.	1391	48	28.97	6-63	3	1	—
Mendis, G.D.	76	1	76.00	1-65	—	—	—
Merry, W.G.	1724	52	33.15	4-24	—	—	—
Merrick, T.A.	1665	66	25.22	5-54	4	—	—
Metcalfe, A.A.	85	0	—	—	—	—	—
Middleton, T.C.	39	1	39.00	1-13	—	—	—
Miller, A.J.T.	10	1	10.00	1-4	—	—	—
Miller, G.	20910	772	27.08	8-70	36	6	—
Moir, D.G.	6795	206	32.98	6-60	9	1	—
Moles, A.J.	198	5	39.60	2-57	—	—	—
Monkhouse, G.	4682	173	27.06	7-51	2	—	—
Monkhouse, S.	95	2	47.50	1-34	—	—	—
Morris, H.	144	1	144.00	1-45	—	—	—
Morris, J.E.	373	2	186.50	1-35	—	—	—
Mortensen, O.H.	4283	163	26.27	6-27	5	1	—
Moseley, E.A.	4579	194	23.60	6-23	6	—	—
Moxon, M.D.	972	17	57.17	3-26	—	—	—
Munton, T.A.	940	32	29.37	4-60	—	—	—
Murphy, A.J.	685	22	31.13	3-67	—	—	—
Neale, P.A.	201	1	201.00	1-15	—	—	—
Needham, A.	4429	104	42.58	6-30	5	—	—
Newell, M.	95	1	95.00	1-38	—	—	—
Newman, P.G.	6679	205	32.58	7-104	3	—	—
Newport, P.J.	4405	161	27.36	6-48	9	1	—
Nicholas, M.C.J.	2013	48	41.93	5-45	1	—	—
North, P.D.	209	5	41.80	4-49	—	—	—

	Runs	Wkts	Avge	Best	5wI	10wM	100wS
Old, C.M.	25127	1070	23.48	7-20	39	2	—
Ontong, R.C.	21359	721	29.62	8-67	28	4	—
O'Shaughnessy, S.J.	3592	103	34.87	4-66	—	—	—
Page, H.A.	2489	133	18.71	5-31	3	—	—
Palmer, G.V.	2891	62	46.62	5-38	1	—	—
Pandit, C.S.	42	1	42.00	1-26	—	—	—
Parker, P.W.G.	566	10	56.60	2-21	—	—	—
Parks, R.J.	110	0	—	—	—	—	—
Parsons, G.J.	11147	367	30.37	9-72	9	1	—
Patel, A.S.	96	2	48.00	2-55	—	—	—
Patel, D.N.	14022	393	35.67	7-46	14	—	—
Patel, T.	12	0	—	—	—	—	—
Patil, S.M.	2023	60	33.71	6-20	1	—	—
Patterson, B.P.	4805	171	28.09	7-24	8	2	—
Pauline, D.B.	662	18	36.77	5-52	1	—	—
Payne, I.R.	1917	45	42.60	5-13	1	—	—
Penn, C.	1807	45	40.15	5-65	1	—	—
Phillipson, C.P.	5213	153	34.07	6-56	4	—	—
Pick, R.A.	3939	108	36.47	6-68	3	1	—
Pickles, C.S.	385	6	64.16	2-31	—	—	—
Pierson, A.R.K.	720	10	72.00	3-92	—	—	—
Pigott, A.C.S.	8359	298	28.05	7-74	13	1	—
Plumb, S.G.	124	3	41.33	2-47	—	—	—
Pocock, P.I.	42648	1607	26.53	9-57	60	7	1
Pont, I.L.	1039	27	38.48	5-103	1	—	—
Pont, K.R.	3189	96	33.21	5-17	2	—	—
Potter, L.	2075	62	33.46	4-52	—	—	—
Prabhakar, M.	1977	75	26.36	5-28	3	—	—
Price, D.G.	18	0	—	—	—	—	—
Prichard, P.J.	5	0	—	—	—	—	—
Pridgeon, A.P.	15636	477	32.77	7-35	9	1	—
Pringle, D.R.	10489	381	27.53	7-32	11	1	—
Pringle, N.J.	48	0	—	—	—	—	—
Prior, J.A.	119	3	39.66	2-7	—	—	—
Quinlan, J.D.	1004	14	71.71	4-76	—	—	—
Radford, N.V.	11467	424	27.04	9-70	19	4	1
Radley, C.T.	160	8	20.00	2-38	—	—	—
Randall, D.W.	383	12	31.91	3-15	—	—	—
Reeve, D.A.	5488	197	27.85	5-22	4	—	—
Rice, C.E.B.	17777	800	22.22	7-62	20	1	—
Richards, C.J.	198	5	39.60	2-42	—	—	—
Richards, I.V.A.	7684	177	43.41	5-88	1	—	—
Riddell, N.A.	5	0	—	—	—	—	—
Roberts, B.	2065	56	36.87	4-32	—	—	—
Robinson, P.E.	127	0	—	—	—	—	—
Robinson, R.T.	120	2	60.00	1-22	—	—	—
Roebuck, P.M.	2189	43	50.90	6-50	1	—	—
Romaines, P.W.	211	3	70.33	3-42	—	—	—
Roope, G.R.J.	8404	225	37.35	5-14	2	—	—
Rose, B.C.	289	8	36.12	3-9	—	—	—
Rose, G.D.	419	16	26.18	6-41	1	—	—
Rudd, C.F.B.P.	90	0	—	—	—	—	—
Rutherford, K.R.	174	3	58.00	1-13	—	—	—

	Runs	Wkts	Avge	Best	5wI	10wM	100wS
Rutnagur, R.S.	1256	29	43.31	5-112	1	—	—
Rydon, R.A.	471	5	94.20	3-106	—	—	—
Sadiq Mohammad	7476	235	31.81	7-34	8	—	—
Sainsbury, G.E.	4780	153	31.24	7-38	7	—	—
Saxelby, K.	6513	211	30.86	6-64	5	1	—
Scott, A.M.G.	1693	43	39.37	5-68	1	—	—
Sharma, C.	4272	160	26.70	7-83	10	1	—
Sharma, R.	407	11	37.00	3-72	—	—	—
Sharp, K.	602	11	54.72	2-13	—	—	—
Shastri, R.J.	8327	273	30.50	9-101	11	2	—
Shaw, C.	2311	68	33.98	5-38	2	—	—
Sidebottom, A.	10131	415	24.41	8-72	15	2	—
Simmons, J.	24671	895	27.56	7-59	35	5	—
Slack, W.N.	581	19	30.57	3-17	—	—	—
Small, G.C.	11841	399	29.67	7-42	13	—	—
Smith, C.L.	2207	37	59.64	3-35	—	—	—
Smith, D.M.	1520	30	50.66	3-40	—	—	—
Smith, G.	132	2	66.00	1-38	—	—	—
Smith, I.	265	2	132.50	1-18	—	—	—
Smith, I.D.S.	38	0	—	—	—	—	—
Smith, P.A.	4105	90	45.61	4-25	—	—	—
Smith, R.A.	320	7	45.71	2-11	—	—	—
Srikkanth, K.	567	8	70.87	2-39	—	—	—
Standing, D.K.	568	4	142.00	2-28	—	—	—
Steele, J.F.	15793	584	27.04	7-29	16	—	—
Stephenson, F.D.	2561	110	23.28	6-19	6	1	—
Stephenson, J.P.	5	0	—	—	—	—	—
Stevenson, A.W.J.	186	6	31.00	4-66	—	—	—
Stevenson, G.B.	14008	486	28.82	8-57	18	2	—
Stewart, A.J.	98	0	—	—	—	—	—
Stirling, D.A.	4917	150	32.78	6-75	4	—	—
Storie, A.C.	51	0	—	—	—	—	—
Stovold, A.W.	218	4	54.50	1-0	—	—	—
Such, P.M.	4159	141	29.49	6-123	6	—	—
Surridge, D.	2660	89	29.88	5-78	1	—	—
Swallow, I.G.	1882	35	53.77	4-52	—	—	—
Swan, R.G.	0	0	—	—	—	—	—
Sygrove, M.R.	85	2	42.50	1-19	—	—	—
Sykes, J.F.	790	19	41.57	4-102	—	—	—
Tavaré, C.J.	400	4	100.00	1-3	—	—	—
Taylor, J.P.	487	10	48.70	4-81	—	—	—
Taylor, L.B.	12231	501	24.41	7-28	15	1	—
Taylor, N.R.	760	14	54.28	2-20	—	—	—
Taylor, N.S.	2775	79	35.12	7-44	2	—	—
Taylor, R.W.	75	1	75.00	1-23	—	—	—
Tennant, L.	35	0	—	—	—	—	—
Terry, V.P.	39	0	—	—	—	—	—
Thomas, D.J.	10011	296	33.82	6-36	6	1	—
Thomas, J.G.	7915	250	31.66	5-56	6	1	—
Thorne, D.A.	2009	41	49.00	5-39	1	—	—
Todd, P.A.	7	0	—	—	—	—	—
Tomlins, K.P.	360	4	90.00	2-28	—	—	—
Toogood, G.J.	1067	25	42.68	8-52	1	1	—

	Runs	Wkts	Avge	Best	5wI	10wM	100wS
Topley, T.D.	1208	49	24.65	5-52	2	—	—
Tremellen, J.M.	32	0	—	—	—	—	—
Tremlett, T.M.	8277	337	24.56	6-82	8	—	—
Tufnell, P.C.R.	479	5	95.80	2-47	—	—	—
Turner, D.R.	338	9	37.55	2-7	—	—	—
Turner, M.S.	788	15	52.53	4-74	—	—	—
Turner, S.	21351	821	26.00	6-26	27	1	—
Twizell, P.H.	136	2	68.00	2-65	—	—	—
Underwood, D.L.	48698	2420	20.12	9-28	152	47	10
Varey, D.W.	4	0	—	—	—	—	—
Vengsarkar, D.B.	126	1	126.00	1-31	—	—	—
Walker, A.	3796	105	36.15	6-50	1	—	—
Walsh, C.A.	8613	388	22.19	9-72	26	6	1
Waring, I.C.	45	1	45.00	1-16	—	—	—
Warner, A.E.	4160	113	36.81	5-27	2	—	—
Watkin, S.L.	82	2	41.00	2-74	—	—	—
Watkinson, M.	5184	139	37.29	6-39	5	—	—
Watson, W.	1863	58	32.12	5-36	1	—	—
Wells, A.P.	86	1	86.00	1-42	—	—	—
Wells, C.M.	6855	203	33.76	5-25	2	—	—
Weston, M.J.	1913	46	41.58	4-44	—	—	—
Whitaker, J.J.	135	1	135.00	1-41	—	—	—
Wild, D.J.	1742	36	48.38	4-4	—	—	—
Willey, P.	19466	654	29.76	7-37	25	3	—
Williams, N.F.	7588	255	29.75	7-55	4	1	—
Williams, R.G.	9485	276	34.36	7-73	7	—	—
Winterborne, G.	47	0	—	—	—	—	—
Wood, L.J.	277	6	46.16	4-124	—	—	—
Wright, A.J.	13	0	—	—	—	—	—
Wright, J.G.	239	2	119.50	1-4	—	—	—
Wyatt, J.G.	63	2	31.50	1-0	—	—	—
Yadav, N.S.	7675	228	33.66	6-30	9	—	—
Younis Ahmed	1899	41	46.31	4-10	—	—	—

COUNTY BENEFITS AWARDED IN 1987

Derbyshire	J.G. Wright
Gloucestershire	A.W. Stovold
Hampshire	M.D. Marshall
Kent	K.B.S. Jarvis
Leicestershire	D.I. Gower
Middlesex	C.T. Radley
Northamptonshire	B.J. Griffiths (Testimonial)
Nottinghamshire	E.E. Hemmings
Somerset	C.H. Dredge
Surrey	S.T. Clarke
Sussex	Imran Khan
Warwickshire	G.W. Humpage

No benefits have been awarded by Essex, Glamorgan, Lancashire, Worcestershire or Yorkshire.

TEST CAREER RECORDS

ENGLAND

BATTING AND FIELDING

	Tests	*I*	*NO*	*HS*	*Runs*	*Avge*	*100*	*50*	*Ct/St*
Agnew, J.P.	3	4	3	5	10	10.00	—	—	—
Allott, P.J.W.	13	18	3	52*	213	14.20	—	1	4
Amiss, D.L.	50	88	10	262*	3612	46.30	11	11	24
Athey, C.W.J.	13	24	0	96	536	22.33	—	4	8
Bairstow, D.L.	4	7	1	59	125	20.83	—	1	12/1
Balderstone, J.C.	2	4	0	35	39	9.75	—	—	1
Benson, M.R.	1	2	0	30	51	25.50	—	—	—
Botham, I.T.	89	142	4	208	4825	34.96	14	21	106
Broad, B.C.	10	18	2	162	768	48.00	3	2	6
Butcher, A.R.	1	2	0	20	34	17.00	—	—	—
Butcher, R.O.	3	5	0	32	71	14.20	—	—	3
Cook, G.	7	13	0	66	203	15.61	—	2	9
Cook, N.G.B.	9	15	1	26	101	7.21	—	—	5
Cowans, N.G.	19	29	7	36	175	7.95	—	—	9
Cowdrey, C.S.	5	6	1	38	96	19.20	—	—	5
DeFreitas, P.A.J.	4	5	1	40	77	19.25	—	—	1
Dilley, G.R.	26	37	11	56	371	14.26	—	2	7
Downton, P.R.	27	43	7	74	701	19.47	—	4	61/5
Edmonds, P.H.	46	58	11	64	809	17.21	—	2	39
Ellison, R.M.	11	16	1	41	202	13.46	—	—	2
Emburey, J.E.	42	63	14	75	865	17.65	—	3	25
Fletcher, K.W.R.	59	96	14	216	3272	39.90	7	19	54
Foster, N.A.	14	21	3	18*	127	7.05	—	—	3
Fowler, G.	21	37	0	201	1307	35.32	3	8	10
French, B.N.	5	7	2	21	55	11.00	—	—	12
Gatting, M.W.	53	92	12	207	3118	38.97	7	16	47
Gifford, N.	15	20	9	25*	179	16.27	—	—	8
Gooch, G.A.	59	105	4	196	3746	37.08	7	21	57
Gower, D.I.	91	156	12	215	6553	45.50	14	32	64
Hemmings, E.E.	5	10	1	95	198	22.00	—	1	4
Lamb, A.J.	51	88	7	137*	2644	32.64	7	10	52
Larkins, W.	6	11	0	34	176	16.00	—	—	3
Lever, J.K.	21	31	5	53	306	11.76	—	1	11
Lloyd, T.A.	1	1	1	10*	10	—	—	—	—
Marks, V.J.	6	10	1	83	249	27.66	—	3	—
Miller, G.	34	51	4	98*	1213	25.80	—	7	17
Moxon, M.D.	2	4	0	74	111	27.75	—	1	1
Parker, P.W.G.	1	2	0	13	13	6.50	—	—	—
Pigott, A.C.S.	1	2	1	8*	12	12.00	—	—	—
Pringle, D.R.	14	25	3	63	413	18.77	—	1	7
Radford, N.V.	2	3	1	12*	13	6.50	—	—	—
Radley, C.T.	8	10	0	158	481	48.10	2	2	4
Randall, D.W.	47	79	5	174	2470	33.37	7	12	31
Richards, C.J.	5	7	0	133	264	37.71	1	—	15/1
Robinson, R.T.	16	28	3	175	1052	42.08	3	3	6
Rose, B.C.	9	16	2	70	358	25.57	—	2	4
Sidebottom, A.	1	1	0	2	2	2.00	—	—	—
Slack, W.N.	3	6	0	52	81	13.50	—	1	3

	Tests	I	NO	HS	Runs	Avge	100	50	Ct/St
Small, G.C.	4	5	2	21*	49	16.33	—	—	1
Smith, C.L.	8	14	1	91	392	30.15	—	2	5
Smith, D.M.	2	4	0	47	80	20.00	—	—	—
Stevenson, G.B.	2	2	1	27*	28	28.00	—	—	—
Tavaré, C.J.	30	55	2	149	1753	33.07	2	12	20
Taylor, L.B.	2	1	1	1*	1	—	—	—	1
Terry, V.P.	2	3	0	8	16	5.33	—	—	2
Thomas, J.G.	5	10	4	31*	83	13.83	—	—	—
Underwood, D.L.	86	116	35	45*	937	11.56	—	—	44
Whitaker, J.J.	1	1	0	11	11	11.00	—	—	1
Willey, P.	26	50	6	102*	1184	26.90	2	5	3

BOWLING

	Balls	Runs	Wkts	Avge	Best	5wI	10wM
Agnew, J.P.	552	373	4	93.25	2-51	—	—
Allott, P.J.W.	2225	1084	26	41.69	6-61	1	—
Balderstone, J.C.	96	80	1	80.00	1-80	—	—
Botham, I.T.	19994	9959	366	27.21	8-34	27	4
Butcher, A.R.	12	9	0	—	—	—	—
Cook, G.	42	27	0	—	—	—	—
Cook, N.G.B.	2990	1212	40	30.30	6-65	4	1
Cowans, N.G.	3452	2003	51	39.27	6-77	2	—
Cowdrey, C.S.	366	288	4	72.00	2-65	—	—
DeFreitas, P.A.J.	850	446	9	49.55	3-62	—	—
Dilley, G.R.	5116	2584	85	30.40	5-68	1	—
Edmonds, P.H.	11473	4054	121	33.50	7-66	2	—
Ellison, R.M.	2264	1048	35	29.94	6-77	3	1
Emburey, J.E.	10226	3633	115	31.59	7-78	6	—
Fletcher, K.W.R.	285	193	2	96.50	1-6	—	—
Foster, N.A.	3023	1480	39	37.94	6-104	3	1
Fowler, G.	18	11	0	—	—	—	—
Gatting, M.W.	482	216	2	108.00	1-14	—	—
Gifford, N.	3084	1026	33	31.09	5-55	1	—
Gooch, G.A.	1419	546	13	42.00	2-12	—	—
Gower, D.I.	36	20	1	20.00	1-1	—	—
Hemmings, E.E.	1468	558	12	46.50	3-68	—	—
Lamb, A.J.	30	23	1	23.00	1-6	—	—
Lever, J.K.	4433	1951	73	26.72	7-46	3	1
Marks, V.J.	1082	484	11	44.00	3-78	—	—
Miller, G.	5149	1859	60	30.98	5-44	1	—
Pigott, A.C.S.	102	75	2	37.50	2-75	—	—
Pringle, D.R.	2411	1128	29	38.89	5-108	1	—
Radford, N.V.	378	219	3	73.00	2-131	—	—
Randall, D.W.	16	3	0	—	—	—	—
Robinson, R.T.	6	0	0	—	—	—	—
Sidebottom, A.	112	65	1	65.00	1-65	—	—
Small, G.C.	856	314	16	19.62	5-48	2	—
Smith, C.L.	102	39	3	13.00	2-31	—	—
Stevenson, G.B.	312	183	5	36.60	3-111	—	—
Tavaré, C.J.	30	11	0	—	—	—	—
Taylor, L.B.	381	178	4	44.50	2-34	—	—
Thomas, J.G.	774	504	10	50.40	4-70	—	—
Underwood, D.L.	21862	7674	297	25.83	8-51	17	6
Willey, P.	1091	456	7	65.14	2-73	—	—

TEST CAREER RECORDS

AUSTRALIA

BATTING AND FIELDING

	Tests	*I*	*NO*	*HS*	*Runs*	*Avge*	*100*	*50*	*Ct/St*
Boon, D.C.	23	42	2	131	1399	34.97	4	7	12
Border, A.R.	89	157	26	196	6917	52.80	21	33	94
Bright, R.J.	25	39	8	33	445	14.35	—	—	13
Davis, S.P.	1	1	0	0	0	0.00	—	—	—
Dyer, G.C.	1	—	—	—	—	—	—	—	2
Gilbert, D.R.	9	12	4	15	57	7.12	—	—	—
Holland, R.G.	11	15	4	10	35	3.18	—	—	5
Hughes, M.G.	5	7	0	16	31	4.42	—	—	3
Jones, D.M.	10	19	2	210	947	55.70	2	4	4
Lawson, G.F.	37	60	10	57*	756	15.12	—	3	8
McDermott, C.J.	17	23	1	36	189	8.59	—	—	5
Marsh, G.R.	14	26	1	118	974	38.96	3	3	8
Matthews, C.D.	2	3	0	11	21	7.00	—	—	1
Matthews, G.R.J.	21	34	6	130	1031	36.82	3	4	13
O'Donnell, S.P.	6	10	3	48	206	29.42	—	—	4
Phillips, W.B.	27	48	2	159	1485	32.28	2	7	52
Reid, B.A.	13	16	8	13	45	5.62	—	—	1
Ritchie, G.M.	30	53	5	146	1690	35.20	3	7	14
Sleep, P.R.	7	12	0	64	149	12.41	—	1	1
Taylor, P.L.	1	2	0	42	53	26.50	—	—	—
Waugh, S.R.	13	21	4	79*	482	28.35	—	4	12
Wellham, D.M.	6	11	0	103	257	23.36	1	—	5
Zoehrer, T.J.	10	14	2	52*	246	20.50	—	1	18/1

BOWLING

	Balls	*Runs*	*Wkts*	*Avge*	*Best*	*5wI*	*10wM*
Boon, D.C.	12	5	0	—	—	—	—
Border, A.R.	1781	699	16	43.68	3-20	—	—
Bright, R.J.	5541	2180	53	41.13	7-87	4	1
Davis, S.P.	150	70	0	—	—	—	—
Gilbert, D.R.	1647	843	16	52.68	3-48	—	—
Holland, R.G.	2889	1352	34	39.76	6-54	3	2
Hughes, M.G.	1047	567	11	51.54	3-134	—	—
Jones, D.M.	6	0	0	—	—	—	—
Lawson, G.F.	8705	4420	145	30.48	8-112	10	2
McDermott, C.J.	3346	1935	53	36.50	8-141	2	—
Matthews, C.D.	421	233	6	38.83	3-95	—	—
Matthews, G.R.J.	3500	1707	39	43.76	5-103	2	1
O'Donnell, S.P.	940	504	6	84.00	3-37	—	—
Reid, B.A.	2959	1368	41	33.36	4-64	—	—
Ritchie, G.M.	6	10	0	—	—	—	—
Sleep, P.R.	1405	697	13	53.61	5-72	1	—
Taylor, P.L.	330	154	8	19.25	6-78	1	—
Waugh, S.R.	1185	618	19	32.52	5-69	1	—

TEST CAREER RECORDS

WEST INDIES

BATTING AND FIELDING

	Tests	I	NO	HS	Runs	Avge	100	50	Ct/St
Best, C.A.	3	4	1	35	78	26.00	—	—	4
Butts, C.G.	3	4	0	17	44	11.00	—	—	—
Dujon, P.J.L.	40	53	4	139	1876	38.28	4	9	130/3
Garner, J.	56	65	14	60	661	12.96	—	1	39
Gomes, H.A.	57	86	10	143	3099	40.77	9	13	17
Gray, A.H.	3	5	1	12*	27	6.75	—	—	2
Greenidge, C.G.	74	122	13	223	5165	47.38	12	28	68
Harper, R.A.	19	25	3	60	352	16.00	—	1	24
Haynes, D.L.	62	102	11	184	3852	42.32	8	24	39
Holding, M.A.	59	75	10	73	910	14.00	—	6	21
Logie, A.L.	13	17	1	130	493	30.81	1	3	7
Marshall, M.D.	48	58	5	92	985	18.58	—	7	23
Patterson, B.P.	6	7	4	9	18	6.00	—	—	2
Payne, T.R.O.	1	1	0	5	5	5.00	—	—	5
Richards, I.V.A.	85	127	8	291	6395	53.73	20	28	80
Richardson, R.B.	23	36	3	185	1502	45.51	6	4	30
Walsh, C.A.	10	13	5	18*	59	7.37	—	—	3

BOWLING

	Balls	Runs	Wkts	Avge	Best	5wI	10wM
Butts, C.G.	642	208	6	34.66	4-73	—	—
Garner, J.	12707	5228	247	21.16	6-56	6	—
Gomes, H.A.	2221	867	13	66.69	2-20	—	—
Gray, A.H.	594	227	14	16.21	4-39	—	—
Greenidge, C.G.	26	4	0	—	—	—	—
Harper, R.A.	2997	1090	40	27.25	6-57	1	—
Haynes, D.L.	18	8	1	8.00	1-2	—	—
Holding, M.A.	12458	5799	249	23.28	8-92	13	2
Logie, A.L.	7	4	0	—	—	—	—
Marshall, M.D.	10564	4905	231	21.23	7-53	14	2
Patterson, B.P.	895	527	22	23.95	4-30	—	—
Richards, I.V.A.	2962	1061	20	53.05	2-20	—	—
Richardson, R.B.	18	5	0	—	—	—	—
Walsh, C.A.	1811	805	32	25.15	4-21	—	—

TEST CAREER RECORDS

NEW ZEALAND

BATTING AND FIELDING

	Tests	I	NO	HS	Runs	Avge	100	50	Ct/St
Blain, T.E.	1	1	0	37	37	37.00	—	—	—
Boock, S.L.	26	37	8	37	192	6.62	—	—	13
Bracewell, J.G.	20	29	7	110	441	20.04	1	1	16
Brown, V.R.	2	3	1	36*	51	25.50	—	—	3
Cairns, B.L.	43	65	8	64	928	16.28	—	2	30
Chatfield, E.J.	29	36	23	21*	137	10.53	—	—	6
Coney, J.V.	49	79	14	174*	2591	39.86	3	16	59
Crowe, J.J.	26	42	2	128	1060	26.50	2	5	32
Crowe, M.D.	32	52	5	188	1807	38.44	5	5	35
Edgar, B.A.	39	68	4	161	1958	30.59	3	12	14
Franklin, T.J.	2	3	0	7	9	3.00	—	—	—
Gillespie, S.R.	1	1	0	28	28	28.00	—	—	—
Gray, E.J.	7	11	0	50	177	16.09	—	1	4
Hadlee, R.J.	66	106	13	103	2397	25.77	1	13	33
Reid, J.F.	19	31	3	180	1296	46.28	6	2	9
Robertson, G.K.	1	1	0	12	12	12.00	—	—	—
Rutherford, K.R.	8	13	2	65	151	13.72	—	2	3
Smith, I.D.S.	33	45	9	113*	808	22.44	1	2	92/6
Snedden, M.C.	11	12	2	32	147	14.70	—	—	2
Stirling, D.A.	6	9	2	26	108	15.42	—	—	1
Troup, G.B.	15	18	6	13*	55	4.58	—	—	2
Watson, W.	2	2	1	8*	9	9.00	—	—	2
Wright, J.G.	49	86	4	141	2635	32.13	5	12	23

BOWLING

	Balls	Runs	Wkts	Avge	Best	5wI	10wM
Boock, S.L.	5620	2102	65	32.33	7-87	4	—
Bracewell, J.G.	4222	1732	58	29.86	6-32	2	1
Brown, V.R.	342	176	1	176.00	1-17	—	—
Cairns, B.L.	10628	4280	130	32.92	7-74	6	1
Chatfield, E.J.	6834	2719	88	30.89	6-73	3	1
Coney, J.V.	2751	936	27	34.66	3-28	—	—
Crowe, J.J.	18	9	0	—	—	—	—
Crowe, M.D.	1113	559	12	46.58	2-25	—	—
Edgar, B.A.	18	3	0	—	—	—	—
Gillespie, S.R.	162	79	1	79.00	1-79	—	—
Gray, E.J.	1344	582	13	44.76	3-73	—	—
Hadlee, R.J.	17179	7520	334	22.51	9-52	27	7
Reid, J.F.	18	7	0	—	—	—	—
Robertson, G.K.	144	91	1	91.00	1-91	—	—
Rutherford, K.R.	76	56	1	56.00	1-38	—	—
Smith, I.D.S.	18	5	0	—	—	—	—
Snedden, M.C.	1878	930	24	38.75	3-21	—	—
Stirling, D.A.	902	601	13	46.23	4-88	—	—
Troup, G.B.	3183	1454	39	37.28	6-95	1	1
Watson, W.	437	196	4	49.00	2-51	—	—
Wright, J.G.	30	5	0	—	—	—	—

TEST CAREER RECORDS

INDIA

BATTING AND FIELDING

	Tests	*I*	*NO*	*HS*	*Runs*	*Avge*	*100*	*50*	*Ct/St*
Amarnath, M.	61	100	9	138	4109	45.15	11	23	44
Arun, B.	2	2	1	2*	4	4.00	—	—	2
Azharuddin, M.	16	25	3	199	1146	52.09	4	4	12
Binny, R.M.H.	24	37	3	83*	756	22.23	—	4	11
Gavaskar, S.M.	121	208	16	236*	9827	51.18	34	42	105
Kapil Dev	83	120	11	163	3486	31.98	5	18	38
Kirmani, S.M.H.	88	124	22	102	2759	27.04	2	12	160/38
Kulkarni, R.R.	1	—	—	—	—	—	—	—	—
Lamba, R.	3	3	0	53	101	33.66	—	1	1
Madan Lal	39	62	16	74	1042	22.65	—	5	15
Maninder Singh	24	25	8	15	73	4.29	—	—	8
More, K.S.	8	9	3	48	181	30.16	—	—	18/2
Pandit, C.S.	3	5	1	39	140	35.00	—	—	4/1
Prabhakar, M.	2	4	1	35*	86	28.66	—	—	—
Sharma, C.	16	16	6	54	237	23.70	—	1	3
Sharma, G.	2	2	1	10*	11	11.00	—	—	1
Shastri, R.J.	49	73	11	142	2266	36.54	6	9	23
Sivaramakrishnan, L.	9	9	1	25	130	16.25	—	—	9
Srikkanth, K.	23	36	1	116	1075	30.71	1	6	18
Vengsarkar, D.B.	90	145	18	166	5547	43.67	14	27	60
Viswanath, S.	3	5	0	20	31	6.20	—	—	11
Yadav, N.S.	31	35	10	43	385	15.40	—	—	9

BOWLING

	Balls	*Runs*	*Wkts*	*Avge*	*Best*	*5wI*	*10wM*
Amarnath, M.	3467	1698	30	56.60	4-63	—	—
Arun, B.	252	116	4	29.00	3-76	—	—
Azharuddin, M.	6	8	0	—	—	—	—
Binny, R.M.H.	2575	1408	39	36.10	5-40	1	—
Gavaskar, S.M.	350	187	1	187.00	1-34	—	—
Kapil Dev	17575	8715	300	29.05	9-83	19	2
Kirmani, S.M.H.	19	13	1	13.00	1-9	—	—
Kulkarni, R.R.	174	114	3	38.00	3-85	—	—
Madan Lal	5997	2846	71	40.08	5-23	4	—
Maninder Singh	5175	2090	57	36.66	7-51	1	1
Prabhakar, M.	174	102	1	102.00	1-68	—	—
Sharma, C.	2586	1529	43	35.55	6-58	3	1
Sharma, G.	516	167	3	55.66	3-115	—	—
Shastri, R.J.	11321	4261	110	38.73	5-75	2	—
Sivaramakrishnan, L.	2367	1145	26	44.03	6-64	3	1
Srikkanth, K.	90	44	0	—	—	—	—
Vengsarkar, D.B.	47	36	0	—	—	—	—
Yadav, N.S.	7380	3179	94	33.81	5-76	3	—

TEST CAREER RECORDS

PAKISTAN

BATTING AND FIELDING

	Tests	*I*	*NO*	*HS*	*Runs*	*Avge*	*100*	*50*	*Ct/St*
Abdul Qadir	41	49	5	54	648	14.72	—	2	12
Ashraf Ali	5	5	3	65	206	103.00	—	2	9/2
Asif Mujtaba	2	4	0	12	32	8.00	—	—	1
Imran Khan	60	89	14	123	2255	30.06	2	9	21
Jalaluddin	6	3	2	2	3	3.00	—	—	—
Javed Miandad	77	121	17	280*	5589	53.74	14	29	65/1
Manzoor Elahi	2	3	1	26	49	24.50	—	—	3
Mohsin Kamal	3	4	3	13*	18	18.00	—	—	—
Mohsin Khan	48	79	6	200	2709	37.10	7	9	34
Mudassar Nazar	60	94	7	231	3514	40.39	8	16	40
Qasim Omar	26	43	2	210	1502	36.63	3	5	15
Ramiz Raja	9	15	1	122	384	27.42	1	2	13
Rizwan-uz-Zaman	4	8	0	42	115	14.37	—	—	1
Salim Jaffer	1	1	0	9	9	9.00	—	—	—
Salim Malik	31	42	8	119*	1447	42.55	5	7	31
Salim Yousuf	6	10	1	61	181	20.11	—	1	25/3
Shoaib Mohammad	6	9	1	80	213	26.62	—	1	4
Tausif Ahmed	16	17	8	23*	109	12.11	—	—	4
Wasim Akram	10	14	4	66	115	11.50	—	1	1
Zakir Khan	1	1	1	0*	0	—	—	—	—
Zulqarnain	3	4	0	13	24	6.00	—	—	8/2

BOWLING

	Balls	*Runs*	*Wkts*	*Avge*	*Best*	*5wI*	*10wM*
Abdul Qadir	10579	4816	146	32.98	7-142	10	2
Asif Mujtaba	18	2	0	—	—	—	—
Imran Khan	14609	6056	282	21.47	8-58	19	4
Jalaluddin	1197	537	11	48.81	3-77	—	—
Javed Miandad	1446	672	17	39.52	3-74	—	—
Manzoor Elahi	138	76	1	76.00	1-74	—	—
Mohsin Kamal	456	265	8	33.12	3-50	—	—
Mohsin Khan	86	30	0	—	—	—	—
Mudassar Nazar	4557	1963	51	38.49	6-32	1	—
Qasim Omar	6	0	0	—	—	—	—
Rizwan-uz-Zaman	102	39	3	13.00	3-26	—	—
Salim Jaffer	174	57	2	28.50	1-23	—	—
Salim Malik	134	63	3	21.00	1-3	—	—
Shoaib Mohammad	18	8	0	—	—	—	—
Tausif Ahmed	3236	1285	49	26.22	6-45	2	—
Wasim Akram	1991	800	34	23.52	6-91	3	1
Zakir Khan	270	150	3	50.00	3-80	—	—

TEST CAREER RECORDS

SRI LANKA

BATTING AND FIELDING

	Tests	I	NO	HS	Runs	Avge	100	50	Ct/St
Ahangama, F.S.	3	3	1	11	11	5.50	—	—	1
Amalean, K.N.	1	2	0	2	2	2.00	—	—	—
Anurasiri, S.D.	3	4	2	8	12	6.00	—	—	—
De Alwis, R.G.	10	17	0	28	144	8.47	—	—	19/2
De Mel, A.L.F.	17	28	5	34	326	14.17	—	—	9
De Silva, E.A.R.	5	8	3	21	72	14.40	—	—	3
De Silva, P.A.	13	24	2	122	626	28.45	2	1	5
Dias, R.L.	19	35	1	109	1260	37.05	3	8	6
Gurusinha, A.P.	6	11	2	116*	329	36.55	1	—	3
Jurangpathy, B.R.	2	4	0	1	1	0.25	—	—	2
Kuruppuarachchi, A.K.	1	1	1	0*	0	—	—	—	—
Labrooy, G.F.	1	1	1	5*	5	—	—	—	—
Madugalle, R.S.	18	34	4	103	933	31.10	1	6	8
Mahanama, R.S.	2	4	0	41	63	15.75	—	—	1
Mendis, L.R.D.	22	40	1	124	1240	31.79	4	7	7
Ranatunga, A.	21	38	2	135*	1339	37.19	2	10	9
Ratnayake, R.J.	13	22	4	56	255	14.16	—	1	5
Ratnayeke, J.R.	17	30	5	93	502	20.08	—	2	1
Silva, S.A.R.	8	14	2	111	336	28.00	2	—	30/1
Warnaweera, K.P.J.	1	2	0	3	3	1.50	—	—	—
Weerasinghe, C.D.U.S.	1	1	0	3	3	3.00	—	—	—
Wettimuny, S.	23	43	1	190	1221	29.07	2	6	10
Wijesuriya, R.G.C.E.	4	7	2	8	22	4.40	—	—	1

BOWLING

	Balls	Runs	Wkts	Avge	Best	5wI	10wM
Ahangama, F.S.	801	348	18	19.33	5-52	1	—
Amalean, K.N.	110	59	3	19.66	3-59	—	—
Anurasiri, S.D.	270	92	4	23.00	4-71	—	—
De Mel, A.L.F.	3518	2180	59	36.94	6-109	3	—
De Silva, E.A.R.	978	413	2	206.50	1-37	—	—
De Silva, P.A.	30	22	0	—	—	—	—
Gurusinha, A.P.	53	67	2	33.50	2-25	—	—
Jurangpathy, B.R.	150	93	1	93.00	1-69	—	—
Kuruppuarachchi, A.K.	152	85	7	12.14	5-44	1	—
Labrooy, G.F.	210	164	1	164.00	1-164	—	—
Madugalle, R.S.	72	32	0	—	—	—	—
Ranatunga, A.	1167	533	9	59.22	2-17	—	—
Ratnayake, R.J.	2633	1433	40	35.82	6-85	2	—
Ratnayeke, J.R.	2880	1498	47	31.87	8-83	4	—
Warnaweera, K.P.J.	51	26	1	26.00	1-26	—	—
Weerasinghe, C.D.U.S.	114	36	0	—	—	—	—
Wettimuny, S.	24	37	0	—	—	—	—
Wijesuriya, R.G.C.E.	586	294	1	294.00	1-68	—	—

LIMITED-OVERS INTERNATIONAL CAREER RECORDS

These Limited-Overs International career records for players contracted to play county cricket in 1987 are complete to 17 January 1987 and are compiled by **Victor Isaacs.**

BATTING AND FIELDING

	M	*I*	*NO*	*HS*	*Runs*	*Avge*	*100*	*50*	*Ct/St*
Agnew, J.P.	3	1	1	2*	2	—	—	—	1
Allott, P.J.W.	13	6	1	8	15	3.00	—	—	2
Amiss, D.L.	18	18	0	137	859	47.72	4	1	2
Athey, C.W.J.	7	7	1	142*	303	50.50	1	1	4
Bailey, R.J.	1	1	1	41*	41	—	—	—	—
Bairstow, D.L.	21	20	6	23*	206	14.71	—	—	17/4
Baptiste, E.A.E. (WI)	29	10	2	28*	119	14.87	—	—	4
Benjamin, W.K.M. (WI)	9	5	1	5	10	2.50	—	—	2
Benson, M.R.	1	1	0	24	24	24.00	—	—	—
Botham, I.T.	82	73	9	72	1411	22.04	—	6	29
Broad, B.C.	4	4	0	97	173	43.25	—	2	2
Butcher, A.R.	1	1	0	14	14	14.00	—	—	—
Butcher, R.O.	3	3	0	52	58	19.33	—	1	—
Clarke, S.T. (WI)	10	8	2	20	60	10.00	—	—	4
Cook, G.	6	6	0	32	106	17.66	—	—	2
Cook, N.G.B.	1	—	—	—	—	—	—	—	1
Cowans, N.G.	23	8	3	4*	13	2.60	—	—	5
Cowdrey, C.S.	3	3	1	46*	51	25.50	—	—	—
Crowe, M.D. (NZ)	56	53	6	105*	1538	32.72	1	10	21
Curran, K.M. (Z)	6	6	0	73	212	35.33	—	2	—
Daniel, W.W. (WI)	18	5	4	16*	49	49.00	—	—	5
Davis, W.W. (WI)	32	4	3	8*	18	18.00	—	—	1
DeFreitas, P.A.J.	3	2	2	13*	13	—	—	—	1
Dilley, G.R.	25	14	4	31*	105	10.50	—	—	1
Downton, P.R.	17	14	4	44*	193	19.30	—	—	12/2
Edmonds, P.H.	27	18	7	20	116	10.54	—	—	4
Ellison, R.M.	14	12	4	24	86	10.75	—	—	2
Emburey, J.E.	20	14	3	20	102	9.27	—	—	5
Fletcher, K.W.R.	24	22	3	131	757	39.84	1	5	4
Foster, N.A.	23	11	5	24	61	10.16	—	—	9
Fowler, G.	26	26	2	81*	744	31.00	—	4	4/2
French, B.N.	3	2	0	7	11	5.50	—	—	3/1
Gatting, M.W.	51	48	11	115*	1080	29.18	1	4	14
Gifford, N.	2	1	0	0	0	0.00	—	—	1
Gooch, G.A.	48	47	3	129*	1665	37.84	4	10	18
Gould, I.J.	18	14	2	42	155	12.91	—	—	15/3
Gower, D.I.	89	86	7	158	2614	33.08	7	9	36
Gray, A.H. (WI)	12	4	3	10*	30	30.00	—	—	—
Greenidge, C.G. (WI)	81	81	7	115	3362	45.43	7	22	31
Hadlee, R.J. (NZ)	91	77	12	79	1259	19.36	—	2	22
Harper, R.A. (WI)	40	20	9	45*	223	20.27	—	—	15
Hemmings, E.E.	5	2	0	3	4	2.00	—	—	1
Holding, M.A. (WI)	99	41	11	64	282	9.40	—	2	28
Humpage, G.W.	3	2	0	6	11	5.50	—	—	2

	M	I	NO	HS	Runs	Avge	100	50	Ct/St
Imran Khan (P)	83	69	20	102*	1396	28.48	1	3	25
Jesty, T.E.	10	10	4	52*	127	21.16	—	1	5
Kallicharran, A.I. (WI)	31	28	4	78	826	34.41	—	6	8
Kapil Dev (I)	97	89	17	175*	1948	27.05	1	9	36
Lamb, A.J.	55	54	8	118	1971	42.84	3	11	12
Larkins, W.	6	6	0	34	84	14.00	—	—	2
Lever, J.K.	22	11	4	27*	56	8.00	—	—	6
Lloyd, C.H. (WI)	87	69	19	102	1977	39.54	1	11	39
Lloyd, T.A.	3	3	0	49	101	33.66	—	—	—
Love, J.D.	3	3	0	43	61	20.33	—	—	1
Marks, V.J.	33	24	3	44	285	15.00	—	—	8
Marshall, M.D. (WI)	79	41	15	66*	456	17.53	—	2	9
Miller, G.	25	18	2	46	136	8.50	—	—	4
Moxon, M.D.	5	5	0	70	132	26.40	—	1	4
Patterson, B.P. (WI)	6	—	—	—	—	—	—	—	1
Pringle, D.R.	13	11	4	49*	183	26.14	—	—	6
Radley, C.T.	4	4	1	117*	250	83.33	1	1	—
Randall, D.W.	49	45	5	88	1067	26.67	—	5	25
Richards, C.J.	9	7	1	50	72	12.00	—	1	5
Robinson, R.T.	10	10	0	55	175	17.50	—	1	2
Rose, B.C.	2	2	0	54	99	49.50	—	1	1
Shastri, R.J. (I)	74	57	11	102	1450	31.52	2	9	21
Slack, W.N.	2	2	0	34	43	21.50	—	—	—
Small, G.C.	4	1	1	8*	8	—	—	—	—
Smith, C.L.	4	4	0	70	109	27.25	—	1	—
Smith, D.M.	1	1	1	10*	10	—	—	—	—
Stevenson, G.B.	4	4	3	28*	43	43.00	—	—	2
Tavaré, C.J.	29	28	2	83*	720	27.69	—	4	7
Taylor, L.B.	2	1	1	1*	1	—	—	—	—
Thomas, J.G.	2	2	1	0*	0	0.00	—	—	—
Underwood, D.L.	26	13	4	17	53	5.88	—	—	6
Walsh, C.A. (WI)	24	3	0	7	9	3.00	—	—	6
Wells, C.M.	2	2	0	17	22	11.00	—	—	—
Willey, P.	26	24	1	64	538	23.39	—	5	4
Wright, J.G. (NZ)	86	85	1	84	2087	24.84	—	12	37

BOWLING

	Balls	Runs	Wkts	Avge	4w	Best	Runs/ Over
Agnew, J.P.	126	120	3	40.00	—	3-38	5.71
Allott, P.J.W.	819	552	15	36.80	—	3-41	4.04
Bailey, R.J.	36	25	0	—	—	—	4.17
Baptiste, E.A.E. (WI)	1476	989	27	36.62	—	2-10	4.02
Benjamin, W.K.M. (WI)	474	250	11	22.72	—	3-21	3.16
Botham, I.T.	4308	2908	109	26.67	1	4-56	4.05
Clarke, S.T. (WI)	524	245	13	18.84	—	3-22	2.81
Cook, N.G.B.	48	34	1	34.00	—	1-34	4.25
Cowans, N.G.	1282	913	23	39.69	—	3-44	4.27
Cowdrey, C.S.	52	55	2	27.50	—	1-3	6.35
Crowe, M.D. (NZ)	996	710	24	29.58	—	2-9	4.28
Curran, K.M. (Z)	350	274	5	54.80	—	3-65	6.35

	Balls	Runs	Wkts	Avge	4w	Best	Runs/ Over
Daniel, W.W. (WI)	912	595	23	25.86	—	3-27	3.91
Davis, W.W. (WI)	1749	1139	36	31.63	1	7-51	3.91
DeFreitas, P.A.J.	170	99	4	24.75	—	3-42	3.49
Dilley, G.R.	1404	886	30	29.53	2	4-45	3.79
Edmonds, P.H.	1414	869	22	39.50	—	3-39	3.69
Ellison, R.M.	696	510	12	42.50	—	3-42	4.40
Emburey, J.E.	1145	711	17	41.82	—	2-22	3-73
Foster, N.A.	1164	842	22	38.27	—	3-39	4.34
Gatting, M.W.	302	250	7	35.71	—	3-32	4.97
Gifford, N.	120	50	4	12.50	1	4-23	2.50
Gooch, G.A.	1003	791	19	41.63	—	2-12	4.73
Gower, D.I.	5	14	0	—	—	—	16.80
Gray, A.H. (WI)	538	285	23	12.39	2	4-36	3.18
Greenidge, C.G. (WI)	60	45	1	12.39	—	1-21	3.18
Hadlee, R.J. (NZ)	4856	2606	126	20.68	5	5-25	3.22
Harper, R.A. (WI)	2034	1346	39	34.51	—	3-24	3.22
Hemmings, E.E.	249	175	5	35.00	—	3-11	4.22
Holding, M.A. (WI)	5326	2967	138	21.50	6	5-26	3.22
Imran Khan (P)	3279	1904	83	22.93	1	6-14	3.48
Jesty, T.E.	108	93	1	93.00	—	1-23	5.17
Kallicharran, A.I. (WI)	105	64	3	21.30	—	2-10	5.17
Kapil Dev (I)	5030	3074	119	25.83	2	5-43	3-67
Larkins, W.	12	21	0	—	—	—	10.50
Lever, J.K.	1152	713	24	29.70	1	4-29	3.71
Lloyd, C.H. (WI)	358	210	8	26.25	—	2-4	3.71
Marks, V.J.	1772	1076	44	24.45	2	5-20	3.64
Marshall, M.D. (WI)	4179	2315	98	23.62	3	4-23	3.64
Miller, G.	1268	813	25	32.52	—	3-27	3.85
Patterson, B.P. (WI)	293	202	6	33.66	—	2-17	4.78
Pringle, D.R.	722	575	13	44.23	—	3-21	4.78
Randall, D.W.	2	2	1	2.00	—	1-2	6.00
Shastri, R.J. (I)	3436	2308	70	32.97	1	4-40	4.03
Small, G.C.	234	168	6	28.00	—	3-28	4.31
Smith, C.L.	36	28	2	14.00	—	2-8	4.67
Stevenson, G.B.	192	125	7	17.85	1	4-33	3.91
Tavaré, C.J.	12	3	0	—	—	—	1.50
Taylor, L.B.	84	47	0	—	—	—	3.36
Thomas, J.G.	90	85	1	85.00	—	1-35	5.67
Underwood, D.L.	1278	734	32	22.93	1	4-44	3.45
Walsh, C.A. (WI)	1183	784	28	28.00	2	5-1	3.45
Willey, P.	1031	659	13	50.69	—	3-33	3.84
Wright, J.G. (NZ)	24	8	0	—	—	—	2.00

MIDDLESEX VALETE

BARLOW, Graham Derek (Ealing GS; Loughborough CE), b Folkestone 26 Mar 1950. 5′9½″. LHB, RM. Debut 1969. Cap 1976. Benefit 1984. **Tests:** 3 (1976-77 and 1977); HS 7*. LOI: 6. Tour: Aus 1976-77; Ind/SL 1976-77. 1000 runs (7); most – 1545 (1983). HS 177 v Lancs (Southport) 1981. BB 1-6. Awards: NWT 3; BHC 2.
ROSE, G.D. – see SOMERSET.

CRICKET RECORDS

FIRST-CLASS MATCHES

UPDATED TO THE END OF THE 1986 ENGLISH SEASON

TEAM RECORDS

Highest Innings Totals

1107	Victoria v New South Wales	Melbourne	1926-27
1059	Victoria v Tasmania	Melbourne	1922-23
951-7d	Sind v Baluchistan	Karachi	1973-74
918	New South Wales v South Australia	Sydney	1900-01
912-8d	Holkar v Mysore	Indore	1945-46
910-6d	Railways v Dera Ismail Khan	Lahore	1964-65
903-7d	England v Australia	The Oval	1938
887	Yorkshire v Warwickshire	Birmingham	1896
849	England v West Indies	Kingston	1929-30

There have been 22 instances of a team scoring over 800 runs in an innings, the most recent being by Sind in 1973-74 (above).

Highest Second Innings Total

770	New South Wales v South Australia	Adelaide	1920-21

Highest Fourth Innings Total

654-5	England v South Africa	Durban	1938-39

Highest Match Aggregate

2376	Maharashtra v Bombay	Poona	1948-49

Record Margin of Victory

Innings and 851 runs: Railways v Dera Ismail Khan at Lahore 1964-65

Most Runs in a Day

721	Australians v Essex	Southend	1948

Most Hundreds in an Innings

6	Holkar v Mysore	Indore	1945-46
5	New South Wales v South Australia	Sydney	1900-01
5	Australia v West Indies	Kingston	1954-55

Lowest Innings Totals

12	†Oxford University v MCC and Ground	Oxford	1877
12	Northamptonshire v Gloucestershire	Gloucester	1907
13	Auckland v Canterbury	Auckland	1877-78
13	Nottinghamshire v Yorkshire	Nottingham	1901
14	Surrey v Essex	Chelmsford	1983
15	MCC v Surrey	Lord's	1839
15	†Victoria v MCC	Melbourne	1903-04
15	†Northamptonshire v Yorkshire	Northampton	1908
15	Hampshire v Warwickshire	Birmingham	1922

†Batted one man short

There have been 26 instances of a team being dismissed for under 20, the most recent being by Surrey in 1983 (above).

Lowest Match Aggregate by One Team

34 (16 and 18)	Border v Natal	East London	1959-60

Lowest Completed Match Aggregate by Both Teams

105	MCC v Australians	Lord's	1878

Fewest Runs in an Uninterrupted Day's Play

95	Australians (80) v Pakistan (15-2)	Karachi	1956-57

Tied Matches

Before 1948 a match was considered to be tied if the scores were level after the fourth innings, even if the side batting last had wickets in hand when play ended. Law 22 was amended in 1948 and since then a match has been tied only when the scores are level after the fourth innings has been completed. There have been 46 tied first-class matches, five of which would not have qualified under the current law. The most recent are:

Victoria (230-5d/245) v New Zealanders (301-9d/174-3d)	Melbourne	1982-83
Muslim Commercial Bank (229/238) v Railways (149/318)	Sialkot	1983-84
Kent (92/243) v Sussex (143/192)	Hastings	1984
Northamptonshire (124/330) v Kent (250-6d/204-5d)	Northampton	1984

BATTING RECORDS

Highest Individual Innings

499†	Hanif Mohammad	Karachi v Bahawalpur	Karachi	1958-59
452*	D.G. Bradman	NSW v Queensland	Sydney	1929-30
443*	B.B. Nimbalkar	Maharashtra v Kathiawar	Poona	1948-49
437	W.H. Ponsford	Victoria v Queensland	Melbourne	1927-28
429	W.H. Ponsford	Victoria v Tasmania	Melbourne	1922-23
428	Aftab Baloch	Sind v Baluchistan	Karachi	1973-74
424	A.C. MacLaren	Lancashire v Somerset	Taunton	1895
385	B. Sutcliffe	Otago v Canterbury	Christchurch	1952-53
383	D.W. Gregory	NSW v Queensland	Brisbane	1906-07
369	D.G. Bradman	S Australia v Tasmania	Adelaide	1935-36
365*	C. Hill	S Australia v NSW	Adelaide	1900-01
365*	G.St. A. Sobers	West Indies v Pakistan	Kingston	1957-58

364	L. Hutton	England v Australia	Oval	1938
359*	V.M. Merchant	Bombay v Maharashtra	Bombay	1943-44
359	R.B. Simpson	NSW v Queensland	Brisbane	1963-64
357*	R. Abel	Surrey v Somerset	Oval	1899
357	D.G. Bradman	S Australia v Victoria	Melbourne	1935-36
356	B.A. Richards	S Australia v W Australia	Perth	1970-71
355	B. Sutcliffe	Otago v Auckland	Dunedin	1949-50
352	W.H. Ponsford	Victoria v NSW	Melbourne	1926-27
350	Rashid Israr	Habib Bank v National Bank	Lahore	1976-77

†In 16 hours 10 minutes – the longest first-class innings.
There have been 95 triple hundreds in first-class cricket, the most recent being 317 by K.R. Rutherford for New Zealanders v D.B. Close's XI at Scarborough in 1986.

Most Hundreds in Successive Innings

6	C.B. Fry	Sussex and Rest of England	1901
6	D.G. Bradman	South Australia and D.G. Bradman's XI	1938-39
6	M.J. Procter	Rhodesia	1970-71
5	E. de C. Weekes	West Indians (in New Zealand)	1955-56

Two Double Hundreds in a Match

244	202*	A.E. Fagg	Kent v Essex	Colchester	1938

Double Hundred and Hundred in a Match Most Times

4	Zaheer Abbas	Gloucestershire	1976-81

Two Hundreds in a Match Most Times

8	Zaheer Abbas	Gloucestershire and PIA	1976-82
7	W.R. Hammond	Gloucestershire, England and MCC	1927-45

Most Hundreds in a Season

18	D.C.S. Compton	1947
16	J.B. Hobbs	1925
15	W.R. Hammond	1938

Most Hundreds in a Career

(*The season in which his 100th hundred was scored is given in brackets*)

197	J.B. Hobbs (1923)	122	T.W. Graveney (1964)
170	E.H. Hendren (1928-29)	117	D.G. Bradman (1947-48)
167	W.R. Hammond (1935)	107	A. Sandham (1935)
153	C.P. Mead (1927)	107	M.C. Cowdrey (1973)
151	G. Boycott (1977)	107	Zaheer Abbas (1982-83)
149	H. Sutcliffe (1932)	104	T.W. Hayward (1913)
145	F.E. Woolley (1929)	103	J.H. Edrich (1977)
129	L. Hutton (1951)	103	G.M. Turner (1982)
126	W.G. Grace (1895)	102	E. Tyldesley (1934)
123	D.C.S. Compton (1952)	102	L.E.G. Ames (1950)
		100	D.L. Amiss (1986)

Most Runs in a Month

1294	(avge 92.42)	L. Hutton	Yorkshire	June 1949

Most Runs in a Season

Runs			*I*	*NO*	*HS*	*Avge*	*100*	*Season*
3816	D.C.S. Compton	Middlesex	50	8	246	90.85	18	1947
3539	W.J. Edrich	Middlesex	52	8	267*	80.43	12	1947
3518	T.W. Hayward	Surrey	61	8	219	66.37	13	1906

The feat of scoring 3000 runs in a season has been achieved on 28 occasions, the most recent instance being by W.E. Alley (3019) in 1961. The highest aggregate in a season since 1969, when the number of County Championship matches was substantially reduced, is 2559 by G.A. Gooch in 1984.

1000 Runs in a Season Most Times

28 W.G. Grace (Gloucestershire), F.E. Woolley (Kent)

Highest Batting Average in a Season

(*Qualification: 12 innings*)

Avge			*I*	*NO*	*HS*	*Runs*	*100*	*Season*
115.66	D.G. Bradman	Australians	26	5	278	2429	13	1938
102.53	G. Boycott	Yorkshire	20	5	175*	1538	6	1979
102.00	W.A. Johnston	Australians	17	16	28*	102	—	1953
100.12	G. Boycott	Yorkshire	30	5	233	2503	13	1971

Fastest Hundred

35 min	P.G.H. Fender, Surrey v Northamptonshire; Northampton	1920
35 min	S.J. O'Shaughnessy, Lancashire v Leicestershire; Manchester	1983

Fastest Double Hundred

113 min	R.J. Shastri	Bombay v Baroda	Bombay	1984-85

Fastest Triple Hundred

181 min	D.C.S. Compton	MCC v NE Transvaal	Benoni	1948-49

Most Sixes in an Innings

15	J.R. Reid	Wellington v N. Districts	Wellington	1962-63
13	Majid Khan	Pakistanis v Glamorgan	Swansea	1967
13	C.G. Greenidge	D.H. Robins' XI v Pakistanis	Eastbourne	1974
13	C.G. Greenidge	Hampshire v Sussex	Southampton	1975
13	G.W. Humpage	Warwickshire v Lancashire	Southport	1982
13	R.J. Shastri	Bombay v Baroda	Bombay	1984-85

Most Sixes in a Match

17	W.J. Stewart	Warwickshire v Lancashire	Blackpool	1959

Most Sixes in a Season

80	I.T. Botham	Somerset and England	1985

Most Boundaries in an Innings

68	P.A. Perrin	Essex v Derbyshire	Chesterfield	1904

Most Runs off One Over

36	G.St. A. Sobers	Nottinghamshire v Glamorgan	Swansea	1968
36	R.J. Shastri	Bombay v Baroda	Bombay	1984-85

Both batsmen hit all six balls of an over (bowled by M.A. Nash and Tilak Raj respectively) for six.

Most Runs in a Day

345 C.G. Macartney, Australians v Nottinghamshire; Nottingham 1921

There have been 17 instances of a batsman scoring 300 or more runs in a day, the most recent being by K.R. Rutherford (317) in 1986.

Highest Partnerships

First Wicket

561	Waheed Mirza/Mansoor Akhtar, Karachi Whites v Quetta; Karachi	1976-77
555	P. Holmes/H. Sutcliffe, Yorkshire v Essex; Leyton	1932
554	J.T. Brown/J. Tunnicliffe, Yorkshire v Derbyshire; Chesterfield	1898

Second Wicket

465*	J.A. Jameson/R.B. Kanhai, Warwickshire v Glos; Birmingham	1974
455	K.V. Bhandarkar/B.B. Nimbalkar, Maharashtra v Kathiawar; Poona	1948-49
451	D.G. Bradman/W.H. Ponsford, Australia v England; The Oval	1934

Third Wicket

456	Khalid Irtiza/Aslam Ali, United Bank v Multan; Karachi	1975-76
451	Mudassar Nazar/Javed Miandad, Pakistan v India; Hyderabad	1982-83
445	P.E. Whitelaw/W.N. Carson, Auckland v Otago; Dunedin	1936-37
434	J.B. Stollmeyer/G.E. Gomez, Trinidad v Br Guiana; Port-of-Spain	1946-47
424*	W.J. Edrich/D.C.S. Compton, Middlesex v Somerset; Lord's	1948

Fourth Wicket

577	V.S. Hazare/Gul Mahomed, Baroda v Holkar; Baroda	1946-47
574*	C.L. Walcott/F.M.M. Worrell, Barbados v Trinidad; Port-of-Spain	1945-46
502*	F.M.M. Worrell/J.D.C. Goddard, Barbados v Trinidad; Bridgetown	1943-44
470	A.I. Kallicharran/G.W. Humpage, Warwicks v Lancs; Southport	1982

Fifth Wicket

405	S.G Barnes/D.G. Bradman, Australia v England; Sydney	1946-47
397	W. Bardsley/C. Kelleway, NSW v South Australia; Sydney	1920-21
393	E.G. Arnold/W.B. Burns, Worcs v Warwicks; Birmingham	1909

Sixth Wicket

487*	G.A. Headley/C.C. Passailaigue, Jamaica v Lord Tennyson's XI; Kingston	1931-32
428	W.W. Armstrong/M.A. Noble, Australians v Sussex; Hove	1902
411	R.M. Poore/E.G. Wynyard, Hampshire v Somerset; Taunton	1899

Seventh Wicket

347	D.St. E. Atkinson/C.C. Depeiza, West Indies v Australia; Bridgetown	1954-55

344 K.S. Ranjitsinhji/W. Newham, Sussex v Essex; Leyton 1902
340 K.J. Key/H. Philipson, Oxford U v Middlesex; Chiswick Park 1887

Eighth Wicket

433 A. Sims/V.T. Trumper, Australians v Canterbury; Christchurch 1913-14
292 R. Peel/Lord Hawke, Yorkshire v Warwickshire; Birmingham 1896
270 V.T. Trumper/E.P. Barbour, NSW v Victoria; Sydney 1912-13

Ninth Wicket

283 J. Chapman/A. Warren, Derbyshire v Warwicks; Blackwell 1910
251 J.W.H.T. Douglas/S.N. Hare, Essex v Derbyshire; Leyton 1921
245 V.S. Hazare/N.D. Nagarwalla, Maharashtra v Baroda; Poona 1939-40

Tenth Wicket

307 A.F. Kippax/J.E.H. Hooker, NSW v Victoria; Melbourne 1928-29
249 C.T. Sarwate/S.N. Bannerjee, Indians v Surrey; The Oval 1946
235 F.E. Woolley/A. Fielder, Kent v Worcestershire; Stourbridge 1909

Most Runs in a Career

	Career	*I*	*NO*	*HS*	*Runs*	*Avge*	*100*
J.B. Hobbs	1905-34	1315	106	316*	**61237**	50.65	197
F.E. Woolley	1906-38	1532	85	305*	**58969**	40.75	145
E.H. Hendren	1907-38	1300	166	301*	**57611**	50.80	170
C.P. Mead	1905-36	1340	185	280*	**55061**	47.67	153
W.G. Grace	1865-1908	1493	105	344	**54896**	39.55	126
W.R. Hammond	1920-51	1005	104	336*	**50551**	56.10	167
H. Sutcliffe	1919-45	1088	123	313	**50138**	51.95	149
G. Boycott	1962-86	1014	162	261*	**48426**	56.83	151
T.W. Graveney	1948-71/2	1223	159	258	**47793**	44.91	122
T.W. Hayward	1893-1914	1138	96	315*	**43551**	41.79	104
M.C. Cowdrey	1950-76	1130	134	307	**42719**	42.89	107
D.L. Amiss	1960-86	1093	123	262*	**42123**	43.42	100
A. Sandham	1911-37/8	1000	79	325	**41284**	44.82	107
L. Hutton	1934-60	814	91	364	**40140**	55.51	129
M.J.K. Smith	1951-75	1091	139	204	**39832**	41.84	69
W. Rhodes	1898-1930	1528	237	267*	**39802**	30.83	58
J.H. Edrich	1956-78	979	104	310*	**39790**	45.47	103
R.E.S. Wyatt	1923-57	1141	157	232	**39405**	40.04	85
D.C.S. Compton	1936-64	839	88	300	**38942**	51.85	123
E. Tyldesley	1909-36	961	106	256*	**38874**	45.46	102
J.T. Tyldesley	1895-1923	994	62	295*	**37897**	40.60	86
J.W. Hearne	1909-36	1025	116	285*	**37252**	40.98	96
L.E.G. Ames	1926-51	951	95	295	**37248**	43.51	102
D. Kenyon	1946-67	1159	59	259	**37002**	33.63	74
W.J. Edrich	1934-58	964	92	267*	**36965**	42.39	86
J.M. Parks	1949-76	1227	172	205*	**36673**	34.76	51
D. Denton	1894-1920	1163	70	221	**36479**	33.37	69
K.W.R. Fletcher	1962-86	1118	164	228*	**36437**	38.19	62
G.H. Hirst	1891-1929	1215	151	341	**36323**	34.13	60
A. Jones	1957-83	1168	72	204*	**36049**	32.89	56
W.G. Quaife	1894-1928	1203	185	255*	**36012**	35.37	72
R.E. Marshall	1945/6-72	1053	59	228*	**35725**	35.94	68
G. Gunn	1902-32	1061	82	220	**35208**	35.96	62

BOWLING RECORDS

All Ten Wickets in an Innings

This feat has been achieved on 70 occasions at first-class level.
Three Times: A.P. Freeman (1929, 1930, 1931)
Twice: V.E. Walker (1859, 1865); H. Verity (1931, 1932); J.C. Laker (1956).

Instances since 1945:

W.E. Hollies	Warwicks v Notts	Birmingham	1946
J.M. Sims	East v West	Kingston/Thames	1948
J.K.R. Graveney	Glos v Derbyshire	Chesterfield	1949
T.E. Bailey	Essex v Lancashire	Clacton	1949
R. Berry	Lancashire v Worcestershire	Blackpool	1953
S.P. Gupte	Bombay v Pakistan Services	Bombay	1954–55
J.C. Laker	Surrey v Australians	Oval	1956
K. Smales	Notts v Glos	Stroud	1956
G.A.R. Lock	Surrey v Kent	Blackheath	1956
J.C. Laker	England v Australia	Manchester	1956
P.M. Chatterjee	Bengal v Assam	Jorhat	1956–57
J.D. Bannister	Warwicks v Combined Services	Birmingham	1959
A.J.G. Pearson	Cambridge U v Leicestershire	Loughborough	1961
N.I. Thomson	Sussex v Warwickshire	Worthing	1964
P.J. Allan	Queensland v Victoria	Melbourne	1965–66
I.J. Brayshaw	Western Australia v Victoria	Perth	1967–68
Shahid Mahmood	Karachi Whites v Khairpur	Karachi	1969–70
E.E. Hemmings	International XI v W Indians	Kingston	1982–83
P. Sunderam	Rajasthan v Vidarbha	Jodhpur	1985–86

Most Wickets in a Match

19	J.C. Laker	England v Australia	Manchester	1956

Most Wickets in a Season

Wkts		*Season*	*M*	*Overs*	*Mdns*	*Runs*	*Avge*
304	A.P. Freeman	1928	37	1976.1	423	5489	18.05
298	A.P. Freeman	1933	33	2039	651	4549	15.26

N.B. The feat of taking 250 wickets in a season has been achieved on 12 occasions, the last instance being by A.P. Freeman as above. 200 or more wickets in a season have been taken on 59 occasions, the last instance being by G.A.R. Lock (212 wkts, avge 12.02) in 1957.

The most wickets taken in a season since the reduction of County Championship matches in 1969 are as follows:

Wkts		*Season*	*M*	*Overs*	*Mdns*	*Runs*	*Avge*
134	M.D. Marshall	1982	22	822	225	2108	15.73
131	L.R. Gibbs	1971	23	1024.1	295	2475	18.89
121	R.D. Jackman	1980	23	746.2	220	1864	15.40

N.B. 100 wickets in a season have been taken on 40 occasions since 1969.

Most Hat-tricks in a Career

7 D.V.P. Wright
6 T.W.J. Goddard, C.W.L. Parker
5 S. Haigh, V.W.C. Jupp, A.E.G. Rhodes, F.A. Tarrant

MOST WICKETS IN A CAREER

	Career	Runs	Wkts	Avge	100w
W. Rhodes	1898-1930	69993	**4187**	16.71	23
A.P. Freeman	1914-36	69577	**3776**	18.42	17
C.W.L. Parker	1903-35	63817	**3278**	19.46	16
J.T. Hearne	1888-1923	54361	**3061**	17.75	15
T.W.J. Goddard	1922-52	59116	**2979**	19.84	16
W.G. Grace	1865-1908	51545	**2876**	17.92	10
A.S. Kennedy	1907-36	61034	**2874**	21.23	15
D. Shackleton	1948-69	53303	**2857**	18.65	20
G.A.R. Lock	1946-71	54710	**2844**	19.23	14
F.J. Titmus	1949-82	63313	**2830**	22.37	16
M.W. Tate	1912-37	50567	**2784**	18.16	13+1
G.H. Hirst	1891-1929	51300	**2739**	18.72	15
C. Blythe	1899-1914	42136	**2506**	16.81	14
W.E. Astill	1906-39	57781	**2431**	23.76	9
D.L. Underwood	1963-86	48698	**2420**	20.12	10
J.C. White	1909-37	43759	**2356**	18.57	14
W.E. Hollies	1932-57	48656	**2323**	20.94	14
F.S. Trueman	1949-69	42154	**2304**	18.29	12
J.B. Statham	1950-68	36995	**2260**	16.36	13
R.T.D. Perks	1930-55	53770	**2233**	24.07	16
J. Briggs	1879-1900	35432	**2221**	15.95	12
D.J. Shepherd	1950-72	47298	**2218**	21.32	12
E.G. Dennett	1903-26	42568	**2147**	19.82	12
T. Richardson	1892-1905	38794	**2105**	18.42	10
T.E. Bailey	1945-67	48170	**2082**	23.13	9
R. Illingworth	1951-83	42023	**2072**	20.28	10
F.E. Woolley	1906-38	41066	**2068**	19.85	8
G. Geary	1912-38	41339	**2063**	20.03	11
D.V.P. Wright	1932-57	49305	**2056**	23.98	10
J.A. Newman	1906-30	51211	**2032**	25.20	9
A. Shaw	1864-97	24579	**2027**	12.12	9
S. Haigh	1895-1913	32091	**2012**	15.94	11
N. Gifford	1960-86	46634	**2001**	23.30	4

ALL-ROUND RECORDS

The 'Double' Event

3000 runs and 100 wickets: J.H. Parks, 1937.
2000 runs and 200 wickets: G.H. Hirst, 1906.
2000 runs and 100 wickets: F.E. Woolley (4), J.W. Hearne (3), G.H. Hirst (2), W. Rhodes (2), T.E. Bailey, D.E. Davies, W.G. Grace, G.L. Jessop, V.W.C. Jupp, James Langridge, F.A. Tarrant, C.L. Townsend, L. F. Townsend.
1000 runs and 200 wickets: M.W. Tate (3), A.E. Trott (2), A.S. Kennedy.
Most 'Doubles': W. Rhodes (16), G.H. Hirst (14), V.W.C. Jupp (10).
'Double' in first season: D.B. Close, 1949. At the age of 18, Close is the youngest player ever to perform this feat.
The feat of scoring 1000 runs and taking 100 wickets has been achieved on 303 occasions, the last instance being R.J. Hadlee in 1984.

WICKET-KEEPING RECORDS

Most Dismissals in an Innings

8 (8 ct)	A.T.W. Grout	Queensland v W Australia	Brisbane	1959-60
8 (8 ct)	D.E. East	Essex v Somerset	Taunton	1985

Most Dismissals in a Match

12 (8 ct, 4 st)	E. Pooley	Surrey v Sussex	Oval	1868
12 (9 ct, 3 st)	D. Tallon	Queensland v NSW	Sydney	1938-39
12 (9 ct, 3 st)	H.B. Taber	NSW v S Australia	Adelaide	1968-69

Most Catches in a Match

11	A. Long	Surrey v Sussex	Hove	1964
11	R.W. Marsh	W Australia v Victoria	Perth	1975-76
11	D.L. Bairstow	Yorkshire v Derbyshire	Scarborough	1982

Most Dismissals in a Season

128 (79 ct, 49 st) L.E.G. Ames 1929

Most Dismissals in a Career

	Career	*Dismissals*	*Ct*	*St*
R.W. Taylor	1960-86	**1648**	1473	175
J.T. Murray	1952-75	**1527**	1270	257
H. Strudwick	1902-27	**1496**	1242	254
A.P.E. Knott	1965-85	**1344**	1211	133
F.H. Huish	1895-1914	**1310**	933	377
D. Hunter	1889-1909	**1265**	914	351
B. Taylor	1949-73	**1294**	1082	212
H.R. Butt	1890-1912	**1228**	953	275
J.H. Board	1891-1914/15	**1207**	852	355
H. Elliott	1920-47	**1206**	904	302
J.M. Parks	1949-76	**1181**	1088	93
R. Booth	1951-70	**1126**	949	177
L.E.G. Ames	1926-51	**1121**	703	418
G. Duckworth	1923-47	**1090**	751	339
H.W. Stephenson	1948-64	**1082**	748	334
J.G. Binks	1955-75	**1071**	895	176
T.G. Evans	1939-69	**1066**	816	250
A. Long	1960-80	**1046**	922	124
G.O. Dawkes	1937-61	**1043**	895	148
R.W. Tolchard	1965-83	**1037**	912	125
W.L. Cornford	1921-47	**1017**	673	344

FIELDING RECORDS

Most Catches

Innings:	7	M.J. Stewart	Surrey v Northants	Northampton	1957
	7	A.S. Brown	Glos v Notts	Nottingham	1966
Match:	10	W.R. Hammond	Glos v Surrey	Cheltenham	1928

Season: 78 W.R. Hammond (1928); 77 M.J. Stewart (1957)

Career: 1018 F.E. Woolley; 874 W.G. Grace; 831 G.A.R. Lock; 819 W.R. Hammond; 813 D.B. Close; 786 J.G. Langridge; 764 W. Rhodes; 758 C.A. Milton; 754 E.H. Hendren

TEST CRICKET RECORDS

Records include all official Test matches played before 30 January 1987. The following series played in 1986-87 are NOT included: India v Pakistan, New Zealand v West Indies.

TEAM RECORDS

HIGHEST INNINGS TOTALS

903-7d	England v Australia	Oval	1938
849	England v West Indies	Kingston	1929-30
790-3d	West Indies v Pakistan	Kingston	1957-58
758-8d	Australia v West Indies	Kingston	1954-55
729-6d	Australia v England	Lord's	1930
701	Australia v England	Oval	1934
695	Australia v England	Oval	1930
687-8d	West Indies v England	Oval	1976
681-8d	West Indies v England	Port-of-Spain	1953-54
676-7	India v Sri Lanka	Kanpur	1986-87
674-6	Pakistan v India	Faisalabad	1984-85
674	Australia v India	Adelaide	1947-48
668	Australia v West Indies	Bridgetown	1954-55
659-8d	Australia v England	Sydney	1946-47
658-8d	England v Australia	Nottingham	1938
657-8d	Pakistan v West Indies	Bridgetown	1957-58
656-8d	Australia v England	Manchester	1964
654-5	England v South Africa	Durban	1938-39
652-8d	West Indies v England	Lord's	1973
652-7d	England v India	Madras	1984-85
652	Pakistan v India	Faisalabad	1982-83
650-6d	Australia v West Indies	Bridgetown	1964-65

The highest innings for the countries not mentioned above are:

622-9d	South Africa v Australia	Durban	1969-70
553-7d	New Zealand v Australia	Brisbane	1985-86
491-7d	Sri Lanka v England	Lord's	1984

LOWEST INNINGS TOTALS

26	New Zealand v England	Auckland	1954-55
30	South Africa v England	Port Elizabeth	1895-96
30	South Africa v England	Birmingham	1924
35	South Africa v England	Cape Town	1898-99
36	Australia v England	Birmingham	1902
36	South Africa v Australia	Melbourne	1931-32
42	Australia v England	Sydney	1887-88
42	New Zealand v Australia	Wellington	1945-46
42†	India v England	Lord's †*Batted one man short*	1974
43	South Africa v England	Cape Town	1888-89
44	Australia v England	Oval	1896
45	England v Australia	Sydney	1886-87
45	South Africa v Australia	Melbourne	1931-32
47	South Africa v England	Cape Town	1888-89
47	New Zealand v England	Lord's	1958

The lowest innings for the countries not mentioned above are:

53	West Indies v Pakistan	Faisalabad	1986-87
62	Pakistan v Australia	Perth	1981-82
93	Sri Lanka v New Zealand	Wellington	1982-83

BATTING RECORDS

HIGHEST INDIVIDUAL INNINGS

365*	G.St A. Sobers	WI v P	Kingston	1957-58
364	L. Hutton	E v A	Oval	1938
337	Hanif Mohammad	P v WI	Bridgetown	1957-58
336*	W.R. Hammond	E v NZ	Auckland	1932-33
334	D.G. Bradman	A v E	Leeds	1930
325	A. Sandham	E v WI	Kingston	1929-30
311	R.B. Simpson	A v E	Manchester	1964
310*	J.H. Edrich	E v NZ	Leeds	1965
307	R.M. Cowper	A v E	Melbourne	1965-66
304	D.G. Bradman	A v E	Leeds	1934
302	L.G. Rowe	WI v E	Bridgetown	1973-74
299*	D.G. Bradman	A v SA	Adelaide	1931-32
291	I.V.A. Richards	WI v E	Oval	1976
287	R.E. Foster	E v A	Sydney	1903-04
285*	P.B.H. May	E v WI	Birmingham	1957
280*	Javed Miandad	P v I	Hyderabad	1982-83
278	D.C.S. Compton	E v P	Nottingham	1954
274	R.G. Pollock	SA v A	Durban	1969-70
274	Zaheer Abbas	P v E	Birmingham	1971
270*	G.A. Headley	WI v E	Kingston	1934-35
270	D.G. Bradman	A v E	Melbourne	1936-37
268	G.N. Yallop	A v P	Melbourne	1983-84
266	W.H. Ponsford	A v E	Oval	1934
262*	D.L. Amiss	E v WI	Kingston	1973-74
261	F.M.M. Worrell	WI v E	Nottingham	1950
260	C.C. Hunte	WI v P	Kingston	1957-58
259	G.M. Turner	NZ v WI	Georgetown	1971-72
258	T.W. Graveney	E v WI	Nottingham	1957
258	S.M. Nurse	WI v NZ	Christchurch	1968-69
256	R.B. Kanhai	WI v I	Calcutta	1958-59
256	K.F. Barrington	E v A	Manchester	1964
255*	D.J. McGlew	SA v NZ	Wellington	1952-53
254	D.G. Bradman	A v E	Lord's	1930
251	W.R. Hammond	E v A	Sydney	1928-29
250	K.D. Walters	A v NZ	Christchurch	1976-77
250	S.F.A.F. Bacchus	WI v I	Kanpur	1978-79

The highest individual innings for other countries are:

236*	S.M. Gavaskar	I v WI	Madras	1983-84
190	S. Wettimuny	SL v E	Lord's	1984

MOST RUNS IN A SERIES

Runs		*Series*	*T*	*I*	*NO*	*HS*	*Avge*	*100*	*50*
974	D.G. Bradman (A v E)	1930	5	7	0	334	139.14	4	—
905	W.R. Hammond (E v A)	1928-29	5	9	1	251	113.12	4	—
834	R.N. Harvey (A v SA)	1952-53	5	9	0	205	92.66	4	3
829	I.V.A. Richards (WI v E)	1976	4	7	0	291	118.42	3	2
827	C.L. Walcott (WI v A)	1954-55	5	10	0	155	82.70	5	2
824	G.St A. Sobers (WI v P)	1957-58	5	8	2	365*	137.33	3	3
810	D.G. Bradman (A v E)	1936-37	5	9	0	270	90.00	3	1
806	D.G. Bradman (A v SA)	1931-32	5	5	1	299*	201.50	4	—

779	E.de C. Weekes (WI v I)	1948-49	5	7	0	194	111.28	4	2
774	S.M. Gavaskar (I v WI)	1970-71	4	8	3	220	154.80	4	3
761	Mudassar Nazar (P v I)	1982-83	6	8	2	231	126.83	4	1
758	D.G. Bradman (A v E)	1934	5	8	0	304	94.75	2	1
753	D.C.S. Compton (E v SA)	1947	5	8	0	208	94.12	4	2

RECORD WICKET PARTNERSHIPS

1st	413	V. Mankad/Pankaj Roy	I v NZ	Madras	1955-56
2nd	451	W.H. Ponsford/D.G. Bradman	A v E	Oval	1934
3rd	451	Mudassar Nazar/Javed Miandad	P v I	Hyderabad	1982-83
4th	411	P.B.H. May/M.C. Cowdrey	E v WI	Birmingham	1957
5th	405	S.G. Barnes/D.G. Bradman	A v E	Sydney	1946-47
6th	346	J.H.W. Fingleton/D.G. Bradman	A v E	Melbourne	1936-37
7th	347	D.St E. Atkinson/C.C. Depeiza	WI v A	Bridgetown	1954-55
8th	246	L.E.G. Ames/G.O.B. Allen	E v NZ	Lord's	1931
9th	190	Asif Iqbal/Intikhab Alam	P v E	Oval	1967
10th	151	B.F. Hastings/R.O. Collinge	NZ v P	Auckland	1972-73

WICKET PARTNERSHIPS OF OVER 300

451	2nd	W.H. Ponsford/D.G. Bradman	A v E	Oval	1934
451	3rd	Mudassar Nazar/Javed Miandad	P v I	Hyderabad	1982-83
446	2nd	C.C. Hunte/G.St A. Sobers	WI v P	Kingston	1957-58
413	1st	V. Mankad/Pankaj Roy	I v NZ	Madras	1955-56
411	4th	P.B.H. May/M.C. Cowdrey	E v WI	Birmingham	1957
405	5th	S.G. Barnes/D.G. Bradman	A v E	Sydney	1946-47
399	4th	G.St A. Sobers/F.M.M. Worrell	WI v E	Bridgetown	1959-60
397	3rd	Qasim Omar/Javed Miandad	P v SL	Faisalabad	1985-86
388	4th	W.H. Ponsford/D.G. Bradman	A v E	Leeds	1934
387	1st	G.M. Turner/T.W. Jarvis	NZ v WI	Georgetown	1971-72
382	2nd	L. Hutton/M. Leyland	E v A	Oval	1938
382	1st	W.M. Lawry/R.B. Simpson	A v WI	Bridgetown	1964-65
370	3rd	W.J. Edrich/D.C.S. Compton	E v SA	Lord's	1947
369	2nd	J.H. Edrich/K.F. Barrington	E v NZ	Leeds	1965
359	1st	L. Hutton/C. Washbrook	E v SA	Jo'burg	1948-49
351	2nd	G.A. Gooch/D.I. Gower	E v A	Oval	1985
350	4th	Mushtaq Mohammad/Asif Iqbal	P v NZ	Dunedin	1972-73
347	7th	D.St E. Atkinson/C.C. Depeiza	WI v A	Bridgetown	1954-55
346	6th	J.H.W. Fingleton/D.G. Bradman	A v E	Melbourne	1936-37
344*	2nd	S.M. Gavaskar/D.B. Vengsarkar	I v WI	Calcutta	1978-79
341	3rd	E.J. Barlow/R.G. Pollock	SA v A	Adelaide	1963-64
338	3rd	E.de C. Weekes/F.M.M. Worrell	WI v E	Pt-of-Spain	1953-54
336	4th	W.M. Lawry/K.D. Walters	A v WI	Sydney	1968-69
331	2nd	R.T. Robinson/D.I. Gower	E v A	Birmingham	1985
323	1st	J.B. Hobbs/W. Rhodes	E v A	Melbourne	1911-12
319	3rd	A. Melville/A.D. Nourse	SA v E	Nottingham	1947
316†	3rd	G.R. Viswanath/Yashpal Sharma	I v E	Madras	1981-82
308	7th	Waqar Hasan/Imtiaz Ahmed	P v NZ	Lahore	1955-56
308	3rd	R.B. Richardson/I.V.A. Richards	WI v A	St John's	1983-84
303	3rd	I.V.A. Richards/A.I. Kallicharran	WI v E	Nottingham	1976
301	2nd	A.R. Morris/D G. Bradman	A v E	Leeds	1948

† 415 runs were added for this wicket in two separate partnerships. D.B. Vengsarkar retired hurt and was replaced by Yashpal Sharma after 99 runs had been added.

4000 RUNS IN TESTS

Runs			*Tests*	*Inns*	*NO*	*HS*	*Avge*	*100*	*50*
9827	S.M. Gavaskar	(I)	121	208	16	236*	51.18	34	42
8114	G. Boycott	(E)	108	193	23	246*	47.72	22	42
8032	G.St A. Sobers	(WI)	93	160	21	365*	57.78	26	30
7624	M.C. Cowdrey	(E)	114	188	15	182	44.06	22	38
7515	C.H. Lloyd	(WI)	110	175	14	242*	46.67	19	39
7249	W.R. Hammond	(E)	85	140	16	336*	58.45	22	24
7110	G.S. Chappell	(A)	87	151	19	247*	53.86	24	31
6996	D.G. Bradman	(A)	52	80	10	334	99.94	29	13
6971	L. Hutton	(E)	79	138	15	364	56.67	19	33
6917	A.R. Border	(A)	89	157	26	196	52.80	21	33
6806	K.F. Barrington	(E)	82	131	15	256	58.67	20	35
6553	D.I. Gower	(E)	91	156	12	215	45.50	14	32
6395	I.V.A. Richards	(WI)	85	127	8	291	53.73	20	28
6227	R.B. Kanhai	(WI)	79	137	6	256	47.53	15	28
6149	R.N. Harvey	(A)	79	137	10	205	48.41	21	24
6080	G.R. Viswanath	(I)	91	155	10	222	41.93	14	35
5807	D.C.S. Compton	(E)	78	131	15	278	50.06	17	28
5589	Javed Miandad	(P)	77	121	17	280*	53.74	14	29
5547	D.B. Vengsarkar	(I)	90	145	18	166	43.67	14	27
5410	J.B. Hobbs	(E)	61	102	7	211	56.94	15	28
5357	K.D. Walters	(A)	74	125	14	250	48.26	15	33
5345	I.M. Chappell	(A)	75	136	10	196	42.42	14	26
5234	W.M. Lawry	(A)	67	123	12	210	47.15	13	27
5165	C.G. Greenidge	(WI)	74	122	13	223	47.38	12	28
5138	J.H. Edrich	(E)	77	127	9	310*	43.54	12	24
5062	Zaheer Abbas	(P)	78	124	11	274	44.79	12	20
4882	T.W. Graveney	(E)	79	123	13	258	44.38	11	20
4869	R.B. Simpson	(A)	62	111	7	311	46.81	10	27
4825	I.T. Botham	(E)	89	142	4	208	34.96	14	21
4737	I.R. Redpath	(A)	66	120	11	171	43.45	8	31
4555	H. Sutcliffe	(E)	54	84	9	194	60.73	16	23
4537	P.B.H. May	(E)	66	106	9	285*	46.77	13	22
4502	E.R. Dexter	(E)	62	102	8	205	47.89	9	27
4455	E.de C. Weekes	(WI)	48	81	5	207	58.61	15	19
4415	K.J. Hughes	(A)	70	124	6	213	37.41	9	22
4399	A.I. Kallicharran	(WI)	66	109	10	187	44.43	12	21
4389	A.P.E. Knott	(E)	95	149	15	135	32.75	5	30
4334	R.C. Fredericks	(WI)	59	109	7	169	42.49	8	26
4108	M. Amarnath	(I)	61	100	9	138	45.14	11	23

MOST HUNDREDS

34	S.M. Gavaskar	(I)	22	G. Boycott	(E)
29	D.G. Bradman	(A)	21	R.N. Harvey	(A)
26	G.St A. Sobers	(WI)	21	A.R. Border	(A)
24	G.S. Chappell	(A)	20	K.F. Barrington	(E)
22	W.R. Hammond	(E)	20	I.V.A. Richards	(WI)
22	M.C. Cowdrey	(E)			

BOWLING RECORDS

NINE OR TEN WICKETS IN AN INNINGS

10-53	J.C. Laker	E v A	Manchester	1956
9-28	G.A. Lohmann	E v SA	Johannesburg	1895-96
9-37	J.C. Laker	E v A	Manchester	1956
9-52	R.J. Hadlee	NZ v A	Brisbane	1985-86
9-69	J.M. Patel	I v A	Kanpur	1959-60
9-83	Kapil Dev	I v WI	Ahmedabad	1983-84
9-86	Sarfraz Nawaz	P v A	Melbourne	1978-79
9-95	J.M. Noreiga	WI v I	Port-of-Spain	1970-71
9-102	S.P. Gupte	I v WI	Kanpur	1958-59
9-103	S.F. Barnes	E v SA	Johannesburg	1913-14
9-113	H.J. Tayfield	SA v E	Johannesburg	1956-57
9-121	A.A. Mailey	A v E	Melbourne	1920-21

FIFTEEN OR MORE WICKETS IN A TEST

19-90	J.C. Laker	E v A	Manchester	1956
17-159	S.F. Barnes	E v SA	Johannesburg	1913-14
16-137	R.A.L. Massie	A v E	Lord's	1972
15-28	J. Briggs	E v SA	Cape Town	1888-89
15-45	G.A. Lohmann	E v SA	Port Elizabeth	1895-96
15-99	C. Blythe	E v SA	Leeds	1907
15-104	H. Verity	E v A	Lord's	1934
15-123	R.J. Hadlee	NZ v A	Brisbane	1985-86
15-124	W. Rhodes	E v A	Melbourne	1903-04

MOST WICKETS IN A SERIES

Wkts			*Series*	*Tests*	*Balls*	*Runs*	*Avge*	*5 wI*	*10 wM*
49	S.F. Barnes	E v SA	1913-14	4	1356	536	10.93	7	3
46	J.C. Laker	E v A	1956	5	1703	442	9.60	4	2
44	C.V. Grimmett	A v SA	1935-36	5	2077	642	14.59	5	3
42	T.M. Alderman	A v E	1981	6	1950	893	21.26	4	—
41	R.M. Hogg	A v E	1978-79	6	1740	527	12.85	5	2
40	Imran Khan	P v I	1982-83	6	1339	558	13.95	4	2
39	A.V. Bedser	E v A	1953	5	1591	682	17.48	5	1
39	D.K. Lillee	A v E	1981	6	1870	870	22.30	2	1
38	M.W. Tate	E v A	1924-25	5	2528	881	23.18	5	1
37	W.J. Whitty	A v SA	1910-11	5	1395	632	17.08	2	—
37	H.J. Tayfield	SA v E	1956-57	5	2280	636	17.18	4	1
36	A.E.E. Vogler	SA v E	1909-10	5	1349	783	21.75	4	1
36	A.A. Mailey	A v E	1920-21	5	1465	946	26.27	4	2
35	G.A. Lohmann	E v SA	1895-96	3	520	203	5.80	4	2
35	B.S. Chandrasekhar	I v E	1972-73	5	1747	662	18.91	4	—

200 WICKETS IN TESTS

Wkts			*Tests*	*Balls*	*Runs*	*Avge*	*5wI*	*10wM*
366	I.T. Botham	(E)	89	19994	9959	27.21	27	4
355	D.K. Lillee	(A)	70	18467	8493	23.92	23	7
334	R.J. Hadlee	(NZ)	66	17179	7520	22.51	27	7
325	R.G.D. Willis	(E)	90	17357	8190	25.20	16	—
309	L.R. Gibbs	(WI)	79	27115	8989	29.09	18	2
307	F.S. Trueman	(E)	67	15178	6625	21.57	17	3
300	Kapil Dev	(I)	83	17576	8715	29.05	19	2
297	D.L. Underwood	(E)	86	21862	7674	25.83	17	6
282	Imran Khan	(P)	60	14610	6056	21.47	19	4
266	B.S. Bedi	(I)	67	21364	7637	28.71	14	1
252	J.B. Statham	(E)	70	16056	6261	24.84	9	1
249	M.A. Holding	(WI)	59	12458	5799	23.28	13	2
248	R. Benaud	(A)	63	19108	6704	27.03	16	1
247	J. Garner	(WI)	56	12707	5228	21.16	6	—
246	G.D. McKenzie	(A)	60	17681	7328	29.78	16	3
242	B.S. Chandrasekhar	(I)	58	15963	7199	29.74	16	2
236	A.V. Bedser	(E)	51	15918	5876	24.89	15	5
235	G.St A. Sobers	(WI)	93	21599	7999	34.03	6	—
231	M.D. Marshall	(WI)	48	10564	4905	21.23	14	2
228	R.R. Lindwall	(A)	61	13650	5251	23.03	12	—
216	C.V. Grimmett	(A)	37	14513	5231	24.21	21	7
202	A.M.E. Roberts	(WI)	47	11136	5174	25.61	11	2
202	J.A. Snow	(E)	49	12021	5387	26.66	8	1
200	J.R. Thomson	(A)	51	10535	5601	28.00	8	—

HAT-TRICKS

F.R. Spofforth	Australia v England	Melbourne	1878-79
W. Bates	England v Australia	Melbourne	1882-83
J. Briggs	England v Australia	Sydney	1891-92
G.A. Lohmann	England v South Africa	Port Elizabeth	1895-96
J.T. Hearne	England v Australia	Leeds	1899
H. Trumble	Australia v England	Melbourne	1901-02
H. Trumble	Australia v England	Melbourne	1903-04
T.J. Matthews (2)*	Australia v South Africa	Manchester	1912
M.J.C. Allom†	England v New Zealand	Christchurch	1929-30
T.W.J. Goddard	England v South Africa	Johannesburg	1938-39
P.J. Loader	England v West Indies	Leeds	1957
L.F. Kline	Australia v South Africa	Cape Town	1957-58
W.W. Hall	West Indies v Pakistan	Lahore	1958-59
G.M. Griffin	South Africa v England	Lord's	1960
L.R. Gibbs	West Indies v Australia	Adelaide	1960-61
P.J. Petherick	New Zealand v Pakistan	Lahore	1976-77

* *In each innings.* † *Four wickets in five balls.*

WICKET-KEEPING RECORDS

MOST DISMISSALS IN AN INNINGS

7	Wasim Bari	Pakistan v New Zealand	Auckland	1978-79
7	R.W. Taylor	England v India	Bombay	1979-80
6	A.T.W. Grout	Australia v South Africa	Johannesburg	1957-58
6	D.T. Lindsay	South Africa v Australia	Johannesburg	1966-67
6	J.T. Murray	England v India	Lord's	1967
6†	S.M.H. Kirmani	India v New Zealand	Christchurch	1975-76
6	R.W. Marsh	Australia v England	Brisbane	1982-83
6	S.A.R. Silva	Sri Lanka v India	Colombo	1985-86

† Including one stumping

MOST DISMISSALS IN A TEST

10	R.W. Taylor	England v India	Bombay	1979-80
9†	G.R.A. Langley	Australia v England	Lord's	1956
9	D.A. Murray	West Indies v Australia	Melbourne	1981-82
9	R.W. Marsh	Australia v England	Brisbane	1982-83
9	S.A.R. Silva	Sri Lanka v India	Colombo (SSC)	1985-86
9†	S.A.R. Silva	Sri Lanka v India	Colombo (SO)	1985-86

† Including one stumping

MOST DISMISSALS IN A SERIES

28	R.W. Marsh	Australia v England	1982-83
26 (inc 3 st)	J.H.B. Waite	South Africa v New Zealand	1961-62
26	R.W. Marsh	Australia v West Indies (6 Tests)	1975-76
24 (inc 2 st)	D.L. Murray	West Indies v England	1963
24	D.T. Lindsay	South Africa v Australia	1966-67
24 (inc 3 st)	A.P.E. Knott	England v Australia (6 Tests)	1970-71

100 DISMISSALS IN TESTS

Total			*Tests*	*Ct*	*St*
355	R.W. Marsh	Australia	96	343	12
269	A.P.E. Knott	England	95	250	19
228	Wasim Bari	Pakistan	81	201	27
219	T.G. Evans	England	91	173	46
198	S.M.H. Kirmani	India	88	160	38
189	D.L. Murray	West Indies	62	181	8
187	A.T.W. Grout	Australia	51	163	24
174	R.W. Taylor	England	57	167	7
141	J.H.B. Waite	South Africa	50	124	17
133†	P.J.L. Dujon	West Indies	40	130	3
130	W.A.S. Oldfield	Australia	54	78	52
114†	J.M. Parks	England	46	103	11

† Including two catches taken in the field.

Most Dismissals for other Countries:

98	I.D.S. Smith	New Zealand	33	92	6
31	S.A.R. Silva	Sri Lanka	8	30	1

FIELDING RECORDS
(Excluding Wicket-Keepers)

MOST CATCHES IN AN INNINGS

5	V.Y. Richardson	Australia v South Africa	Durban	1935-36
5	Yajurvindra Singh	India v England	Bangalore	1976-77

MOST CATCHES IN A TEST

7	G.S. Chappell	Australia v England	Perth	1974-75
7	Yajurvindra Singh	India v England	Bangalore	1976-77

MOST CATCHES IN A SERIES

15	J.M. Gregory	Australia v England	1920-21

100 CATCHES IN TESTS

Total			*Tests*
122	G.S. Chappell	Australia	87
120	M.C. Cowdrey	England	114
110	R.B. Simpson	Australia	62
110	W.R. Hammond	England	85
109	G.St A. Sobers	West Indies	93
106	I.T. Botham	England	89
105	I.M. Chappell	Australia	75
105	S.M. Gavaskar	India	121

MOST TEST APPEARANCES

England	M.C. Cowdrey	114
Australia	R.W. Marsh	96
South Africa	J.H.B. Waite	50
West Indies	C.H. Lloyd	110
New Zealand	R.J. Hadlee	66
India	S.M. Gavaskar	121
Pakistan	Wasim Bari	81
Sri Lanka	S. Wettimuny	23

MOST CONSECUTIVE TEST APPEARANCES

105	S.M. Gavaskar	India	January 1975 to January 1987

SUMMARY OF ALL TEST MATCHES

To 30 January 1987

		Tests	*Won by*								*Tied*	*Drawn*
			E	*A*	*SA*	*WI*	*NZ*	*I*	*P*	*SL*		
England	v Australia	262	88	97	—	—	—	—	—	—	—	77
	v South Africa	102	46	—	18	—	—	—	—	—	—	38
	v West Indies	90	21	—	—	35	—	—	—	—	—	34
	v New Zealand	63	30	—	—	—	4	—	—	—	—	29
	v India	75	30	—	—	—	—	11	—	—	—	34
	v Pakistan	39	13	—	—	—	—	—	3	—	—	23
	v Sri Lanka	2	1	—	—	—	—	—	—	0	—	1
Australia	v South Africa	53	—	29	11	—	—	—	—	—	—	13
	v West Indies	62	—	27	—	19	—	—	—	—	1	15
	v New Zealand	21	—	9	—	—	5	—	—	—	—	7
	v India	45	—	20	—	—	—	8	—	—	1	16
	v Pakistan	28	—	11	—	—	—	—	8	—	—	9
	v Sri Lanka	1	—	1	—	—	—	—	—	0	—	0
South Africa	v New Zealand	17	—	—	9	—	2	—	—	—	—	6
West Indies	v New Zealand	21	—	—	—	7	3	—	—	—	—	11
	v India	54	—	—	—	22	—	5	—	—	—	27
	v Pakistan	22	—	—	—	8	—	—	5	—	—	9
New Zealand	v India	25	—	—	—	—	4	10	—	—	—	11
	v Pakistan	27	—	—	—	—	3	—	10	—	—	14
	v Sri Lanka	5	—	—	—	—	4	—	—	0	—	1
India	v Pakistan	35	—	—	—	—	—	4	6	—	—	25
	v Sri Lanka	7	—	—	—	—	—	2	—	1	—	4
Pakistan	v Sri Lanka	9	—	—	—	—	—	—	5	1	—	3
		1065	229	194	38	91	25	40	37	2	2	407

	Tests	*Won*	*Lost*	*Drawn*	*Tied*	*Toss Won*
England	633	229	168	236	—	311
Australia	472	194	139	137	2	237
South Africa	172	38	77	57	—	80
West Indies	249	91	61	96	1	133
New Zealand	179	25	75	79	—	88
India	241	40	83	117	1	120
Pakistan	160	37	40	83	—	83
Sri Lanka	24	2	13	9	—	13

TEXACO TROPHY 1972-86

(Including the Prudential Trophy)

Highest Total	320-8	England v Australia	Birmingham	1980
Lowest Total	70	Australia v England	Birmingham	1977
Highest Aggregate	593	Eng (320-8) v Aus (273-5)	Birmingham	1980
Largest Victories	9 wkts	England beat India	Leeds	1982
	9 wkts	India beat England	The Oval	1986
	132 runs	England beat Pakistan	Manchester	1978
Narrowest Victories	1 wkt	England beat West Indies	Leeds	1973
	2 runs	Australia beat England	Birmingham	1981
Highest Score	189*	I.V.A. Richards WI v E	Manchester	1984

Hundreds (19)

D.L. Amiss (3)	103	E v A	Manchester	1972
	100	E v NZ	Swansea	1973
	108	E v A	The Oval	1977
C.W.J. Athey	142*	E v NZ	Manchester	1986
G.S. Chappell	125*	A v E	The Oval	1977
R.C. Fredericks	105	WI v E	The Oval	1973
G.A. Gooch (3)	108	E v A	Birmingham	1980
	115	E v A	Birmingham	1985
	117*	E v A	Lord's	1985
D.I. Gower (2)	114*	E v P	The Oval	1978
	102	E v A	Lord's	1985
A.J. Lamb	118	E v P	Nottingham	1982
D. Lloyd	116*	E v P	Nottingham	1974
Majid Khan	109	P v E	Nottingham	1974
C.T. Radley	117*	E v NZ	Manchester	1978
I.V.A. Richards (2)	119*	WI v E	Scarborough	1976
	189*	WI v E	Manchester	1984
G.M. Wood (2)	108	A v E	Leeds	1981
	114*	A v E	Lord's	1985

Fastest Hundred	88 balls – Majid Khan	P v E	Nottingham	1974
Fastest Fifties	35 balls – R.O. Butcher	E v A	Birmingham	1980
	35 balls – Kapil Dev	I v E	Leeds	1982

Highest Partnership for Each Wicket

1st	193	G.A. Gooch, C.W.J. Athey	E v NZ	Manchester	1986
2nd	202	G.A. Gooch, D.I. Gower	E v A	Lord's	1985
3rd	159	A.J. Lamb, D.I. Gower	E v I	The Oval	1982
4th	116	G.A. Gooch, I.T. Botham	E v A	Manchester	1985
5th	113	M.D. Crowe, J.J. Crowe	NZ v E	Manchester	1986
6th	104	R.J. Shastri, Kapil Dev	I v E	Manchester	1986
7th	77	A.W. Greig, A.P.E. Knott	E v A	Lord's	1972
8th	68	B.E. Congdon, B.L. Cairns	NZ v E	Scarborough	1978
9th	47	A.J. Lamb, N.A. Foster	E v WI	Manchester	1984
10th	106*	I.V.A. Richards, M.A. Holding	WI v E	Manchester	1984

Most Wickets	5-18	G.J. Cosier	A v E	Birmingham	1977
	5-20	G.S. Chappell	A v E	Birmingham	1977
	5-28	B.L. Cairns	NZ v E	Scarborough	1978
	5-31	M. Hendrick	E v A	The Oval	1980
	5-50	V.A. Holder	WI v E	Birmingham	1976

Most Economical Bowling

11-4-12-1	L.R. Gibbs	WI v E	The Oval	1973
11-4-12-2	C.M. Old	E v WI	Leeds	1980

Most Expensive Bowling

11-0-84-0	B.L. Cairns	NZ v E	Manchester	1978

Most Wicket-Keeping Dismissals

5 (5 ct)	R.W. Marsh	A v E	Leeds	1981

Most Catches in the Field

3	A.W. Greig	E v WI	Leeds	1973
3	B.S. Bedi	I v E	Leeds	1974
3	Kapil Dev	I v E	The Oval	1986
3	M. Azharuddin	I v E	The Oval	1986

RESULTS SUMMARY 1972-86

	Played	*Won*	*Lost*	*No Result*
ENGLAND	42	24	17	1
AUSTRALIA	14	6	8	—
WEST INDIES	10	7	3	—
NEW ZEALAND	6	1	4	1
INDIA	6	1	5	—
PAKISTAN	6	2	4	—

1987 TEXACO TROPHY VENUES
55-OVERS MATCH RECORDS

THE OVAL, LONDON (Thursday 21 May)

Highest Total	280-3		Kent v Surrey	1976
Lowest Total	94		Camb U v Surrey	1974
Highest Score	125*	G.S. Chappell	Aus v England	1977
Best Bowling	5-21	B.D. Julien	Kent v Surrey	1973
	5-21	P.H.L. Wilson	Surrey v Comb U	1979

TRENT BRIDGE, NOTTINGHAM (Saturday 23 May)

Highest Total	269-5		Notts v Derbys	1980
Lowest Total	89		Surrey v Notts	1984
Highest Score	118	A.J. Lamb	Eng v Pak	1982
Best Bowling	5-28	C.E.B. Rice	Notts v M. Counties	1984

EDGBASTON, BIRMINGHAM (Monday 25 May)

Highest Total	320-8		Eng v Aus	1980
Lowest Total	70		Eng v Aus	1977
Highest Score	143*	G.M. Turner	Worcs v Warwicks	1976
Best Bowling	7-32	R.G.D. Willis	Warwicks v Yorks	1981

LIMITED-OVERS INTERNATIONALS

Compiled by Victor Isaacs

TEAM RECORDS

Highest Innings Totals

338-5	(60 overs)	Pakistan v Sri Lanka	Swansea	1983
334-4	(60 overs)	England v India	Lord's	1975
333-9	(60 overs)	England v Sri Lanka	Taunton	1983
333-8	(45 overs)	West Indies v India	Jamshedpur	1983-84
330-6	(60 overs)	Pakistan v Sri Lanka	Nottingham	1975

Highest Total Batting Second

297-6	(48.5 overs)	New Zealand v England	Adelaide	1982-83

Highest Match Aggregate

626-14	(120 overs)	Pakistàn v Sri Lanka	Swansea	1983

Lowest Innings Totals

(*Excluding Abbreviated Matches*)

45	(40.3 overs)	Canada v England	Manchester	1979
55	(28.3 overs)	Sri Lanka v West Indies	Sharjah	1986-87
63	(25.5 overs)	India v Australia	Sydney	1980-81
64	(35.5 overs)	New Zealand v Pakistan	Sharjah	1985-86
70	(25.2 overs)	Australia v England	Birmingham	1977
70	(26.3 overs)	Australia v New Zealand	Adelaide	1985-86

Lowest Match Aggregate

91-12	(54.2 overs)	England v Canada	Manchester	1979

Largest Margins of Victory

232 runs	Australia beat Sri Lanka	Adelaide	1984-85
206 runs	New Zealand beat Australia	Adelaide	1985-86
202 runs	England beat India	Lord's	1975
10 wickets	India beat East Africa	Leeds	1975
10 wickets	New Zealand beat India	Melbourne	1980-81
10 wickets	West Indies beat Zimbabwe	Birmingham	1983
10 wickets	India beat Sri Lanka	Sharjah	1983-84
10 wickets	West Indies beat New Zealand	Port-of-Spain	1984-85
10 wickets	Pakistan beat New Zealand	Sharjah	1985-86

Tied Match

Australia (222-9) v West Indies (222-5)	Melbourne	1983-84

Smallest Margins of Victory

(*Excluding Abbreviated Matches*)

1 run	New Zealand beat Pakistan	Sialkot	1976-77
1 run	New Zealand beat Australia	Sydney	1980-81
1 wicket	England beat West Indies	Leeds	1973
1 wicket	West Indies beat Pakistan	Birmingham	1975
1 wicket	New Zealand beat West Indies	Christchurch	1979-80

1 wicket	West Indies beat Pakistan	Adelaide	1983-84
1 wicket	Pakistan beat New Zealand	Multan	1984-85
1 wicket	Pakistan beat India	Sharjah	1985-86
1 wicket	Pakistan beat Australia	Perth	1986-87

BATTING RECORDS

Highest Individual Innings

189*	I.V.A. Richards	WI v E	Manchester	1984
175*	Kapil Dev	I v Z	Tunbridge Wells	1983
171*	G.M. Turner	NZ v EA	Birmingham	1975
158	D.I. Gower	E v NZ	Brisbane	1982-83
153*	I.V.A. Richards	WI v A	Melbourne	1979-80

Hundred On Debut

103	D.L. Amiss	E v A	Manchester	1972
148	D.L. Haynes	WI v A	St John's	1977-78

Highest Partnerships For Each Wicket

1st	212	G.R. Marsh/D.C. Boon	A v I	Jaipur	1986-87
2nd	221	C.G. Greenidge/I.V.A. Richards	WI v I	Jamshedpur	1983-84
3rd	224*	D.M. Jones/A.R. Border	A v SL	Adelaide	1984-85
4th	173	D.M. Jones/S.R. Waugh	A v P	Perth	1986-87
5th	152	I.V.A. Richards/C.H. Lloyd	WI v SL	Brisbane	1984-85
6th	144	Imran Khan/Shahid Mahboob	P v SL	Leeds	1983
7th	115	P.J.L. Dujon/M.D. Marshall	WI v P	Gujranwala	1986-87
8th	68	B.E. Congdon/B.L. Cairns	NZ v E	Scarborough	1978
9th	126*	Kapil Dev/S.M.H. Kirmani	I v Z	Tunbridge Wells	1983
10th	106*	I.V.A. Richards/M.A. Holding	WI v E	Manchester	1984

Most Runs in a Career

		I	*NO*	*HS*	*Runs*	*Avge*	*100*	*50*
I.V.A. Richards	WI	109	19	189*	4797	53.33	8	35
D.L. Haynes	WI	112	15	148	4046	41.71	8	25
A.R. Border	A	127	19	127*	3493	32.34	3	23
C.G. Greenidge	WI	81	7	115	3362	45.43	7	22
Javed Miandad	P	102	23	119*	3293	41.68	3	22
D.I. Gower	E	86	7	158	2614	33.08	7	8
Zaheer Abbas	P	60	6	123	2572	47.63	7	13
S.M. Gavaskar	I	88	12	92*	2557	33.64	—	22
D.B. Vengsarkar	I	79	12	105	2393	35.71	1	15
G.S. Chappell	A	71	14	138*	2329	40.86	3	14

BOWLING RECORDS

Most Wickets in an Innings

7-51	W.W. Davis	WI v A	Leeds	1983
6-14	G.J. Gilmour	A v E	Leeds	1975
6-14	Imran Khan	P v I	Sharjah	1984-85
6-15	C.E.H. Croft	WI v E	Kingston	1980-81
6-39	K.H. MacLeay	A v I	Nottingham	1983

Hat-Tricks

Jalaluddin	Pakistan v Australia	Hyderabad	1982-83
B.A. Reid	Australia v New Zealand	Sydney	1985-86

Most Wickets in a Career

		Balls	*Runs*	*Wkts*	*Avge*	*Best*	*4w*
M.A. Holding	WI	5326	2967	138	21.50	5-26	6
J. Garner	WI	4724	2416	136	17.76	5-31	5
R.J. Hadlee	NZ	4856	2606	126	20.68	5-25	5
Kapil Dev	I	5030	3074	119	25.83	5-43	2
I.T. Botham	E	4308	2908	109	26.67	4-56	1
E.J. Chatfield	NZ	4351	2504	105	23.85	5-34	2
D.K. Lillee	A	3593	2145	103	20.83	5-34	6

WICKET-KEEPING RECORDS

Most Dismissals in an Innings

5 (5 ct)	R.G. de Alwis	SL v A	Colombo (SO)	1982-83
5 (5 ct)	S.M.H. Kirmani	I v Z	Leicester	1983
5 (5 ct)	R.W. Marsh	A v E	Leeds	1981
5 (3 ct/2 st)	S. Viswanath	I v E	Sydney	1984-85

Most Dismissals in a Career

R.W. Marsh Australia 123 dismissals (119 ct/4 st) in 91 matches

FIELDING RECORDS

Most Catches in an Innings

4	Salim Malik	P v NZ	Sialkot	1984-85
4	S.M. Gavaskar	I v P	Sharjah	1984-85

Most Catches in a Career

I.V.A. Richards	West Indies	59 in 120 matches
A.R. Border	Australia	47 in 136 matches

ALL-ROUND RECORDS

Fifty Runs and Four Wickets in a Match

69*/4-42	D.A.G. Fletcher	Z v A	Nottingham	1983
82/4-48	S.R. Waugh	A v P	Perth	1986-87

1000 Runs and 100 Dismissals

I.T. Botham	England	1411 runs	109 wickets
R.J. Hadlee	New Zealand	1259 runs	126 wickets
Kapil Dev	India	1948 runs	119 wickets
R.W. Marsh	Australia	1220 runs	123 dismissals (119 ct/4 st)

RESULTS SUMMARY

Updated to 17 January 1987

		Matches	*E*	*A*	*I*	*NZ*	*P*	*SL*	*WI*	*C*	*EA*	*Z*	*Tied*	*NR*
Ėngland	v Australia	34	18	15	—	—	—	—	—	—	—	—	—	1
	v India	17	11	—	6	—	—	—	—	—	—	—	—	—
	v New Zealand	23	11	—	—	9	—	—	—	—	—	—	—	3
	v Pakistan	18	12	—	—	—	6	—	—	—	—	—	—	—
	v Sri Lanka	4	3	—	—	—	—	1	—	—	—	—	—	—
	v West Indies	23	6	—	—	—	—	—	17	—	—	—	—	—
	v Canada	1	1	—	—	—	—	—	—	—	—	—	—	—
	v East Africa	1	1	—	—	—	—	—	—	—	—	—	—	—
ustralia	v India	26	—	15	9	—	—	—	—	—	—	—	—	2
	v New Zealand	30	—	18	—	10	—	—	—	—	—	—	—	2
	v Pakistan	18	—	7	—	—	9	—	—	—	—	—	—	2
	v Sri Lanka	10	—	5	—	—	—	3	—	—	—	—	—	2
	v West Indies	41	—	11	—	—	—	—	29	—	—	—	1	—
	v Canada	1	—	1	—	—	—	—	—	—	—	—	—	—
	v Zimbabwe	2	—	1	—	—	—	—	—	—	—	1	—	—
ndia	v New Zealand	18	—	—	7	11	—	—	—	—	—	—	—	—
	v Pakistan	18	—	—	8	—	9	—	—	—	—	—	—	1
	v Sri Lanka	15	—	—	11	—	—	3	—	—	—	—	—	1
	v West Indies	14	—	—	3	—	—	—	11	—	—	—	—	—
	v East Africa	1	—	—	1	—	—	—	—	—	—	—	—	—
	v Zimbabwe	2	—	—	2	—	—	—	—	—	—	—	—	—
lew Zealand	v Pakistan	14	—	—	—	7	6	—	—	—	—	—	—	1
	v Sri Lanka	13	—	—	—	10	—	3	—	—	—	—	—	—
	v West Indies	10	—	—	—	1	—	—	8	—	—	—	—	1
	v East Africa	1	—	—	—	1	—	—	—	—	—	—	—	—
akistan	v Sri Lanka	17	—	—	—	—	13	3	—	—	—	—	—	1
	v West Indies	31	—	—	—	—	7	—	24	—	—	—	—	—
	v Canada	1	—	—	—	—	1	—	—	—	—	—	—	—
i Lanka	v West Indies	8	—	—	—	—	—	—	8	—	—	—	—	—
'est Indies	v Zimbabwe	2	—	—	—	—	—	—	2	—	—	—	—	—
		414	63	73	47	49	51	13	99	0	0	1	1	17

	Matches	*Won*	*Lost*	*Tied*	*NR*
ngland	121	63	54	—	4
ustralia	162	73	79	1	9
dia	111	47	60	—	4
ew Zealand	109	49	53	—	7
kistan	117	51	61	—	5
i Lanka	67	13	50	—	4
est Indies	129	99	28	1	1
anada	3	—	3	—	—
ast Africa	3	—	3	—	—
mbabwe	6	1	5	—	—

THE 1987 SEASON

We welcome Pakistan for only their second full, five-Test match tour of England. They promise to provide somewhat stronger opposition than they did on their first such mission 25 years ago. Then, led by Javed Burki, an Oxford blue, they were outplayed in every Test, losing four and being rescued by rain in the other. They won only four of their 29 first-class fixtures and lost to four of the counties.

Under the shrewd and commanding leadership of Imran Khan, Pakistan have become very much a force to be reckoned with. Crucially, he has brought the best out of his dynamic wizard of leg-spin, that whirly-wristed little genius, Abdul Qadir. The very name has a ring of Eastern magic. When the rest of his side are gaudily attired in those obscene blue and green one-day outfits, he should be permitted a special sorcerer's cloak; a black silk gown with stars and crescents. May he find some hard, bouncy pitches on which to display his art. Lamentably, throughout his travels in Britain he will meet no rival of even the most modest ability.

Sadly this will be Imran's final tour. He has found the continuous treadmill of international cricket impossible for an all-rounder who is a genuinely fast bowler. And no wonder he has found his physical and mental fitness under acute stress. As these notes are being written, Pakistan are embarking on a five-Test tour of India. Since October they have already played West Indies and competed in one-day tournaments in Sharjah and Perth. After their visit here they return home to act as joint hosts for the Reliance World Cup. 'Overkill' scarcely does justice to such a schedule.

After Pakistan have completed their series, the international season ends with the centrepiece of the MCC's celebrations, the Lord's Bicentenary match. Played with the full panoply of a five-day Test it will be between the MCC, selected from all those of every nationality currently playing in English first-class cricket and captained by Mike Gatting, and a Rest of the World XI led by Allan Border.

ENGLAND v PAKISTAN

1954 TO 1983-84

Season	Captains: England	Captains: Pakistan	P	Eng	Pak	D
1954	L. Hutton[1]	A.H. Kardar	4	1	1	2
1961-62	E.R. Dexter	Imtiaz Ahmed	3	1	—	2
1962	E.R. Dexter[2]	Javed Burki	5	4	—	1
1967	D.B. Close	Hanif Mohammad	3	2	—	1
1968-69	M.C. Cowdrey	Saeed Ahmed	3	—	—	3
1971	R. Illingworth	Intikhab Alam	3	1	—	2
1972-73	A.R. Lewis	Majid J. Khan	3	—	—	3
1974	M.H. Denness	Intikhab Alam	3	—	—	3
1977-78	J.M. Brearley[3]	Wasim Bari	3	—	—	3
1978	J.M. Brearley	Wasim Bari	3	2	—	1
1982	R.G.D. Willis[4]	Imran Khan	3	2	1	—
1983-84	R.G.D. Willis[5]	Zaheer Abbas	3	—	1	2

	P	Eng	Pak	D
At Lord's	7	2	1	4
At Nottingham	3	2	—	1
At Manchester	1	—	—	1
At The Oval	4	2	1	1
At Birmingham	4	3	—	1
At Leeds	5	3	—	2
At Lahore	5	1	—	4
At Dacca	2	—	—	2
At Karachi	5	—	1	4
At Hyderabad	2	—	—	2
At Faisalabad	1	—	—	1
In England	24	12	2	10
In Pakistan	15	1	1	13
Totals	39	13	3	23

The following deputised for the official captain: [1]D.S. Sheppard (2nd and 3rd). [2]M.C. Cowdrey (3rd). [3]G. Boycott (3rd). [4]D.I. Gower (2nd). [5]D.I. Gower (2nd and 3rd).

HIGHEST INNINGS TOTALS

England	in England	558-6d	Nottingham	1954
	in Pakistan	546-8d	Faisalabad	1983-84
Pakistan	in England	608-7d	Birmingham	1971
	in Pakistan	569-9d	Hyderabad	1972-73

LOWEST INNINGS TOTALS

England	in England	130	The Oval	1954
	in Pakistan	159	Karachi	1983-84
Pakistan	in England	87	Lord's	1954
	in Pakistan	199	Karachi	1972-73

HIGHEST MATCH AGGREGATE

1274 for 25 wickets	Hyderabad	1972-73

LOWEST MATCH AGGREGATE

509 for 28 wickets	Nottingham	1967

HIGHEST INDIVIDUAL INNINGS

England	in England	278	D.C.S. Compton	Nottingham	1954
		183	D.L. Amiss	The Oval	1974
		182	M.C. Cowdrey	The Oval	1962
		172	E.R. Dexter	The Oval	1962
		159	M.C. Cowdrey	Birmingham	1962
		153	T.W. Graveney	Lord's	1962
	in Pakistan	205	E.R. Dexter	Karachi	1961-62
		173*	D.I. Gower	Lahore	1983-84
		165	G. Pullar	Dacca	1961-62
		158	D.L. Amiss	Hyderabad	1972-73
		152	D.I. Gower	Faisalabad	1983-84
Pakistan	in England	274	Zaheer Abbas	Birmingham	1971
		240	Zaheer Abbas	The Oval	1974
		200	Mohsin Khan	Lord's	1982
		187*	Hanif Mohammad	Lord's	1967
	in Pakistan	157	Mushtaq Mohammad	Hyderabad	1972-73

61 hundreds have been scored in this series (England 36, Pakistan 25). At Karachi in 1972-73 three batsmen – Majid Khan, Mushtaq Mohammad and D.L. Amiss – each scored 99; a coincidence unique in Test cricket.

HUNDRED IN EACH INNINGS

Pakistan	111	104	Hanif Mohammad	Dacca	1961-62

HUNDRED ON DEBUT IN SERIES

England	139	K.F. Barrington	Lahore	1961-62
	159	M.C. Cowdrey	Birmingham	1962
	108*	B.W. Luckhurst	Birmingham	1971
	106	C.T. Radley	Birmingham	1978
	100	I.T. Botham	Birmingham	1978
Pakistan	138	Javed Burki	Lahore	1961-62
	274	Zaheer Abbas	Birmingham	1971
	122	Haroon Rashid	Lahore	1977-78
	114	Mudassar Nazar	Lahore	1977-78

HIGHEST AGGREGATE OF RUNS IN A SERIES

England	in England	453 (av. 90.60)	D.C.S. Compton	1954
	in Pakistan	449 (av. 112.25)	D.I. Gower	1983-84
Pakistan	in England	401 (av. 44.55)	Mushtaq Mohammad	1962
	in Pakistan	407 (av. 67.83)	Hanif Mohammad	1961-62

RECORD WICKET PARTNERSHIPS – ENGLAND

1st	198	G. Pullar (165), R.W. Barber (86)	Dacca	1961-62
2nd	248	M.C. Cowdrey (182), E.R. Dexter (172)	The Oval	1962
3rd	201	K.F. Barrington (148), T.W. Graveney (81)	Lord's	1967
4th	188	E.R. Dexter (205), P.H. Parfitt (111)	Karachi	1961-62
5th	192	D.C.S. Compton (278), T.E. Bailey (36*)	Nottingham	1954
6th	153*	P.H. Parfitt (101*), D.A. Allen (79*)	Birmingham	1962
7th	167	D.I. Gower (152), V.J. Marks (83)	Faisalabad	1983-84
8th	99	P.H. Parfitt (119), D.A. Allen (62)	Leeds	1962
9th	76	T.W. Graveney (153), F.S. Trueman (29)	Lord's	1962
10th	79	R.W. Taylor (54), R.G.D. Willis (28*)	Birmingham	1982

RECORD WICKET PARTNERSHIPS – PAKISTAN

1st	173	Mohsin Khan (104), Shoaib Mohammad (80)	Lahore	1983-84
2nd	291	Zaheer Abbas (274), Mushtaq Mohammad (100)	Birmingham	1971
3rd	180	Mudassar Nazar (114), Haroon Rashid (122)	Lahore	1977-78
4th	153	Javed Burki (138), Mushtaq Mohammad (76)	Lahore	1961-62
	153	Mohsin Khan (200), Zaheer Abbas (75)	Lord's	1982
5th	197	Javed Burki (101), Nasim-ul-Ghani (101)	Lord's	1962
6th	145	Mushtaq Mohammad (157), Intikhab Alam (138)	Hyderabad	1972-73
7th	75	Salim Malik (74), Abdul Qadir (40)	Karachi	1983-84
8th	130	Hanif Mohammad (187*), Asif Iqbal (76)	Lord's	1967
9th	190	Asif Iqbal (146), Intikhab Alam (51)	The Oval	1967
10th	62	Sarfraz Nawaz (53), Asif Masood (4*)	Leeds	1974

BEST INNINGS BOWLING ANALYSIS

England	in England	8-34	I.T. Botham	Lord's	1978
	in Pakistan	7-66	P.H. Edmonds	Karachi	1977-78
Pakistan	in England	7-52	Imran Khan	Birmingham	1982
	in Pakistan	6-44	Abdul Qadir	Hyderabad	1977-78

BEST MATCH BOWLING ANALYSIS

England	in England	13-71	D.L. Underwood	Lord's	1974
	in Pakistan	11-83	N.G.B. Cook	Karachi	1983-84
Pakistan	in England	12-99	Fazal Mahmood	The Oval	1954
	in Pakistan	10-194	Abdul Qadir	Lahore	1983-84

HIGHEST AGGREGATE OF WICKETS IN A SERIES

England	in England	22 (av 19.95)	F.S. Trueman	1962
	in Pakistan	14 (av 31.71)	N.G.B. Cook	1983-84
Pakistan	in England	21 (av 18.57)	Imran Khan	1982
	in Pakistan	19 (av 23.73)	Abdul Qadir	1983-84

FIRST-CLASS UMPIRES 1987

*__BIRD,__ Harold Dennis (**'Dickie'**) (Raley SM, Barnsley), b Barnsley, Yorkshire 19 Apr 1933. RHB, RM. Yorkshire 1956-59. Leicestershire 1960-64 (cap 1960). 1000 runs (1): 1028 (1960). HS 181* Yorks v Glam (Bradford) 1959. F-c career: 93 matches; 3314 runs @ 20.71, 2 hundreds. Appointed 1970. Umpired 35 Tests (1973 to 1986).

BIRKENSHAW, Jack (Rothwell GS), b Rothwell, Yorkshire 13 Nov 1940. LHB, OB. Yorkshire 1958-60. Leicestershire 1961-80 (cap 1965; benefit of £13,000 in 1974). Worcestershire 1981. Tests: 5 (1972-73 to 1973-74); 148 runs @ 21.14, HS 64 v Ind (Kanpur) 1972-73; 13 wickets @ 36.07, BB 5-57 v Pak (Karachi) 1972-73. Tours: WI 1969-70 (DN), 1973-74; Ind/Pak/SL 1967-68 (Int XI), 1972-73. HS 131 Leics v Surrey (Guildford) 1969. BB 8-94 Leics v Somerset (Taunton) 1972. F-c career: 490 matches; 12,780 runs @ 23.57, 4 hundreds; 1073 wickets @ 27.28. Appointed 1982. Umpired 1 Test (1986).

*__CONSTANT, David__ John, b Bradford-on-Avon, Wiltshire 9 Nov 1941. LHB, SLA. Kent 1961-63. Leicestershire 1965-68. HS 80 Leics v Glos (Bristol) 1966. F-c career: 61 matches; 1517 runs @ 19.20; 1 wicket @ 36.00. Appointed 1969. Umpired 32 Tests (1971 to 1986). Bowls for Gloucestershire 1984-86.

DUDLESTON, Barry (Stockport S), b Bebington, Cheshire 16 Jul 1945. RHB, SLA. Leicestershire 1966-80 (cap 1969; benefit of £25,000 in 1980). Gloucestershire 1981-83. Rhodesia 1976-80. 1000 runs (8): most – 1374 (1970). HS 202 Leics v Derbys (Leicester) 1979. BB 4-6 Leics v Surrey (Leicester) 1972. F-c career: 295 matches; 14,747 runs @ 32.48, 32 hundreds; 47 wickets @ 29.04. Appointed 1984.

EVANS, David Gwilliam Lloyd, b Lambeth, London 27 Jul 1933. RHB, WK. Glamorgan 1956-69 (cap 1959; benefit of £3500 in 1969). HS 46* v Oxford U (Oxford) 1961. F-c career: 270 matches; 2875 runs @ 10.53; 558 dismissals (502 ct, 56 st). Appointed 1971. Umpired 9 Tests (1981 to 1985).

HAMPSHIRE, John Harry (Oakwood THS, Rotherham), b Thurnscoe, Yorkshire 10 Feb 1941. RHB, LB. Son of John (Yorks 1937); brother of A.W. (Yorks 1975). Yorkshire 1961-81 (cap 1963; benefit of £28,425 in 1976; captain 1979-80). Derbyshire 1982-84 (cap 1982). Tasmania 1967-69, 1977-79. Tests: 8 (1969 to 1975); 403 runs @ 26.86, HS 107 v WI (Lord's) 1969 on debut (only England player to score hundred at Lord's on debut in Tests). Tours: Aus 1970-71; SA 1972-73 (DHR), 1974-75 (DHR); WI 1964-65 (Cavs); NZ 1970-71; Pak 1967-68 (Cwlth XI); SL 1969-70; Zim 1980-81 (Leics XI). 1000 runs (15): most – 1596 (1978). HS 183* Yorks v Sussex (Hove) 1971. BB 7-52 Yorks v Glam (Cardiff) 1963. F-c career: 577 matches; 28,059 runs @ 34.55, 43 hundreds; 30 wickets @ 54.56; 445 ct. Appointed 1985.

HARRIS, John Humphrey, b Taunton 13 Feb 1936. LHB, RFM. Somerset 1952-59. Suffolk 1960-62. Devon 1975. HS 41 v Worcs (Taunton) 1957. BB 3-29 v Worcs (Bristol) 1959. F-c career: 15 matches; 154 runs @ 11.00; 19 wickets @ 32.57. Appointed 1983.

HOLDER, John Wakefield (Combermere S, Barbados), b St. George, Barbados 19 Mar 1945. RHB, RFM. Hampshire 1968-72. HS 33 v Sussex (Hove) 1971. BB 7-79 v Glos (Gloucester) 1972. F-c career: 47 matches; 374 runs @ 10.68; 139 wickets @ 24.56. Appointed 1983.

JAMESON, John Alexander (Taunton S), b Bombay, India 30 Jun 1941. RHB, RM/OB, WK. Brother of T.E.N. (Cambridge U and Warwicks 1970). Warwickshire 1960-76 (cap 1964; benefit of £13,500 in 1974). Tests: 4 (1971 to 1973-74); 214 runs @ 26.75, HS 82 v Ind (Oval) 1971; 1 wkt. Tours: Rhodesia 1972-73 (Int Wand); WI 1973-74. 1000 runs (11): most – 1948 (1973). HS 240* v Glos (Birmingham) 1974, sharing world-record 2nd wicket partnership of 465 (unbroken) with R.B. Kanhai. BB 4-22 v Oxford U (Oxford) 1971. F-c career: 361 matches; 18,941 runs @ 33.34; 33 hundreds; 89 wickets @ 42.49. Appointed 1984.

JONES, Allan Arthur (St. John's C, Horsham), b Horley, Surrey 9 Dec 1947. RHB, RFM. Sussex 1966-69. Somerset 1970-75 (cap 1972). Northern Transvaal 1972-73. Middlesex 1976-79 (cap 1976). Orange Free State 1976-77. Glamorgan 1980-81. HS 33 Middx v Kent (Canterbury) 1978. BB 9-51 Somerset v Sussex (Hove) 1972. F-c career: 214 matches; 799 runs @ 5.39; 549 wickets @ 28.07. Appointed 1985.

JULIAN, Raymond (Wigston SM), b Cosby, Leicestershire 23 Aug 1936. RHB, WK. Leicestershire 1953-71 (cap 1961). HS 51 v Worcs (Worcester) 1962. F-c career: 192 matches; 2581 runs @ 9.73; 421 dismissals (382 ct, 39 st). Appointed 1972.

KITCHEN, Mervyn John (Backwell SM, Nailsea), b Nailsea, Somerset 1 Aug 1940. LHB, RM. Somerset 1960-79 (cap 1966; testimonial of £6000 in 1973). Tour: Rhodesia 1972-73 (Int Wand). 1000 runs (7): most – 1730 (1968). HS 189 v Pakistanis (Taunton) 1967. BB 1-4. F-c career: 354 matches; 15,230 runs @ 26.25, 17 hundreds; 2 wickets @ 54.50. Appointed 1982.

LEADBEATER, Barrie (Harehills SS), b Harehills, Leeds 14 Aug 1943. RHB, RM. Yorkshire 1966-79 (cap 1969; joint benefit sharing £33,846 with G.A. Cope in 1980). Tour: WI 1969-70 (DN). HS 140* v Hants (Portsmouth) 1976. F-c career: 147 matches; 5373 runs @ 25.34, 1 hundred; 1 wicket @ 5.00. Appointed 1981.

LLOYD, David (Accrington Secondary Technical S), b Accrington, Lancashire 18 March 1947. LHB, SLA. Lancashire 1965-83 (cap 1968; captain 1973-77; benefit of £40,171 in 1978). Cumberland 1984-86. Tests: 9 (1974 and 1974-75); 552 runs @ 42.46, HS 214* v Ind (Birmingham) 1974. Tours: Aus 1974-75; SA (DHR) 1975-76; NZ 1974-75. 1000 runs (11): most – 1510 (1972). HS 214* (Tests). BB 7-38 v Glos (Lydney) 1966. F-c career: 407 matches; 19,269 runs @ 33.33, 38 hundreds; 237 wickets @ 30.26; 334 ct. Appointed 1987.

LYONS, Kevin James (Lady Mary's HS), b Cardiff 18 Dec 1946. RHB, RM. Glamorgan 1967-77. Tour: WI 1969-70 (Glam). HS 92 v Cambridge U (Cambridge) 1972. F-c career: 62 matches; 1673 runs @ 19.68; 2 wickets @ 126.00. Appointed 1985.

***MEYER, Barrie** John (Boscombe SS), b Bournemouth 21 Aug 1932. RHB, WK. Gloucestershire 1957-71 (cap 1958; benefit 1971). HS 63 v Indians (Cheltenham) 1959, 63 v Oxford U (Bristol) 1962, and 63 v Sussex (Bristol) 1964. F-c career: 406 matches; 5367 runs @ 14.16; 826 dismissals (707 ct, 119 st). Soccer for Bristol Rovers, Plymouth Argyle, Newport County and Bristol City. Appointed 1973. Umpired in 18 Tests (1978 to 1986).

OSLEAR, Donald Osmund, b Cleethorpes, Lincolnshire 3 Mar 1929. No appearances at first-class level. Soccer for Grimsby Town, Hull City and Oldham Athletic. Also played Ice Hockey. Appointed 1975. Umpired in 5 Tests (1980 to 1984).

***PALMER, Kenneth** Ernest (Southbroom SM, Devizes), b Winchester 22 Apr 1937. RHB, RFM. Brother of Roy (Somerset 1965-70) and father of G.V. (Somerset 1982-). Somerset 1955-69 (cap 1958; testimonial of £4000 in 1968). Tours: WI 1963-64 (Cavs); Pak 1963-64 (Cwlth XI). Tests: 1 (1964-65; while coaching in South Africa); 10 runs; 1 wicket. 1000 runs (1): 1036 (1961). 100 wickets (4); most – 139 (1963). HS 125* v Northants (Northampton) 1961. BB 9-57 v Notts (Nottingham) 1963. F-c career: 314 matches; 7761 runs @ 20.64, 2 hundreds; 866 wickets @ 21.34. Appointed 1972. Umpired in 13 Tests (1978 to 1986).

PALMER, Roy (Southbroom SM), b Devizes, Wiltshire 12 Jul 1942. RHB, RFM. Brother of K.E. (above). Somerset 1965-70. HS 84 v Leics (Taunton) 1967. BB 6-45 v Middx (Lord's) 1967. F-c career: 74 matches; 1037 runs @ 13.29; 172 wickets @ 31.62. Appointed 1980.

PLEWS, Nigel Trevor, b Nottingham 5 Sep 1934. Former policeman (Fraud Squad). No first-class appearances. Appointed 1982. Umpired Texaco Trophy International 1986.

***SHEPHERD, David** Robert (Barnstaple GS; St. Luke's C, Exeter), b Bideford, Devon 27 Dec 1940. RHB, RM. Gloucestershire 1965-79 (cap 1969; joint benefit with J. Davey 1978). Scored 108 on debut (v OU). Devon 1959-64. 1000 runs (2): most – 1079 (1970). HS 153 v Middx (Bristol) 1968. F-c career: 282 matches; 10,672 runs @ 24.47, 12 hundreds; 2 wickets @ 53.00. Appointed 1981. Umpired 4 Tests (1985 and 1986).

WHITE, Robert Arthur (Chiswick GS), b Fulham, London 6 Oct 1936. LHB, OB. Middlesex 1958-65 (cap 1963). Nottinghamshire 1966-80 (cap 1966; benefit of £11,000 in 1974). 1000 runs (1): 1355 (1963). HS 116* Notts v Surrey (Oval) 1967. BB 7-41 Notts v Derbys (Ilkeston) 1971. F-c career; 413 matches; 12,452 runs @ 23.18, 5 hundreds; 693 wickets @ 30.50. Appointed 1983.

***WHITEHEAD, Alan** Geoffrey Thomas, b Butleigh, Somerset 28 Oct 1940. LHB, SLA. Somerset 1957-61. HS 15 v Hants (Southampton) 1959, and 15 v Leics (Leicester) 1960. BB 6-74 v Sussex (Eastbourne) 1959. F-c career: 38 matches; 137 runs @ 5.70; 67 wickets @ 34.41. Appointed 1970. Umpired 3 Tests (1982 to 1986).

WIGHT, Peter Bernard, b Georgetown, British Guiana 25 Jun 1930. RHB, OB. Brother of G.L. (West Indies), H.A. and N. (all British Guiana). British Guiana 1950-51. Somerset 1953-65 (cap 1954; benefit of £5000 in 1963). Canterbury 1963-64. 1000 runs (10): most – 2375 (1960). HS 222* v Kent (Taunton) 1959. BB 6-29 v Derbys (Chesterfield) 1957. F-c career: 333 matches 17,773 runs @ 33.09, 28 hundreds; 68 wickets @ 33.26. Appointed 1966.

RESERVE LIST

P.J. EELE, B. HASSAN, M. HENDRICK, H.J. RHODES, K. TAYLOR and D.S. THOMPSETT.

* On Test Match and Texaco Trophy Panel for 1987.
See page 72 for key to abbreviations.

PRINCIPAL FIXTURES 1987

**Including Sunday play*

Saturday 18 April

Other Match
Fenners: Cambridge U v Essex

Wednesday 22 April

Other Matches
The Parks: Oxford U v Kent
Fenners: Cambridge U v Lancs
Lord's: MCC v Essex

Saturday 25 April

Britannic Assurance Championship
*Chesterfield: Derbys v Sussex
*Bristol: Glos v Essex
*Southampton: Hants v Northants
*Lord's: Middx v Yorks
*Trent Bridge: Notts v Surrey
*Taunton: Somerset v Lancs
*Edgbaston: Warwicks v Glam
*Worcester: Worcs v Kent
Other Match
Fenners: Cambridge U v Leics

Wednesday 29 April

Britannic Assurance Championship
Chelmsford: Essex v Warwicks
Canterbury: Kent v Glam
Old Trafford: Lancs v Middx
The Oval: Surrey v Derbys
Hove: Sussex v Glos
Other Matches
The Parks: Oxford U v Hants
Fenners: Cambridge U v Northants

Thursday 30 April

Tourist Match
Arundel: Lavinia Duchess of Norfolk's XI v Pakistanis (one day)

Saturday 2 May

Benson & Hedges Cup
Derby: Derbys v Northants
Swansea: Glam v Sussex
Bristol: Glos v Notts
Canterbury: Kent v Minor Counties
Taunton: Somerset v Essex
Edgbaston: Warwicks v Yorks
Worcester: Worcs v Lancs
The Parks: Combined U v Hants
Tourist Match
*The Oval: Surrey v Pakistanis

Sunday 3 May

Refuge Assurance League
Derby: Derbys v Northants
Cardiff: Glam v Sussex
Leicester: Leics v Hants
Trent Bridge: Notts v Kent
Taunton: Somerset v Essex
Edgbaston: Warwicks v Yorks
Worcester: Worcs v Lancs

Wednesday 6 May

Britannic Assurance Championship
Swansea: Glam v Lancs
Leicester: Leics v Essex
Lord's: Middx v Northants
Taunton: Somerset v Surrey
Worcester: Worcs v Sussex
Headingley: Yorks v Hants
Tourist Match
Canterbury: Kent v Pakistanis
Other Match
Fenners: Cambridge U v Derbys

Saturday 9 May

Benson & Hedges Cup
Bristol: Glos v Leics
Southampton: Hants v Middx
Trent Bridge: Notts v Derbys
Taunton: Somerset v Combined U
The Oval: Surrey v Kent
Hove: Sussex v MCCA
Headingley: Yorks v Lancs
*Perth (North Inch): Scotland v Warwicks
Tourist Match
*Chelmsford: Essex v Pakistanis

Sunday 10 May

Refuge Assurance League
Southampton: Hants v Surrey
Canterbury: Kent v Worcs
Old Trafford: Lancs v Glam
Hove: Sussex v Derbys
Headingley: Yorks v Northants

Tuesday 12 May

Benson & Hedges Cup
Chelmsford: Essex v Middx
Southampton: Hants v Somerset
Canterbury: Kent v Sussex
Southport: Lancs v Scotland
Leicester: Leics v Notts
Northampton: Northants v Glos
The Oval: Surrey v Glam
Headingley: Yorks v Worcs
Tourist Match
Derby: Derbys v Pakistanis (one day)

Thursday 14 May

Benson & Hedges Cup
Chelmsford: Essex v Hants
Old Trafford: Lancs v Warwicks
Leicester: Leics v Derbys
Lord's: Middx v Combined U
Trent Bridge: Notts v Northants
Hove: Sussex v Surrey
Worcester: Worcs v Scotland
Oxford (Christ Church): MCCA v Glam
Tourist Match
Taunton: Somerset v Pakistanis (one day)

Saturday 16 May

Benson & Hedges Cup
Derby: Derbys v Glos
Cardiff: Glam v Kent
Lord's: Middx v Somerset
Northampton: Northants v Leics
Edgbaston: Warwicks v Worcs
Oxford (Christ Church): MCCA v Surrey
Fenners: Combined U v Essex
*Glasgow (Hamilton Crescent): Scotland v Yorks
Tourist Match
*Hove: Sussex v Pakistanis

Sunday 17 May

Refuge Assurance League
Chelmsford: Essex v Leics
Swansea: Glam v Kent
Bristol: Glos v Warwicks
Lord's: Middx v Somerset
Northampton: Northants v Hants
The Oval: Surrey v Lancs

Wednesday 20 May

Britannic Assurance Championship
Chelmsford: Essex v Glam
Bournemouth: Hants v Notts
Dartford: Kent v Sussex
Leicester: Leics v Lancs
Edgbaston: Warwicks v Surrey
Worcester: Worcs v Derbys
Headingley: Yorks v Somerset
Other Matches
The Parks: Oxford U v Glos
Fenners: Cambridge U v Middx

Thursday 21 May

TEXACO TROPHY
The Oval: ENGLAND v PAKISTAN (First One-day International)

Saturday 23 May

TEXACO TROPHY
Trent Bridge: ENGLAND v PAKISTAN (Second One-day International)
Britannic Assurance Championship
Derby: Derbys v Warwicks
Cardiff: Glam v Yorks
Old Trafford: Lancs v Worcs
Northampton: Northants v Leics
Taunton: Somerset v Glos
The Oval: Surrey v Essex
Hove: Sussex v Middx
Other Match
The Parks: Oxford U v Notts

Sunday 24 May

Refuge Assurance League
Derby: Derbys v Worcs
Cardiff: Glam v Yorks
Canterbury: Kent v Middx
Old Trafford: Lancs v Hants
Taunton: Somerset v Glos
The Oval: Surrey v Essex

Monday 25 May

TEXACO TROPHY
Edgbaston: ENGLAND v PAKISTAN (Third One-day International)

Wednesday 27 May

Benson & Hedges Cup
Quarter-finals

Tourist Match
Headingley or Dublin (Rathmines): Yorks (three days) or Ireland (two days) v Pakistanis

Saturday 30 May

Britannic Assurance Championship
Chesterfield: Derbys v Glam
Southampton: Hants v Glos
Leicester: Leics v Somerset
Northampton: Northants v Kent
Worcester: Worcs v Essex
Middlesbrough: Yorks v Notts
Tourist Match
*Lord's: Middx v Pakistanis
Other Match
The Parks: Oxford U v Warwicks

Sunday 31 May

Refuge Assurance League
Southampton: Hants v Glos
Old Trafford: Lancs v Somerset
Northampton: Northants v Sussex
Trent Bridge: Notts v Leics
Edgbaston: Warwicks v Derbys
Worcester: Worcs v Essex
Middlesbrough: Yorks v Kent

Wednesday 3 June

Britannic Assurance Championship
Swansea: Glam v Hants
Bristol: Glos v Lancs
Tunbridge Wells: Kent v Surrey
Lord's: Middx v Essex
Taunton: Somerset v Notts
Edgbaston: Warwicks v Leics
Sheffield: Yorks v Worcs

Thursday 4 June

CORNHILL INSURANCE TEST SERIES
Old Trafford: ENGLAND v PAKISTAN
(First Test Match)

Saturday 6 June

Britannic Assurance Championship
*Swansea: Glam v Somerset
Tunbridge Wells: Kent v Essex
Leicester: Leics v Worcs
Lord's: Middx v Glos
Northampton: Northants v Surrey
Trent Bridge: Notts v Lancs
Horsham: Sussex v Hants
Harrogate: Yorks v Derbys

Sunday 7 June

Refuge Assurance League
Leicester: Leics v Worcs
Lord's: Middx v Glos
Northampton: Northants v Notts
The Oval: Surrey v Warwicks
Horsham: Sussex v Hants
Sheffield: Yorks v Derbys

Wednesday 10 June

Benson & Hedges Cup
Semi-finals
Other Match
Harrogate: Tilcon Trophy (three days)

Thursday 11 June

Tourist Match
Glasgow (Titwood): Scotland v Pakistanis (one day)

Saturday 13 June

Britannic Assurance Championship
Ilford: Essex v Kent
Cardiff: Glam v Warwicks
*Old Trafford: Lancs v Yorks
Bath: Somerset v Middx
The Oval: Surrey v Hants
Worcester: Worcs v Leics
Tourist Match
*Bletchley (Manor Fields): Northants v Pakistanis

Sunday 14 June

Refuge Assurance League
Ilford: Essex v Kent
Ebbw Vale: Glam v Notts
Swindon: Glos v Sussex
Southampton: Hants v Derbys
Leicester: Leics v Surrey
Bath: Somerset v Warwicks
Worcester: Worcs v Middx

Monday 15 June

Downpatrick: Ireland v Glos (one day)

Tuesday 16 June

Downpatrick: Ireland v Glos (one day)

Wednesday 17 June

Britannic Assurance Championship
Derby: Derbys v Lancs
Ilford: Essex v Northants
Basingstoke: Hants v Yorks
Bath: Somerset v Kent
Hove: Sussex v Glam
Edgbaston: Warwicks v Notts
Worcester: Worcs v Glos
Other Match
Fenners: Cambridge U v Surrey

Thursday 18 June

CORNHILL INSURANCE TEST SERIES
Lord's: ENGLAND v PAKISTAN (Second Test Match)

Saturday 20 June

Britannic Assurance Championship
Southampton: Hants v Middx
Liverpool: Lancs v Kent
Hinckley: Leics v Sussex
Luton: Northants v Warwicks
Trent Bridge: Notts v Worcs
Headingley: Yorks v Essex
Other Match
The Parks: Oxford U v Glam

Sunday 21 June

Refuge Assurance League
Ilkeston: Derbys v Glos
Basingstoke: Hants v Middx
Old Trafford: Lancs v Kent
Luton: Northants v Glam
Trent Bridge: Notts v Worcs
Bath: Somerset v Sussex
Edgbaston: Warwicks v Essex
Headingley: Yorks v Surrey

Wednesday 24 June

NatWest Bank Trophy
First Round
High Wycombe: Bucks v Somerset
Wisbech: Cambridgeshire v Derbys
Darlington: Durham v Middx
Cardiff: Glam v Cheshire
Southampton: Hants v Dorset
Old Trafford: Lancs v Glos
Leicester: Leics v Oxfordshire
Northampton: Northants v Ireland
Jesmond: Northumberland v Essex
Trent Bridge: Notts v Suffolk
Edinburgh (Myreside): Scotland v Kent
Burton upon Trent (Ind Coope): Staffs v Warwicks
The Oval: Surrey v Herts
Hove: Sussex v Cumberland
Trowbridge: Wilts v Yorks
Worcester: Worcs v Devon
Tourist Match
Oxford: Combined U v Pakistanis

Saturday 27 June

Britannic Assurance Championship
Chelmsford: Essex v Somerset
Gloucester: Glos v Worcs
Canterbury: Kent v Notts
Old Trafford: Lancs v Derbys
Lord's: Middx v Glam
Northampton: Northants v Yorks
Guildford: Surrey v Sussex
Edgbaston: Warwicks v Hants
Tourist Match
*Leicester: Leics v Pakistanis

Sunday 28 June

Refuge Assurance League
Gloucester: Glos v Worcs
Canterbury: Kent v Somerset
Old Trafford: Lancs v Derbys
Lord's: Middx v Glam
Guildford: Surrey v Northants
Hove: Sussex v Notts
Edgbaston: Warwicks v Hants

Wednesday July 1

Britannic Assurance Championship
Swansea: Glam v Northants
Gloucester: Glos v Hants
Canterbury: Kent v Yorks
Old Trafford: Lancs v Essex
Leicester: Leics v Derbys
The Oval: Surrey v Middx
Edgbaston: Warwicks v Somerset
Kidderminster: Worcs v Notts
Other Match
Lord's: Oxford U v Cambridge U

Thursday 2 July

CORNHILL INSURANCE TEST SERIES
Headingley: ENGLAND v PAKISTAN (Third Test Match)

Saturday 4 July

Britannic Assurance Championship
*Heanor: Derbys v Hants
Swansea: Glam v Glos
Northampton: Northants v Lancs
Trent Bridge: Notts v Yorks
The Oval: Surrey v Leics
Hove: Sussex v Kent
Worcester: Worcs v Warwicks

Sunday 5 July

Refuge Assurance League
Chelmsford: Essex v Sussex
Lord's: Middx v Leics
Tring: Northants v Lancs
Trent Bridge: Notts v Yorks
Worcester: Worcs v Warwicks

Wednesday 8 July

NatWest Bank Trophy
Second Round
Leicester or Oxford (Morris Motors): Leics/Oxon v Hants/Dorset
Glasgow (Titwood) or Canterbury: Scotland/Kent v Cambridgeshire/Derbys
Hove or Kendal (Netherfield): Sussex/Cumberland v Lancs/Glos
Trowbridge or Headingley: Wilts/Yorks v Glam/Cheshire
Sunderland or Uxbridge: Durham/Middx v Notts/Suffolk
Northampton or Dublin: Northants/Ireland v Surrey/Herts
Stone or Edgbaston: Staffs/Warwicks v Bucks/Somerset
Jesmond or Chelmsford: Northumberland/Essex v Worcs/Devon
Tourist Match
Burton upon Trent (Ind Coope): Minor Counties v Pakistanis (two days)

Saturday 11 July

Benson & Hedges Cup
Lord's: Final
Tourist Match
Trent Bridge, Old Trafford or Edgbaston: Notts, Lancs or Warwicks v Pakistanis
Other Match
*Dublin (Malahide): Ireland v Northants (two days)

Sunday 12 July

Refuge Assurance League
Cheadle: Derbys v Glam
Chelmsford: Essex v Glos
Southampton: Hants v Worcs
Old Trafford: Lancs v Leics
The Oval: Surrey v Somerset
Edgbaston: Warwicks v Notts
Scarborough: Yorks v Middx

Wednesday 15 July

Britannic Assurance Championship
Derby: Derbys v Kent
Southend: Essex v Hants
Bristol: Glos v Middx
Trent Bridge: Notts v Leics
Taunton: Somerset v Worcs
The Oval: Surrey v Yorks
Nuneaton: Warwicks v Sussex
Tourist Match
Cardiff: Glam v Pakistanis

Thursday 16 July

Lord's: England v Australia (WCA Silver Jubilee – one day)

Saturday 18 July

Britannic Assurance Championship
Southend: Essex v Derbys
Cardiff: Glam v Surrey
Bristol: Glos v Northants
*Bournemouth: Hants v Warwicks
Lord's: Middx v Notts
Taunton: Somerset v Leics
Hastings: Sussex v Yorks
Tourist Match
*Worcester: Worcester v Pakistanis
Other Match
*Coleraine: Ireland v Scotland (three days)

Sunday 19 July

Refuge Assurance League
Southend: Essex v Derbys
Cardiff: Glam v Surrey
Bristol: Glos v Yorks
Canterbury: Kent v Northants
Trent Bridge: Notts v Middx
Taunton: Somerset v Leics
Hastings: Sussex v Lancs

Wednesday 22 July

Britannic Assurance Championship
Derby: Derbys v Notts
Portsmouth: Hants v Sussex
Folkestone: Kent v Glos
Southport: Lancs v Warwicks
Leicester: Leics v Middx
Northampton: Northants v Somerset
The Oval: Surrey v Worcs
Headingley: Yorks v Glam

Thursday 23 July

CORNHILL INSURANCE TEST SERIES
Edgbaston: ENGLAND v PAKISTAN (Fourth Test Match)

Saturday 25 July

Britannic Assurance Championship
Bristol: Glos v Derbys
Portsmouth: Hants v Essex
Old Trafford: Lancs v Notts
Leicester: Leics v Yorks
Lord's: Middx v Kent
Northampton: Northants v Sussex
Worcester: Worcs v Somerset

Sunday 26 July

Refuge Assurance League
Swansea: Glam v Warwicks
Portsmouth: Hants v Essex
Old Trafford: Lancs v Notts
Leicester: Leics v Yorks
Lord's: Middx v Derbys
Finedon: Northants v Glos
Worcester: Worcs v Somerset

Wednesday 29 July

NatWest Bank Trophy
Quarter-finals

Thursday 30 July

Jesmond: England XI v Rest of the World (one day)

Friday 31 July

Jesmond: England XI v Rest of the World (one day)

Saturday 1 August

Britannic Assurance Championship
Cheltenham: Glos v Leics
Canterbury: Kent v Derbys
Lord's: Middx v Surrey
Weston-super-Mare: Somerset v Glam
Eastbourne: Sussex v Notts
Edgbaston: Warwicks v Northants
Headingley: Yorks v Lancs
Tourist Matches
*Southampton: Hants v Pakistanis
Worcester: England v Australia (four days) Women's Test Match

Sunday 2 August

Refuge Assurance League
Cheltenham: Glos v Leics
Canterbury: Kent v Derbys
Lord's: Middx v Surrey
Weston-super-Mare: Somerset v Glam
Eastbourne: Sussex v Worcs
Edgbaston: Warwicks v Northants
Scarborough: Yorks v Lancs

Wednesday 5 August

Britannic Assurance Championship
Chesterfield: Derbys v Yorks
Abergavenny: Glam v Leics
Cheltenham: Glos v Surrey
Canterbury: Kent v Middx
Old Trafford: Lancs v Northants
Worksop: Notts v Warwicks
Weston-super-Mare: Somerset v Hants
Eastbourne: Sussex v Essex
Other Match
Lord's: MCC v Ireland (two days)

Thursday 6 August

CORNHILL INSURANCE TEST SERIES
The Oval: ENGLAND v PAKISTAN (Fifth Test Match)

Saturday 8 August

Britannic Assurance Championship
Chesterfield: Derbys v Surrey
Cheltenham: Glos v Kent
Southampton: Hants v Lancs
Hinckley: Leics v Warwicks
Lord's: Middx v Worcs
Northampton: Northants v Essex
Trent Bridge: Notts v Somerset
Sheffield: Yorks v Sussex

Sunday 9 August

Refuge Assurance League
Chesterfield: Derbys v Surrey
Cheltenham: Glos v Kent
Bournemouth: Hants v Glam
Leicester: Leics v Warwicks
Lord's: Middx v Lancs
Northampton: Northants v Essex
Trent Bridge: Notts v Somerset
Hull: Yorks v Sussex
Other Matches
Arundel: Lavinia Duchess of Norfolk's XI v Rest of the World (one day)
Welshpool: Wales v Ireland (three days)

Wednesday 12 August

NatWest Bank Trophy
Semi-finals
Tourist Match
Trent Bridge, Old Trafford or Edgbaston: Notts, Lancs or Warwicks v Rest of the World (three days)
Other Match
Aberdeen (Mannofield): Scotland v MCC (three days)

Saturday 15 August

Britannic Assurance Championship
Derby: Derbys v Leics
Chelmsford: Essex v Middx
Trent Bridge: Notts v Northants
Taunton: Somerset v Yorks
The Oval: Surrey v Kent
Hove: Sussex v Warwicks
Worcester: Worcs v Glam
Other Match
*Bristol: Glos v Rest of the World (three days)

Sunday 16 August

Refuge Assurance League
Derby: Derbys v Leics
Chelmsford: Essex v Middx
Swansea: Glam v Worcs
Trent Bridge: Notts v Hants
Taunton: Somerset v Yorks
The Oval: Surrey v Kent
Hove: Sussex v Warwicks

Wednesday 19 August

Britannic Assurance Championship
Chelmsford: Essex v Notts
Cardiff: Glam v Middx
Bournemouth: Hants v Kent
Lytham: Lancs v Sussex
Northampton: Northants v Worcs
The Oval: Surrey v Somerset
Edgbaston: Warwicks v Glos
Scarborough: Yorks v Leics

Thursday 20 August

Lord's: MCC BICENTENARY MATCH
MCC v REST OF THE WORLD XI (five days)

Saturday 22 August

Britannic Assurance Championship
Derby: Derbys v Essex
Neath: Glam v Worcs
Bournemouth: Hants v Somerset
Wellingborough School: Northants v Middx
Trent Bridge: Notts v Glos
Hove: Sussex v Surrey
Edgbaston: Warwicks v Lancs

Sunday 23 August

Refuge Assurance League
Neath: Glam v Essex
Moreton-in-Marsh: Glos v Notts
Bournemouth: Hants v Somerset
Leicester: Leics v Kent
Wellingborough School: Northants v Middx
Hove: Sussex v Surrey
Edgbaston: Warwicks v Lancs
Worcester: Worcs v Yorks

Wednesday 26 August

Britannic Assurance Championship
Maidstone: Kent v Lancs
Leicester: Leics v Notts
Uxbridge: Middx v Warwicks
Northampton: Northants v Derbys
The Oval: Surrey v Glam
Hove: Sussex v Somerset
Worcester: Worcs v Hants
Headingley: Yorks v Glos

Saturday 29 August

Britannic Assurance Championship
Colchester: Essex v Surrey
Maidstone: Kent v Hants
Old Trafford: Lancs v Glos
Leicester: Leics v Northants
Uxbridge: Middx v Sussex
Trent Bridge: Notts v Derbys
Edgbaston: Warwicks v Worcs
Other Match
Hove: England v Australia (four days) Women's Test Match

Sunday 30 August

Refuge Assurance League
Derby: Derbys v Notts
Colchester: Essex v Yorks
Maidstone: Kent v Hants
Old Trafford: Lancs v Glos
Leicester: Leics v Northants
Lord's: Middx v Sussex
Hereford: Worcs v Surrey
Other Matches
Edgbaston: Warwick Under 25 Final (one day)

Wednesday 2 September

Britannic Assurance Championship
Colchester: Essex v Worcs
Cardiff: Glam v Derbys
Bristol: Glos v Somerset
Southampton: Hants v Leics
Trent Bridge: Notts v Sussex
The Oval: Surrey v Northants
Edgbaston: Warwicks v Kent
Other Match
Scarborough: Yorks v MCC (three days)

Saturday 5 September

NatWest Bank Trophy
Lord's: Final

Sunday 6 September

Refuge Assurance League
Canterbury: Kent v Sussex
Leicester: Leics v Glam
Trent Bridge: Notts v Essex
Taunton: Somerset v Northants
The Oval: Surrey v Glos
Edgbaston: Warwicks v Middx
Headingley: Yorks v Hants
Other Match
Scarborough: Asda Cricket Challenge Lancs v Derbys (one day)

Monday 7 September

Venue to be arranged: Bain Dawes Trophy Final (one day)
Scarborough: Asda Cricket Challenge Yorks v Hants (one day)

Tuesday 8 September

Scarborough: Asda Cricket Challenge Final (one day)

Wednesday 9 September

Britannic Assurance Championship
Old Trafford: Lancs v Surrey
Leicester: Leics v Glos
Lord's: Middx v Hants
Trent Bridge: Notts v Glam
Taunton: Somerset v Derbys
Hove: Sussex v Northants
Scarborough: Yorks v Warwicks

Saturday 12 September

Britannic Assurance Championship
Derby: Derbys v Middx
Chelmsford: Essex v Lancs
Bristol: Glos v Glam
Canterbury: Kent v Leics
Worcester: Worcs v Northants

Sunday 13 September

Refuge Assurance League
Derby: Derbys v Somerset
Chelmsford: Essex v Lancs
Bristol: Glos v Glam
Canterbury: Kent v Warwicks
The Oval: Surrey v Notts
Hove: Sussex v Leics
Worcester: Worcs v Northants

MINOR COUNTIES CRICKET ASSOCIATION – FIXTURES, 1987

(E) *Eastern Division* (W) *Western Division*

MAY		**BENSON & HEDGES CUP**
Sat 2	Canterbury	Kent v Minor Counties
Sat 9	Hove	Sussex v Minor Counties
		FRIENDLY
Sun 10	Arundel	Duchess of Norfolk's XI v Minor Counties
		BENSON & HEDGES CUP
Thu 14	Christ Church (Oxford)	Minor Counties v Glamorgan
Sat 16	Christ Church (Oxford)	Minor Counties v Surrey
		CHAMPIONSHIP
Sun 24	Sleaford	(E) Lincolnshire v Hertfordshire
	Jesmond	(E) Northumberland v Bedfordshire
Tue 26	Carlisle	(E) Cumberland v Bedfordshire
	Hartlepool	(E) Durham v Hertfordshire
Wed 27	Framlingham College	(E) Suffolk v Cambridgeshire
Sun 31	Shrewsbury	(W) Shropshire v Somerset II
		KNOCKOUT, *Qualifying Round*
Sun 31	Hurst, Nr. Reading	Berkshire v Oxfordshire
	West Herts C.C., Watford	Hertfordshire v Bedfordshire
	Appleby Frodingham	Lincolnshire v Durham
JUNE		**CHAMPIONSHIP**
Tue 2	Warrington	(W) Cheshire v Somerset II
Sun 7	Barrow	(E) Cumberland v Cambridgeshire
	Bourne	(E) Lincolnshire v Durham
Mon 8	Toft	(W) Cheshire v Cornwall
Tue 9	Jesmond	(E) Northumberland v Cambridgeshire
Wed 10	Watford Town C.C.	(E) Hertfordshire v Staffordshire
	Shifnal	(W) Shropshire v Cornwall
		KNOCKOUT, *First Round*
Sun 14	Reading School or Christ Church	Berkshire or Oxfordshire v Staffordshire
	Beaconsfield	Buckinghamshire v Shropshire
	Cambridge (Trinity Old)	Cambridgeshire v Hertfordshire or Bedfordshire
	Oxton	Cheshire v Cumberland
	Truro	Cornwall v Wiltshire
	Instow	Devon v Dorset
	Market Rasen or Durham City	Lincolnshire or Durham v Northumberland
	To be arranged	Suffolk v Norfolk
		CHAMPIONSHIP
Wed 17	Wisbech	(E) Cambridgeshire v Norfolk
Thu 18	Taunton	(W) Somerset II v Buckinghamshire
Sun 21	Henlow	(E) Bedfordshire v Staffordshire
	Jesmond	(E) Northumberland v Lincolnshire
Sun 28		**KNOCKOUT,** *Quarter Finals*
		CHAMPIONSHIP
Tue 30	Knypersley	(E) Staffordshire v Lincolnshire

JULY

Sun 5	Slough	(W) Buckinghamshire v Shropshire
	Falmouth	(W) Cornwall v Devon
	Hitchin	(E) Hertfordshire v Bedfordshire
	Burghley Park	(E) Lincolnshire v Norfolk
	Jesmond	(E) Northumberland v Cumberland
	Christ Church	(W) Oxfordshire v Cheshire
Mon 6	Brewood	(E) Staffordshire v Durham
Tue 7	Hertford C.C.	†(E) Hertfordshire v Cambridgeshire
	Devizes	†(W) Wiltshire v Cheshire
		REPRESENTATIVE MATCH (2 days)
Thu 9	Burton on Trent (Ind Coope)	Minor Counties v Pakistan
Sun 12		**KNOCKOUT,** ***Semi Finals***
		CHAMPIONSHIP
Sun 12	Morris Motors	*(W) Oxfordshire v Berkshire
Tue 14	Bury St Edmunds	(E) Suffolk v Hertfordshire
Wed 15	Sidmouth	(W) Devon v Dorset
	Leek	(E) Staffordshire v Cambridgeshire
Sun 19	Chester, Boughton Hall	(W) Cheshire v Dorset
	Truro	(W) Cornwall v Berkshire
	Chester-le-Street	(E) Durham v Northumberland
	Grimsby Town	(E) Lincolnshire v Suffolk
	Aston Rowant	(W) Oxfordshire v Buckinghamshire
		CHAMPIONSHIP
Mon 20	Trowbridge	(W) Wiltshire v Somerset II
Tue 21	Torquay	(W) Devon v Berkshire
	Wellington	(W) Shropshire v Dorset
Sun 26	To be arranged	**KNOCKOUT FINAL**
		CHAMPIONSHIP
Sun 26	Falkland C.C., Newbury	*(W) Berkshire v Wiltshire
	Banbury XX	*(W) Oxfordshire v Shropshire
Mon 27	Lakenham	*(E) Norfolk v Bedfordshire
	Ipswich School	*(E) Suffolk v Cumberland
Tue 28	Wadebridge	(W) Cornwall v Buckinghamshire
	Stone	(E) Staffordshire v Northumberland
	Chippenham	(W) Wiltshire v Shropshire
Wed 29	Fenners	(E) Cambridgeshire v Bedfordshire
	Lakenham	(E) Norfolk v Cumberland
Thu 30	Finchampstead	(W) Berkshire v Dorset
	Exmouth	(W) Devon v Buckinghamshire
Fri 31	Lakenham	(E) Norfolk v Suffolk

AUGUST

Sun 2	St George's Telford	(W) Shropshire v Cheshire
Mon 3	Lakenham	(E) Norfolk v Staffordshire
	Taunton	(W) Somerset II v Devon

Wed 5	Fenners	(E)	Cambridgeshire v Lincolnshire
	Sherborne School	(W)	Dorset v Somerset II
	Lakenham	(E)	Norfolk v Hertfordshire
	Mildenhall	(E)	Suffolk v Staffordshire
	Marlborough College	(W)	Wiltshire v Oxfordshire
Sun 9	Bedford (Goldington Bury)	(E)	Bedfordshire v Lincolnshire
	Kidmore End	(W)	Berkshire v Shropshire
	High Wycombe	(W)	Buckinghamshire v Cheshire
	Millom	(E)	Cumberland v Durham
	Ransome & Reavell, Ipswich	(E)	Suffolk v Northumberland
Mon 10	Falmouth	(W)	Cornwall v Oxfordshire
	Swindon	(W)	Wiltshire v Dorset
Tue 11	Bracknell	(W)	Berkshire v Cheshire
	St Albans	(E)	Hertfordshire v Northumberland
Wed 12	Bovey Tracey	(W)	Devon v Oxfordshire
	Stockton-on-Tees	(E)	Durham v Suffolk
Thu 13	Dorchester	(W)	Dorset v Buckinghamshire
	Bristol Imperial	(W)	Somerset II v Berkshire
Sun 16	Luton (Wardown Park)	(E)	Bedfordshire v Durham
	Marlow	(W)	Buckinghamshire v Wiltshire
	Weymouth	(W)	Dorset v Oxfordshire
	Lincoln Lindum	(E)	Lincolnshire v Cumberland
Tue 18	Southill Park	(E)	Bedfordshire v Suffolk
	March	(E)	Cambridgeshire v Durham
	Bowdon	(W)	Cheshire v Devon
	Dorchester	(W)	Dorset v Cornwall
	Potters Bar	(E)	Hertfordshire v Cumberland
	Tor Leisure (Glastonbury C.C.)	(W)	Somerset II v Oxfordshire
Thu 20	Bridgnorth	(W)	Shropshire v Devon
	Taunton	(W)	Somerset II v Cornwall
Sun 23	St Austell	(W)	Cornwall v Wiltshire
	Jesmond	(E)	Northumberland v Norfolk
	Netherfield (Kendal)	(E)	Cumberland v Staffordshire
Tue 25	Newton Abbot	(W)	Devon v Wiltshire
	Sunderland	(E)	Durham v Norfolk
Sun 30	Amersham	(W)	Buckinghamshire v Berkshire
SEPTEMBER			
Thu 10	Worcester		**CHAMPIONSHIP FINAL**

† These fixtures are dependent upon progress in the NatWest Trophy.
* These fixtures could be affected by progress in the Knockout Competition.

MINOR COUNTIES CHAMPIONS

1895	Norfolk Durham Worcestershire
1896	Worcestershire
1897	Worcestershire
1898	Worcestershire
1899	Northamptonshire Buckinghamshire
1900	Glamorgan Durham Northamptonshire
1901	Durham
1902	Wiltshire
1903	Northamptonshire
1904	Northamptonshire
1905	Norfolk
1906	Staffordshire
1907	Lancashire II
1908	Staffordshire
1909	Wiltshire
1910	Norfolk
1911	Staffordshire
1912	In abeyance
1913	Norfolk
1920	Staffordshire
1921	Staffordshire
1922	Buckinghamshire
1923	Buckinghamshire
1924	Berkshire
1925	Buckinghamshire
1926	Durham
1927	Staffordshire
1928	Berkshire
1929	Oxfordshire
1930	Durham
1931	Leicestershire II
1932	Buckinghamshire
1933	Undecided
1934	Lancashire II
1935	Middlesex II
1936	Hertfordshire
1937	Lancashire II
1938	Buckinghamshire
1939	Surrey II
1946	Suffolk
1947	Yorkshire II
1948	Lancashire II
1949	Lancashire II
1950	Surrey II
1951	Kent II
1952	Buckinghamshire
1953	Berkshire
1954	Surrey II
1955	Surrey II
1956	Kent II
1957	Yorkshire II
1958	Yorkshire II
1959	Warwickshire II
1960	Lancashire II
1961	Somerset II
1962	Warwickshire II
1963	Cambridgeshire
1964	Lancashire II
1965	Somerset II
1966	Lincolnshire
1967	Cheshire
1968	Yorkshire II
1969	Buckinghamshire
1970	Bedfordshire
1971	Yorkshire II
1972	Bedfordshire
1973	Shropshire
1974	Oxfordshire
1975	Hertfordshire
1976	Durham
1977	Suffolk
1978	Devon
1979	Suffolk
1980	Durham
1981	Durham
1982	Oxfordshire
1983	Hertfordshire
1984	Durham
1985	Cheshire
1986	Cumberland

1987 RELIANCE WORLD CUP

Sponsored by Reliance Industrial, the Bombay textile company, cricket's fourth World Cup begins in India and Pakistan on 9 October. The final will take place at Eden Gardens, Calcutta, on 7 November.

Oct 9
Madras: I v A
Hyderabad (Ind): NZ v Zim
Hyderabad (Pak): P v SL
Gujranwala: E v WI

12
Bangalore: I v NZ
Madras: A v Zim
Rawalpindi: P v E
Faisalabad: WI v SL

15
Bombay: I v Zim
Indore: A v NZ
Lahore: P v WI
Peshawar: E v SL

19
Calcutta: NZ v Zim
Delhi: I v A

19
Kanpur: SL v WI
Karachi: P v E

23
Ahmedabad: I v Zim
Chandigarh: A v NZ
Jaipur: WI v E
Faisalabad: P v SL

27
Cuttack: A v Zim
Nagpur: I v NZ
Poona: E v SL
Karachi: P v WI

Nov 1
Lahore } SEMI-FINALS
Bombay }

Nov 7
Calcutta: FINAL

FUTURE TOURS

1987
Pakistan to India
West Indies to New Zealand
Pakistan to England
MCC Bicentenary Match (MCC v The Rest of the World)
Australia to Sri Lanka
World Cup in India and Pakistan

1987-88
England to Pakistan and New Zealand (to Australia for Australian Bicentenary only)
West Indies to India
New Zealand to Australia
Sri Lanka to Australia

1988
Pakistan to West Indies
West Indies to England
Sri Lanka to England
Australia to Pakistan
New Zealand to India

1988-89
England to Sri Lanka and India
West Indies and Pakistan to Australia

1989
India to West Indies
Pakistan to New Zealand
Pakistan to Sri Lanka*
Australia to England

1989-90
Sri Lanka and Pakistan to Australia
India to Pakistan

1990
England to West Indies
India to New Zealand and Sri Lanka
New Zealand and India to England
New Zealand to Pakistan

1990-91
England to Australia
West Indies to Sri Lanka and India
Sri Lanka to Pakistan

1991
New Zealand to Australia*
Pakistan to India*
Sri Lanka to New Zealand*
Australia to West Indies*
West Indies to England

* *Tours not confirmed.*

YOUNG CRICKETER OF THE YEAR

Every September since 1950 the Cricket Writers' Club has selected their best young cricketer of the season. In 1986 their ballot resulted in a dead heat for the first time. Only five of their selections have ended their first-class careers without a Test cap.

1950	R. Tattersall
1951	P.B.H. May
1952	F.S. Trueman
1953	M.C. Cowdrey
1954	P.J. Loader
1955	K.F. Barrington
1956	B. Taylor
1957	M.J. Stewart
1958	A.C.D. Ingleby-Mackenzie
1959	G. Pullar
1960	D.A. Allen
1961	P.H. Parfitt
1962	P.J. Sharpe
1963	G. Boycott
1964	J.M. Brearley
1965	A.P.E. Knott
1966	D.L. Underwood
1967	A.W. Greig
1968	R.M.H. Cottam
1969	A. Ward
1970	C.M. Old
1971	J. Whitehouse
1972	D.R. Owen-Thomas
1973	M. Hendrick
1974	P.H. Edmonds
1975	A. Kennedy
1976	G. Miller
1977	I.T. Botham
1978	D.I. Gower
1979	P.W.G. Parker
1980	G.R. Dilley
1981	M.W. Gatting
1982	N.G. Cowans
1983	N.A. Foster
1984	R.J. Bailey
1985	D.V. Lawrence
1986	A.A. Metcalfe J.J. Whitaker

A Queen Anne Press Book

Cover photograph: John Emburey (umpire Arthur Jepson)
by Adrian Murrell
All-Sport Photographic

First published in Great Britain in 1987 by
Queen Anne Press, Macdonald & Co (Publishers) Ltd,
Greater London House, Hampstead Road,
London NW1 7QX
A BPCC plc Company

British Library Cataloguing in Publication Data

Playfair cricket annual.—1987
1. Cricket—Periodicals
I. Frindall, Bill
796.35'8'05 GV911

ISBN 0-356-14214-0

Typeset by Wessex Typesetters
(Division of The Eastern Press Ltd)
Frome, Somerset

Printed and bound in Great Britain by
Hazell, Watson & Viney Limited,
Member of the BPCC Group,
Aylesbury, Bucks